THE DEPARTMENT OF STATE
AND AMERICAN DIPLOMACY

GARLAND REFERENCE LIBRARY
OF SOCIAL SCIENCE
(VOL. 333)

JX
1706
.Z956
1986

THE DEPARTMENT OF STATE
AND AMERICAN DIPLOMACY
A Bibliography

Robert U. Goehlert
Elizabeth R. Hoffmeister

GARLAND PUBLISHING, INC. • NEW YORK & LONDON
1986

332127

© 1986 by Robert U. Goehlert and Elizabeth R. Hoffmeister
All rights reserved

Library of Congress Cataloging-in-Publication Data

Goehlert, Robert, 1948–
   The Department of State and American diplomacy.

   (Garland reference library of social science ;
vol. 333)
   Includes indexes.
   1. United States—Foreign relations—Bibliography.
2. United States. Dept. of State—Bibliography.
I. Hoffmeister, Elizabeth R.   II. Title.   III. Series:
Garland reference library of social science ;
v. 333.
Z6465.U5G63   1986 [JX1706]   016.3530089   86-2107
ISBN 0-8240-8591-4 (alk. paper)

Printed on acid-free, 250-year-life paper
Manufactured in the United States of America

CONTENTS

Contents

OUTLINE OF INTRODUCTION

Part I   Objectives of Bibliography
    Scope
    Arrangement
    Compilation

Part II   Research Guides
    State Department Publications
    Guides to U.S. Documents
    Bibliographies

INTRODUCTION

SCOPE

This bibliography is designed to assist librarians, researchers, and government personnel interested in the Department of State and American diplomacy. The bibliography includes citations drawn from a variety of fields, including political science, law, history, public administration, and the general social sciences. We feel that the scope and arrangement of the bibliography make it unique. It is the first bibliography to focus exclusively on the Department of State and its activities.

Our aim in compiling this volume was to prepare a comprehensive bibliography on the Department of State including its history, functions, organization, structure, and procedures. The bibliography includes books, articles, dissertations, essays, research reports and selected documents. As there is a wealth of documents dealing with the Department of State and foreign affairs, we felt that it would be best to leave these out of the volume. One can identify documents by using a number of indexes which we have identified in the section on Research Guides.

Since the bibliography is intended primarily for an English-speaking audience, all the citations are to English-language works. In general, the time period covered by the bibliography extends primarily from 1945 to 1984. While most of the citations identified were published within the last forty years, there are some citations to earlier works, especially if they provide coverage for areas that have not been extensively researched. This is especially true in the second half of the bibliography which provides biographical materials for each Secretary of State.

The chief criteria we used to determine which materials to include were that they be analytical and scholarly in nature and not merely descriptive. Consequently, the emphasis is on research monographs, articles from major journals, and dissertations. Because of the enormous amount of descriptive material aimed at policymakers, we selectively included such materials in some categories, especially when there was little scholarly work done in those areas. Generally, we included only materials that were commercially available and that could be found in larger academic libraries.

ARRANGEMENT

We have divided the bibliography into four major sections. The first section has be subdivided into ten topical categories covering all aspects of the Department of State. The second major section includes materials that focus on the role of the State Department in the conduct of foreign policy. The materials in this section have been arranged by five major theoretical categories. The third section is arranged by geographical areas, providing a survey of the conduct of American diplomacy throughout the world. The last section contains biographical materials. The first part of this section includes biographical materials about diplomats and foreign service officers. This is arranged alphabetically by author. The second part provides biographical materials about each of the Secretaries of State. This part is arranged by Secretary in alphabetical order. We have also included a subject index, which identifies more specific subjects and indexes all entries according to the topics used in the first section. There is also an author index.

The arrangement of the bibliography reflects the nature of the literature. Most of the citations in the first three sections are theoretical and comparative in nature, while the last section contains materials that are biographical. Consequently, the bibliography can be used to quickly find materials on either a particular topic, individual, or country.

COMPILATION

In compiling this bibliography, we checked a variety of sources, including numerous older bibliographies on American foreign affairs. Primarily, we searched nine indexes: **Index to Legal**

Periodicals, United States Political Science
Documents, Social Sciences Index, Humanities Index,
Public Affairs Information Service Bulletin, ABC
PolSci, Writings on American History, America:
History and Life and International Political
Science Abstracts. For dissertations, we made an
exhaustive key word search of Comprehensive
Dissertation Index. For books and research
reports, we checked all relevant bibliographies on
American foreign policy and diplomacy, plus Books
in Print, Cumulative Book Index, American Book
Publishing Record, Public Affairs Information
Service Bullentin and Biography Index as well as
the holdings of the Indiana University Libraries.

The nine indexes were chosen to incorporate a
variety of disciplines, including history, political science, and law, and they provide the best
coverage of the Department of State. We hope that
this bibliography will prove beneficial to
researchers and students in the field of American
diplomatic history. This bibliography is also
intended to generate interest in the Department of
State by surveying what has been done and pointing
out areas of neglected research.

RESEARCH GUIDES

STATE DEPARTMENT PUBLICATIONS

The Department of State, so named in 1789 following
the election of George Washington, is the oldest
department of the executive branch. The Constitution places the whole of the diplomatic corps
under the command of the president. The Department
of State is one of the most voluminous publishers
in the executive branch. Its publications cover
many aspects of foreign affairs and diplomacy. The
best indexes for identifying these are the Monthly
Catalog and GPO Sales Publications Reference File.
Two publications put out by the Department of State
are especially useful.

Department of State Bulletin. Washington, D.C.:
U.S. Government Printing Office, 1939-.

From 1939 to 1977, the Bulletin was a weekly
publication with semiannual indexes. Since then it

has been issued monthly with an annual index. As the official record of foreign policy, it is an invaluable tool for studying treaties. Documents included in the **Bulletin** are presidential addresses, remarks, radio and television excerpts, correspondence and memoranda, exchanges and greetings with foreign dignitaries and official joint communiques, messages and reports to Congress, and news conferences and proclamations relating to foreign affairs. There are also sections in each issue devoted to the ratification of treaties and announcing executive agreements. In addition to its own index, the **Bulletin** is also indexed in **Public Affairs Information Service Bulletin**, the **Index to U.S. Government Periodicals**, and **Reader's Guide to Periodical Literature**.

The Foreign Relations of the United States, Diplomatic Papers. Washington, D.C.: U.S. Government Printing Office, 1861-.

This series, usually published on an annual basis, contains records on foreign policy and diplomatic practice. A variety of materials can be found in this set, including presidential documents, some treaties, and diplomatic correspondence and reports.

Whether referred to as an accord, protocol, compact, or convention, any international agreement between two or more nations that is governed by international law submitted to the Senate by the president is a treaty. Four compilations provide complete texts for all treaties and executive agreements for 1776 to the present:

U.S. Department of State. **Treaties in Force.** Washington, D.C.: U.S. Government Printing Office, 1929-.

This annual publication, referred to as TIF, lists treaties and agreements of the United States when the treaty is still in effect. The first part lists bilateral treaties and other agreements by country and then by topic. The second part lists multinational agreements arranged by subject and then by country under the subject. The series also cites superceding and terminations of treaty

articles and notes amendments and supplementary
treaties. The monthly **Department of State Bulletin**
will keep you up to date.

U.S. Department of State. **Treaties and Other
International Acts Series**. Washington, D.C.: U.S.
Government Printing Office, 1945-.

This series, referred to as TAIS, is a continuation
of **Treaty Series,** which covers the years 1908-1945
and the **Executive Agreement Series,** which covers
the years 1929-1945. Consequently, the serially
numbered treaties and agreements begin with the
number 1501. Each text is published separately in
pamphlet form six to twelve months after it is in
force. The text, printed in English and the
language of the other country, includes important
dates in its development, the president's
proclamation, and correspondence.

U.S. Department of State. **United States Treaties
and Other International Agreements.** Washington,
D.C.: U.S. Government Printing Office, 1950-.

This annual publication, referred to as UST, provides the text of treaties and agreements proclaim-
ed during the preceding year in the language of the
original instrument. It contains a subject and
country index. Before 1950, the treaties and
agreements were published in the **United States
Statutes at Large**. This annual multivolume set
(UST) cumulates and replaces TAIS.

Bevans, Charles I. **Treaties and Other International
Agreements of the United States of America 1776-
1949.** Washington, D.C.: U.S. Government Printing
Office, 1968-.

This compilation contains all of the treaty and
agreement texts prior to 1950 and is the most
comprehensive collection of treaties. Each volume
has an index, and there are cumulative analytical
indexes. This set is commonly referred to as
"Bevans."

While TIF, TIAS, UST, and Bevans are the primary
sources for finding treaties, there are several
commercial guides that also provide useful
information.

Kavas, Igor I., and M. A. Michael, comps. **United
States Treaties and Other International Agreements
Cumulative Index, 1776-1949.** Buffalo: William S.
Stein, 1975.

This four-volume set can be used to identify
treaties and agreements by their TIAS number, date,
country, and subject.

Kavas, Igor I., and Adolph Sprudas, comps. **UST
Cumulative Index, 1950-1970.** Buffalo: William S.
Stein, 1973-1977.

This five-volume set provides the same kind of
access as the above entry. This series is also
updated by a looseleaf service, which is cumulated
every five years.

Wiktor, Christian L. **Unperfected Treaties of the
United States, 1976-.** Dobbs Ferry, NY: Oceana,
1976.

This set is an annotated compilation of treaties
that were not approved by the Senate or ratified by
the President.

The best sources for finding information about
current treaty developments are the **Department of
State Bulletin,** the **Weekly Compilation of Presidential Documents, TIAS,** and the **Monthly Catalog.**
The following volumes provide a listing of
treaties, agreements, and other international acts
for various time periods. While all of these can
be found in the titles just cited, the following
may be easier to use for specific time periods or
subject matters.

Bryan, Henry L. **Compilation of Treaties in Force.**

Washington, D.C.: U.S. Government Printing Office, 1899.

Davis, J. C. Bancroft. **Treaties and Conventions Concluded Between the United States of American and Other Powers Since July 4, 1776.** Washington, D.C.: U.S. Government Printing Office, 1871.

Elliot, Jonathan, ed. **The American Diplomatic Code: Embracing a Collection of Treaties and Conventions Between the United States and Foreign Powers from 1778 to 1834.** 2 vols. Washington, D.C.: by the editor, 1834.

Executive Agreement Series. Washington, D.C.: U.S. Government Printing Office, 1926-1946.

Hasse, Adelaide R. **Index to United States Documents Relating to Foreign Affairs, 1828-1861.** Washington, D.C.: Carnegie Institute, 1914-1921.

Haswell, John H. **Treaties and Conventions Concluded Between the United States of American and Other Powers Since July 4, 1776.** Washington, D.C.: U.S. Government Printing Office, 1889.

A List of Treaties and Other International Acts of the United States of America in Force on December 31, 1932. Washington, D.C.: U.S. Government Printing Office, 1933.

A List of Treaties and Other International Acts of the United States of American in Force on December 31, 1941. Washington, D.C.: U.S. Government Printing Office, 1944.

List of Treaties Submitted to the Senate, 1789-1934. Washington, D.C.: U.S. Government Printing Office, 1935.

List of Treaties Submitted to the Senate, 1789-1931, Which Have not Gone into Force October 1, 1932. Washington, D.C.: U.S. Government Printing Office, 1932.

List of Treaties Submitted to the Senate, 1935-1944. Washington, D.C.: U.S. Government Printing Office, 1945.

Miller, David Hunter, comp. **Treaties and Other International Acts of the United States of America.** 8 vols. Washington, D.C.: U.S. Government Printing Office, 1931-1948.

Numerical List of the Treaty Series, Executive Agreement Series and Treaties and other International Acts Series. Washington, D.C.: U.S. Government Printing Office, 1950.

Rockhill, W. W., ed. **Treaties, Conventions, Agreements, Ordinances, etc., Relating to China and Korea (October 1904-January 1908).** Washington, D.C.: U.S. Government Printing Office, 1908.

Rockhill, W. W., ed. **Treaties and Conventions with or Concerning China and Korea, 1894-1904, Together with Various State Papers and Documents Affecting Foreign Interests.** Washington, D.C.: U.S. Government Printing Office, 1904.

Treaties, Conventions, International Acts, Protocols, and Agreements Between the U.S.A. and Other Powers, 1776-1937. Washington, D.C.: U.S. Government Printing Office, 1910-1938.

United States Treaty Series. Washington, D.C.: U.S. Government Printing Office, 1908-1946.

U.S. Congress, House Committee on Foreign Affairs. **Collective Defense Treaties.** Committee Print. 91st Cong., 1st sess., 1969.

U.S. Department of State. **A Decade of American Foreign Policy: Basic Documents, 1941-1949.** Washington, D.C.: U.S. Government Printing Office, 1950.

U.S. Department of State. **American Foreign Policy: Current Documents.** Edited by Peter V. Curl. Washington, D.C.: U.S. Government Printing Office, 1956.

U.S. Department of State. **American Foreign Policy, 1950-1955: Basic Documents.** Washington, D.C.: U.S. Government Printing Office, 1957.

United States Department of State Catalogue of
Treaties 1814-1918. Washington, D.C.: U.S.
Government Printing Office, 1919.

The following collections of diplomatic correspondence are useful for the study of treaties for
the periods covered.

Richardson, James D., comp. A Compilaton of the
Messages and Papers of the Confederacy, Including
the Diplomatic Correspondence, 1861-1865. 2 vols.
Nashville: United States Publishing Co., 1905.

Diplomatic Correspondence of the United States:
Concerning the Independence of the Latin-American
Nations. 3 vols. Edited by William R. Manning. New
York: Oxford University Press, 1925.

Diplomatic Correspondence of the United States:
Inter-American Affairs, 1831-1860. 12 vols. Edited
by William R. Manning. Washington, D.C.: Carnegie
Endowment for International Peace, 1932-1939.

The Diplomatic Correspondence of the United States
of America: From the Signing of the Definitive
Treaty of Peace, 10th September, 1783, to the
Adoption of the Constitution, March 4, 1789. 3
vols. 2nd ed. Edited by F. P. Blair and John C.
Rives. Washington, D.C.: Blair and Rives, 1837.

Journal Index to the Published Volumes of the
Diplomatic Correspondence and Foreign Relations of
the United States, 1861-1899. Washington, D.C.:
U.S. Government Printing Office, 1902.

The Revolutionary Diplomatic Correspondence of the
United States. 6 vols. Edited by Francis Wharton.
Washington, D.C.: U.S. Government Printing Office,
1889.

GUIDES TO U.S. DOCUMENTS

Because detailed guides to the technical and
bibliographical aspects of government publications
are readily available, we will keep our discussion
of documents brief. For those interested in such

research, we have provided three annotated entries on the best guides to documents, both for current and historical materials. Researchers should also familiarize themselves with the list of general guides to government documents.

Bitner, Harry, Miles O. Price, and Shirley R. Bysiewicz. **Effective Legal Research.** 4th ed. Boston: Little, Brown, 1969.

This work gives an excellent description of all the tools related to legal research. There are chapters on finding federal statutes, treaties, and other international acts; federal administrative law; and the rules and decision of federal courts and administrative and regulatory agencies.

Morehead, Joe. **Introduction to United States Public Documents.** 3rd ed. Littleton, Colo.: Libraries Unlimited, 1983.

This work, a textbook for library school students and professional librarians, is a valuable guide for anyone interested in researching federal documents. There is a lengthy chapter on the documents of the presidency and the Executive Office of the President and the Department of State. The book is especially useful for learning about the depository system and for identifying the work of the Superintendent of Documents and the Government Printing Office.

Schmeckebeir, Laurence F., and Roy B. Eastin. **Government Publications and Their Use.** 2nd rev ed. Washington, D.C.: Brookings Institution, 1969.

This is a well-known and respected reference work containing extensive information on all forms of government publications. This work contains much information not available elsewhere. Though the volume does not include the numerous reference tools published in the last decade, Schmeckebeir does provide an excellent descripton and analysis of documents published prior to 1900.

Many other research guides to political science and government publications contain sections or chapters on the Department of State. Most of these are available in any college or university library.

Boyd, Anne Morris. **United States Government Publications.** 3rd rev ed. New York: Wilson, 1949.

Brock, Clinton. **The Literature of Political Science: A Guide for Students, Librarians and Teachers.** New York: R. R. Bowker, 1969.

Holler, Frederick L. **The Information Sources of Political Science.** 4th ed. Santa Barbara, Calif.: ABC-Clio, 1985.

Jacobstein, J. Myron, and Roy M. Mersky. **Ervin H. Pollack's Fundamentals of Legal Research.** 4th ed. Mineola, N.Y.: Foundation Press, 1973.

Larson, Donna R. **Guide to U.S. Government Directories.** Phoenix: Oryx Press, 1981.

Lu, Joseph K. **U.S. Government Publications Relating to the Social Sciences: A Selected Annotated Guide.** Beverly Hills, Calif.: Sage Publicatons, 1975.

Mason, John Brown. **Research Resources: Annotated Guide to the Social Sciences.** 2 vols. Santa Barbara, Calif.: ABC-Clio, 1968-1971.

O'Hara, Frederic J. **Guide to Publications of the Executive Branch.** Ann Arbor, Mich.: Pierian Press, 1979.

Palic, Vladimir M. **Government Publications: A Guide to Bibliographic Tools.** 4th ed. Washington, D.C.: U.S. Government Printing Office, 1975.

Vose, Clement E. **A Guide to Library Resources in Political Science: American Government.** Washington, D.C.: American Political Science Associaton, 1975.

Wynar, Lubomyr R. **Guide to Reference Materials in Political Science.** Rochester, N.Y.: Libraries Unlimited, 1967.

Zirwin, Jerold. **Congressional Publications: A Research Guide to Legislation, Budgets and Treaties.** Littleton, Colo.: Libraries Unlimited, 1983.

The following are general indexes to government publications. The first six are especially useful for identifying documents of the eighteenth and nineteenth centuries.

Poore, Ben Perley. **Descriptive Catalog of the Government Publicatons of the United States, September 5, 1774-March 4, 1881.** Washington, D.C.: U.S. Government Printing Office, 1885.

This publication, known as **Poore's Descriptive Catalogue,** attempted to list all governmental publications, but omitted many department publicatons. It is a chronological, annotated list of government publications dated from September, 1774 to March, 1881.

Ames, John Griffith. **Comprehensive Index to the Publications of the United States Government, 1881-1893.** 2 vols. Washington, D.C.: U.S. Government Printing Office, 1905.

This is known as **Ames Comprehensive Index.** Entries are arranged alphabetically by subject. There is an index of names. Some departmental publications were omitted.

Greely, Adolphus Washington. **Public Documents of the First Fourteen Congresses, 1789-1817. Papers Relating to Early Congressional Documents.** Washington, D.C.: U.S. Government Printing Office, 1900.

This is a chronological list of government publications. It includes messages and state papers of presidents that were omitted from Richardson's **Compilation of Presidential Papers.** There is an index of names. Additional information is provided in **Supplement, 1904.** It includes a preliminary list of papers of the first two congresses.

Checklist of United States Public Documents, 1789-
1975. Arlington, Va.: U.S. Historical Documents
Institute, 1976.

This is the single most comprehensive
bibliographical source for U.S. government
documents. All entries provide full bibliographic
citations. The work includes all of the entries in
the 1789-1910 Checklist, the Document Catalog, the
Monthly Catalog, 1895-1976, and the shelflist of
G.P.O.'s Public Documents Library.

Lester, Daniel, and Sandra Faull, comps. Cumulative
Title Index to United States Public Documents,
1789-1976. Arlington, VA: U.S. Historical Documents
Institute, 1978.

This lists all of the titles in the Checklist of
United States Public Documents, 1789-1976.

Catalog of the Public Documents of the [53rd to
76th] Congress and of all Departments of the
Government of the United States [for the Period of
March 4, 1893 through December 31, 1940].
Washington, D.C.: U.S. Government Printing Office,
1896-1945.

Known as the Document Catalog, this was the first
truly systematic record of U.S. public documents
and is the only complete list of executive orders
from 1893 to 1940. It also contains proclamations.
The entries are in alphabetical order. There are
entries from authors, subjects, and some titles.

U.S. Superintendent of Documents. Monthly Catalog
of United States Government Publications.
Washington, D.C.: U.S. Government Printing Office,
1895-.

The Monthly Catalog is the Reader's Guide of U.S.
government publications. While it does not include
all publications, it does index the majority of the
most important ones issued by the federal
government.

Cumulative Subject Index to the Monthly Catalog of
U.S. Government Publications, 1895-1899. 2 vols.

Compiled by Edna A. Kanley. Arlington, Va.: Carrollton Press, 1978.

Cumulative Subject Index to the Monthly Catalog of United States Government Publications, 1900-1971. Compiled by William W. Buchanon and Edna A. Kanley. Arlington, Va.: Carrollton Press, 1975.

The Declassified Documents, Retrospective Collection. 2 vols. Executive ed., Annadel Wile. Operations ed., Elizabeth Jones. Arlington, Va.: Carrollton Press, 1976-1977.

The first part of this work is a catalog of abstracts; the second part is a cumulative subject index.

U.S. Library of Congress. **Popular Names of U.S. Government Reports: A Catalog.** 3rd ed. Washington, D.C.: U.S. Government Printing Office, 1974.

The selected entries in this work are photographic reproductions of Library of Congress catalog cards and are arranged alphabetically by popular name.

Bibliographic Guide to Government Publications: U.S. Boston: G. K. Hall, 1975 -.

This guide includes entries for documents cataloged by the Research Libraries of the New York Public Libraries and from the Library of Congress. The annual editions serve as a supplement to the **Catalog of Government Publications** of the Research Libraries of the New York Public Libraries (40 volumes, G. K. Hall, 1972).

BIBLIOGRAPHIES

The bibliographies and guides listed below are useful in a variety of ways. In addition to providing citiations to secondary materials, especially books and articles, they also contain information on many of the treaty compilations previously cited. They also contain references to other sources of information relating to the study of foreign affairs such as archives, manuscript collections, documentary collections, yearbooks, atlases, oral histories, and special collections. All three of these guides are superb reference tools and should be consulted in any study of the Department of State.

Burns, Richard Dean, ed. **Guide to American Foreign Relations Since 1700.** Santa Barbara, Calif.: ABC-Clio, 1983.

Bemis, Samuel Flagg. **Guide to the Diplomatic History of the United States, 1775-1921.** Washington, D.C.: U.S. Government Printing Office, 1935.

Plishke, Elmer. **U.S. Foreign Relations: A Guide to Information Sources.** Detroit: Gale Research Co., 1980.

In addition to the above reference works, there are a variety of more specialized bibliographies on foreign affairs in general and American diplomacy.

American Historical Association. **The American Historical Association's Guide to Historical Literature.** New York: Macmillan, 1961.

Basler, Roy P., et al., eds. **A Guide to the Study of the United States of America.** Washington, D.C..: Library of Congress, 1960.

Bemis, Samuel Flagg, and Griffin, Grace Gardner, eds. **Guide to the Diplomatic History of the United States, 1775-1921.** Washington, D.C.: U.S. Government Printing Office, 1935.

Beers, Henry P., ed. **Bibliographies in American History: Guide to Materials for Research.** New York: Wilson, 1942.

Billington, Ray A. **Guides to American History Manuscript Collections in Libraries of the United States.** New York: Peter Smith, 1952.

Boyce, Richard F., and Boyce, Katherine Randall. **American Foreign Service Authors: A Bibliography.** Metuchen, N.J.: Scarecrow, 1973.

Carman, Harry J., and Thompson, Arthur W. A Guide to the Principal Sources for American Civilization, 1800-1900, in the City of New York: Printed Materials. New York: Columbia University Press, 1962.

Conover, Helen F. A Guide to Bibliographical Tools for Research in Foreign Affairs. 2nd rev. ed. Washington, D.C.: Library of Congress, 1958.

Coulter, Edith M., and Gerstenfeld, Melanie. Historical Bibliographies: A Systematic and Annotated Guide. Berkeley: University of California Press, 1935.

Council on Foreign Relations. Catalog of the Foreign Relations Library. 9 vols. Boston: G. K. Hall, 1969.

DeConde, Alexander, ed. American Diplomatic History in Transformation. Washington, D.C.: American Historical Association, 1976.

Dexter, Byron, with Bryant, Elizabeth H., and Murray, Janice L., eds. The Foreign Affairs Fifty-Year Bibliography: New Evaluation of Significant Books on International Relations, 1920-1970. New York: Bowker, 1972.

Foreign Affiars Bibliography: A Selected and Annotated List of Books on International Relations. New York: Harper, 1933-.

Fowler, Wilton B. American Diplomatic History since 1890. Northbrook, Ill.: AHM, 1975.

Freidel, Frank, ed. Harvard Guide to American History. 2 vols. Cambridge: Harvard University Press, 1974.

Graebner, Norma A. American Diplomatic History before 1900. Arlington Heights, Ill: AHM, 1978

Griffin, Grace G., ed. A Guide to Manuscripts Relating to American History in British Repositories Reproduced for the Library of Congress. Washington, D.C.: Library of Congress, 1946.

Groom, A. J. R., and Mitchell, C. R., eds. International Relations Theory: A Bibliography. New York: Nichols, 1978.

Gustafson, Milton O., ed. The National Archives and Foreign Relations Research. Athens: Ohio University Press, 1974.

Haines, Gerlad K., and Walker, J. Samuel, eds. American Foreign Relations: A Historical Review. Westport, Conn.: Greenwood, 1981.

Hamer, Philip M., ed. A Guide to Archives and Manuscripts in the United States. New Haven: Yale University Press, 1961.

Hanningan, Jane A., comp. Publications of the Carnegie Endowment for International Peace, 1910-1967, Including International Conciliation, 1924-1967. New York: Carnegie Endowment, 1971.

Harmon, Robert B. The Art and Practice of Diplomacy: A Selected and Annotated Guide. Metuchen, N.J.: Scarecrow, 1971.

LaBarr, Dorothy F., and Singer, J. David. The Study of International Politics: A Guide to the Sources for the Student, Teacher, and Researcher. Santa Barbara, Calif.: ABC-Clio, 1976.

Lowenstein, Linda, comp. Government Resources Available for Foreign Affairs Research. Washington, D.C.: U.S. Government Printing Office, 1965.

Matthews, William. American Diaries in Manuscript, 1580-1954: A Descriptive Bibliography. Athens: University of Georgia Press, 1974.

Morgan, Dole, L., and Hammond, George P., eds. A Guide to the Manuscript Collections of the Bancroft Library. Berkeley: University of California Press, 1963-.

Orr, Oliver H., Jr., A Guide to the Study of the United States of America: Supplement 1956-1965. Washington, D.C.: Library of Congress, 1976.

Pfaltzgraff, Robert L. The Study of International

xxviii Department of State and American Diplomacy

Relations: A Guide to Information Sources. Detroit:
Gale, 1977.

Poulton, Helen J. **The Historian's Handbook: A
Descriptive Guide to Reference Works.** Norman:
University of Oklahoma Press, 1972.

U.S. Library of Congress. **The National Union Catalog of Manuscript Collections.** Hamden, Conn.: Shoe
String Press, 1962.

Ulibarri, George S., and Harrison, John P. **Guide to
Materials on Latin America in the National Archives
of the United States.** Washington, D.C.: National
Archives and Records Service, 1974.

Wright, Moorhead; David, Jane; and Clarke, Michael.
**Essay Collections in International Relations: A
Classified Bibliography.** New York: Garland, 1977.

The Department of State and American Diplomacy

DEPARTMENT OF STATE AND
DIPLOMATIC SERVICE

DEPARTMENT OF STATE

General Studies

1. Barron, Bryton. **The State Department: Blunders or Treason?** Springfield, Va.: Cestwood, 1965.
2. _____. **The Untouchable State Department.** Springfield Va.: Crestwood, 1962.
3. Bendiner, Robert. **The Riddle of the State Department.** New York: Farrar and Rinehart, 1942.
4. Bess, Demaree C. "Why Americans Hate the State Department." **Saturday Evening Post** 223 (August 1950): 20-23, 77-78, 80, 83.
5. Blaney, Harry C. "Global Challenges and the Fudge Factory." **Foreign Service Journal** 51 (September 1974): 13-14, 26.
6. Briggs, Ellis O. **Farewell to Foggy Bottom: The Recollections of a Career Diplomat.** New York: McKay, 1964.
7. Brown, Ben H. "Congress and the Department of State" **Annals of the American Academy of Political and Social Science** 289 (September 1953): 100-107.
8. Calkin, Homer L. **Women in the Department of State: Their Role in American Foreign Affairs.** 2nd ed. Washington, D.C.: Government Printing Office, 1978.
9. Campbell, John F. **The Foreign Affairs Fudge Factory.** New York: Basic Books, 1971.
10. Chu, Francis Yu-Ou. "The American Department of State and Foreign Service." Ph.D. dissertation, University of Wisconsin, 1936.
11. David, Joan. **Inside the State Department: How It Works at Home and Abroad.** New York: Manhattan, 1952.
12. Elder, Robert E. **The Policy Machine: The Department of State and American Foreign Policy.** Syracuse, N.Y.: Syracuse University Press, 1960
13. Estes, Thomas S., and E. Allen Lightner. **The Department of State.** New York: Praeger, 1976.
14. Frankel, Charles R. **High on Foggy Bottom: An Outsider's View of the Government.** New York: Harper and Row, 1968.

15. Garnham, David. "State Department Rigidity: Testing a Hypothetical Hypothesis." **International Studies Quarterly** 18 (March 1974): 31-39.
16. Gerber, William. **The Department of State of the United States**. Washington, D.C.: Government Printing Office, 1942.
17. Halberstam, David. **The Best and the Brightest**. New York: Random House, 1972.
18. Harr, John E. "The Issue of Competence in the State Department." **International Studies Quarterly** 14 (March 1970): 95-101.
19. Herring, Hubert C. "The Department of State." **Harper's Magazine** 174 (February 1937): 225-238.
20. Hulen, Bertram D. **Inside the Department of State**. New York: McGraw Hill, 1939.
21. Krogh, Peter F. "The State Department at Home." **Annals of the American Academy of Political and Social Science** 380 (November 1968): 118-124.
22. Leacacos, John P. **Fires in the In-Basket: The ABC's of the State Department**. Cleveland: World, 1968.
23. Leonidov, A. "Twilight of the Gods: The Glory and Decline of the State Department." **New Times** 39 (September 1960): 9-12.
24. Miller, August C. "The New State Department." **American Journal of International Law** 33 (July 1939): 500-518.
25. Pringle, Robert. "Creeping Irrelevance of Foggy Bottom." **Foreign Policy** 29 (Winter 1977-78): 128-139.
26. Pritt, Denis N. **The State Department and the Cold War**. New York: International Publishers, 1948.
27. Simpson, Smith. **Anatomy of the State Department**. Boston: Beacon Press, 1967.
28. _____. **The Crisis in the American Diplomacy: A Shot Across the Bow of the State Department**. North Quincy, Mass.: Christopher, 1979.
29. Spaulding, E. Wilder, and George Verne Blue. **The Department of State of the United States**. Washington, D.C.: Government Printing Office, 1936.
30. Terrell, John U. **The United States Depart-**

ment of State: **A Story of Diplomats, Embassies and Foreign Policy.** New York: Duell, Sloan, and Pearce, 1964.

31. U.S. Department of State. **Department of State--1963: A Report to the Citizen.** Washington, D.C.: Government Printing Office, 1963.

32. _____. **The Department of State, 1930-1955.** Washington, D.C.: Government Printing Office, 1955.

33. _____. **The Department of State of the United States.** Washington, D.C.: Government Printing Office, 1933.

34. _____. **The Department Today.** Washington, D.C.: Government Printing Office, 1951.

35. _____. **Foreign Policy and the Department of State.** Washington, D.C.: Government Printing Office, 1976.

36. Webb, James E. "Department of State." **Air Affairs** 3 (Autumn 1949): 34-43.

37. Willis, Davis K. **The State Department.** Boston: Christian Science Publishing Society, 1968.

Organization

38. Alger, Chad F. "The External Bureaucracy in United States Foreign Affairs: Utilizing Data from a Study of the Participation of Private Experts in the Conduct of United States Foreign Affairs." **Administrative Science Quarterly** 7 (June 1962): 50-78.

39. Bacchus, William I. **Foreign Policy and the Bureaucratic Process: The State Department's Country Director System.** Princeton, N.J.: Princeton University Press, 1974.

40. _____. "Foreign Affairs Officials: Professionals Without Professions." **Public Administration Review** 37 (November/December 1977): 641-650.

41. Ball, Harris H. "An Examination of the Major Efforts for Organizational Effectiveness in the Department of State from 1924 to 1971." Master's thesis, George Washington University, 1971.

42. Barron, Bryton. **Inside the State Department: A Candid Appraisal of the Bureaucracy.** New York: Comet, 1956.

43. Bilder, Richard B. "The Office of the Legal Adviser: The State Department Lawyer and Foreign Affairs." **American Journal of International Law** 56 (July 1962): 633-684.

44. Bruce, Diana A. "The Office of Congressional Relations of the Department of State, 1959-1960." Master's thesis, University of California, 1961.

45. Burke, Lee H. **The Department of State's Congressional Relations Office.** Washington, D.C.: U.S. Department of State, Office of the Historian, 1977.

46. Destler, I. M. "State and Presidential Leadership." **Foreign Service Journal** 48 (September 1971): 26, 31-32, 43.

47. Esterline, John H., and Robert B. Black. **Inside Foreign Policy: The Department of State Political System and Its Subsystems.** Palo Alto, Calif.: Mayfield, 1975.

48. Hannah, Norman B. "Craftsmanship and Responsibility: A Restatement of the Generalist-Specialist Problem." **Foreign Service Journal** 39 (April 1962): 21-24.

49. Healey, Maryanne F. "Witness, Participant, and Chronicler: The Role of Herbert Feis as Economic Adviser to the State Department, 1931-1943." Ph.D. dissertation, Georgetown University, 1973.

50. Macomber, William B. "Management Strategy: A Program for the Seventies." **Department of State Bulletin** 62 (February 1970): 130-141.

51. Maddox, William P. "Foreign Service Institute of the U.S. Department of State." **Higher Education** 4 (October 1947): 37-40.

52. Marrow, Alfred J. **Making Waves in Foggy Bottom: How a New and More Scientific Approach Changed the Management of the State Department.** Washington D.C.: NTL Institute, 1974.

53. Nelson, O. L. **Report on the Organization of the Department of State.** Washington, D.C.: U.S. Department of State, 1946.

54. Norton, Henry K. "Foreign Office Organization." **Annals of the American Academy of Political and Social Science** 143 (May 1929): 1-83.

55. "Organization of the Department of State."

Department of State Bulletin 20 (June
1949): 835.

56. Osborne, John. "Is the State Department
Manageable?" **Fortune** 55 (March 1957): 110-
112, 267-268, 270, 272, 276, 278.

57. Peurifoy, John E. "The Department of State:
A Reflection of U.S. Leadership." **Department of State Bulletin** 21 (October 1949):
671-674.

58. Richardson, Elliot L. "The Office of the
Under Secretary for Western Hemisphere
Affairs." **Department of State Bulletin** 62
(April 1970): 498-499.

59. Scott, Andrew M. "The Department of State:
Formal Organization and Informal Culture."
International Studies Quarterly 13 (Spring
1969): 1-18.

60. Shoup, Laurence H. "Shaping the National
Interest: The Council on Foreign Rela-
tions, the Department of State, and the
Origins of the Postwar World, 1939-1943."
Ph.D. dissertation, Northwestern Univer-
sity, 1974.

61. Silberman, Lawrence H. "Toward Presidential
Control of the State Department." **Foreign
Affairs** 57 (Spring 1979): 872-893.

62. Stowell, Ellery C. **The Economic Adviser of
the Department of State.** Washington, D.C.:
Digest Press, 1935.

63. _____. **The Legal Adviser of the Department
of State.** Washington, D.C.: Digest Press,
1936.

64. Stuart, Graham H. **The Department of State: A
History of Its Organization, Procedure and
Personnel.** New York: Macmillan, 1949.

65. U.S. Bureau of the Budget. **The Organization
and Administration of the Department of
State.** Washington, D.C.: Bureau of the
Budget, 1945.

66. Warwick, Donald P. "Bureaucratization in a
Government Agency: The Case of the U.S.
State Department." **Sociological Inquiry** 44
(Spring 1974): 75-92.

67. _____. **A Theory of Public Bureaucracy:
Politics, Personality, and Organization in
the State Department.** Cambridge, Mass.:
Harvard University Press, 1975.

Functions

68. Bolles, Blair. **Who Makes Our Foreign Policy?**
     New York: Foreign Policy Association,
     1947.
69. _____., and O. K. D. Ringwood. "Modern
     Functions and Tasks of the State Depart-
     ment. "**Foreign Policy Reports** 23 (August
     1947): 144.
70. Bowie, Robert R. "Planning in the Depart-
     ment." **Foreign Service Journal** 38 (March
     1961): 20-24.
71. Bowling, John W. "How We Do Our Things:
     Policy Formulation." **Foreign Service
     Journal** 47 (January 1970): 19-22, 48.
72. Casey, William J. "The Economic Role of the
     State Department." **Department of State
     Bulletin** 68 (June 1973): 849-852.
73. Clubb, O. Edmund. "Security Risks: National
     Security and the State Department."
     Foreign Service Journal 50 (December
     1973): 13-15.
74. Cooper, Joseph D. "Decision Making and the
     Action Process in the Department of
     State." Ph.D. dissertation, American
     University, 1951.
75. Coulter, Elliot B. "Visa Work of the Depart-
     ment of State and the Foreign Service."
     Department of State Bulletin 28 (February
     1953): 195-203.
76. Curran, R. T. "The State Department's Revo-
     lution in Executive Management." **Foreign
     Service Journal** 49 (October 1972):
     4,6,8,12.
77. Davis, David H. "Bureaucratic Exchange in
     Policy Formulation: The State Department's
     Relations with Three Domestic Agencies in
     the Foreign Affairs Arena." Ph.D. disser-
     tation, Johns Hopkins University, 1971.
78. "The Department of State, 1930-1955: Expand-
     ing Functions and Responsibilities."
     Department of State Bulletin 32 (March
     1955): 470-486, 528-544.
79. Gimlin, Hoyt. "State Department and Policy
     Making." **Editorial research Reports** 1
     (June 1969): 467-484.
80. Gross, Ernest A. "Operation in the Legal
     Adviser's Office." **American Journal of**

International Law 43 (January 1949): 122-127.

81. Hunt, Gaillard. **The Department of State in the United States:Its History and Functions**. New Haven, Conn.: Yale University Press, 1914.

82. Kennan, George F. "Planning in the Department." **Foreign Service Journal** 38 (March 1961): 20-24.

83. Knight,Jonathan. "The State Department Budget, 1933-1965: A Research Note." **American Journal of Political Science** 12 (November 1968): 587-598.

84. Lee, D. E. "State Department and Foreign Policy." **Proceedings of the American Academy of Political and Social Science** 25 (May 1952): 100-108.

85. McCleod, Scott. "Security in the Department of State." **Department of State Bulletin** 30 (March 1954): 469-472.

86. Madar, Daniel R. "Foreign Policy Planning: Its Practice and Problems in the U.S. Department of State." Ph.D. dissertation, University of Toronto, 1974.

87. Manning, Robert J. "Policy and People." **Department of State Bulletin** 49 (October 1963): 639-644.

88. Michael, William H. **History of the Department of State of the United States: Its Functions and Duties, Together with Biographies of its Present Officers and Secretaries from the Beginning**. Washington, D.C.: Government Printing Office, 1901.

89. Morgan, George A. "Planning in Foreign Affairs: The State of the Art." **Foreign Affairs** 39 (January 1961): 271-278.

90. Morgenstern, Oskar. "Decision Theory and the State Department." **Foreign Service Journal** 37 (December 1960): 19-22.

91. Perkins, Edward J. "The Priorities Policy Group: A Case Study of the Institutionalization of a Policy Linkage and Resource Allocation Mechanism in the Department of State." D.P.A., University of Southern California, 1978.

92. "Planning in the Department: Views of Those Who Have Directed the Department's Policy

Planning Staff Since its Inception in 1947." **Foreign Service Journal** 38 (March 1961): 20-24.

93.   Pruitt, Dean G. **Problem Solving in the Department of State.** Denver: University of Denver, 1964.

94.   Robinson, James A. "Process Satisfaction and Policy Approval in State Department-Congressional Relations." **American Journal of Sociology** 67 (November 1961): 278-283.

95.   Rockman, B. A. "America's Departments of State: Irregular and Regular Syndromes of Policy Making." **American Political Science Review** 75 (December 1981): 911-927.

96.   Stempel, John D. "Policy/Decision Making in the Department of State: The Vietnamese Problem, 1961-1965." Ph.D. dissertation, University of California, Berkeley, 1965.

97.   Wilkinson, Vernon L. "Department of State: Its Functions, Its History, and Its Operation." Ph.D. dissertation, American University, 1933.

Historical Studies

98.   Baram, Philip J. **The Department of State in the Middle East. 1919-1945.** Philadelphia: University of Pennsylvania Press, 1978.

99.   Chittick, William O. **State Department, Press, and Pressure Groups: A Role Analysis.** New York: Wiley Interscience, 1970.

100.   Chitversus, W. O. "State Department-Press Antagonism: Opinion versus Policy-Making Needs?" **Journal of Politics** 31 (August 1969): 756-771.

101.   Jablon, Howard. "The State Department and Collective Security, 1933-1934." **Historian** 33 (February 1971): 248-263.

102.   Kuhn, Arnold J. "The State Department's Presentation to the American People of American-Soviet Relations, 1945-1947." Ph.D. dissertation, University of Chicago, 1950.

103.   Lowenfeld, A. F. "Act of State and Department of State: First National City Bank v. Banco Nacional de Cuba." **American Journal of International Law** 66 (October 1972):

795-814.
104. Mashberg, Michael. "Documents Concerning the
      American State Department and the State-
      less European Jews, 1942-1944." **Jewish
      Social Studies** 39 (Winter-Spring 1977):
      163-182.
105. Messer, Robert L. "Paths Not Taken: The
      United States Department of State and
      Alternatives to Containment, 1945-1946."
      Diplomatic History 1 (Fall 1977): 297-320.
106. Metzger, S. D. "State Department's Role in
      the Judicial Administration of the Act of
      State Doctrine." **American Journal of In-
      ternational Law** 66 (January 1972): 94-101.
107. Niven, John. "Gideon Welles and Naval Admin-
      istration During the Civil War." **American
      Neptune** 35 (January 1975): 53-66.
108. Spiers, Ronald I. "International Security
      Affairs and the Department of State."
      Department of State Bulletin 66 (April
      1972): 591-597.
109. Utley, Jonathan G. "Upstairs, Downstairs at
      Foggy Bottom: Oil Exports and Japan, 1940-
      1941." **Prologue** 8 (Spring 1976): 17-28.
110. Warshawsky, Howard. "The Department of State
      and Human Rights Policy: A Case Study of
      the Human Rights Bureau." **World Affairs**
      142 (Winter 1980): 188-215.
111. West, Rachel. **The Department of State on the
      Eve of the First World War.** Athens:
      University of Georgia Press, 1978.

Great Seal

112. Burke, Lee H. **Homes of the Department of
      State, 1774-1976: The Buildings Occupied
      by the Department of State and its
      Predecessors.** Washington, D.C.: Historical
      Office, U.S. Department of State, 1977.
113. Cigrand, Bernard J. **Story of the Great Seal
      of the United States; or History of
      American Emblems.** Chicago: Cameron,
      Ambers, 1908.
114. Gustafson, Milton O. "Archival Implications
      of State Department Recordkeeping."
      Prologue 7 (Spring 1975): 36-38.
115. _____. "State Department Records in the
      National Archives: A Profile." **Prologue** 2

(Winter 1970): 175-180.

116. Hunt, Gaillard. **The History of the Seal of the United States.** Washington, D.C.: U.S. Department of State, 1892.

117. _____. **The Seal of the United States: How It Was Developed and Adopted.** Washington, D.C.: Government Printing Office 1909.

118. Hurst, Carlton B. **The Arms Above the Door.** New York: Dodd, Mead, 1932.

119. Lander, E. T. "The Great Seal of the United States." **Magazine of American History** 29 (May-June 1893): 471-491.

120. Leopold, Richard W. "The Foreign Relations Series: A Centennial Estimate." **Journal of American History** 49 (March 1963): 595-612.

121. _____. "The Foreign Relations Series Revisited: One Hundred Plus Ten." **Journal of American History** 59 (March 1973): 935-957.

122. Lossing, Benson J. "The Great Seal of the United States." **Harper's Magazine** 13 (July 1856): 178-186.

123. Patterson, Richard S. "The Seal of the Department of State." **Department of State Bulletin** 21 (December 1949): 894-896.

124. _____., and Richardson Dougall. **The Eagle and the Shield: A History of the Great Seal of the United States.** Washington, D.C.: Government Printing Office, 1976.

125. U.S. Department of State. **The Seal of the United States.** Washington, D.C.: Government Printing Office, 1957.

Secretary of State

126. Bemis, Samuel F., ed. **The American Secretaries of State and Their Diplomacy.** 10 vols. New York: Knopf, 1927-1929.

127. DeConde, Alexander. **The American Secretary of State: An Interpretation.** New York: Praeger, 1962.

128. Dougall, Richardson, and Richard S. Patterson. "The Numbering of the Secretaries of State." **Department of State Bulletin** 41 (July 1959): 80-82.

129. Falkowski, Lawrence. **Presidents, Secretaries of State, and Crises in U.S. Foreign Relations.** Boulder, Colo.: Westview, 1978.

130. "Function of Secretary of State in National

Elections." **Department of State Bulletin** 18 (November 1948): 587.

131. Graebner, Norman A., ed. **An Uncertain Tradition: American Secretaries of State in the Twentieth Century.** New York: McGraw-Hill, 1961.

132. Greenberg, Myron A. "The Secretary of State and Secretarial Belief Systems: An Inquiry into the Relationship Between Knowledge and Action." Ph.D. dissertation, University of Cincinnati, 1979.

133. Gustafson, Merlin. "Our Part-Time Chief of State." **Presidential Studies Quarterly** 9 (Spring 1979): 163-171.

134. Heller, David. **Paths of Diplomacy: America's Secretaries of State.** Philadelphia: Lippincott, 1967.

135. Hill, Norman L. **Mr. Secretary of State.** New York: Random House, 1963.

136. "How the Secretary of State Apportions His Time." **Department of State Bulletin** 54 (April 1966): 651-654.

137. Jackson, Henry M., ed. **The Secretary of State and the Ambassador: Jackson Subcommittee Papers on the Conduct of American Foreign Policy.** New York: Praeger, 1966.

138. Price, Don K., ed. **The Secretary of State.** Englewood Cliffs, N.J.: Prentice-Hall, 1960.

139. Rigert, Joseph C. "The Office of the Assistant Secretary of State for Congressional Relations: A Study of an Aspect of Executive-Legislative Relations in the Formulation of Foreign Policy." Master's thesis, Georgetown University, 1959

140. Taylor, John M. "Autographs of American Diplomats: The Secretaries of State." **American Book Collector** 25 (July-August 1974): 16-19.

141. Tessendorf, K. C. "Mr. Secretary, May We Have Your Remittance, Please?" **Foreign Service Journal** 47 (August 1970): 39-41.

142. U.S. Department of State. **The Secretaries of State: Portraits and Biographical Sketches.** Compiled by Lee H. Burke and Jan K. Herman. Washington, D.C.: Government Printing Office, 1978.

143. Weil, Martin. **A Pretty Good Club: The Found-**

ing Fathers of the U.S. Foreign Service.
New York: Norton, 1978.

144. Wriston, Henry M., "The Secretary of State
Abroad." **Foreign Affairs** 34 (July 1956):
523-541.

Reform

145. Argyris, Chris. **Some Causes of Organizational Ineffectiveness within the Department of State.** Washington, D.C.: Government Printing Office, 1967.
146. Attwood, William. "The Labyrinth in Foggy
Bottom: A Critique of the State Department." **Atlantic** 219 (February 1967): 45-
50.
147. Bolles, Blair. "Reorganization of the State
Department." **Foreign Policy Reports** 23
(August 1947): 134-143.
148. Briggs, Ellis O. "The Sad State of the
Department of State: Part I. The Hog-Tied
Ambassador." **Esquire** 60 (September 1963):
100-101, 150-151.
149. Brown, MacAlister. "The Demise of State
Department Public Opinion Polls: A Study
in Legislative Oversight." **Midwest
Journal of Political Science** 5 (February
1961): 1-17.
150. Epernay, Mark. "The Sad State of the Department of State: Part II. The How-Wild
Machine." **Esquire** 60 (September 1963):
102-103, 151-153.
151. Evans, A. D. "Reorganization of the American
Foreign Service." **International Affairs**
24 (April 1948): 206-217.
152. Felix, David. "Three Suggestions for Strengthening the Foreign Service." **Foreign
Service Journal** 32 (December 1955): 30-31,
42-45.
153. Graves, Harold N. "State Department--New
Model." **Reporter** 1 (November 1949): 27-
29.
154. Johnson, Richard A. "A Proposal for Reorgan-
izing the High Command of the Department
of State." **Foreign Service Journal** 48
(October 1971): 19-20, 38.
155. Kennedy, Aubrey L. "Reorganization of the
Foreign Service." **Quarterly Review** 566

(October 1945): 397-413.
156. Laves, Walter H. C., and Francis O. Wilcox. "The Reorganization of the Department of State." **American Political Science Review** 38 (April 1944): 289-301.
157. _____. "The State Department Continues Its Reorganization." **American Political Science Review** 39 (April 1945): 309-317.
158. Macomber, William B. "Change in Foggy Bottom: An Anniversary Report on Management Reform and Modernization in the Department of State." **Department of State Bulletin** 66 (February 1972): 206-212.
159. _____. "Diplomacy for the Seventies: A Program of Management Reform for the Department of State." **Department of State Bulletin** 63 (December 1970): 775-793.
160. Mead, Lawrence M. "Foreign Service Reform; A View from HEW." **Foreign Service Journal** 52 (October 1975): 21-24.
161. Mosher, Frederick C. "Some Observations About Foreign Service Reform: Famous First Words." **Public Administration Review** 29 (November-December 1969): 600-610.
162. Myers, Denys, and Charles F. Ransom. "Reorganization of the State Department." **American Journal of International Law** 31 (October 1937): 713-720.
163. Saltzman, Charles E. "Progress Report on the Wriston Committee Recommendations." **Foreign Service Journal** 32 (January 1955): 18-21, 42.
164. Scott, Andrew M. "Environmental Change and Organizational Adaptation: The Problem of the State Department." **Foreign Service Journal** 47 (June 1970): 25-27, 63.
165. Simpson, Smith. "Perceptives of Reform: Part I. The Era of Wilbur Carr." **Foreign Service Journal** 48 (August 1971): 17-19, 41.
166. _____. "Perspectives of Reform: Part II. The Post-Carr Period." **Foreign Service Journal** 48 (September 1971): 21-25.
167. _____. "Reform From Within: The Importance of Attitudes." **Foreign Service Journal** 47 (May 1970): 33-34, 47.
168. Stuart, Graham H. "A Streamlined State Department." **Current History** 18 (February 1950): 71-75.

169. Sylvester, John. "Will Candor Survive the Leaking Ship of State?" **Foreign Service Journal** 52 (June 1975): 15-16, 32.

170. U.S. Department of State. **Directive to Improve the Personnel Program of the Department of State and the United Foreign Service of the United States.** Washington, D.C.: Government Printing Office, 1951.

171. Vogelsang, Sandy. "Feminism in Foggy Bottom: Man's World, Woman's Place?" **Foreign Service Journal** 49 (August 1972): 4, 6, 8, 10-11.

Relations with International Organizations

172. Baer, Peter R. **The Role of a National Delegation in the General Assembly.** New York: Carnegie Endowment, 1970.

173. Bailie, Robert H. "The UNESCO Relations Staff of the Department of State: A Study of Agency Response to Public and Private Pressures." Ph.D. dissertation, University of Pittsburgh, 1964.

174. Beichman, Arnold. **The "Other" State Department: The United States Mission to the United Nations--Its Role in the Making of Foreign Policy.** New York: Basic Books, 1967.

175. Bloomfield, Lincoln P. "The Department of State and the United Nations." **International Organization** 4 (August 1950): 400-411.

176. Bloomfield, Lincoln P. "The United Nations in Crisis: the Role of the United Nations in United States Foreign Policy." **Daedalus** 91 (Fall 1962): 749-765.

177. Cleveland, Harlan. "The Future Role of the United States in the United Nations." **Annals of the American Academy of Political and Social Science** 342 (July 1962): 69-79.

178. Downing, Marvin L. "Hugh B. Wilson and American Relations with the League of Nations, 1927-1937." Ph.D. dissertation, University of Oklahoma, 1970.

179. Edel, Wilbur. "The State Department, the Public and the United Nations Concept, 1939-1945." Ph.D. dissertation, Columbia

University, 1951.
180. Gershman, C. "Andrew Young Affair." **Commentary** 68 (November 1979): 25-33.
181. Goldberg, Arthur J. "Public Diplomacy at the U.N." **Department of State Bulletin** 57 (August 1967): 262-265.
182. Gross, Franz. B., ed. **The United States and the United Nations.** Norman: University of Oklahoma Press, 1964.
183. Haviland, H. Field. "The United States and the United Nations." **International Organization** 19 (Summer 1965): 643-665.
184. Hyde, James N. "U.S. Participation in the UN." **International Organization** 10 (Feburary 1956): 22-34.
185. Joyce, J. A. "Will USA quit ILO?" **Contemporary Review** 228 (April 1976): 169-174.
186. Kahan, Gilbert N. "Pressure Group Influence on Foreign Policy Decision Making: A Case Study of the United States' Efforts to Join the World Court, 1935." Ph.D. dissertation, New York University, 1972.
187. MacVane, John. **Embassy Extraordinary: The U.S. Mission to the United Nations.** New York: Public Affairs Committee, 1961.
188. Mangone, Gerard J. "The United Nations and United States Foreign Policy." **Texas Quarterly** 6 (Spring 1963): 11-18.
189. Maynes, Charles W. "A U.N. Policy for the Next Administration." **Foreign Affairs** 54 (July 1976): 804-819.
190. Mazuzan, George T. "America's U.N. Commitment, 1943-1953." **Historian** 40 (February 1978): 309-330.
191. Meck, John F., and Louis W. Koenig. **The Administration of United States Participation in International Organizations.** Washington, D.C.: American Society for Public Administration, 1950.
192. Ostrower, Garry B. "American Ambassador to the League of Nations--1933: A Proposal Postponed." **International Organization** 25 (Winter 1971): 46-58.
193. Parker, Chauncey G. "The Ambassadorship to the United Nations." **Yale Review** 63 (Autumn 1973): 1-9.
194. Patterson, David S. "The United States and the Origins of the World Court." **Politi-**

cal Science **Quarterly** 91 (Summer 1976): 279-295.
195. Pederson, Richard F. "National Representation in the United Nations." **International Organization** 15 (Spring 1951): 255-266.
196. Richardson, Channing B. "The United States Mission to the United Nations." **International Organization** 7 (February 1953): 22-34.
197. Snyder, Charles K. "The Department of State and the Congress: A Study of the Effect of Foreign Policies of Positive Internationalism and Membership in the United Nations on Organization and Procedure." Ph.D. dissertation, Cornell University, 1953.
198. U.S. Department of State. **U.S. Participation in the UN.** Washington, D.C.: Government Printing Office, 1946.
199. Wilcox, Francis O., and H. Field Haviland. **The United States and the United Nations.** Baltimore: Johns Hopkins University Press, 1961.
200. Young, Andrew. **Andrew Young at the United Nations.** Edited by Lee Clement. Salisbury, N.C.: Documentary Publications, 1978.

Diplomacy

Historical Studies

201. Adams, John. **Letters From a Distinguished American: Twelve Essays By John Adams on American Foreign Policy, 1780.** Washington, D.C.: Government Printing Office, 1978.
202. Anderson, George L., ed. **Issues and Conflicts: Studies in Twentieth Century American Diplomacy.** Lawrence: University of Kansas Press, 1959.
203. Armstrong, Willis C. "The Trade Policy Crisis." **Foreign Service Journal** 48 (November 1971): 14-18.
204. Ayres, Philip W. "The Diplomatic Relations of the United States with Great Britain During the Revolution, the Confederation, and Washington's First Administration." Ph.D. dissertation, Johns Hopkins University, 1888.

205. Badeau, John S. "Diplomacy and Medicine."
     Bulletin of the New York Academy of Medi-
     cine 46 (May 1970): 303-312.
206. Bailey, Thomas A. **The Art of Diplomacy:**
     American Experience. New York: Appleton-
     Century-Crofts, 1968.
207. Ball, George W. **The Discipline of Power:**
     Essentials of a Modern World Structure.
     Boston: Little, Brown, 1968.
208. _____. "The New Diplomacy." **Department of**
     State Bulletin 52 (June 1965): 1042-1048.
209. Barragy, Terrence J. "American Maritime
     Otter Diplomacy." Ph.D. dissertation,
     University of Wisconsin, Madison, 1974.
210. Beaulac, Willard L. "U.S. Diplomacy in a
     Changing World." **Department of State**
     Bulletin 33 (August 1955): 335-338.
211. Bell, Sidney. **Righteous Conquest: Woodrow**
     Wilson and the Evolution of the New Diplo-
     macy. Port Washington, N.Y.: Kennikat,
     1972.
212. Bemis, Samuel F. **The Diplomacy of the**
     American Revolution. Bloomington: Indiana
     University Press, 1957.
213. Berry, Nicholas O. "The Management of
     Foreign Penetration." **Orbis** 17 (Summer
     1973): 598-619.
214. Bishop, William W., et al. "Report of Ad-
     visory Committee on Foreign Relations,
     1964." **American Journal of International**
     Law 59 (October 1965): 914-918.
215. Black, Eugene R. **The Diplomacy of Economic**
     Development. Cambridge, Mass.: Harvard
     University Press, 1960.
216. Bliven, Bruce. "The New Techniques of
     Diplomacy." **New Republic** 29 (November
     1943): 782-784.
217. Bohlen, Charles E. "Economic Assistance in
     United States Foreign Policy." **Department**
     of State Bulletin 42 (March 1960): 495-
     501.
218. _____. "The Importance of Foreign Rela-
     tions." **Department of State Bulletin** 46
     (June 1962): 1012-1018.
219. Bowles, Chester. "A Balance Sheet on U.S.
     Foreign Policy." **Department of State**
     Bulletin 46 (February 1962): 252-258.
220. _____. "It Is Time to Reaffirm Our National

Purpose." **Department of State Bulletin** 45 (November 1961): 875-880.

221. _____. "Foreign Policy Under President Kennedy." **Progressive** 26 (April 1962): 10-13.

222. _____. "Total Diplomacy." **Department of State Bulletin** 46 (April 1962): 677-678.

223. _____. "Toward a New Diplomacy." **Foreign Affairs** 40 (January 1962): 244-251.

224. Bowman, Albert H. "Pichon, The United States, and Louisiana." **Diplomatic History** 1 (Summer 1977): 257-270.

225. Brauer, Kinley J. "The Slavery Problem in the Diplomacy of the American Civil War." **Pacific Review** 46 (August 1977): 439-469.

226. Butrow, R. J. C. "Backdoor Diplomacy in the Pacific: The Proposal for a Konaye-Roosevelt Meeting, 1941." **Journal of American History** 59 (June 1972): 48-72.

227. Buzanski, Peter M. "Alaska and Nineteenth Century American Diplomacy." **Journal of the West** 6 (July 1967): 451-467.

228. Cabot, John M. **Toward Our Common American Destiny.** Medford, Mass.: Fletcher School of Law and Diplomacy, 1955.

229. Calvert, P. A. R. "Murray Contract: An Episode in International Finance and Diplomacy." **Pacific Historical Review** 35 (May 1966): 203-224.

230. Chittick, William O. "American Foreign Policy Elites: Attitudes Toward Secrecy and Publicity." **Journalism Quarterly** 47 (Winter 1970): 689-696.

231. Clifford, John G. "President Truman and the Peter the Great's Will." **Diplomatic History** 4 (Fall 1980): 371-385.

232. Cohen, Warren I. "Revisionism Between World Wars: A Study in American Diplomatic History." Ph.D. dissertation, University of Washington, 1962.

233. Coughlin, M. "California Ports: A Key to Diplomacy for the West Coast, 1820-1845." **Journal of the West** 5 (April 1966): 153-172.

234. Culbertson, William S. **International Economic Policies: A Survey of the Economics of Diplomacy.** New York: Appleton, 1925.

235. Daniels, Josephus. **The Wilson Era: Years of**

Peace, 1910-1917. Chapel Hill: University of North Carolina Press, 1944.

236. _____. Wilson Era: Years of War and After, 1917-1923. Chapel Hill: University of North Carolina Press, 1946.

237. Darnell, Michael R. "Henry P. Fletcher and American Diplomacy, 1902-1929." Ph.D. dissertation, University of Colorado, 1972.

238. Davis, C. D. "British Diplomat and the American Civil War: Edward Malet in the United States." South Atlantic Quarterly 77 (Spring 1978): 159-178.

239. Dennis, Alfred L. P. Adventures in American Diplomacy, 1896-1906. New York: Dutton, 1928.

240. Dennis, Donnie L. "A History of American Diplomatic History." Ph.D. dissertation, University of California, Santa Barbara, 1971.

241. Farer, Tom J. Toward Humanitarian Diplomacy: A Primer for Policy. New York: New York University Press, 1980.

242. Ferrell, Robert H. American Diplomacy in the Great Depression. New Haven, Conn.: Yale University Press, 1957.

243. Findley, Paul. "The Impact and Potential of American Diplomacy." Annals of the American Academy of Political and Social Science 366 (July 1966): 68-77.

244. Flack, Michael J. "Cultural Diplomacy: Blindspot in International Affairs Textbooks." International Educational and Cultural Exchange 8 (Winter 1972/73): 11-18.

245. Foster, John W. A Century of American Diplomacy. Boston: Houghton Mifflin, 1900.

246. _____. The Practice of Diplomacy as Illustrated in the Foreign Relations of the United States. Boston: Houghton Mifflin, 1906.

247. Foster, H. Schuyler. "American Public Opinion and U.S. Foreign Policy." Department of State Bulletin 41 (November 1959): 796-803.

248. Gallaher, John G. "An Evaluation of the Revolution of 1848 by American Diplomats." Ph.D. dissertation, St. Louis University,

1960.
249. Gardner, Lloyd C. **Economic Aspects of New Deal Diplomacy.** Madison: University of Wisconsin Press, 1964.
250. Gerand, Andre. "Diplomacy Old and New." **Foreign Affairs** 23 (January 1945): 256-270.
251. Gibson, Hugh S. **The Road to Foreign Policy.** Garden City, N.Y.; Doubleday, 1944.
252. Graebner, Norman A. **Cold War Diplomacy: America's Foreign Policy, 1945-1975.** 2nd ed. New York: Van Nostrand, 1977.
253. Graham, Malbone W. **American Diplomacy in the International Community.** Baltimore: Johns Hopkins University Press, 1948.
254. Greene, J. A. "Crawford Affair: International Implications of the Geronimo Campaign." **Journal of the West** 11 (January 1972): 143-153.
255. Grenville, John A., and George B. Young. **Politics, Strategy, and American Diplomacy: Studies in Foreign Policy, 1783-1917.** New Haven, Conn.: Yale University Press, 1966.
256. Grew, Joseph C. **Turbulent Era: A Diplomatic record of Forty Years, 1904-1945.** Edited by Walter Johnson. Boston: Houghton Mifflin, 1952.
257. Hagan, Kenneth J. "Protecting American Commerce and Neutrality: The Global Gunboat Diplomacy of the Old Navy, 1877-1889." Ph.D. dissertation, Claremont Graduate School, 1970.
258. Halle, Louis J. "Significance of the Institute of Inter-American Affairs in the Conduct of U.S. Foreign Policy." **Department of State Bulletin** 18 (May 1948): 659-662.
259. Hannigan, Robert E. "Dollars and Diplomacy: United States Foreign Policy, 1909-1913." Ph.D. dissertation, Princeton University, 1978.
260. Harper, Elizabeth J. **The Role of Women in International Diplomacy.** Washington, D.C.: U.S. Department of State, 1972.
261. Hutson, James H. "Early American Diplomacy: A Reappraisal." **Quarterly Journal of the Library of Congress** 33 (July 1976): 183-198.

262. James, Elizabeth M. "State Department Adaptation to Independent Africa, 1952-1962: A Study in Thought and Practice." Ph.D. dissertation, George Washington University, 1969.

263. Kennan, George F. **American Diplomacy: 1900-1950.** Chicago: Unviersity of Chicgao Press, 1951.

264. _____. "America's Administration Response to Its World Problems." **Daedalus** 87 (May 1958): 4-25.

265. _____. "Foreign Aid as a National Policy." **Proceedings of the Academy of Political Science** 30 (June 1971): 175-183.

266. _____. "The Future of Our Professional Diplomacy." **Foreign Affairs** 33 (July 1955): 566-586.

267. Kertesz, Stephen D., ed. **American Diplomacy in a New Era.** Notre Dame, Ind.: University of Notre Dame Press, 1961.

268. _____. "Diplomacy in the Atomic Age." **Review of Politics** 21 (January 1959): 151-188.

269. La Feber, Walter. "'Ah, If We Had Studied It More Carefully': The Fotrunes of American Diplomatic History." **Prologue** 11 (Summer 1979): 121-131.

270. Langley, Lester D. "The Diplomactic Historians: Bailey and Bemis." **History Teacher** 6 (November 1972): 51-70.

271. Lasch, Christopher. "The Historian as Diplomat." **Nation** 24 (November 1962): 348-353.

272. Lazorchick, Daniel C. "Foreign Policy and Diplomatic Initiative in Washington." **Annals of the American Academy of Political and Social Science** 380 (November 1968): 105-111.

273. Lee, Robert E. "Education for the New Diplomacy." **Department of State Bulletin** 48 (March 1963): 423-427.

274. Lefgren, Charles A. "Force and Diplomacy, 1846-1848: The View from Washington." **Military Affairs** 31 (Summer 1967): 57-64.

275. Lindsay, Franklin A. "Program Planning: The Missing Element." **Foreign Affairs** 39 (January 1961): 279-290.

276. Logan, John A. "The Origins of the No-Transfer Principle in American Diplomacy,

1775-1823." Ph.D. dissertation, Yale
University, 1954.

277. Lombard, H. C. C. Washington Waltz: Diplomatic People and Policies. New York: Knopf,
1941.

278. Lowenheim, Francis L., ed. The Historian and
the Diplomat: The Role of History and Historians in American Foreign Policy. New
York: Harper 1967.

279. McCamy, James L. Conduct of the New Diplomacy. New York: Harper and Row, 1964.

280. McKenna, Joseph C. Diplomatic Protest in
Foreign Policy; Analysis and Case Studies.
Chicago: Loyola University Press, 1962.

281. Mayer, Arno J. Political Origins of the New
Diplomacy, 1917-1918. New Haven, Conn.:
Yale University Press, 1959.

282. Merchant, Livingston T. "Diplomacy and the
Modern World." Department of State Bulletin 43 (November 1960): 707-713.

283. Merli, Frank J., and Theodore A. Wilson.
Makers of American Diplomacy: From
Benjamin Franklin to Henry Kissinger. New
York: Scribner, 1974.

284. Millett, Richard. "The State Department's
Navy: A History of the Special Service
Squadron, 1920-1940." American Fortune 35
(April 1975): 181-38.

285. Millington, Herbert. "American Diplomacy and
the War of the Pacific." Ph.D. dissertation, Columbia University, 1948.

286. Moore, John B. The Principles of American
Diplomacy. New York: Harper 1918.

287. Muller, Steve. "Revival of Diplomacy."
World Policy 15 (July 1963): 647-654.

288. Murphy, Robert D. "What Is Past Is Prologue." Department of State Bulletin 41
(December 1959): 898-902.

289. Nicolson, Harold. "Diplomacy Then and Now."
Foreign Affairs 40 (October 1961): 39-49.

290. Ninkovich, Frank. "The Currents of Cultural
Diplomacy: Art and the State Department,
1938-1947." Diplomatic History 1 (Summer
1977): 215-238.

291. Norton, Nile B. "Frank R. McCoy and American
Diplomacy, 1928-1932." Ph.D. dissertation, University of Denver, 1966.

292. Offner, Arnold A. "William F. Dodd: Romantic

Historian and Diplomatic Cassandra."
Historian 24 (August 1962): 451-469.

293. Perkins, Dexter. The Diplomacy of the New
Age: Major Issues in U.S. Policy Since
1945. Bloomington: Indiana University
Press, 1967.

294. Phelan, Edward J. "Diplomacy Old and New:
Study of Its Gradual Evolution." Century
120 (April 1930): 243-255.

295. Phillips, Howard J. "The United States
Diplomatic Establishment in the Critical
Period, 1783-1789." Ph.D. dissertation,
University of Notre Dame, 1968.

296. Plischke, Elmer. "The New Diplomacy: A
Changing Process.' Virginia Quarterly
Review 49 (Summer 1973): 321-345.

297. Reuter, Paul H. "William Phillips and the
Development of Foreign Policy, 1933-1947."
Ph.D. dissertation, Southern Mississippi
University, 1979.

298. Rossiter, Clinton L. "The Old Conservatism
and the New Diplomacy." Virginia
Quarterly Review 32 (Winter 1956): 28-49.

299. Rossow, Robert. "The Professionalization of
the New Diplomacy." World Politics 14
(July 1962): 561-575.

300. Rubin, Seymour J. "American Diplomacy: The
Case for Amateurism." Yale Review 45
(March 1956): 321-335.

301. Sands, William F. Our Jungle Diplomacy.
Chapel Hill: University of North Carolina
Press, 1944.

302. Seymour, Charles. American Diplomacy During
the World War. Hamden, Conn.: Archon,
1964.

303. Shepardson, Donald E. "The Devil or
Beelzebub: Diplomacy and Morality."
Midwest Quarterly 18 (Autumn 1976): 36-52.

304. Simpson, Smith. "The Nature and Dimensions
of Diplomacy." Annals of the American
Academy of Political and Social Science
380 (November 1968): 135-144.

305. _____, ed. "Resources and Needs of American
Diplomacy." Annals of the American Aca-
demy of Political and Social Science 380
(November 1968): 1-134.

306. Siracusa, Joseph M., ed. The American Diplomatic Revolution: A Documentary History of

the Cold War, 1941-47. Port Washington, N.Y.: Kennikat, 1977.

307. _____. New Left Diplomatic Histories and Historians: A Critical Analysis of Recent Trends in American Diplomacy Historiography, 1960-1970." Ph.D. dissertation, University of Colorado, 1971.

308. Stoler, Mark A. "The Politics of the Second Front American Military Planning and Diplomacy, 1941-1944." Ph.D. dissertation, University of Wisconsin, 1971.

309. Storch, Neil T. "Congressional Politics and Diplomacy, 1775-1783." Ph.D. dissertation, University of Wisconsin, 1969.

310. Stupak, Ronald J., and David S. McLellan. "The Bankruptcy of Super-Activism and the Resurgence of Diplomacy and the Department of State." Foreign Service Journal 52 (April 1975): 23-28.

311. Thompson, Kenneth W. "The New Diplomacy and the Quest for Peace." International Organization 19 (Summer 1965): 394-409.

312. _____. "The Prospects and Limitations of Diplomacy." Review of Politics 36 (April 1974): 298-305.

313. U.S. Library of Congress. Congressional Research Service. Science, Technology, and American Diplomacy: Science, Technology, and Diplomacy in the Age of Interdependence. Washington, D.C.: Government Printing Office, 1976.

314. Vogelgesang, Stanley. "Diplomacy of Human Rights." International Studies Quarterly 23 (June 1979): 216-245.

315. Welles, Sumner. Seven Decisions that Shaped History. New York: Harper 1951.

316. Williams, Benjamin H. American Diplomacy: Policies and Practice. New York: McGraw-Hill, 1936.

317. Winkler, Fred H. "Some Suggested Laws of Diplomatic History." Social Studies 58 (March 1967): 114-119.

318. Woodward, E. L. "The Old and the New Diplomacy." Yale Review 36 (Spring 1947): 405-422.

319. Young, Andrew. "The United States and Africa: Victory for Diplomacy." Foreign Affairs 59 (1981): 648-666.

320. Young, George B. **Diplomacy Old and New.**
London: Swarthmore, 1921.

Concepts and Analysis

321. American Foreign Service Association. **Toward
a Modern Diplomacy: A Report to the
American Foreign Service Association.**
Washington, D.C.: American Foreign Service
Association, 1968.
322. Aron, Raymond. "Reflections on American Diplomacy." **Daedalus** 91 (Fall 1962): 713-
732.
323. Bacchus, William I. "Diplomacy for the 70s:
An Afterview and Appraisal." **American
Political Science Review** 68 (June 1974):
736-748.
324. Bardes, Barabara, and Robert Oldendick.
"Beyond Internationalism: A Case for Multiple Dimensions in the Structure of
Foreign Policy Attitudes." **Social Science
Quarterly** 59 (December 1978): 496-508.
325. Bastert, Russell H. "The Two American Diplo-
macies." **Yale Review** 49 (June 1960): 518-
538.
326. Beaulac, Willard L. "Technical Cooperation
as an Instrument of Foreign Policy--No
Substitute for Traditional Diplomacy."
Department of State Bulletin 32 (June
1955): 964-969.
327. Bell, Harry H. "Modern Analytical Tech-
niques." **Foreign Service Journal** 38
(October 1961): 23-25.
328. Bowles, Chester. "Evaluation of American
Foreign Policy." **India Quarterly** 17
(July/September 1971): 215-226.
329. Butner, John C. "Congressmen-Diplomats:
Legislative-Executive Collaboration in the
Conduct of American Foreign Relations."
Ph.D. dissertation, University of
Maryland, 1977.
330. Cheever, Daniel S., and H. Field Haviland.
"The New Diplomacy and World Order." In
their **Organizing for Peace: International
Organization in World Affairs**, pp. 815-
822. Boston: Houghton Mifflin, 1954.
331. Cleveland, Harlan. "Delights and Dilemmas of
Diplomacy." **Michigan Quarterly Review** 3

(Fall 1964): 237-272.

332. Davis, Donald H. **How the Bureaucracy Makes Foreign Policy: An Exchange Analysis.** Lexington, Mass.: Heath, 1972.

333. Dillon, Douglas. "American Foreign Policy Today." **Department of State Bulletin** 42 (May 1960): 723-729.

334. Doenecke, Justus D. "Revisionists, Oil and Cold War Diplomacy." **Iranian Studies** 3 (Winter 1970): 23-33.

335. Gallois, Pierre M. **The Balance of Terror: Strategy for the Nuclear Age.** Boston: Houghton Mifflin, 1961.

336. Grow, Mary M. "Boundaries and United States Diplomacy: Two Case Studies." Ph.D. dissertation, Fletcher School of Law and Diplomacy, Tufts University, 1969.

337. Guerrant, Edward O., ed. **Modern American Diplomacy.** Albuquerque: University of New Mexico Press, 1954.

338. Hammond, Thomas T. "'Atomic Diplomacy' Revisited." **Orbis** 19 (Winter 1976): 1403-1428.

339. Howe, Fisher. "Policy-Planning in the New Diplomacy." **Annals of the American Academy of Political and Social Science** 380 (November 1968): 39-49.

340. Hutson, James H. "Intellectual Foundations of Early American Diplomacy." **Diplomatic History** 1 (Winter 1977): 1-19.

341. Kennan, George F. "After the Cold War: American Foreign Policy in the 1970s." **Foreign Affairs** 51 (October 1972): 210-277.

342. _____. **The Cloud of Danger: Current Realities of American Foreign Policy.** Boston: Little, Brown, 1977.

343. _____. "History and Diplomacy as Viewed by a Diplomatist." **Review of Politics** 18 (April 1956): 170-177.

344. Lacy, William S. B. "Usefulness of Classical Diplomacy." **Department of State Bulletin** 38 (March 1958): 326-327.

345. Macomber, William B. **The Angels' Game: A Handbook of Modern Diplomacy.** New York: Stein and Day, 1975.

346. Marshall, James. "Citizen Diplomacy." **American Political Science Review** 43

(February 1949): 83-90.
347. Martin, William M. "Human Rights and Foreign
     Policy: The Relationship of Theory and Ac-
     tion." **Parameters** 8 (September 1978): 30-
     40.
348. Mooney, Anne L. "Dexter Perkins: A Study in
     American Diplomatic Philosophy." Ph.D.
     dissertation, St. Louis University, 1965.
349. Murphy, Robert D. "The Interrelationship of
     Military Power and Foreign Policy." **De-
     partment of State Bulletin** 31 (August
     1954): 291-294.
350. Nichols, Jeannette P. "Dollar Strength as a
     Liability in United States Diplomacy."
     **Proceedings of the American Philosophical
     Society** 111 (February 1967): 46-56.
351. Nicolson, Harold. "The Faults of American
     Diplomacy." **Harper's Magazine** 210 (Jan-
     uary 1955): 52-58.
352. Outland, John W. "Law and the Lawyer in the
     State Department's Administration of
     Foreign Policy." Ph.D. dissertation,
     Syracuse University, 1970.
353. Phillips, William. **Ventures in Diplomacy.**
     Boston: Beacon, 1953.
354. Plischke, Elmer. **Conduct of American Diplo-
     macy.** 3rd ed. Princeton, N.J.: Van
     Nostrand, 1967.
355. Ponsonby, Arthur. **Democracy and Diplomacy: A
     Plea for Popular Control of Foreign
     Policy.** London: Methuen, 1915.
356. Potter, Pitman B. "Control of American
     Diplomacy." **India Quarterly** 6 (June 1950):
     162-178.
357. Rappaport, Armin, ed. **Issues in American
     Diplomacy.** 2 vols. New York: Macmillan,
     1965.
358. Singer, J. David. "Popular Diplomacy and
     Policy Effectiveness: A Note on the Mech-
     anisms and Consequences." **Comparative
     Studies in Society and History** 12 (July
     1970): 320-326.
359. Small, Melvin. "The Appplicability of Quan-
     titative International Politics to Diplo-
     matic History." **Historian** 38 (February
     1976): 281-304.
360. Staley, Eugene. "Scientific Developments and
     Foreign Policy." **Bulletin of Atomic**

Scientists 16 (January 1960): 7-13.

361. Stearns, Monteagle. "Democratic Diplomacy and the Role of Propaganda. **Foreign Service Journal** 30 (October 1953): 24, 25, 62-64.

362. _____. "Making American Diplomacy Relevant." **Foreign Affairs** 52 (October 1973): 153-167.

363. Stevenson, Adlai E. "Science, Diplomacy, and Peace." **Department of State Bulletin** 45 (September 1961): 402-407.

364. Thompson, Kenneth W. "American Democracy and the Third World: Convergence and Contradictions." **Review of Politics** 41 (April 1979): 256-272.

365. _____. **American Diplomacy and Emergent Patterns.** New York: New York University Press, 1962.

366. Ullman, Richard H. "Education and Training for Our New Diplomacy." **Annals of the American Academy of Political and Social Science** 380 (November 1968): 82-88.

367. U.S. Department of State. **Diplomacy for the 70s: A Program of Management Reform for the Department of State--Summary.** Washington, D.C.: Government Printing Office, 1970.

368. Vansittart, Lord. "The Decline of Diplomacy." **Foreign Affairs** 28 (January 1950): 177-188.

369. Webb, James E. "U.S. Organization for the Conduct of Foreign Affairs." **Department of State Bulletin** 24 (February 1951): 273-276.

370. Wilson, Philip W. "Open Methods in Modern Diplomacy." **Current History** 35 (October 1931): 111-118.

371. Wriston, Henry M. **Diplomacy in a Democracy.** New York: Harper, 1956.

372. Entry deleted.

Negotiations and Treaty Making

373. Bingham, Jonathan B. **Shirt-Sleeve Diplomacy: Point 4 in Action.** New York: Day, 1954.

374. Brewer, John C. "Lend-Lease: Foreign Policy Weapon in Politics and Diplomacy, 1941-1945." Ph.D. dissertation, University of Texas, Austin, 1974.

375. Brookens, Benoit O. "Diplomatic Protection of Foreign Economic Interests: The Changing Structure of International Law in the New International Economic Order." **Journal of Interamerican Studies and World Affairs** 20 (February 1978): 37-68.

376. Cardozo, Michael H. Diplomats in International Cooperation: Stepchildren of the Foreign Service. Ithaca, N.Y.: Cornell University Press, 1962.

377. Chesterton, G. K. "The Real Secret Diplomacy." **North American Review** 207 (April 1918): 505-515.

378. Choate, Joseph H. The Two Hague Peace Conferences. Princeton, N.J.: Princeton University Press, 1913.

379. Clarfield, Gerard. "John Adams: The Marketplace, and American Foreign Policy." **New England Quarterly** 52 (September 1979): 345-357.

380. _____. "Protecting the Frontiers: Defense Policy and the Tariff Question in the First Washington Administration." **William and Mary Quarterly** 32 (July 1975): 443-464.

381. Cleveland, Harlan. "Crisis Diplomacy." **Foreign Affairs** 41 (July 1963): 638-649.

382. Crabb, Cecil V. "American Diplomatic Tactics and Neutralism." **Political Science Quarterly** 78 (September 1963): 418-443.

383. Creaghe, John. "Personal Qualities and Effective Diplomatic Negotiations." Ph.D. dissertation, University of Maryland, 1965.

384. Curti, Merle E., and Kendall Birr. **Prelude to Point Four: American Technical Missions Overseas, 1838-1938.** Madison: University of Wisconsin Press, 1954.

385. Dai, Poeliu. "The Diplomacy of Cooperative Action in China, with Special Reference to the Washington Conference and Its Aftermath." Ph.D. dissertation, Johns Hopkins University, 1934.

386. Davis, Gerald H. "Ancona Affair: A Case of Preventive Diplomacy." **Journal of Modern History** 38 (September 1966): 267-277.

387. Eller, George. **Secret Diplomacy.** London: Swift, 1912.

388. Etzold, Thomas H. **The Conduct of American Foreign Relations: The Other Side of Diplomacy.** New York: New Viewpoints, 1977.

389. Gardner, Richard N. "Outer Space, the Atmospheric Sciences, and U.S. Foreign Policy." **Department of State Bulletin** 47 (October 1962): 496-500.

390. Harvey, George. "Diplomats of Diplomacy." **North American Review** 199 (February 1914): 161-174.

391. Heston, Thomas J. "Sweet Subsidy: The Economic and Diplomatic Effects of the U.S. Sugar Acts, 1934-1974." Ph.D. dissertation, Case Western Reserve University, 1975.

392. Hindman, E. James. "The General Arbitration Treaties of William Howard Taft." **Historian** 36 (November 1973): 52-65.

393. Hutson, James H. "John Adams and the Diplomacy of the American Revoltuion." Ph.D. dissertation, Yale University, 1964.

394. Ilchman, Warren F. **Professional Diplomacy in the United States, 1779-1939: A Study in Administrative History.** Chicago: University of Chicago Press, 1961.

395. Johnson, Frank J. **No Substitute for Victory.** New York: Regnery, 1962.

396. Kennan, George F. "Foreign Policy and the Professional Diplomat." **Wilson Quarterly** 1 (Winter 1977): 148-157.

397. Kihl, Mary R. "A Failure of Ambassadorial Diplomacy." **Journal of American History** 57 (December 1970): 636-653.

398. Kohler, Foy D. "Negotiation as an Effective Instrument of American Foreign Policy." **Department of State Bulletin** 38 (June 1958): 901-910.

399. Kurtz, S. G. "French Mission of 1799-1800: Concluding Chapter in the Statecraft of John Adams." **Political Science Quarterly** 80 (December 1965): 543-557.

400. _____. "Political Science of John Adams, a Guide to His Statecraft." **William and Mary Quarterly** 25 (October 1968): 605-613.

401. Lael, Richard L. "Struggle for Ratification: Wilson, Lodge, and the Thomson-Urrutia Treaty." **Diplomatic History** 2 (Winter 1978): 81-102.

402. Link, Arthur S. **Wilson the Diplomatist; A
     Look at His Major Foreign Policies.** New
     York: New Viewpoints, 1957.
403. Low, Maurice A. "The Vice of Secret
     Diplomacy." **North American Review** 207
     (February 1918): 209-220.
404. Macdonell, John. "Secret or Constructive
     Diplomacy." **Contemporary Review** 109 (June
     1916): 718-724.
405. Merillat, Herbert C. L., ed. **Legal Advisers
     and Foreign Affairs.** Dobbs Ferry, N.Y.:
     Oceana, 1964.
406. Mitchell, Kell F. "Diplomacy and Prejudice:
     The Morris-Shidehara Negotiations, 1920-
     1921." **Pacific Historical Review** 39
     (February 1970): 85-104.
407. Nadelmann, K. B. "United States Joins the
     Hague Conference on Private International
     Law: A History with Comments." **Law and
     Contemporary Problems** 30 (Spring 1965):
     291-325.
408. Namier, Lewis B. "Diplomacy, Secret and
     Open." **Nineteenth Century** 123 (January
     1938): 36-45.
409. "Operations of the Department of State in
     Connection with Progress of the Economic
     Cooperation Administration." **Department
     of State Bulletin** 18 (May 1948): 718-719.
410. Pearson, Drew, and Constantine Brown. **The
     American Diplomatic Game.** Garden City,
     N.Y.: Doubleday, 1935.
411. Petrie, Charles. "The Place of the Profes-
     sional in Modern Diplomacy." **Quarterly
     Review** 605 (July 1955): 295-308.
412. Quester, George H. **Nuclear Diplomacy: The
     First Twenty-five Years.** New York: Dunel-
     len, 1970.
413. Ranger, Robert R. "Death of a Treaty: A
     Diplomatic Obituary?" **International
     Relations** 3 (April 1969): 482-497.
414. Reinsch, Paul S. **Secret Diplomacy: How Far
     Can It Be Eliminated?** New York: Harcourt,
     Brace, 1922.
415. Schwartz, Abba P. "The Role of the State
     Department in the Administration and En-
     forcement of the New Immigration Law."
     **Annals of the American Academy of Poli-
     tical and Social Science** 367 (September

1966): 93-104.
416. Scott, James B. **American Addresses at the Second Hague Peace Conference, Delivered by Joseph H. Choate, General Horace Porter, James Brown Scott.** Boston: Ginn, 1910.
417. Semmel, A. K. "Some Correlates of Attitudes of Multilateral Diplomacy in th U.S. Department of State." **International Studies Quarterly** 20 (June 1976): 301-324.
418. Sherwood, Robert E. **Roosevelt and Hopkins: An Intimate History.** rev. ed. New York: Harper 1950.
419. Singer, J. David. "The Return to Multilateral Diplomacy." **Yale Review** 53 (October 1963): 36-48.
420. Wainwright, William H. "The Paris Peace Talks: Diplomacy and Stagecraft." **Antioch Review** 29 (Winter 1969-70): 505-514.
421. Winham, Gilbert R., and H. E. Bovis. "Agreement and Breakdown in Negotiation: Report on a State Department Training Simulation." **Journal of Peace Research** 15 (1978): 285-303.
422. Worsnop, Richard L. "Heads-of-State Diplomacy." **Editorial Research Reports** 2 (December 1962): 873-892.
423. ———. "Presidential Diplomacy." **Editorial Research Reports** 11 (September 1971): 737-758.

Communications and Reporting

424. Alger, Chadwick F. "The Role of the Private Expert in the Conduct of American Foreign Affairs." Ph.D. dissertation, Princeton University, 1958.
425. Anthony, William H. "Public Diplomacy and the Nixon Doctrine, Reaction by Foreign and American Media and the U.S. Information Agency's Role." Ph.D. dissertation, George Washington University, 1976.
426. Ben-Eliezer, M. "Public and Instant Diplomacy." **ETC** 36 (Winter 1979): 357-364.
427. Berding, Andrew H. "Foreign Policy and News Responsibility." **Department of State Bulletin** 43 (December 1960): 883-888.
428. Bergman, Helen A. **The Communications System**

of the United States Department of State
as It Pertains to the Foreign Service.
Minneapolis: University of Minnesota
Press, 1948.

429.   Blair, William D. "Communications: The Weak
Link in Our Foreign Relations."
Department of State Bulletin 63 (November
1970): 580-586.

430.   _____. "Department Discusses National
Security Information System." **Department
of State Bulletin** 66 (April 1972): 523-
525.

431.   Cassar, Paul. "'Medical' Despatches from
American Consuls in Malta, 1804-1865."
Bulletin of the History of Medicine 54
(Winter 1980): 554-560.

432.   Charlick, Carl. "Diplomatic Caretaker."
Foreign Service Journal 32 (October 1955):
20-23, 40, 42, 44, 46.

433.   Chittick, William O. "The Domestic Informa-
tion Activities of the Department of
State." Ph.D. dissertation, Johns Hopkins
University, 1964.

434.   Collins, Michael. "Communicating About
Foreign Policy.' **Department of State
Bulletin** 62 (March 1970): 393-396.

435.   Cooper, James F. "Toward a Professional Political Analysis in Foreign Service Reporting." **Foreign Service Journal** 48
(February 1971): 24-27.

436.   Elder, Robert E. "A Career Service for
USIA?" **Foreign Service Journal** 33
(February 1956): 26-27, 40, 42, 44.

437.   English, Gary C. "United States Media-
Diplomacy: Problems in the Politics of Ad-
ministration." Ph.D. dissertation, Emory
University, 1968.

438.   Groth, Alexander J. "On the Intelligence
Aspects of Personal Diplomacy." **Orbis** 7
(Winter 1964): 833-848.

439.   Hall, Harold E. "The Job of Economic Reporting." **Foreign Service Journal** 32 (April
1955): 24-25, 46-47.

440.   Keller, Suzanne. "Diplomacy and Communication." **Public Opinion Quarterly** 20
(September 1956): 176-182.

441.   Keogh, James. "Information and Modern Diplomacy." **Department of State Bulletin** 70

(January 1974): 57-63.

442. London, Kurt. "Diplomatic Communication." In his **How Foreign Policy Is Made**, pp. 194-201. New York: Van Nostrand, 1949.

443. Ludden, Howard R. "The International Information Program of the United States: State Department Years, 1945-1953." Ph.D. dissertation, Princeton University, 1966.

444. Plischke, Elmer. "Diplomatic Reporting." In his **Conduct of American Diplomacy**, pp. 291-333. Princeton, N.J.: Van Nostrand, 1967.

445. _____., ed. **Modern Diplomacy: The Art and the Artisans**. Washington, D.C.: American Enterprise Institute, 1979.

446. Regala, Robert. **The Trends in Modern Diplomatic Practice**. Dobbs Ferry, N.Y.: Oceana, 1959.

447. Rosenau, James N. "Public Protest, Political Leadership and Diplomatic Strategy." **Orbis** 14 (Fall 1970): 557-571.

448. Simpson, Smith. "Diplomacy: Some Professional and Political Perspectives." **Foreign Service Journal** 53 (August 1976): 15-19.

449. Speakman, Cummins E. "Political Reporting by American Diplomatic and Consular Officers." Ph.D. dissertation, Yale University, 1955.

450. Syracuse University. Maxwell Graduate School of Citizenship and Public Affairs. **United States Foreign Policy: The Operational Aspects of United States Foreign Policy**. Washington, D.C.: Government Printing Office, 1959.

451. Vivian, James, F. "The Commercial Bureau of American Republics, 1894-1902: The Advertising Policy, The State Department, and the Governance of the International Union." **Proceedings of the American Philosophical Society** 118 (December 1974): 555-566.

452. Waters, Maurice. "Special Diplomatic Agents of the President." **Annals of the American Academy of Political and Social Science** 307 (September 1956): 124-133.

453. Zorthian, Barry. "A Press Relations Doctrine for the Foreign Service." **Foreign Service**

Journal 48 (February 1971): 20-23, 55-56.

Consular Affairs

454. Banks, Michael. "Professionalism in the Con-
     duct of Foreign Policy." **International
     Affairs** 44 (October 1968): 720-734.
455. Belmont, Perry. "Ambassadorial Rank for Min-
     isters." **Current History** 29 (January
     1929): 629-632.
456. Blair, Leon B. "Amateurs in Diplomacy: The
     American Vice Consuls in North Africa
     1941-1943." **Historian** 35 (August 1973):
     607-620.
457. Boyes, John L. "The Political Adviser
     (Polad): The Role of the Diplomatic Ad-
     viser to Selected United States and North
     Atlantic Alliance Military Commanders."
     Ph.D. dissertation, University of
     Maryland, 1971.
458. Byers, John R., ed. "Selections from the
     Official Consular Despatches of Nathaniel
     Hawthorne from Liverpool, August 1, 1853-
     December 31, 1857." **Essex Institute
     Historical Collections** 113 (October 1977):
     241-332.
459. Cahier, Philippe and Luke T.Lee. "Vienna
     Conventions on Diplomatic and Consular
     Relations." **International Conciliation**
     571 (January 1969): 1-76.
460. Carr, Wilbur J. "American Consular Service."
     American Journal of International Law 1
     (October 1907): 891-913.
461. Cleveland, Harlan, and Gerard J. Mangone,
     eds. **The Art of Overseasmanship: Americans
     at Work Abroad.** Syracuse, N.Y.: Syracuse
     University Press, 1957.
462. Colligan, Francis J. **The In-Service Training
     of Cultural Relations Officers: An Outline
     Guide.** Washington, D.C.: Government Print-
     ing Office, 1949.
463. David, Paul T. **The Administration of Foreign
     Affairs and Overseas Operatons.** Washing-
     ton, D.C.: Brookings Institution, 1951.
464. Etzold, Thomas H. "Understanding Consular
     Diplomacy." **Foreign Service Journal** 52
     (March 1975): 10-12.
465. Feller, Abraham H. and Manley O. Hudson,

eds. A Collection of the Diplomatic and Consular Laws and Regulations of Various Countries. 2 vols. Washington D.C.: Carnegie Endowment, 1933.

466. Gauss, Clarence E. A Notarial Manual for Consular Officers. Washington, D.C.: Government Printing Office, 1921.

467. Gross, Leo. "The Case of United States Diplomatic and Consular Staff in Tehran: Phase of Provisional Measures." American Journal of International Law 74 (April 1980): 395-410.

468. Hinckley, Frank E. American Consular Jurisdiction in the Orient. Washington, D.C.: Lowdermilk, 1906.

469. Horstmann, G. Henry. Consular Reminiscences. Philadelphia: Lippincott, 1886.

470. Johnson, Emory R. "The Early History of the United States Consular Service, 1776-1792." Political Science Quarterly 13 (March 1898): 10-40.

471. Jones, Chester L. The Consular Service of the United States: Its History and Activities. Philadelphia: University of Pennsylvania, 1906.

472. Jones, R. L. "America's First Consular Convention." Southwestern Social Science Quarterly 13 (December 1932): 250-263.

473. Kerbey, Joseph O. An American Consul in Amazonia. New York: Rudge, 1911.

474. Kingsley, Robert E. "The Public Diplomacy of U.S. Business Abroad: The Experience of Latin America." Journal of Interamerican Studies on World Affairs 9 (July 1967): 413-427.

475. Lee, Luke T. Consular Law and Practice. New York: Praeger, 1961.

476. Ludwig, Ernest. Consular Treaty Rights and Comments on the "Most Favored Nation" Clause. Akron, Ohio: New Werner, 1913.

477. Marx, Walter J. "The Consular Service of the United States." Department of State Bulletin 33 (September 1955): 447-448, 450-454.

478. Murphy, Edmund. "Extra Curricular Diplomacy." Foreign Service Journal 33 (January 1956): 22-24, 48, 50.

479. Murphy, George H. Digest of Circular In-

structions to Consular Officers. 2 vols.
Washington, D.C.: Government Printing Office, 1904-1906.

480. Paterson, Thomas G. "American Businessmen and Consular Service Reform, 1890's to 1906." Business History Review 40 (Spring 1966): 77-97.

481. Patterson, Jefferson. Diplomatic Duty and Diversion. Cambridge, Mass.: Riverside, 1956.

482. Plischke, Elmer. "The Overseas Establishment." In his Conduct of American Diplomacy, pp. 262-290. Princeton, N.J.: Van Nostrand, 1967.

483. _____. United States Diplomats and Their Missions: A Profile of American Diplomatic Emissaries Since 1778. Washington, D.C.: American Enterprise Institute, 1975.

484. Puente, Julius I. The Foreign Consul: His Juridical Status in the United States. Chicago: B. J. Smith, 1926.

485. Ritchie, John A. "The Consular Function: The Stepchild of United States Foreign Policy Administration." Ph.D. dissertation, Southern Illinois University, 1969.

486. Sapin, Burton M. "Field Missions." In his The Making of United States Foreign Policy, pp. 246-286. Washington, D.C.: Brookings Institutions, 1966.

487. Sayre, Francis B. Experiments in International Administration. New York: Harper, 1919.

488. Scidmore, George H. Outline Lectures on the History, Organization, Jurisdiction and Practice of the Ministerial and Consular Courts of the United States of America in Japan. Tokyo: Igerisu Horitsu Gakko, 1887.

489. Serpell, David R. "American Consular Activities in Egypt, 1849-1863." Journal of Modern History 10 (September 1938): 344-363.

490. Seward, George F. The United States' Consulates in China: A Letter with Inclosures of the Consul-General in China to the Secretary of State. Washington, D.C.: Privately printed, 1867.

491. Sheppard, Eli T. American Consular Service. Berkeley: University of California Press,

1901.

492. Simmons, John F. "How We Work With Other Nations." Department of State Bulletin. 33 (July 1955): 91-94.

493. Stewart, Irvin, Consular Privileges and Immunities. New York: Columbia University Press, 1926.

494. Stowell, Ellery C. Consular Cases and Opinions. Washington, D.C.: Byrne, 1909.

495. Stuart, Graham H. American Diplomatic and Consular Practices. 2nd ed. New York: Appleton-Century-Crofts. 1952.

496. _____. "The American Embassy in Paris." Current History 21 (October 1951): 220-224.

497. Szajkowski, Z. "Consul and the Immigrant: A Case of Bureaucratic Bias." Jewish Social Studies 36 (January 1974): 3-18.

498. Thayer, Charles W. "How to Organize an Embassy: American Embassy in Russia." Atlantic Monthly 186 (November 1950): 58-60.

499. U.S. Department of State. The American Consul. Washington, D.C.: Government Printing Office, 1955.

500. _____. The American Cultural Attache. Washington, D.C.: Government Printing Office, 1957.

501. _____. The Rank of the Counselor Historically in the Department of State. Washington, D.C.: Department of State, 1961.

502. Warden, David B. On the Origin, Nature, Progress and Influence of Consular Establishment. Paris: Smith, 1813.

Foreign Service

General

503. Atwater, Elton. "The American Foreign Service Since 1939." American Journal of International Law 41 (January 1947): 73-102.

504. Bacchus, William I. "Obstacles to Reform in Foreign Affairs: The Case of NSAM 341." Orbis 18 (Spring 1974): 266-276.

505. Bailey, Thomas A. "A Hall of Fame for American Diplomats." Virginia Quarterly Review 36 (Summer 1960): 390-404.

506. Billman, Calvin J. "Backrounds and Policies

of Selected United States Diplomats to Latin America, 1898-1938." Ph.D. dissertation, Tulane University, 1955.

507. Bohlen, Charles E. "The Foreign Service and the Panorama of Change." **Department of State Bulletin** 44 (June 1961): 964-969.

508. Cabot, John M. "Understanding Our Foreign Service." **Department of State Bulletin** 30 (March 1954): 353-358.

509. Cantrell, William A. "Culture Shock and the Foreign Service Child." **Foreign Service Journal** 51 (December 1974): 4, 6, 8, 28-29.

510. Carlsen, Charles R., ed. **Bibliography: The Generalist and the Specialist in the U.S. Foreign Service.** Minneapolis: University of Minnesota, 1965.

511. Childs, James R. **American Foreign Service.** New York: Holt, 1948.

512. Commission on Organization of the Executive Branch of the Government. **Task Force on Foreign Affairs (Appendix H.).** Washington, D.C.: Government Printing Office, 1949.

513. Craig, Gordon A., and Gelix Gilbert, eds. **The Diplomats, 1919-1939.** Princeton, N.J.: Princeton University Press, 1953.

514. Ellison, W. J. "Paul Robeson and the State Department." **Crisis** 84 (May 1977): 184-189.

515. Ferris, Norman B. "An American Diplomatist Confronts Victorian Society, 1861." **History Today** 15 (August 1965): 550-558.

516. Finney, Charles G. **The Old China Hands.** Garden City, N.Y.: Doubleday. 1961.

517. Fiszman, J. R. "Development of Administrative Roles: The Labor Attache Program of the U.S. Foreign Service." **Public Administration Review** 25 (September 1965): 203-212.

518. Ford, Gerald R. "Fiftieth Anniversary of the Foreign Service." **Department of State Bulletin** 71 (July 1974): 145-147.

519. "Foreign Service Act of 1946." **Foreign Service Journal** 23 (September 1946): 7-21.

520. Grabill, Josephy L. "Missionaries and Diplomats," **Illinois Quarterly** 32 (April 1970): 4-15.

521. Harr, John E. **The Anatomy of the Foreign**

Service: A Statistical Profile. New York: Carnegie Endowment, 1965.

522. Henderson, Loy. "The Foreign Service--First Line of Defense." Department of State Bulletin 32 (May 1955): 849-853.

523. Hopkins, R. F. "International Role of Domestic Bureaucracy." International Organization 30 (Summer 1976): 405-432.

524. Kahn, Ely J. The China Hands: America's Foreign Service Officers and What Befell Them. New York: Viking, 1975.

525. Kelly, Henry W., and Dorothy Kelly. Dancing Diplomats. Albuquerque: University of New Mexico Press, 1950.

526. Lavine, David. Outposts of Adventure: The Story of the Foreign Service. Garden City, N.Y.: Doubleday, 1966.

527. Lay, Tracy H. The Foreign Service of the United States. New York: Prentice-Hall, 1925.

528. Lazalier, James H. "Surrogate Diplomancy: Franklin D. Roosevelt's Personal Envoys, 1941-1945." Ph.D. dissertation, University of Oklahoma, 1973.

529. Livermore, Seward W. "'Deserving Democrats': The Foreign Service Under Woodrow Wilson." South Atlantic Quarterly 69 (Winter 1970): 144-160.

530. McKnight, Joseph A. "English Life and American Diplomats: A Study of the Observations of American Diplomats on Certain Phases of English Civilization, 1785-1836." Ph.D. dissertation, Johns Hopkins University, 1936.

531. Moss, Ambler H. "The Foreign Service Illusion." Foreign Service Journal 49 (June 1972): 6, 8, 10, 12.

532. National Civil Service Reform League. Report on the Foreign Service. New York: The League, 1919.

533. Plischke, Elmer. "United States Diplomats Since 1778: Bicentennial Review and Future Projection." World Affairs 138 (Winter 1975-76): 205-218.

534. Rinden, Robert W., and S. I. Nadler. Life and Love in the Foreign Service. Washington, D.C.: Foreign Service Journal, 1969.

535. Rubottom, Roy, R. The People Who Wage the

Peace: An Account of the History and Mission of the Foreign Service. Washington, D.C.: Government Printing Office, 1958.

536. Spaulding, E. Wilder. **Ambassadors Ordinary and Extraordinary.** Washington, D.C.: Public Affairs Press, 1961.

537. Stowell, Ellery C. "Cramping Our Foreign Service." **American Journal of International Law** 29 (April 1935): 314-317.

538. _____. "The Moses-Linthicum Act on the Foreign Service." **American Journal of International Law** 25 (July 1931): 516-520.

539. Strauss, W. Patrick. "Pioneer American Diplomats in Polynesia, 1820-1840." **Pacific Historical Review** 31 (February 1962): 21-30.

540. Swayne, Kingdon, W. "Horse and Buggy Political Science in the Jet Age." **Foreign Service Journal** 45 (March 1968): 17-19, 46.

541. Tracy, Thomas M. "Automation and the Foreign Service." **Foreign Service Journal** 48 (February 1971): 21-22.

542. "The U.S. Foreign Service." **Fortune** 34 (July 1946): 81-87, 198-207.

543. U.S. Department of State. **The Foreign Service of the Seventies.** Washington, D.C.: Government Printing Office, 1970.

544. _____. **Toward a Stronger Foreign Service: Report of the Secretary of State's Public Committee on Personnel.** Washington, D.C.: Government Printing Office, 1954.

545. Van Dyne, Frederick. **Our Foreign Service: The "ABC" of American Diplomacy.** Rochester, N.Y.: Lawyers Cooperative, 1909.

546. Williams, Carman C. "The Wasted Resource: Foreign Service Wives." **Foreign Service Journal** 52 (May 1975): 6-7, 20-21.

547. Willson, Beckles. **America's Ambassadors to England (1785-1929).** New York: Stokes, 1929.

548. Welch, Holmes. "The Real Life of the Foreign Service Officer." **Harper's Magazine** 224 (March 1962): 82-85.

549. Werking, Richard H. **The Master Architects: Building the United States Foreign Service, 1890-1913.** Lexington: University of

Kentucky Press, 1978.

550.   _____. "Selling the Foreign Service: Bureaucratic Rivalry and Foreign-Trade Promotion, 1903-1912." **Pacific Historical Review** 45 (May 1976): 185-207.

Career and Recuitment

551.   Angel, Juvenal L. **Careers in the Diplomatic Service.** 4th ed. New York: World Trade Academy Press, 1961.

552.   Atwater, Elton. **Examinations for the American Foreign Service.** Washington, D.C.: Digest Press, 1936.

553.   Bahti, James H. "Personnel Integration in the Foreign Service." Ph.D. dissertation, University of Michigan, 1959.

554.   Bean, Elizabeth A. "Down in Generation Gap: The Junior Foreign Service Officer Looks at the System." **Annals of the American Academy of Political and Social Science** 380 (November 1968): 76-81.

555.   Churchill, Malcolm. "What Happened to the Career Foreign Service?" **Foreign Service Journal** 47 (December 1970): 38, 50-52.

556.   Cohen, E. M. "Rank Injustice: The Case for Semiautomatic Promotion of Middle Grade Officers." **Foreign Service Journal** 49 (August 1972): 17-19, 27-28.

557.   Davis, Nathaniel P. "Accelerating Promotion." **Foreign Service Journal** 51 (October 1974): 16-17, 57.

558.   _____. **Few Dull Moments: A Foreign Service Career.** Philadelphia: Dunlap, 1967.

559.   Delaney, Robert F. **Your Future in the Foreign Service.** New York: Richards Rosen, 1961.

560.   "Department Announces New Emphasis on Foreign Service Recruitment." **Department of State Bulletin** 65 (October 1971): 350-361.

561.   Fielder, Frances, and Godfrey Harris. **The Quest for Foreign Affairs Officers--Their Recruitment and Selection.** New York: Carnegie Endowment, 1966.

562.   Fisher, Glen H. "The Foreign Service Officer." **Annals of the American Academy of Political and Social Science** 368

(November 1966): 71-82.
563. Fosdick, Dorothy. "For the Foreign Service--
Help Wanted." **New York Time Magazine,** 20
November 1955, pp. 13, 65-69.
564. Harr, John. **The Development of Careers in
the Foreign Service.** New York: Carnegie
Endowment, 1965.
565. Henderson, Loy. "The Foreign Service as a
Career." **Department of State Bulletin** 32
(April 1955): 635-640.
566. Hickman, Martin B., and N. Hollander.
"Undergraduate Origin as a Factor in Elite
Recruitment and Mobility: The Foreign
Service--A Case Study." **Western Political
Quarterly** 19 (June 1966): 337-353.
567. Hoffman, Arthur S. **International Communication and the New Diplomacy.** Bloomington:
Indiana University Press, 1968.
568. Johnson, R. C. "Recruitment and Training for
the Foreign Service of the United States."
India Quarterly 11 (October-December
1955): 376-381.
569. Jones, Arthur G. **The Evolution of Personnel
Systems for U.S. Foreign Affairs: A History of Reform Efforts.** New York: Carnegie
Endowment, 1964.
570. Kux, Dennis, and Michael Burner. "The German
and American Foreign Service." **Foreign
Service Journal** 50 (January 1973): 15-16,
20.
571. Laves, Walter H. C. "Increasing the Number
of Americans Potentially Available for
Foreign Assignments." **American Political
Science Review** 47 (September 1953): 798-
804.
572. McKibbin, Carroll R. "The Career Structure
and Success in the U.S. Foreign Service."
Ph.D. dissertation, University of Kansas,
1968.
573. McNair, Clare H. "Women in the Foreign Service." **Foreign Service Journal** 22 (June
1945): 30-31, 45.
574. Moser, Martin W. "The Personnel System of
the Foreign Service of the United States."
Ph.D. dissertation, University of
Maryland, 1952.
575. Neal, Harry E. **Your Career in Foreign
Service.** New York: Messner 1965.

576. Peters, C. Brooks. "Why Not a Foreign Service Career?" **Reader's Digest** 69 (October 1956): 118-120.

577. Roudybush, Franklin. **An Analysis of the Educational Background and Experience of U.S. Foreign Service Officers.** Washington, D.C.: George Washington University Press, 1944.

578. Sakell, Achilles N. **Career in the Foreign Service.** New York: Walck, 1962.

579. Segal, D. R., and Daniel H. Willick. "Reinforcement of Traditional Career Patterns in Agencies Under Stress." **Public Administration Review** 28 (January 1968): 30-38.

580. Shade, Chloris. **Foreign Service.** 2nd ed. Chicago: Morgan, Dillon, 1940.

581. Stowell, Ellery C. "Examinations for the American Foreign Service." **American Journal of International Law** 24 (July 1930): 577-581.

582. "The U.S. Foreign Service: A Career for Young Americans." **Department of State Bulletin** 26 (April 1952): 549-550.

583. U.S. Department of State. **Career Opportunities on the U.S. Foreign Service.** Washington, D.C.: Government Printing Office, 1958

584. _____. **Facts and Issues Relating to the Amalgamation of the Department of State and the Foreign Service.** Washington, D.C.: Government Printing Office, 1949.

585. _____. **The Foreign Service Officer: A Career in the U.S. Department of State.** Washington, D.C.: Government Printing Office, 1963.

586. U.S. Secretary of State. **An Improved Personnel System for the Conduct of Foreign Affairs: A Report to the Secretary of State by the Secretary's Advisory Committee on Personnel.** Washington, D.C.: U.S. Department of State, 1950.

587. Warwick, Donald, P. "Performance Appraisal and Promotions in the Foreign Service." **Foreign Service Journal** 47 (July 1970): 37-41, 45.

588. Wriston, Henry M. "Young Men and the Foreign Service." **Foreign Affairs** 33 (October 1954): 28-42.

Functions

589. "Academic Training for the Foreign Service."
      Department of State Bulletin 39 (November
      1958): 689-692.
590. Allen, George V. "The Utility of a Trained
      and Permenent Foreign Service." **Foreign
      Service Journal** 31 (March 1954): 20-23,
      49-50.
591. Barnes, William, and John H. Morgan. **The
      Foreign Service of the United States:
      Origins, Development and Functions.**
      Washington, D.C.: Government Printing
      Office, 1961.
592. Hopkins, Frank S. "Training Responsibilities
      in the Department of State." **Public Ad-
      ministration Review** 8 (Spring 1948): 119-
      125.
593. Hunt, Gaillard. **The American Passport: Its
      History and a Digest of Laws, Rulings and
      Regulations Governing Its Issuance by the
      Department of State.** Washington, D.C.:
      Government Printing Office, 1898.
594. Kottman, Richard N. "Hoover and Canada
      Diplomatic Appointments." **Canadian
      Historical Review** 51 (September 1970):
      292-308.
595. Kryza, E. Gregory, and William E. Knight.
      "Management in the Foreign Service."
      Foreign Service Journal 52 (March 1975):
      16-18.
596. Linehan, Patrick E. **The Foreign Service Per-
      sonnel System: An Organizational Analysis.**
      Boulder, Colo.: Westview, 1976.
597. McCamy, James L., and Alessandro Corrandini.
      "The People of the State Department and
      the Foreign Service." **American Political
      Science Review** 47 (December 1954): 1067-
      1082.
598. Perry, Jack. "The Present Challenge to the
      Foreign Service." **Foreign Service Journal**
      51 (October 1974): 18-20.
599. Reed, Theodore L. "Organizational Change in
      the American Foreign Service, 1925-1965:
      The Utility of Cohort Analysis." **American
      Sociological Review** 43 (June 1978): 404-
      421.

600. Saltzman, Charles E. "The Reorganization of
     the American Foreign Service." **Department
     of State Bulletin** 31 (September 1954):
     436-444.

601. Sayre, Wallace S., and Clarence E. Thurber.
     **Training for Specialized Mission Per-
     sonnel.** Chicago: Public Administration
     Service, 1952.

602. Schratz, Paul R. "The Role of the Service
     Secretary in the National Security Organ-
     ization." **United States Naval Institute
     Proceedings** 101 (September 1975): 18-24.

603. Snyder, Richard C., and Edgar S. Furniss.
     "Representation of the United States
     Abroad." **American Foreign Policy:
     Formulation, Principles and Programs,** pp.
     310-344. New York: Rinehart, 1961.

604. Steiner, Zara S. **Present Problems of the
     Foreign Service.** Princeton, N.J.: Center
     of International Studies, Princeton
     University, 1961.

605. _____. **The State Department and the Foreign
     Service: The Wriston Report--Four Years
     Later.** Princeton, N.J.: Center of Interna-
     tional Studies, Princeton University,
     1958.

606. Stewart, Irvin. "Congress, the Foreign Ser-
     vice, and Department of State: Personnel
     Problems." **American Political Science
     Review** 24 (May 1930): 355-366.

607. Stowell, Ellery C. "Reforms in the State
     Department and Foreign Service." **American
     Journal of International Law** 22 (July
     1928): 606-610.

608. Stuart, Graham H. "A Better Foreign Ser-
     vice." **Current History** 21 (September
     1951): 148-150.

609. Summers, Natalia. **Outline of the Functioning
     of the Offices of the Department of State,
     1789-1943.** Washington, D.C.: U.S. National
     Archives, Division of Department of State
     Archives, 1946.

610. U.S. Department of State. **A Management Pro-
     gram for the Department of State, Office
     of the Deputy Under Secretary for Adminis-
     tration.** Washington, D.C.: U.S. Department
     of State, 1966.

611. _____. **Personnel for the New Diplomacy.**

Washington, D.C.: Carnegie Endowment, 1962.

612. _____. The Science Advisor of the Department of State. Washington, D.C.: Government Printing Office, 1960.

613. Walther, Regis. Orientation and Behavioral Styles of Foreign Service Officers. New York: Carnegie Endowment, 1965.

Activities

614. Andrews, Russell P. The Reamericanization of Foreign Service Officers. Syracuse, N.Y.: Inter-University Case Program, 1970.

615. Bowling, John W. "How We Do Our Thing: Crisis in Management." Foreign Service Journal 47 (May 1970): 19-21.

616. _____. "How We Do Our Thing: Innovation." Foreign Service Journal 47 (October 1970): 25-27, 55-56.

617. Carter, Kent C. "Development of the Foreign Service Inspection System." Foreign Service Journal 51 (January 1974): 18-20, 25.

618. Clubb, O. Edmund. "The National Security and Our Foreign Service." Nation 179 (December 1954): 544-547.

619. Coulter, Eliot B. "Visa Work of the Department of State and the Foreign Service." Department of State Bulletin 21 (October 1949): 523-535.

620. Denby, James O. "Suggestions for Improving the Foreign Service and Its Administration to Meet Its War and Postwar Responsibilities." Foreign Service Journal 22 (February 1945): 7-10 (March 1945): 12-15 (April 1945): 12-14 (May 1945) 14-17 (June 1945) 12-14 (July 1945) 13-15.

621. Elder, Robert E. Overseas Representation and Services for Federal Domestic Agencies. New York: Carnegie Endowment, 1965.

622. Estes, Thomas S. "Executive and Administrative Assignments for FSO's." Foreign Service Journal 29 (March 1952): 26, 48.

623. Fuchs, Lawrence H. "Those Peculiar Americans": The Peace Corps and American National Character. New York: Meredith, 1967.

624. Halle, Louis J. "'Policy Making' and the

Career Service." **Foreign Service Journal**
30 (September 1953): 31, 48, 50.

625. Hapgood, David, and Meridian Bennett. **Agents
of Change: A Close Look at the Peace
Corps.** Boston: Little, Brown, 1968.

626. Hilton, Ralph. **Worldwide Mission: The Story
of the United States Foreign Service.** New
York: World, 1970.

627. Ketzel, Clifford P. "Exchange of Persons and
American Foreign Policy: The Foreign
Leader Program of the Department of
State." Ph.D. dissertation, University of
California, Berkeley, 1955.

628. Lowther, Kevin, and C. Payne Lucas. **Keeping
Kennedy's Promise: The Peace Corps—Unmet
Hope of the New Frontier.** Boulder, Colo.:
Westview, 1978.

629. Maddox, William P. "The Foreign Service in
Transition." **Foreign Affairs** 25 (January
1947): 303-313.

630. Mosher, Frederick C. "Personnel Management
in Foreign Affairs." **Public Personnel
Review** 12 (October 1951): 175-186.

631. Osborne, John. "What's the U.S. Foreign Service Worth?" **Fortune** 55 (May 1957): 154-
159, 238, 241-242, 244, 247.

632. Taylor, Maxwell D. "New System for Coping
with Our Overseas Problems." **Foreign Service Journal** 43 (May 1966): 34-36.

633. U.S. Department of State. **Some Facts About
the Foreign Service: A Short Account of
Its Organization and Duties Together with
Pertinent Laws and Regulations.** Washington, D.C.: Government Printing Office,
1950.

634. Ward, Paul V. "Performance Evaluation: The
Annual Inventory." **Foreign Service Journal**
51 (October 1974): 29-31, 52.

635. Waters, Maurice. "The Ad Hoc Diplomat: A
Legal and Historical Analysis." **Wayne Law
Review** 6 (Summer 1960):380-392.

Conduct

636. American Assembly. **The Representation of the
United States Abroad.** New York: American
Assembly, Columbia University, 1956.

637. Andrew, Arthur. "The Diplomat and the Mana-

ger." International Journal 30 (Winter 1974-75): 45-79.

638. Barnett, Vincent M., ed. The Representation of the United States Abroad. New York: Praeger, 1965.

639. Beam, Jacob D. Multiple Exposure: An American Ambassador's Unique Perspective on East-West Issues. New York: Norton, 1978.

640. Brown, R. L. "Rise of the Ambassador." Contemporary Review 210 (April 1967): 196-200.

641. Calvocoressi, P. "The Diplomat." Political Quarterly 28 (October 1957): 352-361.

642. Cleveland, Harlan. "View from the Diplomatic Tightrope." Department of State Bulletin 46 (May 1962): 803-808.

643. Cleveland, Harlan, Gerald J. Mangone, and John C. Adams. The Overseas Americans. New York: McGraw-Hill, 1960.

644. Cochran, William P. "A Diplomat's Moments of Truth." Foreign Service Journal 30 (September 1953): 23, 62.

645. Cunningham, John E. "Are We Administering Away Our Effectiveness?" Foreign Service Journal 36 (February 1959): 19-21.

646. Garnham, David. "Attitude and Personality Patterns of United States Foreign Service Officers." American Journal of Political Science 18 (August 1974): 525-547.

647. _____. "Foreign Service Elitism and US Foreign Affairs." Public Administration Review 35 (January 1975): 44-51.

648. Glassman, Jon D. "The Foreign Service Officer: Observer or Advocate?" Foreign Service Journal 47 (May 1970): 29-30, 45.

649. Grew, Joseph C. "Ambassador Grew on the American Foreign Service." Foreign Service Journal 13 (December 1936): 549-694, 696.

650. Harr, John E. The Professional Diplomat. Princeton, N.J.: Princeton University Press, 1969.

651. Kennan, George F. "The Needs of the Foreign Service." In The Public Service and University Education, edited by Joseph E. McClean, pp. 1-97. Princeton, N.J.: Princeton University Press, 1949.

652. Lenderking, William R. "Dissent, Disloyalty,

and Foreign Service Finkism." **Foreign Service Journal** 51 (May 1974): 13-15.

653. Lichman, Warren F. **Professional Diplomacy in the United States, 1779-1939: A Study in Administrative History.** Chicago: University of Chicago Press, 1961.

654. Luce, Clare B. "The Ambassadorial Issue: Professional or Amateur?" **Foreign Affairs** 36 (October 1957): 105-121.

655. McGhee, George C. "The Changing Role of the American Ambassador." **Department of State Bulletin** 46 (June 1962): 1007-1011.

656. Martin, James V. "The Quiet Revolution in the Foreign Service." **Foreign Service Journal** 37 (February 1960): 19-22.

657. Mendershausen, Horst. "The Diplomat's National and Transnational Commitments." **Foreign Service Journal** 47 (February 1970): 20-22, 31-33.

658. Mennis, Bernard. **American Foreign Policy Officials: Who Are They and What Are They?** Columbus: Ohio State University Press, 1971.

659. Modelski, George A. "The Foreign Ministers as a World Elite." **Peace Research Society Papers** 14 (1970): 31-46.

660. _____. "The World's Foreign Ministers: A Political Elite." **Journal of Conflict Resolution** 14 (June 1970): 135-176.

661. Morris, Roger. "Clientism in the Foreign Service." **Foreign Service Journal** 51 (February 1974): 24-26, 30-31.

662. Moss, Michael A. "The Ambassador as Advisor and Advocate." Ph.D. dissertation, Yale University, 1966.

663. Osborne, John. "The Importance of Ambassadors." **Fortune** 55 (April 1957): 146-147, 150-151, 184, 186, 189, 190, 192, 194.

664. Schulzinger, Robert D. **The Making of the Diplomatic Mind: The Training, Outlook, and Style of United States Foreign Service Officers, 1908-1931.** Middletown, Conn.: Wesleyan University Press, 1975.

665. Stern, Thomas. "Management: A New Look." **Foreign Service Journal** 49 (March 1972): 14-15.

666. Spector, Paul, and Harley O. Preston. **Working Effectively Overseas.** Washington,

D.C.: Institute for Institute for International Service, 1961.

667. Taylor, A. J. P. "The Judgment of the Diplomat." **Saturday Review** 11 (December 1954): 9-10, 54-56.

668. Thayer, Charles W. "Our Ambassadors: An Intimate Appraisal of the Men and the System." **Harper's Magazine** 219 (September 1959): 29-35.

669. Thayer, Robert H. "Cultural Diplomacy and the Development of Mutual Understanding." **Department of State Bulletin** 41 (August 1959): 310-316.

670. U.S. Department of State. **The American Ambassador.** Washington, D.C.: Government Printing Office, 1957

671. Walters, Maurice. **The Ad Hoc Diplomat.** The Hague: Nijhoff, 1963.

672. Wriston, Henry M. "The Special Envoy." **Foreign Affairs** 38 (January 1960): 219-237.

673. Yardley, Edward. "Identification Pass System for the Department of State." **Foreign Service Journal** 18 (October 1941): 554-555.

Protocol

674. Davis, Robert R. "Diplomatic Plumage: American Court Dress in the Early National Period." **American Quarterly** 20 (Summer 1968): 164-179.

675. _____. "Diplomatic Gifts and Emoluments: The Early National Experience." **Historian** 32 (May 1970): 376-391.

676. _____. "Manners and Diplomacy: A History of American Diplomatic Etiquette and Protocol During the Early National Period." Ph.D. dissertation, Michigan State University, 1967.

677. _____. "Republican Simplicity: The Diplomatic Costume Question." **Civil War History** 15 (March 1969): 19-29.

678. Duke, Angier B. "Perspectives in Protocol." **Department of State Bulletin** 44 (March 1961): 414-418.

679. _____. "Protocol and Peacekeeping." **Department of State Bulletin** 51 (November 1964): 736-739.

680.   _____. "Protocol and the Conduct of Foreign
        Affairs." **Department of State Bulletin** 49
        (November 1963): 700-704.
681.   Holzheimer, Hermann. "Protocol as a Function
        of Foreign Policy." **Aussenpolitik** 27
        (1976): 349-360.
682.   U.S. Department of State. **Guidebook to Di-
        plomatic Reception Rooms in Department of
        State.** Washington, D.C.: Government Print-
        ing Office, 1969.
683.   Woodward, Stanley. "Protocol: What It Is and
        What It Does." **Department of State
        Bulletin** 21 (October 1949): 501-503.

Privileges and Treatment

684.   Becker, Joseph D. "The State Department
        White List and Diplomatic Immunity."
        American Journal of International Law 47
        (October 1953): 704-706.
685.   Bovis, H. E. and Gilbert R. Winham. "Distri-
        bution of Benefits in Negotiation: Report
        on a State Department Training Simula-
        tion." **Journal of Conflict Resolution** 23
        (September 1979): 408-424.
686.   Gordon, J. C. "Diplomatic Immunity." **Foreign
        Service Journal** 29 (January 1952): 23, 46-
        47.
687.   Leigh, Michael. "Sovereign Immunity--the
        Case of the Imias." **American Journal of
        International Law** 68 (April 1974): 289-
        298.
688.   Lent, Ernest S. **The Recall or Withholding of
        U.S. Ambassadors to Influence Other
        Governments or Express Disapproval of
        Their Actions: Some Specific Cases.**
        Washington, D.C.: U.S. Library of Con-
        gress, 1969.
689.   Macomber, William B. "Department Discusses
        Grievance Procedures for the Foreign Ser-
        vice." **Department of State Bulletin** 67
        (October 1972): 505-515.
690.   Nixon, Richard M. "President Nixon Deline-
        ates Authority of American Ambassadors."
        Department of State Bulletin 62 (January
        1970): 30-31.
691.   Sweeney, Joseph M. **The International Law of
        Sovereign Immunity.** Washington, D.C.: U.S.

Department of State, 1964.
692.   U.S. Department of Justice. "Legislation
       Proposed to Protect U.S. Officials and
       Foreign Diplomats." **Department of State
       Bulletin** 65 (September 1971): 268-270.

CONDUCT OF
U.S. FOREIGN POLICY

THEORETICAL AND SYSTEMATIC STUDIES

General Studies

693. Adelman, Kenneth L. "Black Man's Burden." **Foreign Policy** 28 (Fall 1977): 86-109.
694. Appleton, Sheldon. **United States Foreign Policy: An Introduction with Cases.** Boston: Little, Brown, 1968.
695. Aptheker, Herbert. **American Foreign Policy and the Cold War.** New York: New Century Publishers, 1962.
696. Armacost, Michael H. **The Foreign Relations of the United States.** Belmont, Calif.: Dickenson, 1969.
697. Armstrong, Hamilton F., ed. **Fifty Years of Foreign Affairs.** New York: Praeger, 1972.
698. Aruga, Tadash. "The American Revolution and the Origin of American Foreign Policy." **American Studies International** 15 (Winter 1976): 35-42.
699. Ashabranner, Brent K. **A Moment in History.** New York: Doubleday, 1971.
700. Barber, Hollis W. **Foreign Policies of the United States.** New York: Dryden 1953.
701. Barker, C. A. "Another American Dilemma: Multilateral Authority Versus Unilateral Power." **Virginia Quarterly Review** 54 (Spring 1969): 230-252.
702. Beloff, Max. **Foreign Policy and the Democratic Process.** Baltimore: Johns Hopkins University Press, 1955.
703. Bemis, Samuel F. "American Foreign Policy and the Blessings of Liberty." **American Historical Review** 67 (January 1962): 291-305.
704. Berding, Andrew H. **The Making of Foreign Policy.** Washington, D.C.: Potomac, 1956.
705. Berle, Adolf A. **Tides of Crisis: A Primer of Foreign Relations.** New York: Reynal, 1957.
706. Boggs, J. "Beyond Nationalism." **Monthly Review** 25 (January 1974): 34-45.
707. Bohlen, Charles E. **The Transformation of American Foreign Policy.** New York: Norton, 1969.
708. Brewster, Kingman. "Reflections on Our National Purpose." **Foreign Affairs** 50 (April 1972): 399-415.

709.   Buchan, Alastair. "Partners and Allies."
       Foreign Affairs 41 (July 1963): 621-637.
710.   Bundy, McGeorge. "Americans and the World."
       Daedalus 107 (Winter 1978): 289-303.
711.   _____, ed. The Pattern of Responsibility.
       Boston: Houghton Mifflin, 1952.
712.   Bundy, William P. "Dictatorships and
       American Foreign Policy." Proceedings of
       the American Philosophical Society 119
       (August 1975): 251-256.
713.   _____, ed. Two Hundred Years of American
       Foreign Policy. New York: New York
       University Press, 1977.
714.   Carleton, William G. "American Foreign
       Policy: Myths and Realities." Virginia
       Quarterly Review 37 (Spring 1961): 177-
       197.
715.   _____. "A New Departure in Foreign Policy."
       Virginia Quarterly Review 44 (Autumn
       1968): 559-579.
716.   _____. The Revolution in American Foreign
       Policy: Its Global Range. New York: Random
       House, 1963.
717.   Chamberlain, Lawrence H., and Richard C.
       Snyder. American Foreign Policy. New York:
       Rinehart, 1948.
718.   Claude, I. L. "Casual Commitment to
       International Relations." Political
       Science Quarterly 96 (Fall 1981): 367-379.
719.   Cleveland, Harlan. "America's Not-So-
       Manifest Destiny." Atlantic Community
       Quarterly 14 (Fall 1976): 285-305.
720.   _____. Managing U.S. Foreign Policy in a
       Leaderless World. New York: Bernard M.
       Baruch College, 1975.
721.   _____. The Obligations of Power. New York:
       Harper and Row, 1966.
722.   Davis, Saville. "Patterns and Problems in
       U.S. Foreign Policy." International
       Affairs 41 (October 1965): 634-636.
723.   DeConde, Alexander. A History of American
       Foreign Policy. New Jersey: Scribner,
       1963.
724.   Degler, Carl N. "The American Past: An
       Unsuspected Obstacle in Foreign Affairs."
       American Scholar 32 (Spring 1963): 192-
       209.
725.   _____. "The Great Revolution in American

Foreign Policy." **Virginia Quarterly Review** 38 (Summer 1962): 380-399.

726. Denitch, B., E. Kohak, and D. H. Wrong. "Democracy and American Power." **Dissent** 22 (Fall 1975): 351-365.

727. Diebold, William. **The United States and the Industrial World.** New York: Praeger, 1972.

728. Diesing, P. "National Self-Determination and U.S. Foreign Policy." **Ethics** 77 (January 1977): 85-94.

729. Dingman, R. "1950: The Fate of a Grand Design." **Pacific Historical Review** 47 (August 1978): 465-471.

730. Divine, Robert A., ed. **American Foreign Policy Since 1945.** Chicago: Quadrangle, 1969.

731. _____. **The Illusion of Neutrality.** Chicago: University of Chicago Press, 1962.

732. Doran, Charles F. "Change, Uncertainty, and Balance: A Dynamic View of United States Foreign Policy." **International Journal** (Toronto) 35 (Summer 1980): 563-579.

733. Edwards, M. "Foreign Policy: The Case for a Third Option." **World Affairs** 144 (Summer 1981): 3-13.

734. Ehrlich, T., and C. Gwin. "Third World Strategy." **Foreign Policy** 42 (Fall 1981): 145-166.

735. Ekirch, Arthur A. **Ideas, Ideals, and American Diplomacy: A History of Their Growth and Interaction.** New York: Appleton, 1966.

736. Feis, Herbert. **Seen From E.A.: Three International Episodes.** New York: Knopf, 1947.

737. Field, John E. "Fears and Aspirations in American Foreign Policy." **Atlantic Community Quarterly** 8 (Fall 1970): 383-392.

738. Fitzsimons, M.A. "Fifteen Years of American Foreign Policy." **Review of Politics** 23 (January 1961): 3-19.

739. Fleming, D. F. "The Broken Dialogue on Foreign Affairs." **Annals of the American Academy of Political and Social Science** 344 (November 1962): 128-140.

740. _____. "The Costs and Consequences of the Cold War." **Annals of the American Academy**

of Political and Social Science 366 (July 1966): 127-138.

741. Foreign Policy Association. **A Cartoon History of United States Foreign Policy: 1776-1976.** New York: Morrow, 1976.

742. Franck, Thomas M., and Edwards Weisband, eds. **Secrecy and Foreign Policy.** New York: Oxford University Press, 1974.

743. Friedlander, Robert A. "American Foreign Policy: Illusion and Reality." **South Atlantic Quarterly** 63 (Autumn 1964): 468-477.

744. Friedmann, W. "United States Policy nd the Crisis of International Law." **American Journal of International Law** 59 (October 1965): 857-871.

745. Fulbright, J. William. "American Foreign Policy in the 20th Century Under an 18th Century Constitution." **Cornell Law Review** 47 (Fall 1961): 1-13.

746. _____. "Price of Empire." **North American Review** 4 (November 1967): 12-18.

747. _____. "Toward a More Creative Foreign Policy." **Progressive** 23 (November 1959): 20-23.

748. Furniss, Edgar S., and Richard C. Snyder. **An Introduction to American Foreign Policy.** New York: Rinehart, 1955.

749. Gaddis, John L. **The United States and the Origins of the Cold War: 1941-1947.** New York: Columbia University Press, 1972.

750. Galnoor, Itzhak, ed. **Government Secrecy in Democracies.** New York: Harper and Row, 1976.

751. Garrett, Stephen A. "Foreign Policy and the Democracies: De Tocqueville Revisited." **Virginia Quarterly Review** 48 (Autumn 1972): 481-500.

752. Gelb, L. H., and A. Lake. "Washington Dateline: A Tale of Two Compromises." **Foreign Policy** 22 (Spring 1976): 224-237.

753. Gelber, Harry G. "America, the Global Balance." **Asian Survey** 19 (December 1979): 1147-1158.

754. Gelber, Lionel. "The American Role and World Order." **Yale Review** 56 (June 1967): 524-536.

755. Gilbert, Felix. "Bicentennial Reflections."

Foreign Affairs 54 (July 1976): 635-644.

756. Glazer, Nathan. "American Values and American Foreign Policy." Commentary 62 (July 1976): 32-37.

757. Gordon, Morton, and Kenneth N. Vines, eds. Theory and Practice of American Foreign Policy. New York: Crowell, 1955.

758. Guttman, Allen. "Democracy's Undemocratic Foreign Policy." Michigan Quarterly Review 5 (Fall 1966): 233-235.

759. Hammond, Paul Y. "The Political Order and the Burden of External Relations." World Politics 19 (April 1967): 443-464.

760. Hartmann, Frederick H. The New Age of American Foreign Policy. New York: Macmillan, 1970.

761. Hickman, Martin B., ed. Problems of American Foreign Policy. 2nd ed. Beverly Hills, Calif.: Glencoe, 1975.

762. Hoffmann, Stanley. "Hell of Good Intentions." Foreign Policy 29 (Winter 1977/78): 3-26.

763. _____. Primacy or World Order: American Foreign Policy Since the Cold War. New York: McGraw-Hill, 1978.

764. _____. "The Uses of American Power." Foreign Affairs 56 (October 1977): 27-48.

765. Holbo, Paul S. "Perspectives on American Foreign Policy, 1890-1916: Expansion and World Power." Social Studies 59 (November 1967): 246-255.

766. Houghton, Neal D. "The Challenge to Intellectual Leadership in Recent American Foreign Policy." Social Science 36 (June 1961): 167-176.

767. Hughes, Thomas L. "Relativity in Foreign Policy." Foreign Affairs 45 (July 1967): 670-682.

768. Jacobson, Harold K., ed. America's Foreign Policy. 2nd ed. New York: Random House, 1965.

769. Jacobson, Harold K., and William Zimmermann, eds. The Shaping of Foreign Policy. New York: Atherton, 1969.

770. Jessup, Philip C. The Birth of Nations. New York: Columbia University Press, 1974.

771. Juergensmeyer, John E. "Democracy's Diplomacy: The People-to-People Program--A

Study of Attempts to Focus the Effects of Private Contracts in International Politics." Ph.D. dissertation, Princeton University, 1960.

772. Kaiser, P. "Hegemonism and Great-Power Policy." **World Marxist Review** 22 (April 1979): 112-121.

773. Kaplan, Morton A. "Old Realities and New Myths." **World Politics** 17 (January 1965): 334-347.

774. Kennedy, T. C. "Charles A. Beard in Midpassage." **Historian** 30 (February 1968): 179-198.

775. Kintner, William R. "A Program for America: Freedom and Foreign Policy." **Orbis** 21 (Spring 1977): 139-156.

776. Kirkpatrick, J. J. "Dictatorships and Double Standards." **Commentary** 68 (November 1979): 34-45.

777. Knappen, Marshall. **An Introduction to American Foreign Policy.** New York: Harper, 1956.

778. Knauth, Oliver D. **U.S. Foreign Policy in a Changing World.** Washington, D.C.: National Planning Association, 1960.

779. Krogh, Peter F. "New Directions in American Foreign Policy." **Foreign Service Journal** 50 (September 1973): 13-16.

780. Lebergott, Stanley. "The Returns to U.S. Imperialism, 1890-1929." **Journal of Economic History** 40 (June 1980): 229-252.

781. Leonard, L. Larry. **Elements of American Foreign Policy.** New York: McGraw-Hill, 1953.

782. Leopold, Richard W. **The Growth of American Foreign Policy: A History.** New York: Knopf, 1962.

783. Lerche, Charles O. **Foreign Policy of the American People.** 3rd ed. Englewood Cliffs, N.J.: Prentice-Hall, 1967.

784. Lint, Gregg L. "The American Revolution and the Law of Nations, 1776-1789." **Diplomatic History** 1 (Winter 1977): 20-34.

785. Liska, George. **The New Statescraft: Foreign Aid in American Foreign Policy.** Chicago: University of Chicago Press, 1960.

786. Lord, W. "America's Role in the World: A City Upon a Hill." **Atlantic Community**

Quarterly 14 (Winter 1976-77): 447-460.
787. McCloy, John J. The Challenge to American Foreign Policy. Cambridge, Mass.: Harvard University Press, 1953.
788. Maechling, Charles. "The Next Decade in American Foreign Policy." Virginia Quarterly Review 45 (Summer 1969): 369-385.
789. Manning, Bayless. The Conduct of United States Foreign Policy in the Nation's Third Century. New York: Foreign Policy Association, 1976.
790. Marshall, Charles B. "Changing Concepts of Peace: An American Focus." Social Research 42 (Spring 1975): 52-63.
791. _____. "The Golden Age in Perspective." Journal of International Affairs 17 (1963): 9-17.
792. Marzani, Carl. "Reflections on American Foreign Policy." Monthly Review 12 (January 1961): 481-487.
793. Masters, Roger D. "The Lockean Tradition in American Foreign Policy. Journal of International Affairs 21 (1967): 253-277.
794. May, Ernest R. Lessons of the Past: The Use and Misuse of History in American Foreign Policy. New York: Oxford University Press, 1974.
795. Needler, Martin C., ed. Dimensions of American Foreign Policy: Readings and Documents. Princeton, N.J.: Van Nostrand, 1966.
796. Oliver, Covey T. "United States and the World." Annals of the American Academy of Political and Social Science 426 (July 1976): 166-212.
797. Ostrower, Garry B. "Historical Studies in American Internationalism." International Organization 25 (Autumn 1971): 899-916.
798. Overholt, W. H. "From the Politics of Weakness to the Politics of Strength." Orbis 18 (Spring 1974): 27-49.
799. Parenti, Michael J. Trends and Tragedies in American Foreign Policy. Boston: Little, Brownm, 1971.
800. Perkins, Dexter. The American Approach to Foreign Policy. Cambridge, Mass.: Harvard University Press, 1952.

801. Posvar, Wesley W. "Reshaping Our Foreign
      Policy." **Annals of the American Academy of
      Political and Social Science** 396 (July
      1971): 105-114.
802. Quigley, Carroll. "Major Problems of Foreign
      Policy." **Current History** 55 (October
      1968): 199-206, 242.
803. Rainey, Gene E. **Patterns of American Foreign
      Policy.** Boston: Allyn and Bacon, 1975.
804. Ransom, Harry H., ed. **An American Foreign
      Policy Reader.** New York: Crowell, 1965.
805. Rosenau, James N., ed. **Domestic Sources of
      Foreign Policy.** New York: Free Press,
      1967.
806. Rostow, Eugene V. "Best Is Yet to Be."
      Atlantic Community Quarterly 11 (Winter
      1973-74): 438-447.
807. Rothstein, Robert L. "On the Costs of
      Realism." **Political Science Quarterly** 87
      (September 1972): 347-362.
808. Rourke, Francis E. **Secrecy and Publicity:
      Dilemmas of Democracy.** Baltimore: Johns
      Hopkins University Press, 1961.
809. Rubin, A. P. "Perils of Proximity." **American
      Journal of Interntional Law Proceedings** 68
      (1974): 1-16.
810. Russett, Bruce. "The Americans' Retreat from
      World Power." **Political Science Quarterly**
      90 (Spring 1975): 1-21.
811. Schlesinger, Arthur M. "America's Need for
      Allies." **Round Table** 58 (July 1968): 229-
      242.
812. Schurman, Franz. **The Logic of World Power:
      Secrecy and Foreign Policy.** New York:
      Pantheon, 1974.
813. Sellen, Robert W. "The American Museum,
      1787-1792." **Pennsylvania Magazine of
      History and Biography** 93 (April 1969):
      179-189.
814. Shulman, M. D. "On Learning to Live with
      Authoritarian Regimes." **Foreign Affairs** 55
      (January 1977): 325-338.
815. Slater, Jerome. "Is United States Foreign
      Policy 'Imperialist' or 'Imperial'?"
      Political Science Quarterly 91 (Spring
      1976): 63-87.
816. Stebbins, Richard P., ed. **Documents on
      American Foreign Relations, 1960.** New

York: Harper, 1961.
817. Stevenson, Adlai E. "Putting First Things First: A Democractic View." **Foreign Affairs** 38 (January 1960): 191-208.
818. Stewart, R. B. "Report of the Eleventh Annual Meeting of the Advisory Committee on Foreign Relations of the United States." **American Journal of International Law** 62 (July 1968): 723-729.
819. Stoke, Harold W. **The Foreign Relations of the Federal State**. Baltimore: Johns Hopkins University Press, 1931.
820. Strausz-Hupe, Robert. **A Forward Strategy for America**. New York: Harper, 1961.
821. Sulzberger, Cyrus L. **What's Wrong with U.S. Foreign Policy?** New York: Harcourt, Brace, 1959.
822. Tanham, G. K. "United States View." **International Affairs** 42 (April 1966): 194-206.
823. Thompson, Kenneth W. "Moral Reasoning in American Thought on War and Peace." **Review of Politics** 39 (July 1977): 386-399.
824. _____. **Political Realism and the Crisis of World Politics: An American Approach to Foreign Policy**. Princeton, N.J.: Princeton University Press, 1960.
825. Turpin, William N. "Foreign Relations, Yes; Foreign Policy, No." **Foreign Policy** 8 (Fall 1972): 50-61.
826. Tuthill, John W. "Operation Topsy." **Foreign Policy** 8 (Fall 1972): 62-85.
827. Tyler, Robert L. "Realism, Morality, and Foreign Policy." **North Dakota Quarterly** 47 (Autumn 1979): 11-19.
828. Urbany, R. "International Politics and Moral Standards." **World Marxist Review** 20 (June 1977): 5-12.
829. Varg, Paul A. "Imperialism and the American Orientation Toward World Affairs." **Antioch Review** 26 (Spring 1966): 43-55.
830. Watts, W., and L. A. Free. "Nationalism, Not Isolationism: A New National Survey." **Foreign Policy** 23 (Fall 1976): 3-26.
831. Ways, Max. **Beyond Survival**. New York: Harper, 1959.
832. Wilcox, Wayne. "United States: Imperial Recessional." **International Affairs** 49

(October 1973): 539-553.
833. Williams, William A. "Empire, New Style."
      Monthly Review 11 (July/August 1959): 83-
      93.
834. Wilson, L. C. "Liberty and Union: An
      Analysis of Three Concepts Involved in the
      Nullification Controversy." **Journal of
      Southern History** 33 (August 1967): 331-
      355.
835. Young, Kenneth T. "Implications for United
      States Policy." **Asian Studies** 11 (April
      1971): 422-427.
836. Yost, Charles W. **The Age of Triumph and
      Frustration: Modern Dialogues.** New York:
      Speller, 1964.
837. _____. **The Conduct and Misconduct of
      Foreign Affairs.** New York: Random House,
      1972.
838. _____. **The Insecurity of Nations:
      International Relations in the Twentieth
      Century.** New York: Praeger, 1968.
839. Zevin, R. "Interpretation of American
      Imperialism." **Journal of Economic History**
      22 (March 1972): 316-360, 385-392.

                    Decision-Making

840. Alsop, Joseph, and Stewart Alsop. "How Our
      Foreign Policy Is Made." **Saturday Evening
      Post** 30 (April 1949): 30-31, 113-116.
841. Baldwin, David A. "Making American Foreign
      Policy: A Review." **Journal of Conflict
      Resolution** 12 (September 1968): 386-392.
842. Berding, Andrew H. **Foreign Affairs and You!
      How American Foreign Policy Is Made and
      What It Means to You.** Garden City, N.Y.:
      Doubleday, 1962.
843. Berkowitz, Morton, P. G. Bock, and Vincent
      J. Fuccillo. **The Politics of American
      Foreign Policy: The Social Context of
      Decisions.** Englewood Cliffs, N.J.:
      Prentice-Hall, 1977.
844. Bishop, D. G. **The Administration of United
      States Foreign Policy Through the United
      Nations.** Dobbs Ferry, N.Y.: Oceana, 1967.
845. Bloomfield, Lincoln P. **The Foreign Policy
      Process: Making Theory Relevant.** Beverly
      Hills, Calif.: Sage, 1974.

346. _____. "Planning Foreign Policy: Can It Be Done?" **Political Science Quarterly** 93 (Fall 1978): 369-391.

847. Bonham, G. M. "Cognitive Process Model of Foreign Policy Decision-Making." **Simulation and Games** 7 (June 1976): 123-152.

848. Braybrooke, David, and Charles E. Lindblom. "Types of Decision Making." In **International Politics and Foreign Policy,** edited by James Rosenau, pp. 207-216. 2nd ed. New York: Free Press, 1969.

849. Coplin, William D., and J. Martin Rochester. **Foreign Policy Decision-Making.** Chicago: Markham, 1971.

850. Cox, Robert W., and Harold K. Jacobson. **Decision Making in International Organization.** New Haven, Conn.: Yale University Press, 1972.

851. Dangerfield, Royden J. "Studies in the Administration of U.S. Foreign Affairs." **Public Administration Review** 11 (August 1951): 275-282.

852. Day, Arthur R. "Planning in the Conduct of Foreign Affairs." **Polity** 1 (Summer 1969): 411-426.

853. de Boubon-Busset, Jacques. "Decision-Making in Foreign Policy." In **Diplomacy in a Changing World,** edited by Stephen D. Kertesz and M. A. Fitzsimons, pp. 77-100. Notre Dame, Ind.: University of Notre Dame Press, 1959.

854. _____. "How Decisions Are Made in Foreign Policy: Psychology in International Relations." **Review of Politics** 20 (October 1958): 591-614.

855. Fox, Douglas, M., comp. **The Politics of U.S. Foreign Policy Making: A Reader.** Pacific Palisades, Calif.: Goodyear, 1971.

856. Frankel, Joseph. **The Making of Foreign Policy: An Analysis of Decision Making.** New York: Oxford University Press, 1963.

857. _____. "Towards a Decision-Making Model in Foreign Policy." **Political Studies** 7 (February 1959): 1-11.

858. Friedman, Saul. "The Rand Corporation and Our Policy Makers." **Atlantic** 212 (September 1963): 61-68.

859. Friedrich, Carl J. **Foreign Policy in the Making.** New York: Norton, 1938.
860. Fuchs, Kenneth R. "Foreign Policy Decision-Maker Lines."Ph.D. dissertation, State University of New York, Buffalo, 1974.
861. Fulbright, J. William. "What Makes U.S. Foreign Policy." **Reporter** 20 (May 1959): 18-21.
862. Gardner, Lloyd C. **Architects of Illusion: Men and Ideas in American Foreign Policy, 1941-1949.** New York: New Viewpoints, 1970.
863. George, Alexander L. "The Case for Multiple Advocacy in Making Foreign Policy." **American Political Science Review** 66 (September 1972): 751-795.
864. Gilboa, Eytan. "The Scholar and the Foreign Policy Maker in the United States." Ph.D. dissertation, Harvard University, 1974.
865. Gold, Huam. "Foreign Policy Decision-Making and the Environment." **International Studies Quarterly** 22 (December 1978): 569-586.
866. Hadwen, John G., and Johan Kaufman. **How United Nations Decisions Are Made.** Leiden, The Netherlands: Sythoff, 1960.
867. Halper, Thomas. **Foreign Policy Crises: Appearances and Reality in Decisionmaking.** Columbus, Ohio: Merrill, 1971.
868. Hamilton, William C. "Some Problems of Decision-Making in Foreign Affairs." **Department of State Bulletin** 37 (September 1957): 432-436.
869. Hammond, Paul Y. "Foreign Policy-Making and Administrative Politics." **World Politics** 17 (July 1965): 656-671.
870. Hill, Norman L. **The New Democracy in Foreign Policy Making.** Lincoln: University of Nebraska Press, 1970.
871. Hoerch, H., and M. M. Lavin. **Simulation of Decision Making in Crises: Three Manual Gaming Experiments.** Santa Monica, Calif.: Rand, 1964.
872. Holsti, Ole R. "Cognitive Process Approaches to Decision-Making: Foreign Policy Actors Viewed Psychologically." **American Behavioral Scientist** 20 (September-October 1976): 11-32.
873. Hopkins, Raymond, and Richard W. Mansbach.

Structure and Process in International Politics. New York: Harper and Row, 1973.

874. Johnson, Richard A. **The Administration of United States Foreign Policy.** Austin: University of Texas Press, 1971.

875. Landheer, Batholomeus. **Ethical Values in International Decision Making.** The Hague: Nijhoff, 1960.

876. Langer, William L. "The Mechanism of American Foreign Policy." **International Affairs** 24 (July 1948): 319-328.

877. Levitan, David M. "Constitutional Developments in the Control of Foreign Affairs: A Quest for Democratic Control." **Journal of Politics** 7 (February 1945): 58-92.

878. London, Kurt. **How Foreign Policy Is Made.** New York: Van Nostrand, 1949.

879. Marshall, Charles B. "Making Foreign Policy on the New Frontier." **Annals of the American Academy of Political and Social Science** 342 (July 1962): 138-146.

880. _____. "Scholarship and the Real World of the Policy-maker." **Orbis** 15 (Spring 1971): 283-291.

881. Mathews, John M. **The Conduct of American Foreign Relations.** New York: Century, 1922.

882. Mennis, Bernard. "An Empirical Analysis of the Background and Political Preferences of American Foreign Policy Decision-Makers." Ph.D. dissertation, University of Michigan, 1967.

883. Myers, Denys P. "The Control of Foreign Relations." **American Political Science Review** 11 (February 1917): 24-58.

884. Ostrom, Charles W. "Evaluating Alternative Foreign Policy Decision-Making Models." **Journal of Conflict Resolution** 21 (June 1977): 235-266.

885. Plischke, Elmer. **Foreign Relations Decisionmaking: Options Analysis.** Beirut, Lebanon: Catholic Press, 1973.

886. Poole, DeWitt C. **The Conduct of Foreign Relations Under Modern Democratic Conditions.** New Haven, Conn.: Yale University Press, 1924.

887. Price, Thomas J. "Constraints on Foreign

Policy Decision Making." **International Studies Quarterly** 22 (September 1978): 357-376.

888. Rochester, J. Martin, and Michael Segalla. "What Foreign Policy Makers Want From Foreign Policy Researchers." **International Studies Quarterly** 22 (September 1978): 435-461.

889. Rosenau, James N. "The Premises and Promises of Decision-Making Analysis." In **Contemporary Political Analysis**, edited by James C. Charlesworth, pp. 189-211. New York: Free Press, 1967.

890. Sapin, Burton M. **The Making of United States Foreign Policy**. Washington, D.C.: Brookings Institution, 1966.

891. Schwab, R. W. "America's Golden Triangle." **Journal of Contemporary Asia** 8 (1978): 584-596.

892. Schwebel, Stephen M., ed. **The Effectiveness of International Decisions**. Dobbs Ferry, N.Y.: Oceana, 1971.

893. Scott, Andrew M. "Decision-Making." In his **The Functioning of the International Political System**, pp. 80-105. New York: Macmillan, 1967.

894. Sidjanski, Dusan, ed. **Political Decision-Making Processes: Studies in National, Comparative, and International Politics**. San Francisco: Jossey-Bass, 1973.

895. Smith, Daniel M. "Authoritarianism and American Policy Makers in Two World Wars." **Pacific Historical Review** 43 (August 1974): 303-323.

896. Snyder, Richard C., H. W. Bruck, and Burton M. Sapin, eds. **Foreign Policy Decision Making: An Approach to the Study of International Politics**. New York: Free Press, 1962.

897. Strauss, Lewis T. **Men and Decisions**. New York: Doubleday, 1962.

898. Trivers, Howard. **Three Crises in American Foreign Affairs and a Continuing Revolution**. Carbondale: Southern Illinois University Press, 1972.

899. Walker, Lannon. "Our Foreign Affairs Machinery: Time for an Overhaul." **Foreign Affairs** 47 (January 1969): 309-320.

900. Westerfield, H. Bradford. **The Instruments of America's Foreign Policy.** New York: Crowell, 1963.
901. Wright, Quincy. **The Control of American Foreign Relations.** New York: Macmillan, 1922.

Policy Formulation

902. Andriole, Stephen J. "Public Policy Relevance and Contemporry Social Scientific Inquiry: The Case of Foreign Policy Analysis." Ph.D. dissertation, University of Maryland, 1974.
903. Batchelder, Robert C. **The Irreversible Decision, 1939-1950.** New York: Macmillan, 1961.
904. Bauer, Raymond A., and Kenneth J. Gergen, eds. **The Study of Policy Formation.** New York: Free Press, 1968.
905. Beard, Charles A. **American Foreign Policy in the Making, 1932-1940: A Study in Responsibilities.** New Haven, Conn.: Yale University Press, 1946.
906. Bliss, Howard, and M. Glen Johnson. **Beyond the Water's Edge: America's Foreign Policies.** Philadelphia: Lippincott, 1975.
907. Bloomfield, Lincoln P., and Cornelius J. Gearin. "Games Foreign Policy Experts Play: The Political Exercise Comes of Age." **Orbis** 16 (Winter 1973): 1008-1031.
908. Bowie, Robert R. "Formulation of American Foreign Policy." **Annals of the American Academy of Political and Social Science** 330 (July 1960): 1-10.
909. _____. **Shaping the Future: Foreign Policy in an Age of Transition.** New York: Columbia University Press, 1964.
910. Briggs, V. M., and W. Gordon. "Position Papers: United States Border Policy." **Social Science Quarterly** 56 (December 1975): 476-491.
911. Cannon, Jessica C. "Conceptual and Empirical Analysis of the Policy Implementation Process." Ph.D. dissertation, Ohio State University, 1976.
912. Caputo, David A., ed. **The Politics of Policy Making in America: Five Case Studies.** San

Francisco: Freeman, 1977.
913. Cerf, Jay H., and Walter Pozen, eds.
Strategy for the '60s. New York: Praeger,
1961.
914. Chittick, William O. The Analysis of Foreign
Policy Outputs. Columbus, Ohio: Merrill,
1975.
915. Cobbledick, James R. Choice in American
Foreign Policy: Options for the Future.
New York: Crowell, 1973.
916. Crabb, Cecil V. Policy-Makers and Critics:
Conflicting Theories of American Foreign
Policy. New York: Holt, Rinehart, and
Winston, 1976.
917. Deconde, Alexander. "Themes in the History
of American Foreign Policy." American
Studies International 14 (Spring 1976): 3-
22.
918. Diebold, John. "Computers, Program
Management and Foreign Affairs." Foreign
Affairs 45 (October 1966): 125-134.
919. Elliott, William Y. "The Control of Foreign
Policy Decisions." Social Science 30
(October 1955): 209-216.
920. Gange, John. American Foreign Relations:
Permanent Problems and Changing Policies.
New York: Ronald, 1959.
921. Goldbloom, Maurice J. "Foreign Policy."
Commentary 39 (June 1965): 47-55.
922. Green, D. "Language, Values, and Policy
Perspectives in Inter-American Research."
Latin American Research Review 10 (Fall
1975): 177-190.
923. Halper, Thomas. "Appearance and Reality in
Five American Foreign Policy Crises."
Ph.D. dissertation, Vanderbilt University,
1970.
924. _____. Foreign Policy Crises: Appearance
and Reality in Decision-Making. Columbus,
Ohio: Merrill, 1971.
925. Hamilton, J. A. "To Link or Not to Link."
Foreign Policy 42 (Fall 1981): 127-144.
926. Haviland, H. Field, ed. The Forumation and
Administration of United States Foreign
Policy. Washington, D.C.: Brookings
Institution, 1960.
927. Henderson, Loy W. Foreign Policies: Their
Formulation and Enforcement. Washington,

D.C.: Government Printing Office, 1946.
928. Immerman, Robert M. "The Formulation and
      Administration of U.S. Foreign Policy."
      Foreign Service Journal 37 (April 1960):
      21-23.
929. Irish, Martin D. **U.S. Foreign Policy:
      Context, Conduct, and Content.** New York:
      Harcourt Brace Jovanovich, 1975.
930. Kaplan, Morton A. "Toward the 1980's: A
      Policy Vision in Search of a Projection."
      Orbis 15 (Spring 1971): 275-282.
931. Kegley, Charles W., and Eugene R. Wittkopf.
      **American Foreign Policy: Pattern and
      Process.** New York: St. Martin's, 1979.
932. Laqueur, Walter. "America and the World: The
      Next Four Years, Confronting the
      Problems." **Commentary** 63 (March 1977): 33-
      41.
933. Lovell, John P. **Foreign Policy in
      Perspective: Strategy, Adaptation,
      Decision Making.** New York: Hold, Rinehart,
      and Winston, 1970.
934. Manning, Bayless. "Goals, Ideology and
      Foreign Policy." **Foreign Affairs** 54
      (January 1976): 271-281.
935. Mathews, John M. **American Foreign Reltions:
      Conduct and Policies.** 2nd ed. New York:
      Appleton-Century-Crofts, 1938.
936. Merritt, Richard L., ed. **Foreign Policy
      Analysis.** Lexington, Mass.: Lexington
      Books, 1975.
937. Miller, Linda B. "America in World Politics:
      Linkerage or Leverage?" **World Today** 30
      (July 1974): 296-277.
938. Modelski, George A. **A Theory of Foreign
      Policy.** New York: Praeger, 1962.
939. Morray, J. P. "Dr. Herbert Aptheker's
      Critique of American Foreign Policy."
      Science and Society 27 (Spring 1963): 203-
      211.
940. Moynihan, Daniel P. "Further Thoughts on
      Words and Foreign Policy." **Atlantic
      Community Quarterly** 17 (Fall 1979): 346-
      351.
941. Osgood, Robert E. "Carter Policy in
      Perspective." **SAIS Review** 24 (Winter
      1981): 11-22.
942. Petras, J. "U.S. Foreign Policy: The Revival

of Inter-Ventionism." **Monthly Review** 31 (February 1980): 15-27.

943. Rainey, Gene E. "Foreign Policymaking and Implementation." In his **Patterns of American Foreign Policy,** pp. 139-229. Boston: Allyn and Bacon, 1975.

944. Ravenal, Earl C. **Never Again: Learning From America's Foreign Policy Failures.** Philadelphia: Temple University Press, 1978.

945. Rosenfield, Stephen S. "Pluralism and Policy." **Foreign Affairs** 52 (January 1974): 263-272.

946. Rostow, Walt W. "American Strategy on the World Scene." **Department of State Bulletin** 46 (April 1962): 625-631.

947. _____. "The Planning of Foreign Policy." **Department of State Newsletter** 38 (June 1964): 3-5, 45.

948. Rothstein, Robert L. **Planning, Prediction, and Policymaking in Foreign Affairs: Theory and Practice.** Boston: Little, Brown, 1972.

949. Russell, Francis H. "Formulating Foreign Policy." **Orbis** 17 (Winter 1974): 1344-1353.

950. Seabury, Paul. "Thoughts on a New Foreign Policy Agenda." **Orbis** 20 (Fall 1976): 565-578.

951. Secrest, Donald E. "Containing Communism with Communism." **Midwest Quarterly** 14 (October 1972): 11-25.

952. Smith, Roger. "Restraints on American Foreign Policy." **Daedalus** 91 (Fall 1962): 705-716.

953. Snyder, Richard C. "The Nature of Foreign Policy." **Social Science** 27 (April 1952): 61-69.

954. Snyder, Richard C., and Edgar S. Furniss. **American Foreign Policy: Formulation, Principles, and Programs.** New York: Rinehart, 1954.

955. Spanier, John W. **American Foreign Policy Since World War II.** New York: Praeger, 1960.

956. Spanier, John W., and Eric M. Uslaner. **How American Foreign Policy Is Made.** New York: Holt, Rinehart, and Winston, 1978.

957. Sullivan, Michael P. "The Question of
     'Relevance' in Foreign Policy Studies."
     Western Political Quarterly 26 (June
     1973): 314-324.
958. Unger, L. "Derecognition Worked." **Foreign
     Policy** 36 (Fall 1979): 105-121.
959. Vayrynen, Raimo. "Notes on Foreign Policy
     Research." **Cooperation and Conflict** 7
     (1972): 87-96.
960. Vile, M. J. C. "The Formulation and
     Execution of Policy in the United States."
     Political Quarterly 33 (Spring 1962): 160-
     171.
961. Wendzel, Robert L. **International Relations:
     A Policymaker Focus.** New York: Wiley,
     1977.
962. Yarmolinsky, Adam. "Lessons of Vietnam."
     Round Table 245 (January 1972): 85-92.

Analytic Techniques

963. Barton, A. H. "Consensus and Conflict Among
     American Leaders." **Public Opinion
     Quarterly** 38 (Winter 1974/75): 507-530.
964. Bowman, James S. "Perspectives on American
     Foreign Policy: Past, Present and Future."
     Rocky Mountain Social Science Journal 11
     (October 1974): 119-124.
965. Brecher, Michael, Blema Steinberg, and
     Janice Stein. "A Framework for Research on
     Foreign Policy Behavior." **Journal of
     Conflict Resolution** 13 (March 1969): 75-
     102.
966. Chace, J. "Is a Foreign Policy Consensus
     Possible?" **Foreign Affairs** 57 (Fall 1978):
     1-16.
967. Cleveland, Harlan. "Irrelevance of Anti-
     Commitment." **Atlantic Community Quarterly**
     6 (Winter 1968-69): 520-530.
968. Coplin, William D., Michael K. O'Leary, and
     Patrick McGowan. **American Foreign Policy:
     An Introduction to Analysis and
     Evaluation.** North Scituate, Mass.:
     Duxbury, 1974.
969. Courtright, Margaret A. F. "Times of
     Transition: Issues and Alternatives in
     Late Victorian and Contemporary American
     Foreign Policies." Ph.D. dissertation,

Johns Hopkins University, 1975.

970. Crane, Robert D. "New Directions for American Foreign Policy: Some Thoughts for Macromodeling." **Orbis** 13 (Summer 1969): 455-475.

971. Eaton, Joseph W. "Symbolic and Substantive Evaluative Research." **Administrative Science Quarterly** 6 (March 1962): 421-442.

972. Finnegan, Richard B. "International Relations: The Disputed Search for Method." **Review of Politics** 34 (January 1972): 40-66.

973. Frankel, Joseph. "Rational Decision-Making in Foreign Policy." **Yearbook of World Affairs** 14 (1960): 40-66.

974. Gerbing, William P. **United States Foreign Policy: Perspectives and Analysis.** New York: McGraw-Hill, 1966.

975. Gross, Feliks. **Foreign Policy Analysis.** New York: Philosophical Library, 1954.

976. Hammond, Paul Y. **Foreign Policymaking: Pluralistic Politics or Unitary Analysis?** Santa Monica, Calif.: Rand, 1965.

977. Hanrieder, Wolfram F. "Compatability and Consensus: A Proposal for the Conceptual Linkage of External and Internal Dimensions of Foreign Policy." **American Political Science Review** 61 (December 1967): 971-982.

978. Harsanyi, John C. "Rational-Choice Models of Political Behavior vs. Functionalist and Conformist Theories." **World Politics** 21 (July 1969):513-538.

979. Hermann, Charles F. **Crisis in Foreign Policy: A Simulation Analysis.** Indianapolis: Bobbs-Merrill, 1969.

980. _____. "What Is a Foreign Policy Event?" In **Comparative Foreign Policy: Theoretical Essays,** edited by Wolfram F. Hanrieder, pp.295-321. New York: McKay, 1971.

981. Hilsman, Roger. "The Foreign Policy Consensus: An Interim Research Report." **Journal of Conflict Resolution** 3 (December 1959): 361-382.

982. Hitchens, Harold L. "American Foreign Policy--The Ends and the Means." **Air University Review** 24 (January-February 1973): 80-86.

983. Hoagland, J. H. "Changing Patterns of Insurgency and American Response." **Journal of International Affairs** 25 (1971): 120-141.

984. Holsti, Kalevi J. **International Politics: A Framework for Analysis**. Englewood Cliffs, N.J.: Prentice-Hall, 1967.

985. _____. "National Role Conceptions in the Study of Foreign Policy." **International Studies Quarterly** 14 (September 1970): 233-309.

986. _____. "On Understanding American Foreign Policy: Will the Real Explanation Please Identify Itself?" **Canadian Review of American Studies** 11 (Winter 1980): 389-397.

987. Houghton, Neal D. "Historical Bases for Prediction in International Relations: Some Implications for American Foreign Policy." **Western Political Quarterly** 17 (December 1964): 632-658.

988. _____. "Perspective for Foreign Policy Objectives in Areas--and in an Era--of Rapid Social Change." **Western Political Quarterly** 16 (December 1963): 844-884.

989. Hughes, Thomas L. "Policy-Making in a World Turned Upside Down." **Foreign Affairs** 45 (January 1867): 202-214.

990. Huntington, Samueal P. "American Foreign Policy: The Changing Political Universe." **Washington Quarterly** 2 (Autumn 1979): 32-44.

991. Johnston, Whittle. "Radical Revisionism and the Disintegration of the American Foreign Policy Consensus." **Orbis** 20 (Spring 1976): 179-205.

992. Jones, Roy E. **Analysing Foreign Policy: An Introduction to Some Conceptual Problems**. New York: Humanities, 1967.

993. Mandel, Robert. "Political Gaming and Foreign Policy Making During Crises." **World Politics** 29 (July 1977): 610-625.

994. March, James G. "An Introduction to the Theory and Measurement of Influence." **American Political Science Review** 49 (June 1955): 431-451.

995. May, Ernest R. "The Nature of Foreign Policy: The Calculated Versus the

Axiomatic." **Daedalus** 91 (Fall 1962): 653-667.

996. Moore, David W. "Foreign Policy and Empirical Democratic Theory." **American Political Science Review** 68 (September 1974): 1192-1197.

997. Needler, Martin C. **Understanding Foreign Policy.** New York: Holt, Rinehart, and Winston, 1966.

998. O'Leary, Michael K. "Quest for Relevance: Quantitative International Relations Research and Government Foreign Affairs Analysis." **International Studies Quarterly** 18 (June 1974): 211-237.

999. O'Leary, Michael K., and William D. Coplin. **Quantitative Techniques in Foreign Policy Analysis and Forecasting.** New York: Praeger, 1975.

1000. Possony, Stefan T. "Foreign Policy and Rationality." **Orbis** 12 (Spring 1968): 132-160.

1001. Raucher, Alan. "The First Foreign Affairs Think Tanks." **American Quarterly** 30 (Fall 1978): 493-513.

1002. Rosenau, James N. "Paradigm Lost: Five Actors in Search of the Interactive Effects of Domestic and Foreign Affairs." **Policy Sciences** 4 (December 1973): 415-436.

1003. _____. **The Scientific Study of Foreign Policy.** New York: Free Press, 1971.

1004. Salmore, Stephen A. "Foreign Policy and National Attributes: A Multi-Variate Analysis." Ph.D. dissertation, Princeton University, 1972.

1005. Singer, J. David, ed. **Human Behavior and International Politics: Contributions from the Social-Psychological Sciences.** Chicago: Rand McNally, 1965.

1006. _____. **The Scientific Study of Politics: An Approach to Foreign Policy Analysis.** Morristown, N.J.: General Learning, 1972.

1007. Stupad, Ronald J. **American Foreign Policy: Assumptions, Processes, and Projections.** New York: Harper and Row, 1976.

1008. Sylvan, Donald A. "Planning Foreign Policy Systematically: Mathematical Foreign Policy Planning." **Journal of Conflict**

Resolution 23 (March 1979): 139-183.
1009. Vocke, William C., ed. **American Foreign Policy: An Analytical Approach.** New York: Free Press, 1976.
1010. Ways, Max. "What U.S. Foreign Policy Has Done Right." **Atlantic Community Quarterly** 6 (Summer 1968): 278-283.
1011. Weisband, Edward. **The Ideology of American Foreign Policy: A Paradigm of Lockian Liberalism.** Beverly Hills, Calif.: Sage, 1973.
1012. Winham, Gilbert R. "Quantitative Methods in Foreign Policy Analysis." **Canadian Journal of Political Science** 2 (June 1969): 187-199.
1013. Zinnes, Dina A. **Contemporary Research in International Relations: A Perspective and a Critical Assessment.** New York: Free Press, 1976.

Functional Studies

1014. Adelman, Kenneth L. "Speaking of America: Public Diplomacy in Our Time." **Foreign Affairs** 59 (Spring 1981): 913-936.
1015. Alger, Chadwick F. "Foreign Policies of U.S. Publics." **International Studies Quarterly** 21 (June 1977): 277-318.
1016. Allison, Graham T., and Peter Szanton. **Remaking Foreign Policy: The Organizational Connection.** New York: Basic Books, 1976.
1017. Bernstein, Robert A., and Peter D. Weldon. "A Structural Approach to the Analysis of International Relations." **Journal of Conflict Resolution** 12 (June 1968): 159-181.
1018. Blong, Clair K. "External Penetration and Foreign Policy Behavior." Ph.D. dissertation, University of Maryland, 1975.
1019. Brewer, Thomas, L. "Issue and Context Variations in Foreign Policy: Effects on American Elite Behavior." **Journal of Conflict Resolution** 17 (March 1973): 89-114.
1020. Brodin, Katarina. "Belief Systems, Doctrines, and Foreign Policy."

Cooperation and Conflict 7 (1972): 97-112.

1021. Caporaso, James A. "Dependence, Dependency, and Power in the Global System: A Structural and Behavioral Analysis." International Organization 32 (Winter 1978): 13-43.

1022. Chadwick, Richard W. "An Inductive, Empirical Analysis of Intra- and Inter-National Behavior, Aimed at a Partial Extension of Inter-Nation Simulation Theory." Journal of Peace Research 6 (1969): 193-214.

1023. Corning, Peter A. "Some Biological Bases of Behavior and Some Implications for Political Science." World Politics 23 (April 1971): 321-370.

1024. D'Amato, Anthony A. "Psychological Constructs in Foreign Policy Prediction." Journal of Conflict Resolution 11 (September 1967): 294-311.

1025. de Rivera, Joseph H. The Psychological Dimension of Foreign Policy. Columbus, Ohio: Merrill, 1968.

1026. Dreier, John C. "The Organization of American States and United States Policy." International Organization 17 (Winter 1963): 36-53.

1027. East, Maurice A." Size and Foreign Policy Behavior: A Test of Two Models." World Politics 25 (July 1973): 556-576.

1028. Edinger, Lewis J. "Military Leaders and Foreign Policy-Making." American Political Science Review 57 (June 1963): 392-405.

1029. Ellenport, Samuel. "American Foreign Policy and Mass Democracy." American Scholar 36 (Autumn 1967): 589-593.

1030. Elliott, Williams Y. United States Foreign Policy: Its Organization and Control. New York: Columbia University Press, 1952.

1031. Emshoff, James R., and Russell L. Ackoff. "Explanatory Models of Interactive Choice Behavior." Journal of Conflict Resolution 14 (March 1970): 77-89.

1032. Etheredge, Lloyd S. "Personality Effects on American Foreign Policy, 1898-1968: A Test of Interpersonal Generalization Theory." American Political Science Review 72 (June 1978): 434-451.

1033.   Eulau, Heinz. **The Behavioral Persuasion in
        Politics.** New York: Random House, 1963.
1034.   Fraser, D. M. "Freedom and Foreign Policy."
        Foreign Policy 26 (Spring 1977): 140-156.
1035.   Freymond, Jacques. "New Dimensions in
        International Relations." **Review of
        Politics** 37 (October 1975): 464-478.
1036.   Fuchs, Lawrence H. "Minority Groups and
        Foreign Policy." **Political Science
        Quarterly** 74 (June 1959): 161-175.
1037.   Gamson, W. A., and A. Modigliani. "Knowledge
        and Foreign Policy Opinions: Some Models
        for Consideration." **Public Opinion
        Quarterly** 30 (Summer 1966): 187-199.
1038.   George, Alexander L. "The 'Operational
        Code': A Neglected Approach to the Study
        of Political Leaders and Decision-Making."
        International Studies Quarterly 13 (June
        1969): 190-222.
1039.   Gordon, Lincoln. "Organization for the
        Conduct of Foreign Policy." **Foreign
        Service Journal** 32 (August 1955): 18-20,
        46-48.
1040.   Hayes, Louis D., and Ronald D. Hedlund, eds.
        **The Conduct of Political Inquiry:
        Behavioral Political Analysis.** Englewood
        Cliffs, N.J.: Prentice-Hall, 1970.
1041.   Janis, Irving L. **Victims of Groupthink: A
        Psychological Study of Foreign-Policy
        Decisions and Fiascos.** Boston: Houghton
        Mifflin, 1972.
1042.   Katzenstein, Peter J. "International
        Relations and Domestic Structures: Foreign
        Economic Policies of Advanced Industrial
        States." **International Organization** 30
        (Winter 1976): 1-45.
1043.   Kegley, Charles W. **A General Empirical
        Typology of Foreign Policy Behavior.**
        Beverly Hills, Calif.: Sage, 1973.
1044.   _____. "Toward the Construction of an
        Empirically Grounded Typology of Foreign
        Policy Output Behavior." Ph.D.
        dissertation, Syracuse University, 1971.
1045.   Kelman, Herbert C., ed. **International
        Behavior: A Social Psychological Analysis.**
        New York: Holt, Rinehart, and Winston,
        1965.
1046.   Knorr, K. "Social Science Research Abroad:

Problems and Remedies." **World Politics** 19 (April 1967): 465-485.

1047.   Lasswell, Harold D. **The Analysis of Political Behavior: An Empirical Approach.** London: Routledge and Paul, 1947.

1048.   Lefever, Ernest W. **Ethics and United States Foreign Policy.** New York: Meridian, 1957.

1049.   _____. "The Prestige Press, Foreign Policy, and American Survival." **Orbis** 20 (Spring 1976): 207-225.

1050.   Lerche, Charles O. "Crisis in American World Leadership." **Journal of Politics** 28 (May 1966): 308-321.

1051.   Levinson, Daniel J. "Authoritarian Personality and Foreign Policy." **Journal of Conflict Resolution** 1 (March 1957): 37-47.

1052.   Lifka, Thomas E. "The Concept of 'Totalitarianism' and American Foreign Policy, 1922-1949." Ph.D. dissertation, Harvard University, 1973.

1053.   McClelland, C. A. "Anticipation of International Crises: Prospects for Theory and Research." **International Studies Quarterly** 21 (March 1977): 15-38.

1054.   Meek, G. "U.S. Influence in the Organization of American States." **Journal of Interamerican Studies and World Affairs** 17 (August 1975): 311-325.

1055.   Mosher, Frederick C., and John E. Harr. **Programming Systems and Foreign Policy Leadership.** New York: Oxford University Press, 1970.

1056.   Neiburg, Harold, L. **Political Violence: The Behavioral Process.** New York: St. Martin's, 1969.

1057.   Patchen, Martin. "Social Class and Dimensions of Foreign Policy Attitudes." **Socail Science Quarterly** 51 (December 1970): 649-667.

1058.   Pratt, James W. "Leadership Relations in U.S. Foreign Policy Making: Case Studies, 1947-1950." Ph.D. dissertation, Columbia University, 1963.

1059.   Rosen, David J. "Leadership Change and Foreign Policy." Ph.D. dissertation, Rutgers University, 1975.

1060.   Roskin, Michael. "From Pearl Harbor to

Vietnam: Shifting Generational Paradigms and Foreign Policy." **Political Science Quarterly** 89 (Fall 1974):563-588.

1061. Rostow, Eugene V. "New Challenges to American Foreign Policy, 1963-1968." **Atlantic Community Quarterly** 7 (Spring 1969): 118-124.

1062. Rummel, R. J. "Dimensions of Conflict Behavior within Nations, 1946-59." **Journal of Conflict Resolution** 10 (March 1966): 65-73.

1063. _____. "Some Attributes and Behavioral Patterns of Nations." **Journal of Peace Research** 4 (1967): 196-206.

1064. _____. "Some Dimensions in the Foreign Behavior of Nations." **Journal of Peace Research** 3 (1966): 201-224.

1065. _____. "Some Empirical Findings on Nations and Their Behavior." **World Politics** 21 (January 1969): 226-241.

1066. Schilling, Warner R. "The Clarification of Ends, or, Which Interest Is the National." **World Politics** 8 (July 1956): 566-578.

1067. Shapiro, Michael J., and Matthew G. Bonham. "Cognitive Process and Foreign Policy Decision-Making." **International Studies Quarterly** 17 (June 1973): 147-174.

1068. Simon, Jeffrey D. "Social Position and American Policy Attitudes: 1952-1972." **Journal of Peace Research** 17 (1980): 9-28.

1069. Stichting, Grotius S. **Ethical Values in International Decision Making.** The Hague: Nijhoff, 1960.

1070. Terhune, Kenneth W. "From National Character to National Behavior: A Reformulation." **Journal of Conflict Resolution** 14 (June 1970): 203-263.

1071. Thompson, Kenneth W. "American Foreign Policy: Values Renewed or Discovered." **Orbis** 20 (Spring 1976): 123-135.

1072. Thorson, Stuart J. "Adaptation and Foreign Policy Theory." In **Sage International Yearbook of Foreign Policy Studies,** edited by Patrick J. McGowan, vol. 2, pp. 123-139. Beverly Hills, Calif.: Sage, 1974.

1073. Trachtenberg, Marc. "The Social Interpretation of Foreign Policy." **Review of Politics** 40 (July 1978): 328-350.

1074.   Yost, Charles W. "The Instruments of
        American Foreign Policy." **Foreign Affairs**
        50 (October 1971): 59-68.
1075.   Zimmerman, William. "Issue Area and Foreign
        Policy Process: A Research Note in Search
        of a General Theory." **American Political
        Science Review** 67 (December 1973): 1204-
        1212.

FOREIGN AFFAIRS AND THE PRESIDENCY

General Studies

1076. Adelman, Kenneth L. "The Runner Stumbles: Carter's Foreign Policy in the Year One." **Policy Review** 3 (Winter 1978): 89-116.
1077. Adler, Selig. "Franklin D. Roosevelt's Foreign Policy: An Assessment." **International Review of History and Political Science** 15 (May 1978): 1-17.
1078. Allen, H. C. "Quiet Strength? American Foreign Policy under President Carter." **Round Table** 266 (April 1977): 146-152.
1079. Anderson, Isabel W. **Presidents and Pies: Life in Washington 1897-1919** Boston: Houghton Mifflin, 1920.
1080. Aron, Raymond. "Richard Nixon and the Future of American Foreign Policy." **Daedalus** 101 (Fall 1972): 1-24.
1081. Bell, C. "Virtue Unrewarded: Carter's Foreign Policy at Mid-Term." **International Affairs** 54 (October 1978): 559-572.
1082. Belohlavek, John M. "'Let the Eagle Soar!': Democratic Constraints on the Foreign Policy of Andrew Jackson." **Presidential Studies Quarterly** 10 (Winter 1980): 36-50.
1083. Bernstein, Barton J. "Foreign Policy in the Eisenhower Administration." **Foreign Service Journal** 50 (May 1973): 17-20, 38.
1084. Brookings Institution. **The Administration of Foreign Affairs and Overseas Operations.** Washington D.C.: Brookings Institution, 1950.
1085. Bruchey, Stuart. "Beard on Foreign Policy: A Note." **American Historical Review** 73 (February 1968): 759-760.
1086. Caldwell, Dan. "Bureaucratic Foreign Policy-Making." **American Behavioral Scientist** 21 (September-October 1977): 87-110.
1087. Cheever, Daniel S., and H. Field Haviland. "Hoover Commission: A Symposium--Foreign Affairs." **American Political Science Review** 43 (October 1949): 966-978.

1088. Christopher, W. "Ceasefire Between the
       Branches: A Compact in Foreign Affairs."
       Foreign Affairs 60 (Summer 1982): 989-
       1005.
1089. Divine, Robert A. "Cold War and the Election
       of 1948." **Journal of American History** 59
       (June 1972): 90-110.
1090. Fesler, James W. "Administrative Literature
       and the Second Hoover Commission Reports."
       American Political Science Review 51
       (March 1957): 135-157.
1091. Frye, Alton. "Congress and President: The
       Balance Wheels of American Foreign
       Policy." **Yale Review** 69 (Autumn 1979): 1-
       16.
1092. Garrett, Stephen A. "Nixonian Foreign
       Policy: A New Balance of Power or a
       Revived Concert?" **Polity** 8 (Spring 1976):
       389-421.
1093. George, Alexander L. **Presidential Decision
       Making in Foreign Policy: The Effective
       Use of Information and Advice.** Boulder,
       Colo.: Westview, 1980.
1094. Gershman, C. "Rise and Fall of the New
       Foreign Policy Establishment." **Commentary**
       70 (July 1980): 13-24.
1095. Gilboa, Eytan. "Intellectuals in the White
       House and American Foreign Policy." **Yale
       Review** 65 (June 1976): 481-497.
1096. Girling, J. L. S. "Carter's Foreign Policy:
       Realism or Ideology?" **World Today** 33
       (November 1977): 417-424.
1097. Graber, Doris A. **Public Opinion, the
       President, and Foreign Policy: Four Case
       Studies from the Formative Years.** New
       York: Holt, Rinehart, and Winston, 1968.
1098. Hahn, Harlan. "Political Efficacy and
       Foreign Policy Attitudes." **Social Problems**
       17 (Fall 1969): 271-279.
1099. Halperin, Morton H. **Bureaucratic Politics
       and Foreign Policy.** Washington, D.C.:
       Brookings Institution, 1974.
1100. Harriman, W. Averell. **United States
       President's Committee on Foreign Aid:
       European Recovery and American Aid--A
       Report.** Washington, D.C.: Government
       Printing Office, 1947.
1101. Hensley, Carl W. "Harry S. Truman:

Fundamental Americanism in Foreign Policy
Speechmaking, 1945-1946." **Southern Speech
Communication** Journal 40 (Winter 1975):
180-190.
1102. Hughes, Thomas L. "Carter and the Management
of Contradictions." **Foreign Policy** 31
(Summer 1978): 34-55.
1103. Lacqueur, Walter. "World and President
Carter." **Commentary** 65 (February 1978):
56-63.
1104. Landecker, Manfred. **The President and Public
Opinion: Leadership in Foreign Affairs.**
Washington, D.C.: Public Affairs, 1969.
1105. Lenczowski, J. "Foreign Policy for
Reaganauts." **Policy Review** 18 (Fall 1982):
77-95.
1106. Leopold, Richard W. "A Crisis of Confidence:
Foreign Policy Research and the Federal
Government." **American Archivist** 34 (April
1971): 139-155.
1107. McAuliffe, M. S. "Eisenhower, the
President." **Journal of American History** 68
(December 1981): 625-632.
1108. Macmahon, Arthur W. "The Administration of
Foreign Affairs." **American Political
Science Review** 45 (September 1951): 836-
866.
1109. _____. **Administration in Foreign Affairs.**
University: University of Alabama Press,
1953.
1110. _____. "International Policy and Government
Structure." **Proceedings of the American
Philosophical Society** 92 (October 1948):
217-227.
1111. Maechling, Charles. "Foreign Policy Makers:
The Weakest Link?" **Virginia Quarterly
Review** 52 (Winter 1976): 1-23.
1112. _____. "Our Foreign Affairs Establishment:
The Need for Reform." **Virginia Quarterly
Review** 45 (Spring 1969): 193-210.
1113. Moore, James R. "Sources of New Deal
Economic Policy: The International
Dimension." **Journal of American History** 61
(December 1974): 728-744.
1114. Morgan, E. S. "Slavery and Freedom: The
American Paradox." **Journal of American
History** 59 (June 1972): 5-29.
1115. Morris, Richard B., ed. **Great Presidential**

Decisions: State Papers that Changed the Course of History. rev. ed. New York: Harper and Row, 1973.

1116. Muravchik, J. "Kennedy's Foreign Policy: What the Record Shows." **Commentary** 68 (December 1979): 31-43.

1117. Myers, David S. "Foreign Affairs and the Presidential Election of 1964." Ph.D. dissertation, University of Maryland, 1967.

1118. O'Brien, Francis W., ed. **The Hoover-Wilson Wartime Correspondence, September 24, 1914, to November 11, 1918.** Ames: Iowa State University Press, 1974.

1119. Olson, W. C. "World from Both Ends of Pennsylvania Avenue: President Carter's Foreign Policy Problems." **Round Table** 272 (October 1978): 333-339.

1120. Owen, Henry. "Foreign Policy Premises for the Next Administration." **Foreign Affairs** 46 (July 1968): 699-712.

1121. Paterson, Thomas G. "Bearing the Burden: A Critical Look at JFK's Foreign Policy." **Virginia Quarterly Review** 54 (Spring 1978): 193-212.

1122. _____. "Presidential Foreign Policy, Public Opinion, and Congress: The Truman Years." **Diplomatic History** 3 (Winter 1979): 1-18.

1123. Perlmutter, Amos. "Presidential Political Center and Foreign Policy: A Critique of the Revisionist and Bureaucratic-Political Orientations." **World Politics** 27 (October 1974): 87-106.

1124. Plischke, Elmer. "Presidents's Inner Foreign Policy Team." **Review of Politics** 30 (July 1968): 292-307.

1125. Ravenal, Earl C. "Nixon's Challenge to Carter: No More Mr. Nice Guy." **Foreign Policy** 29 (Winter 1977-78): 27-42.

1126. Rostow, Walt W. "The 'New Look' in U.S. World Policy: Advice President Kennedy Is Getting." **U.S. News and World Report** 50 (February 1961): 75-81.

1127. Rowse, Arthur E. "Foreign Policy in National Elections." **Editorial Research Reports** 28 (July 1960): 545-562.

1128. Schelling, Thomas C. "PPBS and Foreign Affairs." **Public Interest** 11 (Spring

1968): 26-36.

1129. Schneider, M. L. "Human Rights Policy under the Carter Administration." **Law and Contemporary Problems** 43 (Spring 1979): 261-267.

1130. Schweigler, G. "Carter's Detente Policy: Change or Continuity?" **World Today** 34 (March 1978): 81-89.

1131. Sellen, Robert W. "Old Assumptions versus New Realities: Lyndon Johnson and Foreign Policy." **International Journal** 28 (Spring 1973): 205-229.

1132. Szulc, Tad. **The Illusion of Peace: Foreign Policy in the Nixon Years.** New York: Viking Press, 1978.

1133. _____. "Springtime for Carter." **Foreign Policy** 27 (Summer 1977): 178-191.

1134. Thayer, F. C. "Presidential Policy Processes and New Administration: A Search for Revised Paradigms." **Public Administration Review** 31 (Summer 1971): 552-561.

1135. Yankelovich, D. "Farewell to President Knows Best." **Foreign Affairs** 56 (1978): 670-693.

1136. Yarmolinsky, Adam. "Bureaucratic Structures and Political Outcomes." **Journal of International Affairs** 23 (1969): 225-235.

1137. Yizhar, Michael. "The Eisenhower Doctrine: A Case Study of American Foreign Policy Formulation and Implementation." Ph.D. dissertation, New School for Social Research, 1969.

1138. Young, George B. "The Influence of Politics on American Diplomacy during Cleveland's Administrations 1885-1889, 1893-1897." Ph.D. dissertation, Yale University, 1939.

Powers and Duties

1139. Barrett, Raymond J. "The War Powers: Constitutional Crisis." **United States Naval Institute Proceedings** 99 (November 1973): 18-25.

1140. Berger, Raoul. "Presidential Monopoly on Foreign Relations." **Michigan Law Review** 71 (November 1972): 1-58.

1141. Bestor, Arthur. "Separation of Powers in the Domain of Foreign Affairs: The Intent of the Constitution Historically Examined."

Seton Hall Law Review 5 (Spring 1974): 527-665.

1142.   Bishop, William W. "The Structure of Federal Power over Foreign Affairs." Minnesota Law Review 36 (March 1952): 299-322.

1143.   Briggs, Ellis O. Anatomy of Diplomacy: The Origin and Execution of American Foreign Policy. New York: Mckay, 1968.

1144.   Brookings Institution. Governmental Mechanism for the Conduct of United States Foreign Relations. Washington, D.C.: Brookings Institution, 1949.

1145.   Bulmer, Charles, and John L. Carmichael. "The War Powers Resolution: A Limitation on Presidential Power?" Georgia Political Science Association Journal 3 (Fall 1975): 54-68.

1146.   Bundy, Harvey H., and James G. Rogers. The Organization of the Government for the Conduct of Foreign Affairs: A Report with Recommendations Prepared for the Commission on Organization of the Executive Branch of the Government. Washington, D.C.: Government Printing Office, 1949.

1147.   Bundy, McGeorge. "Vietman, Watergate and Presidential Powers." Foreign Affairs 58 (Winter 1979-80): 397-407.

1148.   Chai, Jae H. "Presidential Control of the Foreign Policy Bureaucracy: The Kennedy Case." Presidential Studies Quarterly 8 (Fall 1978): 391-402.

1149.   Collier, Ellen C. Powers of the President in the Field of Foreign Policy. Washington, D.C.: U.S. Library of Congress, 1969.

1150.   Corwin, Edward S. The President's Control of Foreign Relations. Princeton, N.J.: Princeton University Press, 1917.

1151.   Cress, Larry D. "The Jonathan Robbins Incident: Extradition and the Separation of Powers in the Adams Administration." Essex Institute Historical Collections 111 (April 1975): 99-121.

1152.   Destler, I. M. Presidents, Bureaucrats, and Foreign Policy: The Politics of Organizational Reform. Princeton, N.J.: Princeton University Press, 1972.

1153.   Driggs, Don W. "The President as Chief

Educator in Foreign Affairs." **Western Political Quarterly** 11 (December 1958): 813-819.
1154. Garner, James W. "Executive Discretion in the Conduct of Foreign Relations." **American Journal of International Law** 31 (April 1937): 289-293.
1155. Geyelin, P. "Impeachment and Foreign Policy." **Foreign Policy** 15 (Summer 1974): 183-190.
1156. Kesselman, Mark. "Presidential Leadership in Congress on Foreign Policy." **American Journal of Political Science** 9 (November 1965): 401-406.
1157. Kessler, Francis P. "Presidential-Congressional Battles: Toward a Truce on the Foreign Policy Front." **Presidential Studies Quarterly** 8 (Spring 1978): 115-127.
1158. Laski, Harold J. "The American President and Foreign Relations." **Journal of Politics** 11 (February 1949): 171-205.
1159. Lee, Jong R. "Presidential Choice: Limits of Leadership in Foreign Policy." Ph.D. dissertation, Yale University, 1975.
1160. Levitt, Albert. **The President and the International Affairs of the United States.** Los Angeles: Parker, 1954.
1161. McCamy, James L. **The Administration of American Foreign Affairs.** New York: Knopf, 1950.
1162. McGee, Gale W. "Executive Power in Foreign Policy-Making." **Capitol Studies** 1 (Fall 1972): 3-8.
1163. Marks, Frederick W. "Foreign Affairs: A Winning Issue in the Campaign for Ratification of the United States Constitution." **Political Science Quarterly** 86 (September 1971): 444-469.
1164. Newhouse, W. J. "Constitutional and International Agreement or Unilateral Action Curbing Peace-Imperiling Propaganda." **Law and Contemporary Problems** 31 (Summer 1966): 506-529.
1165. Oliver, James K. "United States Foreign Policy Formulation and the Budgetary Process in the 1960's." Ph.D. dissertation, American University, 1970.

1166. Olson, W. C. "President, Congress and
       American Foreign Policy: Confrontation or
       Collaboration?" International Affairs 52
       (October 1976): 565-581.
1167. Palmer, John D. "Presidential Leadership and
       Foreign Economic Aid." Ph.D. dissertation,
       University of Texas, 1965.
1168. Ripley, Randall B., and Grace A. Franklin,
       eds. Policy-Making in the Federal
       Executive Branch. New York: Free Press,
       1975.
1169. Roberts, Chalmers M. "Foreign Policy under a
       Paralyzed Presidency." Foreign Affairs 52
       (July 1974): 677-689.
1170. Schwarzer, William W., and Robert R. Wood.
       "Presidential Power and Aggression Abroad:
       A Constitutional Dilemma." American Bar
       Association Journal 40 (May 1954): 394-
       3397.
1171. Sherwood, Foster H. "Foreign Relations and
       the Constitution." Western Political Quar-
       terly 1 (December 1948): 386-399.
1172. Sigelman, L. "Reassessment of the Two
       Presidencies Thesis." Journal of Politics
       41 (November 1979): 1195-1205.
1173. Sofaer, Abrahama D. "The Presidency, War,
       and Foreign Affairs: Practice under the
       Framers." Law and Contemporary Problems 40
       (Spring 1976): 12-38.
1174. Wallace, Don. "The President's Exclusive
       Foreign Affairs Power Over Foreign Aid."
       Duke Law Journal (April - June 1970): 293-
       328, 293-494.
1175. Weinstein, Allen. "Press and Foreign Policy:
       Freedom of Information and Carter Foreign
       Policy: Act One." Washington Quarterly 2
       (Spring 1979): 39-43.
1176. Weiss, Stuart L. "American Foreign Policy
       and Presidential Power: The Neutrality Act
       of 1935." Journal of Politics 30 (August
       1968): 672-695.
1177. Wilcox, Francis O. "President Nixon, the
       Congress, and Foreign Policy." Michigan
       Quarterly Review 9 (Winter 1970): 37-43.
1178. Wilcox, Francis O., and Richard A. Frank,
       eds. The Constitution and the Conduct of
       Foreign Policy. New York: Praeger, 1976.
1179. Wriston, Henry M. Executive Agents in

American Foreign Relations. Baltimore: Johns Hopkins University Press, 1929.
1180. Young, Lowell T. "Franklin D. Roosevelt and the Expansion of the Monroe Doctrine." North Dakota Quarterly 42 (Winter 1974): 23-32.

Diplomatic Role

1181. Accinelli, Robert D. "Was There a 'New' Harding? Warren G. Harding and the World Court Issue, 1920-1923." Ohio History 84 (Autumn 1975): 168-181.
1182. Bhaqwati, Jaqdish. "The United States in the Nixon Era: The End of Innocence." Daedalus 101 (Fall 1972): 25-48.
1183. Buchan, Alastair. Crisis Management: The New Diplomacy. Boulognesur-Seine, France: Atlantic Institute, 1966.
1184. Errico, Charles J. "The New Deal, Internationalism, and the New American Consensus, 1938-40." Maryland Historian 9 (Spring 1978): 17-31.
1185. Eubank, Keith. The Summit Conferences, 1919-1960. Norman: University of Oklahoma Press, 1966.
1186. Galtung, Johan. "Summit Meetings and International Relations." Journal of Peace Research 1 (1964): 36-54.
1187. Graber, Doris A. Crisis Diplomacy: A History of U.S. Intervention Policies and Practices. Washington, D.C.: Public Affairs, 1959.
1188. Hammond, Paul Y. "Presidents, Politics, and International Intervention." Annals of the American Academy of Political and Social Science 386 (November 1969): 10-18.
1189. Hahn, Walter F. "The Nixon Doctrine: Design and Dilemmas." Orbis 16 (Summer 1972): 361-376.
1190. Holbo, Paul S. "Presidential Leadership in Foreign Affairs: William McKinley and the Turpie-Foraker Amendment." American Historical Review 72 (July 1967): 1321-1335.
1191. Howard, Harry N. "The Regional Pacts and the Eisenhower Doctrine." Annals of the American Academy of Political and Social

Science 401 (May 1972): 85-94.
1192. Kanawada, Leo V. "The Ethnic Factor in American Diplomacy During the Presidency of Franklin D. Roosevelt: 1933-1939." Ph.D. dissertation, St. John's University, 1980.
1193. Kaplan, Lawrence S. "NATO and the Nixon Doctrine Ten Years Later." Orbis 24 (Spring 1980): 149-164.
1194. Kaufman, Burton I. "Wilson's 'War Bureaucracy' and Foreign Trade Expansion, 1917-21." Prologue 6 (Spring 1974): 19-31.
1195. Kottman, Richard N. "The Hoover-Bennett Meeting of 1931: Mismanaged Summitry." Annals of Iowa 42 (Winter 1974): 205-221.
1196. Lewis, Flora. "The Nixon Doctrine." Atlantic 226 (November 1970): 6-19.
1197. Lindner, J., and R. Hoyt. "Up from the Summit." Christianity and Crisis 38 (November 1978): 266-272.
1198. Lowenthal, M. M. "Roosevelt and the Coming of the War: The Search for United States Policy 1937-42." Journal of Contemporary History 16 (July 1981): 413-440.
1199. McClure, Wallace M. "The Presidency and World Affairs: Mobilization of Assistance." Journal of Politics 11 (February 1949): 206-217.
1200. Marks, Frederick W. "Morality as a Drive Wheel in the Diplomacy of Theodore Roosevelt." Diplomatic History 2 (Winter 1978): 43-62.
1201. Morgenthau, Hans J. "Dilemma of the Summit." New York Times Magazine November 11, 1962, pp. 117-122.
1202. Pearson, Frederic S., J. Martin Reynolds, and Keith E. Meyer. "The Carter Foreign Policy and the Use of International Organization: The Limits of Policy Innovation." World Affairs 142 (Fall 1979): 75-97.
1203. Plischke, Elmer. "International Conferencing and the Summit: Macro-Analysis of Presidential Participation." Orbis 14 (Fall 1970): 673-713.
1204. _____. "The President's Right to go Abroad." Orbis 15 (Fall 1971): 755-783.
1205. _____. "Recent State Visits to the United

States--A Technique Summit Diplomacy."
World Affairs Quarterly 29 (October 1958):
223-255.

1206. _____. "Summit Diplomacy: Its Uses and
Limitations." **Virginia Quarterly Review** 48
(Summer 1972): 321-344.

1207. Preeg, Ernest H. **Traders and Diplomats: An**
Analysis of the Kennedy Round of
Negotiations under the General Agreement
of Tariffs and Trade. Washington, D.C.:
Brookings Institution, 1970.

1208. Price, Don K. **The New Dimension of**
Diplomacy: The Organization of the U.S.
Government for Its New Role in World
Affairs. New York: Woodrow Wilson
Foundation, 1951.

1209. Rogers, Lindsay. "Of Summits." **Foreign**
Affairs 34 (October 1955): 141-148.

1210. Sears, Arthur M. "The Search for Peace
Through Summit Conferences." Ph.D.
dissertation, University of Colorado,
1972.

1211. Smith, Geoffrey S. "'Harry, We Hardly Know
You': Revisionism, Politics and Diplomacy,
1945-1954." **American Political Science**
Review 70 (June 1976): 560-582.

1212. Steele, Richard W. "Franklin D. Roosevelt
and His Foreign Policy Critics." **Political**
Science Quarterly 94 (Spring 1979): 15-32.

1213. Theoharis, Athan. "Roosevelt and Truman on
Yalta: The Origins of the Cold War."
Political Science Quarterly 87 (June
1972): 210-241.

1214. Thompson, J. A. "From the Monroe Doctrine to
the Marshall Plan." **Historical Journal** 22
(September 1979): 731-745.

1215. Waples, Douglas. "Publicity versus
Diplomacy: Notes on the Reporting of the
'Summit' Conferences." **Public Opinion**
Quarterly 20 (Spring 1956): 308-314.

1216. Ware, Hugh. "New Tools for Crisis
Management." **United States Naval Institute**
Proceedings 100 (August 1974): 19-24.

1217. Warner, Geoffrey. "From Teheran to Yalta:
Reflections on F.D.R.'s Foreign Policy."
International Affairs 43 (July 1967): 530-
536.

1218. _____. "Truman Doctrine and the Marshall

Plan." **International Affairs** 50 (January 1974): 82-92.

1219. Watt, David C. "Return to Americanism? The Foreign Policy of President Carter." **Political Quarterly** 48 (October 1977): 429-439.

1220. Weiner, Bernard. "The Truman Doctrine: Background and Presentation." Ph.D. dissertation, Claremont Colleges, 1967.

1221. Wimer, Kurt, and S. Wimer. "Harding Administration, the League of Nations, and the Separate Peace Treaty." **Review of Politics** 29 (January 1967): 12-24.

1222. _____. "Wilson and Eisenhower: Two Experiences in Summit Diplomacy." **Contemporary Review** 199 (June 1961): 284-295.

1223. Winham, Gilbert R. "Negotiation as a Management Process." **World Politics** 30 (October 1977): 87-114.

National Security

1224. Adler, Emanuel. "Executive Command and Control in Foreign Policy: The CIA's Covert Activities." **Orbis** 23 (Fall 1979): 671-696.

1225. Barnds, William J. "Intelligence and Foreign Policy: Dilemmas of a Democracy." **Foreign Affairs** 47 (January 1969): 281-295.

1226. Brzezinski, Zbigniew. "America in a Hostile World." **Contemporary Review** 299 (November 1976): 225-244.

1227. _____. "American Foreign Policy in a Rapidly Changing World." **Atlantic Community Quarterly** 17 (Spring 1979): 6-123.

1228. _____. "Deceptive Structure of Peace." **Foreign Policy** 14 (Spring 1974): 35-55.

1229. _____. "Recognizing the Crisis." **Foreign Policy** 17 (Winter 1974-75): 63-74.

1230. _____. "U.S. Foreign Policy: The Search for Focus." **Foreign Affairs** 51 (July 1973): 708-727.

1231. Bullington, James R. "America's Battered Spirit: Our Security and Foreign Policy Dilemma." **Parameters** 9 (March 1979): 46-51.

1232. Clark, Keith C., and Laurence J. Legere, eds. The President and the Management of National Security. New York: Praeger, 1969.
1233. Cline, R. S. "Policy without Intelligence." Foreign Policy 17 (Winter 1974-75): 121-135.
1234. Cuff, Robert D. "We Band of Brothers-- Woodrow Wilson's War Managers." Canadian Review of American Studies 5 (Fall 1974): 135-148.
1235. Destler, I. M. "National Security Advice to US Presidents: Some Lessons from Thirty Years." World Politics 29 (January 1977): 143-176.
1236. Deutsch, Karl W. "Another Look at the National Decision System." In his The Analysis of International Relations, pp. 101-110. Englewood Cliffs, N.J.: Prentice-Hall, 1968.
1237. Falk, R. A. "President Gerald Ford, CIA Covert Operations, and the Status of Internationsl Law." American Journal of International Law 69 (April 1975): 354-358.
1238. Falk, Stanley. "The National Security Council under Truman, Eisenhower and Kennedy." Political Science Quarterly 79 (September 1964): 403-434.
1239. Halperin, Morton, H. "Why Bureaucrats Play Games." Foreign Policy 5 (May 1971): 70-90.
1240. _____. National Security Policy-Making: Analyses, Cases, and Proposals. Lexington, Mass.: Lexington, 1975.
1241. Halperin, Morton H., and Daniel N. Hoffman. Top Secret: National Security and the Right to Know. New York: Simon and Schuster, 1977.
1242. Harrigan, A. "American Security: A Timely Assessment." Modern Age 20 (Winter 1976): 78-85.
1243. Hilsman, Roger. Strategic Intelligence and National Dceisions. Glencoe, Ill.: Free Press, 1956.
1244. King, Alwyntt. "Flexible National Interests and US Foreign Policy." Military Review 57 (April 1977): 80-91.

1245. Lake, A. "Defining the National Interest."
       Procedings of the Academy of Political
       Science 34 (1981): 202-213.
1246. Lipson, L. "Where Do Our Vital Interests
       Lie?" Atlantic Community Quarterly 7
       (Summer 1969): 165-183.
1247. Mowrer, Paul S. Our Foreign Affairs: A Study
       in National Interest and the New
       Diplomacy. New York: Dutton, 1924.
1248. Nuechterlein, D. E. "Concept of National
       Interest: A Time for New Approaches."
       Orbis 23 (Spring 1979): 73-92.
1249. Possony, Stefan T. "US Intelligence at the
       Crossroads." Orbis 9 (Fall 1965): 587-612.
1250. Posvar, Wesley W. "National Security Policy:
       The Realm of Obsecurity." Orbis 9 (Fall
       1965): 694-713.
1251. Ransom, Harry H. Government Secrecy and
       National Security: An Analysis. Boston:
       Harvard Defense Seminar, 1958.
1252. Rochester, J. Martin. "Paradigm Debate in
       International Relations and Its
       Implications for Foreign Policy Making:
       Toward a Redefinition of the National
       Interest." Western Political Quarterly 31
       (March 1978): 48-58.
1253. Sand, G. William. "Clifford and Truman: A
       Study in Foreign Policy and National
       Security, 1945-1949." Ph.D. dissertation,
       St. Louis University, 1973.
1254. Serfaty, S. "Brzezinski: Play It Again,
       Zbig." Foreign Policy 32 (Fall 1978): 3-
       21.
1255. Snyder, William P. Making U.S. National
       Security Policies. Carlisle Barracks, Pa.:
       U.S. Army War College, 1971.
1256. Sondermann, F. A. "Concept of the National
       Interest." Orbis 21 (Spring 1977): 121-
       138.
1257. Sorensen, Theodore C. "Watergate and
       American Foreign Policy." World Today 30
       (December 1974): 497-503.
1258. Taylor, Maxwell D. "Exposed Flank of
       National Security." Orbis 18 (Winter
       1975): 1011-1022.
1259. _____. "The Legitimate Claims of National
       Security." Foreign Affairs 52 (April
       1974): 577-594.

1260. Urban, George. "A Long Conversation with Dr. Zbigniew Brzezinski: 'The Perils of Foreign Policy.'" **Encounter** 56 (May 1981): 12-30.

FOREIGN AFFAIRS AND THE CONGRESS

General Studies

1261. Allen, Howard W. "Republican Reformers and Foreign Policy, 1913-1917." **Mid-America** 44 (October 1962): 222-229.

1262. Baldwin, David A. "Congressional Initiative in Foreign Policy." **Journal of Politics** 28 (November 1966): 754-733.

1263. Barrie, Robert W. "Congress and the Executive: The Making of U.S. Foreign Trade Policy." Ph.D. dissertation, University of Minnesota, 1968.

1264. Bax, Frans R. "The Legislative-Executive Relationship in Foreign Policy: New Partnership or New Competition?" **Orbis** 20 (Winter 1977): 881-904.

1265. Bennet, Douglas J. "Congress in Foreign Policy: Who Needs It?" **Foreign Affairs** 57 (Fall 1978): 40-50.

1266. Benson, Robert S. "The Military on Capitol Hill: Prospects in the Quest for Funds." **Annals of the American Academy of Political and Social Science** 406 (March 1973): 48-58.

1267. Berry, John M. "Foreign Policymaking and the Congress." **Editorial Research Reports** 1 (April 1967): 283-300.

1268. Bolles, Blair. "Congress and Foreign Policy." **Foreign Policy Reports** 20 (January 1945): 266-275.

1269. Bradshaw, Mary E. "Congress and Foreign Policy since 1900." **Annals of the American Academy of Political and Social Science** 289 (September 1953): 40-48.

1270. Buckwalter, Doyle W. "The Concurrent Resoloution: A Search for Foreign Policy Influence." **Midwest Journal of Political Science** 14 (August 1970): 434-458.

1271. Burns, Richard D., and W. Addams Dixon. "Foreign Policy and the 'Democratic Myth': The Debate on the Ludlow Admendment." **Mid-America** 47 (October 1965): 288-306.

1272. Clark, Joseph S. "The Influence of Congress in the Formulation of Disarmament Policy."

Annals of the American Academy of
Political and Social Science 342 (July
1962): 147-153.

1273. Cohen, Benjamin V. "The Evolving Role of
Congress in Foreign Affairs." Proceedings
of the American Philosophical Society 92
(October 1948): 211-216.

1274. Colegrove, Kenneth W. "The Role of Congress
and Public Opinion in Formulating Foreign
Policy." American Poplitical Science
Review 38 (October 1944): 956-969.

1275. Committee for Economic Developoment.
Congressional Decision Making for National
Security: A Statement on National Policy.
New York: Committee For Economic
Development, 1974.

1276. Cooper, John M. "Progressivism and American
Foreign Policy: A Reconsideration." Mid-
America 51 (October 1969): 260-277.

1277. Dahl, Robert A. Congress and Foreign Policy.
New York: Norton, 1964.

1278. Fairlie, H. "Senator and World Power."
Encounter 30 (May 1968): 57-66.

1279. Fascell, Dante B. "Congress and Foreign
Policy." Congressional Studies 7 (Winter
1980): 5-9.

1280. Fortenberry, Joseph E. "James Kimble Vardamn
and American Foreign Policy 1913-1919."
Journal of Mississippi History 35 (May
1973): 127-140.

1281. Frank, Thomas M., and Edward Weisband.
Foreign Policy by Congress. New York:
Oxford University Press, 1979.

1282. Frankel, Charles R. Morality and U.S.
Foreign Policy. New York: Foreign Policy
Association, 1975.

1283. Fry, Alton. Responsible Congress: The
Politics of National Security. New York:
McGraw-Hill, 1975.

1284. Gareau, Frederick H. "Congressional
Representatives to the UN General
Assembly: 'Corruption' by Foreign Gentry?"
Orbis 21 (Fall 1977): 701-726.

1285. Gelb, L. H., and A. Lake. "Congress:
Politics and Bad Policy." Foreign Policy
20 (Fall 1975): 232-238.

1286. Gibbons, William C. "Political Action
Analysis as an Approach to the Study of

Congress and Foreign Policy." Ph.D. dissertation, Princeton University, 1961.

1287. Gibbs, Hubert S. "Domestic Diplomacy: A Study of 'Bipartisan' Foreign Policy." Ph.D. dissertation, Johns Hopkins University, 1952.

1288. Goebel, Dorothy B. "Congress and Foreign Relations before 1900." **Annals of the American Academy of Political and Social Science** 289 (September 1958): 22-39.

1289. Grassmuck, George L. **Sectional Biases in Congress on Foreign Policy.** Baltimore: Johns Hopkins University Press, 1951.

1290. Griffith, Ernest S. "The Place of Congress in Foreign Relations." **Annals of the American Academy of Political and Social Science** 289 (September 1953): 11-21.

1291. Gustafson, Milton O. "Congress and Foreign Aid: The First Phase, 1943-1947." Ph.D. dissertation, University of Nebraska, 1966.

1292. Halperin, Morton H. "The Gaither Committee and the Policy Process." **World Politics** 13 (April 1961): 360-384.

1293. Henkin, Louis. **Foreign Affairs and the Constitution.** Mineola, N.Y.: Foundation Press, 1972.

1294. Henschel, Richard L. "The Committee on Foreign Relations." **Washington World** 4 (April 1964): 13-17.

1295. Hero, Alfred O. "Liberalism-Conservatism Revisited: Foreign vs. Domestic Federal Policies, 1937-1967." **Public Opinion Quarterly** 33 (Fall 1969): 399-408.

1296. Holbo, Paul S. "Isolationist Critics of American Foreign Policy." **Air University Review** 19 (March-April 1968): 48-57.

1297. Javits, Jacob K. "The Congressional Presence in Foreign Relations." **Foreign Affairs** 48 (January 1970): 221-234.

1298. Kennedy, Padraic C. "La Follette's Foreign Policy: From Imperialism to Anti-Imperialism." **Wisconsin Magazine of History** 46 (Summer 1963): 287-293.

1299. Knight, Jonathan. "On the Secretary of State's Relations with Congress: Resources, Skills, and Issues." Ph.D. dissertation, Columbia University, 1969.

1300. Kolodziej, Edward A. "Congress and Foreign Policy: The Nixon Years." **Proceedings of the Academy of Political Science** 32 (1975): 167-179.

1301. _____. "Foreign Policy and the Politics of Interdependence: The Nixon Presidency." **Polity** 9 (Winter 1976): 121-157.

1302. _____. "Formulating Foreign Policy." **Proceedings of the Academy of Political Science** 34 (1981): 174-189.

1303. McCoy, Drew R. "Republicanism and American Foreign Policy: James Madison and the Political Economy of Commercial Discrimination, 1789-1794." **William and Mary Quarterly** 31 (October 1974): 633-646.

1304. Maddox, Robert J. "Another Look at the Legend of Isolationism in the 1920's." **Mid-America** 53 (January 1971): 35-43.

1305. Manley, John F. "The Rise of Congress in Foreign Policy-Making." **Annals of the American Academy of Political and Social Science** 397 (September 1971): 60-70.

1306. Manning, Bayless. "Congress, the Executive and Intermestic Affairs: Three Proposals." **Foreign Affairs** 55 (January 1977): 306-324.

1307. Mazuzan, George T. "Warren R. Austin: A Republican Internationalist and United States Foreign Policy." Ph.D. dissertation, Kent State University, 1969.

1308. Morgenthau, Hans J. "The Founding Fathers and Foreign Policy: Implications for the Late Twentieth Century." **Orbis** 20 (Spring 1976): 15-25.

1309. Munkres, Robert L. "The Use of the Congressional Resolution as an Instrument of Influence over Foreign Policy: 1925-1950." Ph.D. dissertation, University of Nebraska, 1956.

1310. Olson, W. C. "Congressional Competence in Foreign Affairs: The Measure of Information and Analysis." **Round Table** 250 (April 1973): 247-258.

1311. Ornstein, Norman J. "Lobbying for Fun and Policy." **Foreign Policy** 28 (Fall 1977): 156-165.

1312. Patterson, J. W. "Arthur Vandenberg's Rhetorical Strategy in Advancing

Bipartisan Foreign Policy." **Quarterly Journal of Speech** 56 (October 1970): 284-295.

1313. Philipose, Thomas. "The 'Loyal Opposition': Republican Leaders and Foreign Policy, 1943-1946." Ph.D. dissertation, University of Denver, 1972.

1314. Reichard, Gary W. "Divisions and Dissent: Democrats and Foreign Policy, 1952-1956." **Political Science Quarterly** 93 (Spring 1978): 51-72.

1315. Rieselbach, Leroy N. "The Demography of the Congressional Vote on Foreign Aid, 1939-1958." **American Political Science Review** 58 (September 1964): 577-588.

1316. Robinson, James A. **Congress and Foreign Policy-Making: A Study in Legislative Influence and Initiative.** 2nd ed. Homewood, Ill.: Dorsey, 1967.

1317. Rosenberg, J. S., P. Weinberg, and W. M. Pinzler. "Historical and Structural Limitations on Congressional Abilities to Make Foreign Policy." **Boston University Law Review** 50 (Spring 1970): 51-77.

1318. Russell, Willis C. "The Rives Treaty: A Study in American Diplomacy and Party Politics." Ph.D. dissertation, American University, 1932.

1319. Sarros, Panayiotis P. "Congress and the New Diplomacy: The Formulation of Mutual Security Policy: 1953-1960." Ph.D. dissertation, Princeton University, 1964.

1320. Schlesinger, Arthur M. "Congress and the Making of American Foreign Policy." **Foreign Affairs** 51 (October 1972): 78-113.

1321. Sigal, Leon V. "Official Secrecy and Informal Communication in Congressional Bureaucratic Relations." **Political Science Quarterly** 90 (Spring 1975): 71-92.

1322. Tower, J. G. "Congress versus the President: The Formulation and Implementation of American Foreign Policy." **Foreign Affairs** 60 (Winter 1981/82): 229-246.

1323. Westerfield, H. Bradford. "Congress and Closed Politics in National Security Affairs." **Orbis** 10 (Fall 1966): 737-753.

1324. Wiley, Alexander. "The Committee on Foreign Relations." **Annals of the American Academy**

of Political and Social Science 289
(September 1953): 58-65.
1325.   Wilford, W. T. "The Congressional Mandate on
U.S. Foreign Aid: Can It Break the Vicious
Circle of Poverty?" **Journal of Social and
Political Studies** 4 (Fall 1979): 261-268.
1326.   Willick, Daniel H. "Foreign Affairs and
Party Choice." **American Journal of
Sociology** 75 (January 1970): 530-549.
1327.   Wilz, John E. "American Isolationism: Its
Colonial Origins." **Amerikastudien** 21
(1976): 261-280.

House

1328.   Carol, Holbert N. **The House of
Representatives and Foreign Affairs.**
Pittsburgh: University of Pittsburgh
Press, 1958.
1329.   Chiperfield, Robert B. "The Committee on
Foreign Affairs." **Annals of the American
Academy of Political and Social Science**
289 (September 1953): 73-83.
1330.   Cimbala, Stephen J. "Foreign Policy as an
Issue Area: A Roll Call Analysis."
American Political Science Review 63
(March 1969): 148-156.
1331.   Johnson, Victor C. "Congress and Foreign
Policy: Tne House Foreign Affairs and
Senate Foreign Relations Committees."
Ph.D. dissertation, University of
Wisconsin, 1975.
1332.   Kaiser, Fred. "Oversight of Foreign Policy:
The U.S. House Committee on International
Relations." **Legislative Studies Quarterly**
2 (August 1977): 255-279.
1333.   Karns, D. A. "Effect of Inter-Parlimentary
Meetings on the Foreign Policy Attitudes
of United States Congressmen."
International Organization 31 (Summer
1977): 497-513.
1334.   Kolodzeij, Edward A. "Congress and Foreign
Policy: Through the Looking Glass."
Virginia Quarterly Review 42 (Winter
1966): 12-27.
1335.   Moore, Heyward. "Congressional Committees
and the Formulation of Foreign Aid
Policy." Ph.D. dissertation, University of

North Carolina, 1965.
1336. Morrow, William L. "Legislative Control of
      Administrative Discretion: The Case of
      Congress and Foreign Aid." **Journal of
      Politics** 30 (November 1968): 985-1011.
1337. Perkins, James A. "Congressional
      Investigations of Matters of International
      Import." **American Political Science Review**
      34 (April 1940): 284-294.
1338. Richards, James P. "The House of
      Representatives in Foreign Affairs."
      **Annals of the American Academy of
      Political and Social Science** 289
      (September 1953): 66-72.
1339. Stroud, Virgil. "Congressional
      Investigations of the Conduct of War."
      Ph.D. dissertation, New York University,
      1955.
1340. Van Deburg, William L. "Henry Clay, The
      Right of Petition, and Slavery in the
      Nation's Capital." **Register of the
      Kentucky Historical Society** 68 (April
      1970): 132-146.
1341. Westpahal, Albert C. F. **The House Committee
      on Foreign Affairs.** New York: Columbia
      University Press, 1942.

Senate

1342. Andrew, Jean D. "The Effect of Senate
      Foreign Relations Committee Membership in
      Terms of Support of Foreign Policy--1946-
      1966." Ph.D. dissertation, University of
      Connecticut, 1968.
1343. Atwell, Mary W. "A Conservative Response to
      the Cold War: Senator James P. Kem and
      Foreign Aid." **Capitol Studies** 4 (Fall
      1976): 53-65.
1344. Avery, W. P., and D. P. Forsythe. "Human
      Rights, National Security, and the U.S.
      Senate: Who Votes for What, and Why."
      International Studies Quarterly 23 (June
      1979): 303-320.
1345. Berger, Henry W. "Bipartisanship, Senator
      Taft, and the Truman Administration."
      Political Science Quarterly 90 (Summer
      1975): 221-237.
1346. Bozeman, Barry, and Thomas E. James. "Toward

a Comprehensive Model of Foreign Policy Voting in the U.S. Senate." **Western Political Quarterly** 23 (September 1975): 477-495.

1347. Briggs, Philip J. "Senator Vandenberg, Bipartisanship and the Origin of United Nations' Article 51." **Mid-America** 60 (October 1978): 163-169.

1348. Burnette, Ollen L. "The Senate Foreign Relations Committee and the Diplomacy of Garfield, Arthur, and Cleveland." Ph.D. dissertation, University of Virginia, 1952.

1349. Challener, Richard D., ed. **The Legislative Origins of American Foreign Policy: The Senate Foreign Relations Committee in Executive Session.** 10 vols. New York: Garland, 1978.

1350. Colegrove, Kenneth W. **The American Senate and World Peace.** New York: Vanguard, 1944.

1351. Daugham, George C. "From Lodge to Fulbright: The Chairman of the Senate Foreign Relations Committee." Ph.D. dissertation, Howard University, 1968.

1352. Dennison, Eleanor E. **The Senate Foreign Relations Committee.** Stanford, Calif.: Stanford University Press, 1942.

1353. DeWitt, Howard A. "Hiram Johnson and Economic Opposition to Wilsonian Diplomacy: A Note." **Pacific Historian** 19 (Spring 1975): 15-23.

1354. _____. "The 'New' Harding and American Foreign Policy: Warren G. Harding, Hiram W. Johnson, and Pragmatic Diplomacy." **Ohio History** 86 (Spring 1977): 96-114.

1355. _____. "Hiram Johnson and Early New Deal Diplomacy, 1933-1934." **California Historical Quarterly** 53 (Winter 1974): 377-386.

1356. Farnsworth, David N. "A Comparison of the Senate and Its Foreign Relations Committee on Selected Roll Call Votes." **Western Political Quarterly** 14 (March 1961): 168-175.

1357. _____. **The Senate Committee on Foreign Relations.** Urbana: University of Illinois Press, 1961.

1358. Feinstein, Otto. "American Scholars Analyzed

U.S. Foreign Policy: Discussing the Several Studies of American Foreign Policy, Prepared at the Request of the Senate Committee on Foreign Relations." **Bulletin of the Atomic Scientists** 16 (December 1960): 395-399.

1359. Flannagan, J. H. "Disillusionment of a Progressive: U.S. Senator David I. Walsh and the League of Nations Issue, 1981-1920." **New England Quarterly** 41 (December 1968): 483-504.

1360. Gallagher, Hugh G. **Advise and Obstruct: The Role of the United States Senate in Foreign Policy Decisions.** New York: Delacorte, 1969.

1361. Gazell, James A. "Arthur H. Vandenberg, Internationalism, and the United Nations." **Political Science Quarterly** 88 (September 1973): 375-394.

1362. Gillette, Guy M. "The Senate in Foreign Relations." **Annals of the American Academy of Political and Social Science** 289 (September 1953): 49-57.

1363. Gould, James W. "The Origins of the Senate Committee on Foreign Relations." **Western Political Quarterly** 12 (September 1959): 670-682.

1364. Grimmett, Richard F. "Who Were the Senate Isolationists?" **Pacific Historical Review** 42 (November 1973): 479-498.

1365. Grinder, Robert D. "Progressives, Conservatives and Imperialism: Another Look at the Senate Republicans, 1913-1917." **North Dakota Quarterly** 41 (Autumn 1973): 28-39.

1366. Grundy, K. W. "Apprenticeship of J. William Fulbright." **Virginia Quarterly Review** 43 (Summer 1967): 382-399.

1367. Hauptman, Laurence M. "To the Good Neighbor: A Study of the Senate's Role in American Foreign Policy." Ph.D. dissertation, New York University, 1972.

1368. Hill, Thomas M. "The Senate Leadership and International Policy from Lodge to Vandenberg." Ph.D. dissertation, Washington University, 1970.

1369. Hudson, Daryl J. "Vandenberg Reconsidered: Senate Resolution 239 and American Foreign

Policy." **Diplomatic History** 1 (Winter 1977): 46-63.

1370.   Humphrey, Hubert H. "The Senate in Foreign Policy." **Foreign Affairs** 37 (July 1959): 525-536.

1371.   Jewell, Malcolm E. "Evaluating the Decline of Southern Internationalism Through Senatorial Roll Call Votes." **Journal of Politics** 21 (November 1959): 624-646.

1372.   _____. "The Role of Political Parties in the Formation of Foreign Policy in the Senate, 1947-1956." Ph.D. dissertation, Pennsylvania State University, 1958.

1373.   _____. "The Senate Republican Policy Committee and Foreign Policy." **Western Policy Quarterly** 12 (December 1959): 966-980.

1374.   _____. **Senatorial Politics and Foreign Policy.** Lexington: University of Kentucky Press, 1962.

1375.   March, Carl, and Morella Hanson. "A Note on American Participation in Interparliamentary Meetings." **International Organization** 13 (Summer 1959): 431-438.

1376.   Margulies, Herbert F. "The Senate and the World Court." **Capitol Studies** 4 (Fall 1976): 37-51.

1377.   Meyer, Karl E. "Fulbright of Arkansas." **Progressive** 26 (September 1962): 26-31.

1378.   Morgenthau, Hans J. "Senator Fulbright's New Foreign Policy." **Commentary** 37 (May 1964): 68-71.

1379.   Nigro, Felix A. "Senate's Confirmation and Foreign Policy." **Journal of Politics** 14 (May 1952): 281-299.

1380.   Porter, David L. "Senator Warren Austin and the Neutrality Act of 1939." **Vermont History** 42 (Summer 1974): 228-238.

1381.   Shade, William G., Stanley D. Hopper, David Jacobson, and Stephen E. Moiloes. "Partisanship in the United States Senate: 1869-1901." **Journal of Interdisciplinary History** 4 (Autumn 1973): 185-205.

1382.   Tidmarch, Charles M., and Charles M. Sabatt. "Presidential Leadership Change and Foreign Policy Roll-Call Voting in the U.S. Senate." **Western Political Quarterly** 25 (December 1972): 613-625.

1383. Toulmin, Harry A. **Diary of Democracy: The Senate War Investigating Committee.** New York: Smith, 1947.
1384. Wickersham, George W. "The Senate and Our Foreign Relations." **Foreign Affairs** 2 (December 1923): 177-192.
1385. Wilkins, Robert P. "Senator William Langer and National Priorities: An Agrarian Radical's View of American Foreign Policy, 1945-1952." **North Dakota Quarterly** 42 (Autumn 1974): 42-59.

General Studies

1386. Abrams, Richard M. "Unites States Inter-
      vention Abroad: The First Quarter Cen-
      tury." **American Historical Review** 79
      (February 1974): 72-102.
1387. Amory, John F. **Around the Edge of War: A New
      Approach to the Problems of American
      Foreign Policy.** New York: Potter, 1961.
1388. Andrews, Craig N. **Foreign Policy and the New
      American Military.** Beverly Hills, Calif.:
      Sage, 1974.
1389. Berger, E. "Oldest, Cold War." **North
      American Review** 2 (November 1965): 10-18.
1390. Bloomfield, Lincoln P. "Future Small Wars:
      Must the United States Intervene?" **Orbis**
      12 (Fall 1968): 205-228.
1391. Buchan, Alastair. "The United States as a
      Global Power." **International Journal** 24
      (Spring 1969): 205-228.
1392. Bundy, McGeorge. "Friends and Allies."
      Foreign Affairs 41 (October 1962): 1-23.
1393. Busch, Terry J., and Ronald J. Stupak. "The
      U.S. Military: Patterns of Adaptation for
      the 1970's." **Orbis** 16 (Winter 1973): 990-
      1007.
1394. Crabb, Cecil V. **American Foreign Policy in
      the Nuclear Age.** 3rd ed. New York: Harper
      and Row, 1972.
1395. Donovan, John C. **The Cold War: A Policy-
      Making Elite.** Lexington, Mass.: Heath,
      1974.
1396. Draper, Theodore. "Appeasement and Detente."
      Commentary 61 (February 1976): 27-38.
1397. Ekirch, Arthur A. "Charles A. Beard and
      Reinhold Niebuhr: Contrasting Conceptions
      of National Interest in American Foreign
      Policy." **Mid-America** 59 (April 1977): 103-
      116.
1398. Eliot, George F. "Alliance Diplomacy in
      Limited Wars." **United States Naval
      Institute Proceedings** 93 (April 1967): 52-
      57.
1399. Elzy, Martin I. "The Origins of American
      Military Policy, 1945-1950." Ph.D.

dissertation, Miami University, 1975.

1400. Friedmann, W. "Interventionism, Liberalism, and Power-Politics: The Unfinished Revolution in International Thinking." **Political Science Quarterly** 83 (June 1968): 169-189.

1401. Furniss, Edgar S. **American Military Policy: Strategic Aspects of World Political Geography.** New York: Rinehart, 1957.

1402. Gallois, Pierre M. "U.S. Foreign Policy: A Study in Military Strength and Diplomatic Weakness." **Orbis** 9 (Summer 1965): 338-357.

1403. Hahn, Walter F., and John C. Neff, eds. **American Strategy for the Nuclear Age.** New York: Doubleday, 1960.

1404. Halperin, Morton H. "Rise of Militarism, the Decline of Liberty." **Christianity and Crisis** 41 (October 1981): 279-284.

1405. Holt, Robert T., and W. van de Velde. **Strategic Psychological Operations and American Foreign Policy.** Chicago: University of Chicago Press, 1960.

1406. Houghton, Neal D. "Case for Essential Abandonment of Basic U.S. Cold War Objectives." **Western Political Quarterly** 23 (June 1970): 384-411.

1407. Hunter, Robert E. "Troops, Trade and Diplomacy." **Atlantic Community Quarterly** 9 (Fall 1971): 283-292.

1408. Jackson, Henry M. "Organizing for Survival." **Foreign Affairs** 38 (April 1960): 446-456.

1409. Jaffe, Philip J. "The Cold War Revisionists and What They Omit." **Survey** 19 (Autumn 1973): 123-143.

1410. Katzenback, Edward L. "Military Policy as a National Issue." **Current History** 31 (October 1956): 193-198.

1411. Laborde, J. "Imperialism and Border Conflicts." **World Marxist Review** 21 (November 1978): 94-103.

1412. Laqueur, Walter. "From Globalism to Isolationism." **Atlantic Community Quarterly** 10 (Winter 1972-73): 427-436.

1413. _____. "Psychology of Appeasement." **Commentary** 66 (October 1978): 44-50.

1414. Leigh, Michael. "Is There a Revisionist Theses in the Origins of the Cold War?" **Political Science Quarterly** 89 (March

1974): 101-116.
1415. Nash, Henry T. **American Foreign Policy: Changing Perspectives on National Security.** rev. ed. Homewood, Ill.: Dorsey, 1978.
1416. Nitze, Paul H. "Strategy in the Decade of the 1980's." **Foreign Affairs** 59 (Fall 1980): 82-101.
1417. Ransom, Harry H. **Can American Democracy Survive Cold War?** New York: Doubleday, 1963.
1418. Rosenberg, Milton J., ed. **Beyond Conflict and Containment: Critical Studies of Military and Foreign Policy.** New Brunswick, N.J.: Transaction, 1972.
1419. Sapin, Burton M., ed. **Contemporary American Foreign and Military Policy.** Glenview, Ill.: Scott, Foresman, 1970.
1420. Sapin, Burton M., and Richard C. Snyder. **The Role of the Military in American Foreign Policy.** Garden City, N.Y.: Doubleday, 1954.
1421. Scowcroft, Brent. "American Attitudes Toward Foreign Policy." **United States Naval War College War Review** 32 (March-April 1979): 11-19.
1422. Whetten, Lawrence L. **Contemporary American Foreign Policy: Minimal Diplomacy, Defense Strategy, and Detente Management.** Lexington, Mass.: Lexington Books, 1974.
1423. Yarmolinsky, Adam. "American Foreign Policy and the Decision to Intervene." **Journal of International Affairs** 22 (1968): 231-235.
1424. Yergin, D. "Order and Survival." **Daedalus** 107 (Winter 1978): 263-287.

Military Relations

1425. Allison, Graham T. "Military Capabilities and American Foreign Policy." **Annals of the American Academy of Political and Social Science** 406 (March 1973): 17-37.
1426. Beckman, Peter R. "The Influence of the American Military Establishment on American Foreign Policy." Ph.D. dissertation, University of Wisconsin, 1974.
1427. Bennett, John A. "An Examination of the

Foreign Policy Role of American Military Officers in the Light of Contemporary American Military History." Ph.D. dissertation, American University, 1968.

1428. Berger, William E. "The Role of the Armed Services in International Policy." Ph.D. dissertation, University of Nebraska, 1956.

1429. Bernardo, C. Joseph, and Eugene H. Bacon. **American Military Policy: Its Developoment Since 1775**. 2nd ed. Harrisburg, Pa.: Stackpole, 1961.

1430. Blechman, Barry M., and Stephan S. Kaplan. "U.S. Military Forces as a Political Instrument since World War II." **Political Science Quarterly** 94 (Summer 1979): 193-209.

1431. Bletz, Donald F. **The Role of the Military Professional in U.S. Foreign Policy.** New York: Praeger, 1972.

1432. Booth, K. **Navies and Foreign Policy.** New York: Crane, Russak, 1977.

1433. Davis, Vincent. "American Military Policy: Decision-Making in the Executive Branch." **United States Naval War College Review** 22 (May 1970): 4-23.

1434. Holloway, J. K. "The Role of the Services in Support of Foreign Policy." **United States Naval Institute** Proceedings 102 (May 1976): 66-81.

1435. Huntington, Samuel P. "After Containment: The Functions of the Military Establishment." **Annals of the American Academy of Political and Social Science** 406 (March 1973): 1-16.

1436. Kirk, Neville T. "Sentinel for a Century: The **Proceedings,** The Navy, and The Nation, 1873-1973." **United States Naval Institute Proceedings** 99 (October 1973): 97-114.

1437. Owen, Henry. "Elevate Them Guns a Little Lower." **Foreign Policy** 23 (Summer 1976): 149-154.

1438. Pearson, Frederic S. "Geographic Proximity and Foreign Military Intervention." **Journal of Conflict Resolution** 18 (September 1974): 432-433.

1439. Quade, Edward S., ed. **Analysis for Military Decisions.** New York: American Elsevier,

1970.
1440. Sapin, Burton M., Richard C. Snyder, and H.
       W. Bruck. **An Appropriate Role for the
       Military in American Foreign Policy-
       Making: A Research Note.** Princeton, N.J.:
       Princeton University Press, 1954.
1441. Schilling, Warner R. "Admirals and Foreign
       Policy, 1913-1919." Ph.D. dissertation,
       Yale University, 1954.
1442. Stein, Harold, ed. **American Civil-Military
       Decisions: A Book of Case Studies.** Univer-
       sity: University of Alabama Press, 1963.
1443. Steinbrunner, John D. "The Mind and Milieu
       of Policy-Makers: A Case Study of the
       MLF." Ph.D. dissertation, M.I.T., 1968.
1444. Sunderland, Riley. "The Soldier's Relation
       to Foreign Policy." **Unites States Naval
       Institute Proceedings** 69 (September 1943):
       1170-1175.
1445. Taylor, Maxwell D. "Post-Vietnam Role of the
       Military in Foreign Policy." **Air
       University Review** 19 (July-August 1968):
       50-58.
1446. Trager, Frank N. "Wars of National Libera-
       tion: Implications for U.S. Policy and
       Planning." **Orbis** 18 (Spring 1974): 50-105.
1447. Wolf, Charles. "Is United States Foreign
       Policy Being Militarized?" **Orbis** 14
       (Winter 1971): 819-828.
1448. Woodward, Clark H. "Relations between the
       Navy and the Foreign Service." **American
       Journal of International Law** 33 (April
       1939): 283-291.
1449. Wylie, J. C. "The Sixth Fleet and American
       Diplomacy." **Proceedings of the Academy of
       Political Science** 29 (May 1969): 55-60.

Defense Policy

1450. Abel, Theodore. "The Element of Decision in
       the Pattern of War." **American Sociological
       Review** 6 (December 1941): 853-859.
1451. Art, Robert J. **The TFX Decision: McNamara
       and the Military.** Boston: Little, Brown,
       1968.
1452. Ball, George W. "The Nuclear Deterrent and
       the Atlantic Alliance." **Atlantic Community
       Quarterly** 1 (Summer 1963): 199-204.

1453. Beard, Edmund. **Developing the ICBM: A Study in Bureaucratic Politics.** New York: Columbia University Press, 1976.

1454. Bissell, Richard E. "Future of American Alliances." **Orbis** 23 (Fall 1979): 519-523.

1455. Bottome, Edgar M. **The Missile Gap: A Study of the Formulation of Military and Political Policy.** Rutherford, N.J.: Fairleigh Dickinson University Press, 1971.

1456. Carey, Hugh L. "War We Can Win: Health as a Vector of Foreign Policy." **Bulletin of the New York Academy of Medicine** 46 (May 1970): 334-350.

1457. Chayes, Abram, and Jerome B. Wiesner. **ABM: An Evaluation of the Decision to Deploy an Anti-Ballistic Missile System.** New York: Harper and Row, 1969.

1458. Cobb, Stephen A. "Defense Spending and Foreign Policy in the House of Representatives." **Journal of Conflict Resolution** 13 (September 1969): 358-369.

1459. _____. "The Military-Industrial Complex and Foreign Policy." Ph.D. dissertation, Vanderbilt University, 1971.

1460. Dobney, Frederick J. "The Evolution of a Reconversion Policy: World War II and Surplus War Property Disposal." **Historian** 36 (May 1974): 498-519.

1461. Donnelly, Charles H. **United States Defense Policies since World War II.** Washington, D.C.: Government Printing Office, 1957.

1462. Findley, Paul. "Does American Foreign Policy Entail Frequent Wars?" **Annals of the American Academy of Political and Social Science** 384 (July 1969): 45-52.

1463. Fisher, Louis. "Reprogramming of Funds by the Defense Department." **Journal of Politics** 36 (February 1974): 77-102.

1464. Graebner, Norman A. "Cold War Origins and the Continuing Debate: A Review of Recent Literature." **Journal of Conflict Resolution** 13 (March 1969): 123-138.

1465. Gray, Colin S. "Foreign Policy and the Strategic Balance." **Orbis** 18 (Fall 1974): 706-727.

1466. Hammond, Paul Y. "A Functional Analysis of Defense Department Decision Making in the

McNamara Administration." **American Political Science Review** 62 (March 1968): 57-69.
1467. Hilsman,Roger. **The Politics of Policy Making in Defense and Foreign Affairs.** New York: Harper and Row, 1971.
1468. Hitch, Charles J. **Decision Making for Defense.** Berkeley: University of California Press, 1966.
1469. Holsti, Ole R. "Perceptions of Time and Alternatives as Factors in Crisis Decision-Making." **Peace Research Society Papers** 3 (1964): 79-120.
1470. Huntington, Samuel P. "Strategic Planning and the Political Process." **Foreign Affairs** 38 (January 1960): 285-300.
1471. Kintner, William R. "Strategic Triangle of Two and a Half Powers." **Orbis** 23 (Fall 1979): 525-534.
1472. Logan, John A. **No Transfer: An American Security Principle.** New Haven, Conn.: Yale University Press, 1961.
1473. McCarthy, E. J."Look, No Allies." **Foreign Policy** 30 (Spring 1978): 3-16.
1474. McClintock, Robert. **The Meaning of Limited War.** Boston: Houghton Mifflin, 1967.
1475. Marshall, Charles B. "Unconventional Warfare as a Concern of American Foreign Policy." **Annals of the American Academy of Political and Social Science** 341 (May 1962): 93-101.
1476. Nelson, Donald M. **Arsenal of Democracy: The Story of American War Production.** New York: Harcourt, Brace, 1946.
1477. O'Connor, Raymond G., ed. **American Defense Policy in Perspective From Colonial Times to the Present.** New York: Wiley, 1965.
1478. Petras, J., and R. Rhodes. "Reconsolidation of US Hegemony." **New Left Review** 97 (March 1976): 37-53.
1479. Pierre, Andrew J. "Future of America's Commitments and Alliances." **Orbis** 16 (Fall 1972): 696-719.
1480. Reinhardt, George C., and William R. Kintner. "Policy: Matrix of Strategy." **United States Naval Institute Proceedings** 80 (February 1954): 144-155.
1481. Stambuk, George. "Foreign Policy and the

Stationing of American Forces Abroad."
Journal of Politics 25 (August 1963): 472-
488.

1482. Stanley, Timothy W. **American Defense and
National Security.** Washington, D.C.:
Public Affairs, 1956.

Peacekeeping

1483. Andrade, Ernest M. "The United States Navy
and the Washington Conference." **Historian**
31 (May 1969): 345-363.
1484. Bouscaren, A. T. "Acrid Fruits of Detente."
Modern Age 20 (Fall 1976): 419-430.
1485. Brogan, H. "American and the Cold War."
Round Table 245 (January 1972): 119-127.
1486. Chomsky, Noam. "Cold War and the Super-
powers." **Monthly Review** 33 (November
1981): 1-10.
1487. _____. **Towards a New Cold War.** New York:
Pantheon Books, 1982.
1488. Clark, Joseph S. "Prospects for Peace."
Orbis 10 (Spring 1966): 27-41.
1489. Conquest, Robert. "Detente: An Evaluation."
Survey 20 (Spring/Summer 1974): 1-27.
1490. Fitzhugh, David. "Terrorism and Diplomacy."
Foreign Service Journal 54 (February
1977): 14-17.
1491. Gross, G. "Communism Divided: Some Considerations for American Policy." **Russian Review** 28 (April-July 1969): 137-151, 265-
276.
1492. Kennedy, Edward M. "Beyond Detente." **Foreign
Policy** 16 (Fall 1974): 3-29.
1493. Landon, Kenneth P. "1954 Geneva Agreements."
Current History 50 (February 1966): 79-84,
116.
1494. Nathan, James A. "The Missile Crisis: His
Finest Hour Now." **World Politics** 27
(January 1975): 256-281.
1495. Noring, Nina J. "American Coalition Diplomacy and the Armistice, 1918-1919." Ph.D.
dissertation, University of Iowa, 1972.
1496. Pastusiak, Longin. "Objective and Subjective
Premises of Detente." **Journal of Peace
Research** 14 (1977): 185-193.
1497. Rubinstein, Alvin Z. " The Elusive Parameters of Detente." **Orbis** 19 (Winter

1976): 1344-1358.
1498. Schelling, Thomas C. "Deterrence: Military Diplomacy in the Nuclear Age." **Virginia Quarterly Review** 39 (Autumn 1963): 531-547.
1499. Sheldon, Della, ed. **Dimensions of Detente.** New York: Praeger, 1978.
1500. Tucker, R. W. "America and the World: The Next Four Years, Beyond Detente." **Commentary** 63 (March 1977): 42-50.
1501. Wadsworth,James J. **The Price of Peace.** New York: Praeger, 1962.
1502. Wilson, Joan H. "'Peace is a Woman's Job....' Jeannette Rankin and American Foreign Policy: Her Lifework as a Pacifist." **Montana Magazine of Western History** 30 (April 1980): 39-53.
1503. Wooley, W. T. "Quest for Permanent Peace—American Supranationalism, 1945-1947." **Historian** 35 (November 1972): 18-31.

Arms Control and Disarmament

1504. Amrine, Michael. **The Great Decision: The Secret History of the Atomic Bomb.** New York: Putnam, 1959.
1505. Bargman, Abraham. "Nuclear Diplomacy." **Proceedings of the Academy of Political Science** 32 (1977): 159-169.
1506. Barnes, Harley H. "The U.S. Policy-Making Process: The Nuclear Non-Proliferation Treaty of 1968." Ph.D. dissertation, Rutgers University, 1976.
1507. Bay, C. "Return to Dr. Strangelove?" **Monthly Review** 33 (April 1982): 53-54.
1508. Bechhoefer, Bernhard G. "The Disarmament Deadlock: 1946-1955." **Current History** 42 (May 1962): 257-266, 280.
1509. Bernstein, Barton J. "The Challenges and Dangers of Nuclear Weapons: Foreign Policy and Strategy, 1941-1978." **Maryland Historian** 9 (Spring 1978): 73-99.
1510. _____. "Roosevelt, Truman, and the Atomic Bomb, 1941-1945: A Reinterpretation." **Political Science Quarterly** 90 (Spring 1975): 23-69.
1511. Coffey, J. I. " Strategy, Alliance Policy, and Nuclear Proliferation." **Orbis** 11

(Winter 1968): 975-995.
1512. Cohen, S. T. "U.S. Strategic Nuclear Weapon
       Policy." **Air University Review** 26 (January
       1975): 12-25.
1513. Dobrianshy, Lev. E. "The Nuclear Test-Ban
       Treaty and the Cold War." **Ukrainian
       Quarterly** 19 (Summer 1963): 125-132.
1514. Ferrell, Robert H. "Disarmament Conferences:
       Ballets at the Brink." **American Heritage**
       22 (February 1971): 4-7, 96-100.
1515. Finletter, Thomas K. **Power and Policy: U.S.
       Foreign Policy and Military Power in the
       Hydrogen Age.** New York: Harcourt, Brace,
       1954.
1516. Foster, William C. "Arms Control and Dis-
       armament in a Divided World." **Annals of
       the American Academy of Political and
       Social Science** 342 (July 1962): 80-88.
1517. _____. "New Directions in Arms Control and
       Disarmament." **Foreign Affairs** 43 (July
       1965): 587-601.
1518. _____. "Prospects for Arms Control."
       Foreign Affairs 47 (April 1969): 413-421.
1519. Gilpin, Robert. **American Scientists and
       Nuclear Weapons Policy.** Princeton, N.J.:
       Princeton University Press, 1962.
1520. Gray, Colin S. "Rethinking Nuclear Stra-
       tegy." **Orbis** 17 (Winter 1974): 1145-1160.
1521. Halperin, Morton H. "The Decision to Deploy
       the ABM: Bureaucratic and Domestic Poli-
       tics in the Johnson Administration." **World
       Politics** 25 (October 1972): 62-95.
1522. Hammond, Paul Y., David J. Louseher, and
       Michael Salomon. "Controlling U.S. Arms
       Transfers: The Emerging System." **Orbis** 23
       (Summer 1979): 317-352.
1523. Herken, Gregory F. "American Diplomacy and
       the Atomic Bomb, 1945-1947." Ph.D. disser-
       tation, Princeton University, 1973.
1524. Hopmann, P. Terrence. "Bargaining in Arms
       Control Negotiations: The Seabeds Denucle-
       arizaion Treaty." **International Organiza-
       tion** 28 (Summer 1974): 313-343.
1525. Kaplan, Morton A. "Weaknesses of the Non-
       proliferation Treat." **Orbis** 12 (Winter
       1969): 1042-1057.
1526. Kutger, Joseph P. "The Military Assistance
       Program: Symphysis of United States For-

eign and Military Policies." Ph.D. dissertation, University of Colorado, 1961.

1527. Lepper, Mary M. **Foreign Policy Formulation:
A Case Study of the Nuclear Test Ban
Treaty of 1963.** Columbus, Ohio: Merrill,
1971.

1528. Louscher, David J. "The Rise of Military
Sales as a U.S. Foreign Assistance Instrument." **Orbis** 20 (Winter 1977): 933-964.

1529. McGuire, Martin C. **Secrecy and the Arms
Race.** Cambridge, Mass.: Harvard University
Press, 1965.

1530. Maddox, Robert J. "Atomic Diplomacy: A Study
in Creative Writing." **Journal of American
History** 59 (March 1973): 925-934.

1531. Mandelbaum, Michael E. "From Strategy to
Diplomacy: The United States and the
Problem of Nuclear Weapons, 1961-1963."
Ph.D. dissertation, Harvard University,
1975.

1532. Mets, David R. "Arms Control since
Hiroshima." **United States Naval Institute
Proceedings** 99 (December 1973): 18-26.

1533. Nacht, M. "United States in a World of
Nuclear Powers." **Annals of the American
Academy of Political and Social Science**
430 (March 1977): 162-174.

1534. Nitze, Paul H. "Assuring Strategic Stability
in an Era of Detente." **Foreign Affairs** 54
(January 1976): 207-232.

1535. Nye, Joseph S. "Nonproliferation: A Long-
Term Strategy." **Foreign Affairs** 56 (April
1978): 601-623.

1536. Quester, George H. "The Nuclear Nonproliferation Treaty and the International Atomic
Energy Agency." **International Organization**
24 (Spring 1970): 163-182.

1537. Rakove, Milton L.,ed. **Arms and Foreign
Policy in the Nuclear Age.** Chicago:
American Foundation for Continuing
Education, 1964.

1538. Rosenberg, David A. "American Atomic Strategy and the Hydrogen Bomb Decision."
Journal of American History 66 (June
1979): 62-87.

1539. Smith, Bruce L. R., and Victor Gilinsky.
"Civilian Nuclear Power and Foreign
Policy." **Orbis** 12 (Fall 1968): 816-830.

1540.   Sorley, Lewis. **Arms Transfers under Nixon: A Policy Analysis.** Lexington: University of Kentucky Press, 1983.
1541.   Terchek, Ronald J. **The Making of the Test Ban Treaty.** The Hague: Nijhoff, 1970.
1542.   Williams, Raymond C. "Skybolt and American Foreign Policy." **Military Affairs** 30 (Fall 1966): 153-159.
1543.   Winkler, Fred H. "The United States and the World Disarmament Conference, 1926-1935: A Study of the Formulation of Foreign Policy." Ph.D. dissertation, Northwestern University, 1957.

Trade

1544. Atlantic Council of the United States. **Gatt Plus--A Proposal for Trade Reform: With the Text of the General Agreement.** New York: Praeger, 1976.
1545. Baldwin, David A. **Economic Development and American Foreign Policy, 1943-1962.** Chicago: University of Chicago Press, 1966.
1546. Baldwin, Robert E., and David A. Kay. "International Trade and International Relations." **International Organization** 29 (Winter 1975): 99-131.
1547. Baranyuai, Leopold, and J. C. Mills. **International Commodity Agreements.** New York: Committee for Economic Development, 1963.
1548. Bare, C. Gordon. "Trade Policy and Atlantic Partnership: Prospects for New Negotiations."**Orbis** 17 (Winter 1974): 1280-1305.
1549. Benham, Frederic. **Economic Aid to Underdeveloped Countries.** New York: Oxford University Press, 1961.
1550. Bergsten, C. Fred. "Crisis in U.S. Trade Policy." **Foreign Affairs** 49 (July 1971): 619-635.
1551. Bergsten, C. Fred. "The New Economic and U. S. Foreign Policy." **Foreign Affairs** 50 (January 1972): 199-222.
1552. Bergsten, C. Fred, and Lawrence B. Krause. **World Politics and International Economics.** Washington, D.C.: Brookings Institution, 1975.
1553. Bhatachurya, Anindya K. **Foreign Trade and International Development.** Lexington, Mass.: Lexington, 1976.
1554. Blough, Roy. "The Bearing of Foreign Aid on Our Domestic Economy." **Proceedings of the Academy of Political Science** 27 (January 1962): 73-84.
1555. Bonello, Frank, and Thomas Swartz, eds. **Alternative Directions in Economic Policy.** Notre Dame, Ind.: University of Notre Dame

Press, 1978.
1556. Buchanan, Norman S., and Howard S. Ellis. **Approaches to Economic Development.** New York: Twentieth Century Fund, 1955.
1557. Calleo, David P., and Benjamin Rowland. **America and the World Political Economy: Atlantic Dreams and National Realities.** Bloomington: Indiana University Press, 1973.
1558. Cohen, Benjamin J., ed. **American Foreign Economic Policy.** New York: Harper and Row, 1968.
1559. _____. "U.S. Foreign Economic Policy." **Orbis** 15 (Spring 1971): 232-246.
1560. Coutris, Andreas N. "Government Policy-Making and Economic Development." Ph.D. dissertation, Howard University, 1975.
1561. Culbertson, William S. **Reciprocity: A National Policy for Foreign Trade.** New York: McGraw-Hill, 1937.
1562. Dibacco, Thomas V. "Return to Dollar Diplomacy? American Business Reaction to the Eisenhower Foreign Aid Program, 1953-1961." Ph.D. dissertation, American University, 1965.
1563. Diebold, William. **Dollars, Jobs, Trade and Aid.** New York: Foreign Policy Association, 1972.
1564. _____. "U.S. Trade Policy: The New Political Dimensions." **Foreign Affairs** 52 (April 1974): 472-496.
1565. Dillon, Douglas. "Some Economic Aspects of U.S. Foreign Policy." **Department of State Bulletin** 42 (May 1960): 679-683.
1566. Donelan, Michael. "The Trade of Diplomacy." **International Affairs** 45 (October 1969): 605-616.
1567. Erickson, Bonnie H. **International Networks: The Structured Webs of Diplomacy and Trade.** Beverly Hills, Calif.: Sage, 1975.
1568. Evans, John W. **The Kennedy Round in American Trade Policy: The Twilight of the Gatt?** Cambridge, Mass.: Harvard University Press, 1971.
1569. Feraidoon, Shams B. "United States Trade with the Developing World." **Current History** (May/June 1979): 214-217.
1570. Frank, Charles R. **Foreign Trade and Domestic**

Aid. Washington, D.C.: Brookings Institution, 1977.

1571. Gardner, Richard N. Sterling-Dollar Diplomacy in Current Perspective. 3rd ed. New York: Columbia University Press, 1980.

1572. Green, Philip. "Conflict Over Trade Ideologies during the Early Cold War: A Study of American Foreign Economic Policy." Ph.D. dissertation, Duke University, 1979.

1573. Hartmann, Christian D. "Local Currency Programs and United States Foreign Policies." Ph.D. dissertation, Columbia University, 1962.

1574. Hudson, Michael. Super Imperialism: The Economic Strategy of American Empire. New York: Holt, Rinehart and Winston, 1972.

1575. Jameson, Kenneth, and Roger Skurski. U.S. Trade in the Sixties and Seventies. Lexington, Mass.: Lexington Books, 1974.

1576. Kaufman, Burton I. "The Organizational Dimension of United States Economic Foreign Policy, 1900-1920." Business History Review 46 (Spring 1972): 17-44.

1577. Kenen, Peter B. Giant Among Nations: Problems in United States Foreign Economic Policy. Chicago: Rand McNally, 1963.

1578. Kindleberger, Charles P. American in the World Economy. New York: Foreign Policy Association, 1977.

1579. _____. "U.S. Foreign Economic Policy, 1776-1976." Foreign Affairs 55 (January 1977): 395-417.

1580. Krasner, Stephen D. "State Power and the Structure of International Trade." World Politics 28 (April 1976): 317-347.

1581. McKinnon, Ronald I. "America's Role in Stabilizing The World's Monetary System." Daedalus 107 (Winter 1978): 305-324.

1582. Matecki, B. E. Establishment of the International Finance Corporation and United States Policy: A Case Study in International Organization. New York: Praeger, 1957.

1583. Maynes, Charles W. "Who Pays for Foreign Policy." Foreign Policy 15 (Summer 1974): 152-168.

1584. Meier, Gerald M. Problems of Trade Policy. New York: Oxford University Press, 1973.

1585. Meltzer, Ronald I. "The Politics of Policy Reversal: The U.S. Response to Granting Trade Preferences to Developing Countries and Linkages between International Organizations and National Policy Making." **International Organization** 30 (Autumn 1976): 649-668.

1586. _____. "United States Trade Policy: An Overview." **Current History** (May/June 1979): 193-196, 227-229.

1587. Monroe, Wilbur F. **The New Internationalism: Strategy and Initiatives for U.S. Foreign Economic Policy.** Lexington, Mass.: Lexington Books, 1976.

1588. Odell, John S. "The U.S. and the Emergence of Flexible Exchange Rates: An Analysis of Foreign Policy Change." **International Organization** 33 (Winter 1979): 57-81.

1589. Parks, Wallace J. **United States Administration of Its International Economic Affairs.** Baltimore: Johns Hopkins University Press, 1951.

1590. Pearson, James C. **The Reciprocal Trade Agreements Program: The Policy of the United States and Its Effectiveness.** Washington, D.C.: Catholic University Press, 1942.

1591. Reuber, Grant L. "What's New About United States Foreign Economic Policy?" **International Journal** 27 (Spring 1972): 287-305.

1592. Sayre, Francis B. "How Trade Agreements Are Made." **Foreign Affairs** 16 (April 1938): 417-429.

1593. _____. **The Way Forward: The American Trade Agreements Program.** New York: Norton, 1977.

1594. Schultz, George P., and Kenneth W. Dam. **Economic Policy Beyond the Headlines.** New York: Scribners, 1977.

1595. Schuyler, Eugene. **American Diplomacy and the Furtherance of Commerce.** New York: Scribners, 1886.

1596. Snyder, Richard C. **The Most-Favored-Nation Clause.** New York: King's Crown, 1948.

1597. Sorensen, Theodore C. "Most-Favored-Nation and Less Favorite Nations." **Foreign Affairs** 52 (January 1974): 273-286.

1598.   Spero, Joan E. **The Politics of International
        Economic Relations.** New York: St.
        Martin's, 1977.
1599.   Steel, Ronald L., ed. **United States Foreign
        Trade Policy.** New York: Wilson, 1962.
1600.   Yeager, Leland B., and David G. Tuerck.
        **Foreign Trade and U.S. Policy: The Case
        for Free International Trade.** New York:
        Praeger, 1976.

Foreign Aid

1601.   Arnold, Harry J. P. **Aid for Development.**
        Chester Spring, Pa.: Dufour, 1966.
1602.   Asher, Robert E. **Development Assistance in
        the Seventies: Alternatives for the United
        States.** Washington, D.C.: Brookings In-
        stitution, 1970.
1603.   Baldwin, David A. **Foreign Aid and American
        Foreign Policy: A Documentary Analysis.**
        New York: Praeger, 1966.
1604.   Banfield, Edward C. **American Foreign Aid
        Doctrines.** Washington, D.C.: American
        Enterprise Institute, 1963.
1605.   Bird, Richard M. "What's Wrong with the
        United States Foreign Aid Programme?"
        International Journal 25 (Winter 1969-70):
        9-22.
1606.   Black, Lloyd D. **The Strategy of Foreign Aid.**
        New York: Van Nostrand, 1968.
1607.   Blessing, James A. "The Cut-Off of Foreign
        Aid by the United States: A Survey and
        Analysis." Ph.D. dissertation, State
        University of New York, 1975.
1608.   Brady, James R. "Problems of Implementing
        American Foreign Assistance Projects: Per-
        ceptions of the US AID Advisor." Ph.D.
        dissertation, University of Michigan,
        1971.
1609.   Brown, Douglas A. "Three Perspectives on
        U.S. Foreign Aid: Explaining the Alliance
        for Progress." Ph.D. dissertation, Univer-
        sity of Oregon, 1974.
1610.   Brown, George T. "Foreign Policy Legitima-
        tion: The Case of American Foreign Aid,
        1947-1971." Ph.D. dissertation, University
        of Virginia, 1971.
1611.   Brown, Lester R. "Rich Countries and Poor in

a Finite, Interdependent World." **Daedalus** 102 (Fall 1973): 153-164.

1612.   _____. Seeds of Change: The Green Revolution and Development in the 1970s. New York: Praeger, 1970.

1613.   Brown, William A., and Reduers Opie. **American Foreign Assistance** Washington, D.C.: Brookings Institution, 1953.

1614.   Crook, Elizabeth F. "Political Development as a Program Objective of U.S. Foreign Assistance: Title IX of the 1966 Foreign Assistance Act." Ph.D. dissertation, Tufts University, Fletcher School, 1970.

1615.   Daniels, Walter M., ed. **The Point Four Program**. New York: Wilson, 1951.

1616.   Darken, Arthur H. "The Struggle Over Foreign Aid: Major Issues and Competing Theories in the Formulation of United States Foreign Aid Policy." Ph.D. dissertation, Columbia University, 1964.

1617.   Fallowes, James. "Busting Our Mental Blocks on Foreign Aid." **Foreign Service Journal** 50 (June 1973): 19-23.

1618.   Farer, Tom J. "The Sources of United States Policy in the Third World." **Yale Review** 60 (March 1971): 321-332.

1619.   _____. "The United States and the Third World: A Basis for Accommodation." **Foreign Affairs** 54 (October 1975): 79-97.

1620.   Feis, Herbert. **Foreign Aid and Foreign Policy**. New York: St. Martin's, 1964.

1621.   Ferkiss, Victor C. **Foreign Aid: Moral and Political Aspects**. New York: Council on Religion and International Affairs, 1965.

1622.   Graber, Doris A. "Are Foreign Aid Objectives Attainable?" **Western Political Quarterly** 19 (March 1966): 68-84.

1623.   Grant, James P. "Perspectives on Development Aid: World War II to Today and Beyond." **Annals of the American Academy of Political and Social Science** 442 (March 1979): 1-12.

1624.   Goldwin, Robert A., ed. **Why Foreign Aid?** Chicago: Rand McNally, 1963.

1625.   Hayes, Louis D. "Policy Making and Problem Perception: The 1965 Foreign Assistance Act." Ph.D. dissertation, University of Arizona, 1966.

1626. Hayter, Teresa. **Aid as Imperialism.**
Baltimore: Penguin, 1971.
1627. Heusman, Charles R. **Rich Against Poor: The
Reality of Aid.** Baltimore: Penguin, 1975.
1628. Kaplan, Jacob. **The Challenge of Foreign Aid.**
New York: Praeger, 1967.
1629. Kato, Masakatsu. "U.S. Aid and Economic
Development: A Comparative Analysis of the
Priority of the Development Goal." Ph.D.
dissertation, University of Rochester,
1976.
1630. Kiernan, Bernard. "Limitations of U.S.
Policy Toward the Underdeveloped World: A
Note on the Sociology of Revolution."
American Scholar 31 (Spring 1962): 208-
219.
1631. Krause, Walter. **Economic Development: The
Underdeveloped World and American
Interest.** San Francisco: Wadsworth, 1961.
1632. Loeber, Thomas S. **Foreign Aid: Our Tragic
Experiment.** New York: Norton, 1961.
1633. McKinlay, R. D., and R. Little. "A Foreign
Policy Model of U.S. Bilateral Aid Allocation." **World Politics** 30 (October
1977): 58-86.
1634. Maheshwari, Bhanwar L. "Foreign Aid and the
Policy Process: A Study of the Struggle
Over Foreign Aid in Congress, 1961-1965."
Ph.D. dissertation, University of Pennsyl-
vania, 1966.
1635. Marvel, William W. "Foreign Aid and United
States Security: A Study of Demands on the
Postwar Assistance Programs." Ph.D. dissertation, Princeton University, 1951.
1636. Mason, Edward S. **Foreign Aid and Foreign
Policy.** New York: Harper and Row, 1964.
1637. Meier, Gerald M. **Problems of Cooperation for
Development.** New York: Oxford University
Press, 1974.
1638. Millikan, Max. **American Foreign Aid:
Strategy for the 1970's.** New York: Foreign
Policy Association, 1969.
1639. Montgomery, John D. "Evolution of U.S.
Foreign Aid." **Current History** 50 (June
1966): 321-327, 364.
1640. _____. **Foreign Aid in International Politics.** Englewood Cliffs, N.J.: Prentice-
Hall, 1967.

1641.   _____. "The Political Decay of Foreign
        Aid." **Yale Review** 57 (October 1967): 1-15.
1642.   Morenthau, Hans J. "A Political Theory of
        Foreign Aid." **American Political Science
        Review** 56 (June 1962): 301-309.
1643.   Morley, Lorna, and Felix Morley. **The Patch-
        work History of Foreign Aid**. Washington,
        D.C.: American Enterprise Institute, 1961.
1644.   Nau, Henry R. "The Diplomacy of World Food:
        Goals, Capabilities, Issues and Arenas."
        International Organization 32 (Summer
        1978): 775-809.
1645.   Nelson, Joan M. **Aid, Influence and Foreign
        Policy**. New York: Macmillan, 1968.
1646.   O'Leary, Michael K. **The Politics of American
        Foreign Aid**. New York: Atherton, 1967.
1647.   Packenham, Robert A. **Liberal America and the
        Third World: Political Development Ideas
        in Foreign Aid and Social Science**.
        Princeton, N.J.: Princeton University
        Press, 1973.
1648.   _____. "Political-Development Doctrines in
        the American Foreign Aid Program." **World
        Politics** 18 (January 1966): 194-235.
1649.   Palmer, Norman D. "Foreign Aid and Foreign
        Policy: The 'New Statecraft' Reassessed."
        Orbis 13 (Fall 1969): 763-782.
1650.   Paterson, Thomas G. "Foreign Aid under
        Wraps: The Point Four Program." **Wisconsin
        Magazine of History** 56 (Winter 1972-73):
        119-126.
1651.   Pincus, John. **Trade, Aid and Development**.
        New York: McGraw-Hill, 1967.
1652.   Proxmire, William. **Uncle Sam: The Last of
        the Big-Time Spenders**. New York: Simon and
        Schuster, 1972.
1653.   Pye, Lucian. "The Political Impulses and
        Fantasies Behind Foreign Aid." **Proceedings
        of the Academy of Political Science** 27
        (January 1962): 8-27.
1654.   Raichur, Satish, and Craig Liske, eds. **The
        Politics of Aid, Trade, and Investments**.
        New York: Wiley, Halsted, 1976.
1655.   Ranis, Gustav. "The Crisis in Foreign Aid: A
        Proposal." **Yale Review** 53 (Summer 1964):
        522-532.
1656.   Rice, Andrew E. "Building a Constituency for
        the Foreign Aid Program: The Record of the

Eisenhower Years." Ph.D. dissertation, Syracuse University, 1963.

1657. Rothschild, Emma. "Food Politics." **Foreign Affairs** 54 (January 1976): 285-307.

1658. Shaeffer, James M. "United States Foreign Aid: The Additional Goals." Ph.D. dissertation, University of Iowa, 1971.

1659. Shonfield, Andrew. **The Attack on World Poverty.** New York: Random House, 1960.

1660. Sorenson, David S. "Food for Peace—or Defense and Profit? The Role of P. L. 480, 1963-73." **Social Science Quarterly** 60 (June 1979): 62-71.

1661. Sumberg, Theodore A. **Foreign Aid As Moral Obligation?** Beverly Hills, Calif.: Sage, 1973.

1662. Sylvan, Donald A. "Models of Foreign Policy Choice: The Case of Foreign Assistance to Developing Nations." Ph.D. dissertation, University of Minnesota, 1974.

1663. Tendler, Judith. **Inside Foreign Aid.** Baltimore: Johns Hopkins University Press, 1975.

1664. Thorp, Willard L. **The Reality of Foreign Aid.** New York: Prager, 1971.

1665. Toner, Joseph S. "Organization of Our Foreign Aid Program." **Proceedings of the Academy of Political Science** 27 (January 1962): 2-7.

1666. Westwood, Andrew F. **Foreign Aid in a Foreign Policy Framework.** Washington, D.C.: Brookings Institution, 1966.

1667. White, John A. **The Politics of Foreign Aid.** New York: St. Martin's, 1974.

1668. Wiggins, James W., and Helmut Schoeck, eds. **Foreign Aid Reexamined: A Critical Appraisal.** Washington, D.C.: Public Affairs, 1958.

1669. Winham, Gilbert R. "Developing Theories of Foreign Policy Making: A Case Study of Foreign Aid." **Journal of Politics** 32 (February 1970): 41-70.

1670. Wit, Daniel. "A New Strategy; for Foreign Economic Aid." **Orbis** 7 (Winter 1964): 800-820.

1671. Wittkopf, Eugene R. "The Distribution of Foreign Aid in Comparative Perspective: An Empirical Study of the Flow of Foreign

Economic Assistance, 1961-1967." Ph.D. dissertation, Syracuse University, 1971.

1672. _____. **Western Bilateral and Allocations: A Comparative Study of Recipient State Attributes and Aid Received.** Beverly Hills, Calif.: Sage, 1972.

Cultural and Educational Relations

1673. Balzano, Michael P. **The Peace Corps: Myths and Prospects.** Washington, D.C.: American Enterprise Institute, 1978.

1674. Blum, Robert, ed. **Cultural Affairs and Foreign Relations.** Englewood Cliffs, N.J.: Prentice-Hall, 1963.

1675. Braisted, Paul J., ed. **Cultural Affairs and Foreign Relations.** Washington, D.C.: Columbia Book Co., 1968.

1676. Buckley, William F. "Human Rights and Foreign Policy: A Proposal." **Foreign Affairs** 58 (Spring 1980): 775-796.

1677. Burn, B. B., and J. A. Perkins. "International Education in a Troubled World." **Annals of the American Academy of Political and Social Science.** 449 (May 1980): 17-30.

1678. Coombs, Philip H. **The Fourth Dimension in Foreign Policy: Educational and Cultural Affairs.** New York: Harper and Row, 1964.

1679. Deibel, Terry L., and Walter R. Roberts. **Culture and Information: Two Foreign Policy Functions.** Beverly Hills, Calif.: Sage, 1976.

1680. Derian, Patricia M. "Human Rights and American Foreign Policy." **Universal Human Rights** 1 (January/March 1979): 3-9.

1681. Domer, Thomas M. "Sport in Cold War America, 1953-1963: The Diplomatic and Political Use of Sport in the Eisenhower and Kennedy Administration." Ph.D. dissertation, Marquette University, 1978.

1682. Erasmus, Charles J. **Man Takes Control: Cultural Development and American Aid.** Minneapolis: University of Minnesota Press, 1961.

1683. Evans, Luther. **The United States and Unesco.** Dobbs Ferry, N.Y.: Oceana, 1971.

1684. Feingold, Henry L. "The Politics of Rescue:

A Study of American Diplomacy and Politics Related to the Rescue of Refugees, 1938-1944." Ph.D. dissertation, New York University, 1966.

1685. Finger, Seymour M. "United States Policy toward International Institutions." **International Organization** 30 (Spring 1969): 559-588.

1686. Finkelstein, Lawrence S. "International Cooperation in a Changing World: A Challenge to United States Foreign Policy." **International Organization** 23 (Summer 1969): 559-558.

1687. Frankel, Charles R. **The Neglected Aspect of Foreign Affairs: American Educational and Cultural Policy Abroad.** Washington, D.C.: Brookings Institution, 1965.

1688. Franklin, John H. "The American Scholar and American Foreign Policy." **American Scholar** 37 (Autumn 1968): 615-623.

1689. Fraser, D. M. "Human Rights and U.S. Foreign Policy." **International Studies Quarterly** 23 (June 1979): 174-185.

1690. Gange, John. **University Research on International Affairs.** Washington, D.C.: American Council on Education, 1958.

1691. Hills, T. R. "Morality in Foreign Policy: An Expression of American Idealism." **Contemporary Review** 232 (January 1978): 23-30.

1692. Huntington, Samuel P. "Human Rights and American Power." **Commentary** 72 (September 1981): 37-43.

1693. Iriye, Akira. "Culture and Power: International Relations as Intercultural Relations." **Diplomatic History** 3 (Spring 1979): 115-128.

1694. Jacobson, Harold K. "Structuring the Global System: American Contributions to International Organization." **Annals of the American Academy of Political and Social Science** 428 (November 1976): 77-90.

1695. Kristol, Irving. "American Intellectuals and Foreign Policy." **Foreign Affairs** 45 (July 1967): 594-609.

1696. Lauren, Paul G. "Human Rights in History: Diplomacy and Racial Equality." **Diplomatic History** 2 (Summer 1978): 257-278.

1697. Laves, Walter H. C., and Charles A. Thompson. **Cultural Relations and United States Foreign Policy.** Bloomington: Indiana University Press, 1963.

1698. Leff, Nathaniel H. "New Economic Order--Bad Economics, Worse Politics." **Foreign Policy** 24 (Fall 1976): 202-217.

1699. Lillibridge, G. D. "American Impact Abroad: Past and Present." **American Scholar** 35 (Winter 1965-66): 39-63.

1700. Loescher, G. D. "US Human Rights Policy and International Financial Institutions." **World Today** 33 (December 1977): 453-463.

1701. Lopez, George A. "Correlates of the Decision-Making Authority of Secretaries-General: A Comparative Analysis of Intergovernmental Organizations." Ph.D. dissertation, Syracuse University, 1975.

1702. Macmahon, Arthur W. **Memorandum on the Postwar International Information Program of the United States.** Washington, D.C.: U.S. Department of State, 1945.

1703. Moynihan, D. P. "Politics of Human Rights." **Commentary** 64 (August 1977): 19-26.

1704. Schlesinger, Arthur M. "Human Rights and the American Tradition." **Foreign Affairs** 57 (1978): 503-526.

1705. Spiller, Robert E. "American Studies Abroad: Culture and Foreign Policy." **Annals of the American Academy of Political and Social Science** 366 (July 1966): 1-16.

1706. Summers, Robert E. **The United States and International Organizations.** New York: Wilson, 1952.

1707. Thompson, Kenneth W. **Foreign Assistance: A View from the Private Sector.** South Bend, Ind.: Notre Dame University Press, 1972.

1708. _____. "New Reflections on Ethics and Foreign Policy: The Problem of Human Rights." **Journal of Politics** 40 (November 1978): 985-1010.

1709. Vogelgesang, Stanley. "What Price Principle? U.S. Policy on Human Rights." **Foreign Affairs** 56 (July 1978): 819-841.

Scientific and Technological Relations

1710. Basiuk, Victor. "Marine Resources Development, Foreign Policy, and the Spectrum of

Choice." **Orbis** 12 (Spring 1968): 39-72.

1711. _____. "The Oceans--A New Frontier for America's Public Policy?" **Orbis** 10 (Summer 1966): 507-519.

1712. _____. **Technology, World Politics and American Policy.** New York: Columbia University Press, 1977.

1713. Bernstein, Barton J. "The Quest for Security: American Foreign Policy and International Control of Atomic Energy, 1942-46." **Journal of American History** 60 (March 1974): 1003-1004.

1714. Brookstone, Jeffrey M. **The Multinational Businessman and Foreign Policy: Entrepreneurial Politics in East-West Trade and Investment.** New York: Praeger, 1965.

1715. Byrnes, Francis C. **Americans in Technical Assistance: A Study of Attitudes and Responses to Their Role Abroad.** New York: Praeger, 1965.

1716. Churchill, Janice. "U.S. Policy Formulation: A Case Study of Fisheries Jurisdiction." Ph.D. dissertation, American University, 1974.

1717. Denoon, David B. H. "Aid: High Politics, Technology, or Farce?" Ph.D. dissertation, M. I. T., 1975.

1718. Domergue, Maurice. **Technical Assistance: Theory, Practice, and Policies.** New York: Praeger, 1968.

1719. Friedland, Edward, Paul Seabury, and Aaron Wildavsky. "Oil and the Decline of Western Power." **Political Science Quarterly** 90 (Fall 1975): 437-450.

1720. Haskins, Caryl P. "Technology, Science and American Foreign Policy." **Foreign Affairs** 40 (January 1962): 224-243.

1721. Jacobson, Harold K., and Eric Stein. **Diplomats, Scientists, and Politicians: The United States and the Nuclear Ban Negotiations.** Ann Arbor: University of Michigan Press, 1966.

1722. Keohane, R. O. "State Power and Industry Influence: American Foreign Oil Policy in the 1940s." **International Organization** 36 (Winter 1982): 165-183.

1723. Killian, James R. **Sputnik, Scientists, and Eisenhower: A Memoir of the First Special**

Assistant to the President for Science and Technology. Cambridge, Mass.: M. I. T. Press, 1977.

1724. Kim, Young H. "Technical Assistance Programs of the United Nations and of the United States: A Comparative Study." Ph.D. dissertation, University of Southern California, 1961.

1725. Long, T. Dixon. "The Changing Role of Science in the U.S. Foreign Policy Process." Policy Studies Journal 5 (Winter 1976): 193-198.

1726. Merchant, Livingston T. "Importance of the Space Program in International Relations." Department of State Bulletin 42 (February 1960): 213-217.

1727. Nau, Henry R. "Continuity and Change in U.S. Foreign Energy Policy." Policy Studies Journal 7 (Autumn 1978): 121-131.

1728. _____. "Political Interpretation of the Technology Gap Dispute." Orbis 15 (Summer 1971): 507-527.

1729. _____. Technology Transfer and U.S. Foreign Policy. New York: Praeger, 1976.

1730. _____. "U.S. Foreign Policy in the Energy Crisis." Atlantic Community Quarterly 12 (Winter 1974/75): 426-439.

1731. Poats, Rutherford M. "Technology for Developing Nations: New Directions for U.S. Technical Assistance. Washington, D. C.: Brookings Institution, 1972.

1732. Schilling, Warner R. "Scientists, Foreign Policy, and Politics." American Political Science Review 56 (June 1962): 287-300.

1733. Sherwin, Martin J. "The Atomic Bomb, Scientists and American Diplomacy During the Second World War." Ph.D. dissertation, University of California, Los Angeles, 1971.

1734. Skolnikoff, Eugene B. Science, Technology, and American Foreign Policy. Cambridge, Mass.: M. I. T. Press, 1967.

1735. Stanley, Timothy W. Raw Materials and Foreign Policy. Boulder, Colo.: Westview, 1977.

1736. Teaf, Howard M., and Peter G. Franck, eds. Hands Across Frontiers: Case Studies in Technical Cooperation. Ithaca, N.Y.:

Cornell University Press, 1955.
1737. Tucker, R. W. "Oil and American Power—Six Years Later." **Commentary** 68 (September 1979): 35-42.
1738. Wallensteen, P. "Scarce Goods as Political Weapons: The Case of Food." **Journal of Peace Research** 13 (1976): 277-298.
1739. Werner, Roy A. "Oil and U.S. Security Policies." **Orbis** 21 (Fall 1977): 651-670.
1740. White, Irvin L. **Decision-Making for Space: Law and Politics in Air, Sea, and Outer Space.** Lafayette, Ind.: Purdue University Studies, 1970.
1741. Wohlsetter, Albert. "Scientists, Seers and Strategy." **Foreign Affairs** 41 (April 1963): 466-478.

Public Opinion

1742. Axelrod, R. "Structure of Public Opinion on Policy Issues." **Public Opinion Quarterly** 31 (Spring 1967): 51-60.
1743. Bennett, S. E. "Attitude Structures and Foreign Policy Opinions." **Social Science Quarterly** 55 (December 1974): 732-742.
1744. Bray, C. W. "Media and Foreign Policy." **Foreign Policy** 16 (Fall 1974): 109-125.
1745. Caspary, William R. "The 'Mood Theory': A Study of Public Opinion and Foreign Policy." **American Political Science Review** 64 (June 1970): 536-547.
1746. Chasteen, Robert J. "American Foreign Aid and Public Opinion, 1945-1952." Ph.D. dissertation, University of North Carolina, 1958.
1747. Crockett, G. W. "American People Are Misinformed and Lied To." **Freedomways** 21 (1981): 234-241.
1748. Henkin, Louis. "Politics and the Changing Law of the Sea." **Political Science Quarterly** 89 (March 1974): 46-67.
1749. Hero, Alfred O. "Changing Southern Attitudes Toward U.S. Foreign Policy." **Southern Humanities Review** 8 (Summer 1974): 275-295.
1750. Katzenbach, Nicholas. "Foreign Policy, Public Opinion and Secrecy." **Foreign Affairs** 52 (October 1973): 1-19.
1751. Lefever, Ernest W. "Moralism and U.S.

Foreign Policy." **Orbis** 16 (Summer 1972): 396-410.

1752. Lewis, William H. "The Press and Foreign Policy: The Cloning of the American Press." **Washington Quarterly** 2 (Spring 1979): 31-38.

1753. Maggiotto, M. A., and Eugene R. Wittkopf. "American Public Attitudes Toward Foreign Policy." **International Studies Quarterly** 25 (December 1981): 601-631.

1754. Miller, Linda B. "Morality in Foreign Policy: A Failed Consensus?" **Daedalus** 109 (Summer 1980): 143-158.

1755. Packenham, Robert A. "Foreign Aid and the National Interest." **American Journal of Political Science** 10 (May 1966): 214-221.

1756. Reilly, John E. "The American Mood: A Foreign Policy of Self-Interest." **Foreign Policy** 34 (Spring 1979): 74-86.

1757. Roberts, P. C. "Morality and American Foreign Policy." **Modern Age** 21 (Spring 1977): 153-160.

1758. Rogers, William C., Barbara Stuhler, and Donald Koenig. "A Comparison of Informed and General Public Opinion on U.S. Foreign Policy." **Public Opinion Quarterly** 31 (Summer 1967): 242-251.

1759. Rosenau, James N. **National Leadership and Foreign Policy: A Case Study in the Mobilization of Public Support**. Princeton, N.J.: Princeton University Press, 1963.

1760. _____. **Public Opinion and Foreign Policy: An Operational Formulation**. New York: Random, 1961.

1761. _____. "Public Opinion, Foreign Policy, and the Adaptation of National Societies." **Societas** 1 (Spring 1971): 85-100.

1762. Rubin, Barry. "The Press and Foreign Policy: The Press in Its Own Image." **Washington Quarterly** 2 (Spring 1979): 44-53.

1763. Russett, Bruce. "Don't Tread on Me: Public Opinion and Foreign Policy in the Eighties." **Political Science Quarterly** 96 (Fall 1981): 381-399.

1764. Schapsmeier, Frederick H., and Edward L. Schapsmeier. "Walter Lippmann, Critic of American Foreign Policy." **Midwest Quarterly** 7 (October 1965): 123-136.

1765. Schlesinger, Arthur M. "Foreign Policy and
       National Morality." **Foreign Service
       Journal** 38 (October 1961): 20-22.
1766. Schneider, W. "Public Opinion: The Beginning
       of Ideology?" **Foreign Policy** 17 (Winter
       1974-75): 88-120.
1767. Scovel, Don. "The Effect of Public Opinion
       Upon National Security Policy." **United
       States Naval Institute Proceedings** 101
       (May 1975): 118-133.
1768. Secrest, Donald E. "Morality and American
       Foreign Policy." **Midwest Quarterly** 20
       (Winter 1979): 166-176.
1769. Thompson, Kenneth W. "Moral Purpose in
       Foreign Policy: Realities and Illusions."
       Social Research 27 (October 1960): 261-
       276.
1770. Trout, B. T. "Rhetoric Revisited: Political
       Legitimation and The Cold War." **Inter-
       national Studies Quarterly** 19 (September
       1975): 251-284.
1771. Truman, David B. "The Domestic Politics of
       Foreign Aid." **Proceedings of the Academy
       of Political Science** 27 (January 1962):
       62-72.
1772. Windsor, Philip. "America's Moral Confusion:
       Separating the Should from the Good."
       Foreign Policy 13 (Winter 1973-74): 139-
       153.
1773. Woods, R. B. "Black American Press and the
       New Manifest Destiny: The Waller Affair."
       Phylon 38 (March 1977): 24-34.

Interest Groups

1774. Bauer, Raymond A., Ithiel de Sola Pool, and
       Lewis A. Dexter. **American Business and
       Public Policy: The Politics of Foreign
       Trade.** 2nd ed. Chicago: Aldine-Atherton,
       1972.
1775. Becker, William H. **The Dynamics of Business-
       Government Relations: Industry and Ex-
       ports, 1893-1921.** Chicago: University of
       Chicago Press, 1982.
1776. Brady, Linda P., and Charles W. Kegley. "Bu-
       reaucratic Determinants of Foreign Policy:
       Some Empirical Evidence." **International
       Interactions** 2 (March 1977): 33-50.

1777. Castle, Eugene W. **Billions , Blunders and Baloney.** New York: Devin-Adair, 1955.

1778. Dawson, Jerry F. "Southern Baptist Efforts to Influence American Foreign Policy, 1878-1888." **Rocky Mountain Social Science Journal** 4 (April 1967): 78-87.

1779. Fraenkel, Richard, Don F. Hadwinger, and William P. Browne, eds. **American Agriculture and U. S. Foreign Policy.** New York: Praeger, 1979.

1780. Geyer, Alan F. "American Protestantism and World Politics, 1898-1960: A Typological Approach to the Functions of Religion in the Decision Making Processes of Foreign Policy." Ph.D. dissertation, Boston University, 1961.

1781. Hero, Alfred O. "American Negroes and U.S. Foreign Policy: 1937-1967." **Journal of Conflict Resolution** 13 (June 1969): 220-251.

1782. _____. **American in World Affairs.** Boston: World Peace Foundation, 1959.

1783. Hesburgh, T. M. "American Responsibility for Fostering Religious Liberty Internationally." **Journal of Ecumenical Studies** 14 (Fall 1977) 703-713.

1784. Jefferson, Charles J. "Bureaucracy, Diplomacy and the Origins of the Cold War." Ph.D. dissertation, Claremont University, 1975.

1785. Kahler, Miles. "America's Foreign Economic Policy: Is the Old-Time Religion Good Enough?" **International Affairs** (London) 56 (Summer 1980): 458-473.

1786. Lipson, C. H. "Corporate Preferences and Policies: Foreign Aid Sanctions and Investment Protection." **World Politics** 28 (April 1976): 396-421.

1787. Macmahon, Arthur W. "Function and Area in the Administration of International Affairs." In **New Horizons in Public Administration,** pp. 119-145. University: University of Alabama Press, 1945.

1788. McLellan, David S., and Charles E. Woodhouse. "American Business Leaders and Foreign Policy: A Study in Perspectives." **American Journal of Economics and Sociology** 25 (July 1966): 267-280.

1789. McLellan, David S., and Charles E.
       Woodhouse. "The Business Elite and Foreign
       Policy." **Western Political Quarterly** 13
       (March 1960): 172-190.
1790. Mathias, Charles. "Ethnic Groups and Foreign
       Policy." **Foreign Affairs** 59 (Summer 1981):
       975-998.
1791. Nanes, Allan S. "The American Businessman
       and Foreign Policy: Leadership is Needed
       to Eliminate Misconceptions that Form
       Public Attitudes." **Business Horizons** 2
       (Fall 1959): 85-91.
1792. Padgett, Edward R. "The Role of the Minority
       Party in Bipartisan Foreign Policy
       Formulation in the United States, 1945-
       1955." Ph.D. dissertation, University of
       Maryland, 1957.
1793. Preeg, Ernest H. "Economic Blocs and U.S.
       Foreign Policy." **International
       Organization** 28 (Spring 1974): 233-246.
1794. Ray, Dennis M. "Corporations and American
       Foreign Relations." **Annals of the American
       Academy of Political and Social Science**
       403 (September 1972): 80-92.
1795. Remele, Larry. "The Tragedy of Idealism: The
       National Nonpartisan League and American
       Foreign Policy, 1917-1919." **North Dakota
       Quarterly** 42 (Autumn 1975): 78-95.
1796. Reston, James B. "The Press, the President
       and Foreign Policy." **Foreign Affairs** 44
       (July 1966): 553-573.
1797. Werking, Richard H. "Bureaucrats, Business-
       men, and Foreign Trade: The Origins of the
       United States Chamber of Commerce." **Busi-
       ness History Review** 52 (Autumn 1978): 321-
       341.
1798. Wilson, Joan H. **American Business and
       Foreign Policy, 1920-1933.** Lexington:
       University of Kentucky Press, 1971.
1799. Windmuller, J. P. "Foreign Policy Conflict
       in American Labor." **Political Science
       Quarterly** 82 (June 1967): 205-234.
1800. Woodhouse, C. E., and D. S. McLellan.
       "American Business Leaders and Foreign
       Policy: A Study in Perspectives."
       **American Journal of Economics and
       Sociology** 25 (July 1966): 267-280.

GEOGRAPHICAL STUDIES

1801. Ball, George W. "Dangers of Nostalgia." **Atlantic Community Quarterly** 3 (Summer 1965): 167-176.

1802. _____. "NATO and World Responsibility." **Atlantic Community Quarterly** 2 (Summer 1964): 208-217.

1803. Becker, William H. "Foreign Markets for Iron and Steel, 1893-1913: A New Perspective on Williams School of Diplomatic History." **Pacific Historical Review** 44 (May 1975): 233-248.

1804. Bennett, W. S., R. R. Sandoval, and R. G. Shreffler. "A Credible Nuclear-Emphasis Defense for NATO." **Orbis** 17 (Summer 1973): 463-479.

1805. Birnbaum, Karl E. "Human Rights and East-West Relations." **Foreign Affairs** 55 (July 1977): 783-799.

1806. Buchan, Alastair. "The Purpose of NATO and Its Future Development." **Atlantic Community Quarterly** 8 (Spring 1970): 49-56.

1807. Camps, M. "Sources of Strain in Trans-atlantic Relations." **International Affairs** 48 (October 1972): 559-578.

1808. Cleveland, Harlan. "The United States and the Future of NATO." **Atlantic Community Quarterly** 7 (Summer 1969): 216-220.

1809. Cline, William R. **Trade Negotiations in the Tokyo Round: A Quantitative Assessment.** Washington, D.C.: Brookings Institution, 1978.

1810. Crosby, Kenneth W. "The Diplomacy of the United States in Relation to the War of the Pacific, 1879-1884." Ph.D. dissertation, George Washington University, 1949.

1811. Diebold, William. "Economic Aspects of an Atlantic Community." **International Organization** 17 (Summer 1963): 663-682.

1812. Donoff, Marion. "Bonn and Washington: The Strained Relationship." **Foreign Affairs** 57 (Summer 1979): 1052-1064.

1813. Draper, Thomas J. "The Alliance for Progress: Failures and Opportunities." **Yale Review** 55 (December 1965): 182-190.

1814. Dreier, John C. **The Alliance for Progress: Problems and Perspectives.** Baltimore:

Johns Hopkins University Press, 1962.

1815. Edmonds, David C. "The 200-Miles Fishing
Rights Controversy: Ecology or High
Tariffs?" **Inter-American Economic Affairs**
26 (Spring 1973): 3-18.

1816. Ellsworth, Robert. "The Future of the Atlantic Alliance." **Atlantic Community
Quarterly** 7 (Fall 1969): 315-320.

1817. Erler, Fritz. "Atlantic Policy: The Basis of
Partnership." **Foreign Affairs** 42 (October
1963): 84-95.

1818. Francis, Michael J. "The United States and
Chile During the Second World War: The
Diplomacy of Misunderstanding." **Journal of
Latin American Studies** 9 (May 1977): 91-
113.

1819. Gaddis, John L. "Containment: A Reassessment." **Foreign Affairs** 55 (July 1977):
873-887.

1820. Geiger, Theodore. "Ending of an Era in Atlantic Policy." **Atlantic Community
Quarterly** 5 (Spring 1967): 37-98.

1821. Girling, J. L. S. "Reagan and the Third
World." **World Today** 37 (November 1981):
407-413.

1822. Hanson, Simon G. "Experience with the International Coffee Agreement." **Inter-American
Economic Affairs** 19 (Winter 1965): 27-65.

1823. _____. "Success of the International Coffee
Agreement: How the State Department
Deceived the Congress." **Inter-American
Economic Affairs** 21 (Autumn 1967): 55-79.

1824. Hartley, Livingston. "The Atlantic Alliance:
Institutional Developments for the
1970's." **Orbis** 13 (Spring 1969): 299-311.

1825. Henderson, William. "Diplomacy and Intervention in the Developing Countries."
Virginia Quarterly Review 39 (Winter
1963): 26-36.

1826. Herring, George C. "Experiment in Foreign
Aid: Lend-Lease, 1941-1945." Ph.D. dissertation, University of Virginia, 1965.

1827. Hitchens, Harold L. "Influences on the Con-
gressional Decision to Pass the Marshal
Plan." **Western Political Quarterly** 21
(March 1968): 51-68.

1828. Hollick, Ann L. "Canadian-American
Relations: Law of the Sea." **International**

Organization 28 (Autumn 1974): 755-780.
1829. _____. "The Law of the Sea and U.S. Policy
      Initiatives." Orbis 15 (Summer 1971): 670-
      686.
1830. Hoska, Lukas E. "Summit Diplomacy During
      World War II: The Conferences at Tehran,
      Yalta and Potsdam." Ph.D. dissertation,
      University of Maryland, 1966.
1831. Hunter, Robert, E., and John E. Rielly, eds.
      Development Today: A New Look at U.S.
      Relations with the Poor Countries. New
      York: Praeger, 1972.
1832. Huntley, J. R. "Role of Leadership in
      Rebuilding the Atlantic System." Orbis 19
      (Spring 1966): 106-125.
1833. Jones, Randall J. "American Policy Toward
      Generalized Tariff Preferences for
      Developing Countries: The Punta del Este
      Decision of 1967." Ph.D. dissertation,
      University of Texas, 1974.
1834. Kaplan, Lawrence S. "United States and the
      Origins of NATO, 1946-1949." Review of
      Politics 31 (April 1969): 210-222.
1835. Kimball, Warren F. The Most Unsordid Act:
      Lend-Lease, 1939-1941. Baltimore: Johns
      Hopkins University Press, 1969.
1836. Kirkpatrick, J. J. "East/West Relations:
      Toward A New Definition of a Dialogue."
      World Affairs 144 (Summer 1981): 14-30.
1837. Koenig, Louis W. "The Truman Doctrine and
      NATO." Current History 57 (July 1969): 18-
      23.
1838. Kulesar, Peter. "The Helsinki Final Act and
      International Law." New Hungarian
      Quarterly 18 (Spring 1977): 110-119.
1839. Leff, Nathaniel H. "Technology Transfer and
      U.S. Foreign Policy: The Developing
      Countries." Orbis 23 (Spring 1979): 145-
      166.
1840. Levinson, Jerome. The Alliance that Lost Its
      Way: A Critical Report on the Alliance for
      Progress. Chicago: Quadrangle, 1970.
1841. Mangan, Mary. "The Congressional Image of
      Aid to the Underdeveloped Countries (1949-
      1959) as Revealed in the Congressional
      Hearings." Ph.D. dissertation, Yale
      University, 1964.
1842. Meltzer, Ronald I. "The Politics of Policy

Reversal: The American Response to the Issue of Granting Trade Preference to Developing Countries, 1964-1967." Ph.D. dissertation, Columbia University, 1975.

1843. Monnet, J. "America and Ourselves." **Atlantic Community Quarterly** 4 (Fall 1966): 340-348.

1844. Mrozer, Donald J. "Progressive Dissenter: Herbert Hoover's Opposition to Truman's Overseas Military Policy." **Annals of Iowa** 43 (Spring 1976): 275-291.

1845. Nichols, Irby C. "The Russian Ukase and the Monroe Doctrine: A Re-evaluation." **Pacific Historical Review** 36 (February 1967): 13-26.

1846. Pfaltzgraff, Robert L. "The United States and a Strategy for the West." **Strategic Review** 5 (Summer 1977): 10-25.

'1847. Roosevelt, Franklin D. **Wartime Correspondence Between President Roosevelt and Pope Pius XII.** New York: Macmillan, 1947.

1848. Rosecrance, Richard. "Detente or Entente?" **Foreign Affairs** 53 (April 1975): 464-481.

1849. Rostow, Eugene V. "Road Before Us." **Atlantic Community Quarterly** 5 (Summer 1967): 161-172.

1850. _____. "What's to Be Done?" **Atlantic Community Quarterly** 10 (Fall 1972): 331-350.

1851. Ruiz, Ernesto A. "Geography and Diplomacy: The American Geographical and Statistical Society and the Geopolitical Background of American Foreign Policy, 1848-1961." Ph.D. dissertation, Northern Illinois University, 1975.

1852. Schwabe, Klaus. "Woodrow Wilson and Germany's Membership in the League of Nations, 1918-1919." **Central European History** 8 (March 1975): 3-22.

1853. Stanley, Timothy W. "Detente: The Continuation of Tension by Other Means." **Atlantic Community Quarterly** 14 (Winter 1976-77): 411-423.

1854. Thompson, Kenneth W. "America and the World: Looking into the Third Century." **Virginia Quarterly Review** 52 (Winter 1978): 1-18.

1855. Vance, Cyrus R. "Meeting the Challenges of a Changing World." **Atlantic Community Quarterly** 17 (Summer 1979): 129-137.

1856.   Woods, Kenneth F. "'Imperialistic America':
        A Landmark in the Development of U.S.
        Policy Toward Latin America." Inter-
        American Economic Affairs 21 (Winter
        1967): 55-72.
1857.   Wright, Quincy. "How Hostilities Have Ended:
        Peace Treaties and Alternatives." Annals
        of the American Academy of Political and
        Social Science 392 (November 1970): 51-61.

SPECIFIC AREAS

Canada

1858. Brown, Robert J. "Emergence from Isolation: United States-Canadian Diplomatic Relations, 1937-1941." D. S. S., Syracuse University, 1968.
1859. Drouin, M. J., and H. B. Malmgren. "Canada, the United States and the World Economy." **Foreign Affairs** 60 (Winter 1981-82): 393-413.
1860. Duncan, Bingham. "A Letter on the Fur Seal in Canadian-American Diplomacy." **Canadian Historical Review** 43 (March 1965): 42-47.
1861. Farrell, R. B. "Canada and the United States." **Atlantic Community Quarterly** 14 (Spring 1976): 69-75.
1862. Fox, Annette B., and Alfred O. Hero. "Canada and the United States: Their Binding Frontier." **International Organization** 28 (Fall 1974): 999-1014.
1863. Ghent, J. M. "Canada, the United States, and the Cuban Missile Crisis." **Pacific Historical Review** 48 (May 1979): 159-184.
1864. Gluek, Alvin C. "The Passamaquoddy Bay Treaty, 1910: A Diplomatic Sideshow in Canadian-American Relations." **Canadian Historical Review** 47 (March 1966): 1-21.
1865. Holsti, Kalevi J., and Thomas A. Levy. "Bilateral Institutions and Transgovernmental Relations between Canada and the United States." **International Organization** 28 (Autumn 1974): 875-901.
1866. Kottman, Richard N. "The Diplomatic Relations of the United States and Canada, 1927-1941." Ph.D. dissertation, Vanderbilt University, 1958.
1867. Leach, Richard H. "Canada and the United States: A Special Relationship." **Current History** 72 (April 1977): 145-149, 180.
1868. Mahood, Harry R. "The St. Lawrence Seaway Bill of 1954: A Case Study of Decision-Making in American Foreign Policy." Ph.D. dissertation, University of Illinois, 1960.
1869. Merchant, Livingston T., ed. **Neighbors Taken for Granted: Canada and the United States.** New York: Praeger, 1966.

157

1870. Officer, Lawrence H., and Lawrence B. Smith.
       "The Canadian-American Reciprocity Treat
       of 1855 to 1866." **Journal of Economic
       History** 28 (December 1968): 598-623.
1871. Rutan, G. F. "Stresses and Fractures in
       Canadian-American Relations: The Emergence
       of a New Environment." **Orbis** 18 (Summer
       1974): 582-593.
1872. Sigler, John H., and Dennis Goresky. "Public
       Opinion on United States-Canadian Rela-
       tions." **International Organization** 28
       (Autumn 1974): 637-668.
1873. Tynan, Thomas M. "Canadian-American Rela-
       tions in the Artic: The Effect of Environ-
       mental Influences on Territorial Claims."
       Review of Politics 41 (July 1979): 402-
       427.
1874. Wagner, J. Richard. "Congress and Canadian-
       American Relations: The Norman Case."
       Rocky Mountain Social Science Journal 10
       (October 1973): 85-92.

                     Caribbean

1875. Allison, Graham T. "Conceptual Models and
       the Cuban Missile Crisis." **American Poli-
       tical Science Review** 63 (September 1969):
       689-718.
1876. _____. **Essence of a Decision: Explaining
       the Cuban Missile Crisis.** Boston: Little,
       Brown, 1971.
1877. Baker, George W. "The Wilson Administration
       and Cuba, 1913-1921." **Mid-America** 46
       (January 1964): 48-63.
1878. _____. "Woodrow Wilson's Use of the Non-
       Recognition Policy in Costa Rica."
       Americas 22 (July 1965): 3-21.
1879. Bender, Lynn D. "U.S. Cuban Policy Under the
       Nixon Administration: Subtle Modifica-
       tions." **Revista Interamerican** 2 (Fall
       1972): 330-341.
1880. Berle, Adolf A. "The Cuban Crisis: Failure
       of American Foreign Policy." **Foreign
       Affairs** 39 (October 1960): 40-55.
1881. Bernstein, Barton J. "The Cuban Missile
       Crisis: Trading the Jupiters in Turkey?"
       Political Science Quarterly 95 (Spring
       1980): 97-125.
1882. Bonsal, Philip W. **Cuba, Castro and the
       United States.** Pittsburgh: University of

Pittsburgh Press, 1971.

1883. Bras, J. Mari. "Struggle for Puerto Rican
       Independence." **Black Scholar** 8 (December
       1976): 18-26.

1884. Chrisman, R. "Cuba: Forge of the Revolu-
       tion." **Black Scholar** 11 (July 1980): 59-
       71.

1885. Crane, Robert C. "The Cuban Crisis: A Stra-
       tegic Analysis of America and Soviet
       Policy." **Orbis** 6 (Winter 1963): 528-563.

1886. Diez, William E. "Opposition in the United
       States to American Diplomacy in the
       Caribbean, 1898-1932." Ph.D. dissertation,
       University of Chicago, 1946.

1887. Ekman, P. "Coping with Cuba: Divergent
       Policy Preferences of State Political
       Leaders." **Journal of Conflict Resolution**
       10 (June 1966): 180-197.

1888. Esteves, Herman R. "The United States,
       Spain, and the **Maine**, or the Diplomacy of
       Frustration." **Revista Interamericana
       Review** 2 (Winter 1973): 549-558.

1889. Fagen, Richard R. "Calculation and Emotion
       in Foreign Policy: The Cuban Case." **Jour-
       nal of Conflict Resolution** 6 (September
       1962): 214-221.

1890. Fenwick, C. G. "Dominican Republic: Inter-
       vention or Collective Self-Defense."
       American Journal of International Law 60
       (January 1966): 64-67.

1891. Froneck, M. Zygmunta. "Diplomatic Relations
       Between United States and Costa Rica,
       1823-1882." Ph.D. dissertation, Fordham
       University, 1959.

1892. Fry, Joseph A. "William McKinley and the
       Coming of the Spanish-American War: A
       Study of the Besmirching and Redemption of
       an Historical Image." **Diplomatic History** 3
       (Winter 1979): 77-98.

1893. Gillette, H. "Military Occupation of Cuba,
       1899-1902: Workshop for American Progres-
       sivism." **American Quarterly** 25 (October
       1973): 410-425.

1894. Grieb, Kenneth J. "Warren G. Harding and the
       Dominican Republic U.S. Withdrawal, 1921-
       1923." **Journal of Inter-American Studies**
       11 (July 1969): 425-440.

1895. Guggenheim, Harry F. **The United States and**

Cuba: A Study in International Relations. New York: Macmillan, 1934.

1896. Hafner, Donald L. "Bureaucratic Politics and 'Those Frigging Missiles': JFK, Cuba and U.S. Missiles in Turkey." **Orbis** 21 (Summer 1977): 307-333.

1897. Hauptman, Laurence M. "Utah Anti-imperialist: Senator William H. King and Haiti, 1921-34." **Utah Historical Quarterly** 41 (Spring 1973): 116-127.

1898. Hickey, John. "The Role of the Congress in Foreign Policy: Case: The Cuban Disaster." **Inter-American Economic Affairs** 14 (Spring 1961): 67-89.

1899. Hines, Calvin W. "United States Diplomacy in the Caribbean During World War II." Ph.D. dissertation, University of Texas, Austin, 1968.

1900. Hitcfhman, J. H. "American Touch in Imperial Administration: Leonard Wood in Cuba, 1898-1902." **Americas** 24 (April 1968): 394-403.

1901. Holbo, Paul S. "Convergence of Moods and the Cuban-bond Conspiracy of 1898." **Journal of American History** 55 (June 1968): 54-72.

1902. Kahan, Jerome H., and Anne K. Long. "The Cuban Missile Crisis: A Study of Its Strategic Context." **Political Science Quarterly** 87 (December 1972): 564-590.

1903. Kennedy, John F. "The Lesson of Cuba." **Department of State Bulletin** 44 (May 1961): 659-661.

1904. Lane, J. C. "Instrument for Empire: The American Military Government in Cuba, 1899-1902." **Science and Society** 36 (Fall 1972): 314-330.

1905. Lange, P., and M. Vannicelli. "Carter in the Haitian Maze." **Foreign Policy** 33 (Winter 1978/79): 161-173.

1906. Light, Robert E., and Carl Margani. **Cuba versus CIA.** New York: Marzanie and Munsell, 1961.

1907. Logan, Rayford W. "James Weldon Johnson and Haiti." **Phylon** 32 (Winter 1971): 396-402.

1908. Lowenthal, A. F. "Cuba: Time for a Change." **Foreign Policy** 20 (Fall 1975): 65-86.

1909. McMahon, Robert J. "Anglo-American Diplomacy and the Reoccupation of the Netherlands

East Indies." **Diplomatic History** 2 (Winter
1978): 1-24.
1910. MacMichael, David C. "The United States and
the Dominican Republic, 1871-1940: A Cycle
in Caribbean Diplomacy." Ph.D. dissertation, University of Oregon, 1964.
1911. McNaught, Kenneth. "Canada, Cuba, and the
U.S." **Monthly Review** 12 (April 1961): 616-
623.
1912. McWilliams, Tennant. "Procrastination Diplomacy: Hannis Taylor and the Cuban Business
Disputes, 1893-97." **Diplomatic History** 2
(Winter 1978): 63-80.
1913. Matthewson, Timothy M. "Slavery and Diplomacy: The United States and Saint Dominque,
1791-1793." Ph.D. dissertation, University
of California, Santa Barbara, 1976.
1914. May, Robert E. "Lobbyists for Commercial Empire: Jane Cazneau, William Cazneau, and
U.S. Caribbean Policy, 1846-78." **Pacific
Historical Review** 48 (August 1979): 383-
412.
1915. Moineu, H. "Concept of the Caribbean in the
Latin American Policy of the United
States." **Journal of Interamerican Studies
and World Affairs** 15 (August 1973): 285-
307.
1916. Munro, Dana G. **Intervention and Dollar
Diplomacy in the Caribbean, 1900-1921.**
Princeton, N.J.: Princeton University
Press, 1964.
1917. _____. **The United States and the Caribbean
Area.** Boston: World Peace Foundation,
1934.
1918. Norton, Nile B. "American Colonial Administration: Cuba and the Philippines, 1899-
1906." **Rocky Mountain Social Science
Journal** 4 (April 1967): 88-99.
1919. Schreiber, A. P. "Economic Coercion as an
Instrument of Foreign Policy: U.S. Economic Measures Against Cuba and the
Dominican Republic." **World Politics** 25
(April 1973): 387-413.
1920. Shalom, Stephen R. "International Lawyers
and Other Apologists: The Case of the
Cuban Missile Crisis." **Polity** 12 (Fall
1979): 83-109.
1921. Sherwin, Martin J., and Peter Winn. "The

U.S. and Cuba." **Wilson Quarterly** 2 (Winter 1978): 57-68.

1922. Shoemaker, Raymond L. "Diplomacy from the Quarterdeck: The United States Navy in the Caribbean, 1815-1830." Ph.D. dissertation, Indiana University, 1976.

1923. Skillern, William G. "An Analysis of the Decision-Making Process in the Cuban Missile Crisis." Ph.D. dissertation, University of Idaho, 1971.

1924. Tansill, William R. "Diplomatic Relations Between the United States and the Dominican Republic, 1874-1899." Ph.D. dissertation, Georgetown University, 1952.

1925. Toth, Charles W. "Anglo-American Diplomacy and the British West Indies, 1783-1789." **The Americas** 32 (January 1976): 418-436.

1926. Trotter, Richard G. "The Cuban Missile Crisis: An Analysis of Policy Formulation in Terms of Current Decision Making Theory." Ph.D. dissertation, University of Pennsylvania, 1970.

1927. Weigle, Richard D. "The Sugar Interests and American Diplomacy in Hawaii and Cuba, 1893-1903." Ph.D. dissertation, Yale University, 1939.

1928. Wilson, D. P. "Strategic Projections and Policy Options in the Soviet-Cuban Relationship." **Orbis** 12 (Summer 1968): 504-517.

1929. Wilson, L. C. "Monroe Doctrine, Cold War Anachronism: Cuba and the Dominican Republic." **Journal of Politics** 28 (May 1966): 322-346.

1930. Wright, Theodore P. "United States Electoral Intervention in Cuba (1898-1934)." **Inter-American Economic Affairs** 13 (Winter 1959): 50-71.

1931. Wrong, Dennis H. "The American Left and Cuba." **Commentary** 33 (February 1962): 93-103.

Latin America

1932. Aldrich, Richard S. "Development Assistance to Latin America." **Yale Review** 60 (October 1970): 53-62.

1933. Alexander, Robert J. "Diminishing U.S. Aid

in Latin America." **Current History** 77
(July/August 1979): 18-21, 36-37.

1934.   _____. "New Directions: The U.S. and Latin
America." **Current History** 42 (February
1962): 65-70.

1935.   Agor, W. H. "Latin American Inter-State
Politics: Patterns of Cooperation and
Conflict." **Inter-American Economic Affairs**
26 (Autumn 1972): 19-33.

1936.   Astiz, Carlos A. "U.S. Policy and Latin
American Reaction." **Current History** 74
(February 1978): 49-52, 89.

1937.   Bacon, Robert. **For Better Relations with Our
Latin American Neighbors: A Journey to
South America.** Washington, D.C.: Carnegie
Endowment for International Peace, 1915.

1938.   Benton, William. **The Voice of Latin America.**
New York: Harper, 1961.

1939.   Biglow, Frank W. "The Alliance for Progress,
the OAS, and the Kennedy Administration: A
Decision-Making Study of United States
Foreign Policy Objectives in Latin
America, 1960-1963." Ph.D. dissertation,
University of California, 1972.

1940.   Binning, William C. "The Nixon Foreign-Aid
Policy for Latin America." **Inter-American
Economic Affairs** 25 (Summer 1971): 31-46.

1941.   Bode, K. A. "Aspect of United States Policy
in Latin America: The Latin American Diplomats' View." **Political Science
Quarterly** 85 (September 1970): 471-491.

1942.   Bond, R. D. "Regionalism in Latin America:
Prospects for the Latin American Economic
System." **International Organization** 32
(Spring 1978): 401-423.

1943.   Bronheim, D. "Latin American Diversity and
United States Foreign Policy." **Proceeding
of the Academy of Political Science** 30
(August 1972): 167-176.

1944.   _____. "Relations between the United States
and Latin America." **International Affairs**
46 (July 1970): 501-516.

1945.   Bundy, William P. "Who Lost Patagonia?
Foreign Policy in the 1980 Campaign."
Foreign Affairs 58 (Fall 1979): 1-27.

1946.   Busey, James L. "Our Political Gap in Latin
America." **Midwest Quarterly** 3 (April
1962): 219-229.

1947. Cahn, H. "Short Essay on Foreign Policy in
       Latin America." **Texas Quarterly** 9 (Winter
       1966): 15-25.
1948. Cochrane, James D. "U.S. Policy towards
       Recognition of Governments and Promotion
       of Democracy in Latin America since 1963."
       Journal of Latin American Studies 4
       (November 1972): 275-291.
1949. Connell-Smith, Gordon. "The Future of the
       Organization of American States: Signi-
       ficance of the Punta del Este Conference."
       World Today 18 (March 1962): 112-120.
1950. _____. "Latin America in the Foreign
       Relations of the United States: Review
       Article." **Journal of Latin American
       Studies** 8 (May 1976): 137-150.
1951. Dahl, Victor C. "Paraguayan 'Jewel Box'."
       Americas 21 (January 1965): 223-242.
1952. Dominguez, J. I. "Consensus and Divergence:
       The State of the Literature on Inter-
       American Relations in the 1970's." **Latin
       American Research Review** 13 (1978): 87-
       126.
1953. Dreier, John C. "New Wine and Old Bottles:
       The Changing Inter-American System."
       International Organization 22 (Spring
       1968): 477-493.
1954. Eisenhower, Milton. **The Wine Is Bitter: The
       United States and Latin America.** New York:
       Doubleday, 1963.
1955. Fager, Richard R. "The Carter Administration
       and Latin America: Business as Usual?"
       Foreign Affairs 57 (1978): 652-669.
1956. Ferguson, Yale H. "Through Glasses Darkly:
       An Assessment of Various Theoretical
       Approaches to Interamerican Relations."
       **Journal of Interamerican Studies and World
       Affairs** 19 (February 1977): 3-34.
1957. Flickema, T. O. "Sam Ward's Bargain: A
       Tentative Reconsideration." **Hispanic
       American Historical Review** 50 (August
       1970): 538-542.
1958. _____. "Settlement of the Paraguayan-
       American Controversy of 1859: A Reap-
       praisal." **Americas** 25 (July 1968): 49-69.
1959. Francis, Michael J. "United States Policy
       Toward Latin America: An Immoderate Pro-
       posal." **Orbis** 20 (Winter 1977): 991-1006.

1960.   Franck, Thomas M., and Edward Weisband. "Panama Paralysis." **Foreign Policy** 21 (Winter 1975-76): 168-187.

1961.   Gellman, Irwin F. "Prelude to Reciprocity: The Abortive United States-Colombian Treaty of 1933." **Historian** 32 (November 1969): 52-68.

1962.   Gilderhus, Mark T. "United States and Carranza, 1917: The Question of De Jure Recognition." **Americas** 29 (October 1972): 214-231.

1963.   Gomez, M. O. "United States-Latin American Relationship since 1960." **World Today** 30 (December 1974): 513-522.

1964.   Gonzalez, Heliodoro. "US Arms Transfer Policy in Latin America: Failure of a Policy." **Inter-American Economic Affairs** 32 (Autumn 1978): 67-89.

1965.   Goodell, S. "Woodrow Wilson in Latin America: Interpretations." **Historian** 28 (November 1965): 96-127.

1966.   Grayson, George W. "Oil and U.S.-Mexican Relations." **Journal of Inter-American Studies and World Affairs** 21 (November 1979): 427-456.

1967.   Haines, Gerald K. "The Roosevelt Administration Interprets the Monroe Doctrine." **Australian Journal of Politics and History** 24 (December 1978): 322-345.

1968.   Hanson, Simon G. "The Failure of the Stevenson Mission--June 4-22, 1961." **Inter-American Economic Affairs** 15 (Autumn 1961): 53-76.

1969.   _____. "Third Year: Political." **Inter-American Economic Affairs** 18 (Spring 1965): 38-53.

1970.   Harter, Donald. "Contributions of United States Diplomacy in Latin America to Hemispheric Solidarity." Ph.D. dissertation, University of Iowa, 1942.

1971.   Hill, Robert C. "U.S. Policy toward Latin America." **Orbis** 10 (Summer 1966): 390-407.

1972.   Hoffman, Ralph N. "Latin American Diplomacy: The Role of the Assistant Secretary of State, 1957-1969." Ph.D. dissertation, Syracuse University, 1969.

1973.   Hollist, W. Ladd, and Thomas H. Johnson. "Political Consequences of International

Economic Relations: Alternative Expla-
nations of United States/Latin American
Noncooperation." **Journal of Politics** 41
(November 1979): 1125-1155.

1974. Holsinger, M. Paul. "The 'I'm Alone'
Controversy: A Study in Inter-American
Diplomacy, 1929-1935." **Mid-America** 50
(October 1968): 305-313.

1975. Humphrey, Hubert H. "U.S. Policy in Latin
America." **Foreign Affairs** 42 (July 1964):
585-601.

1976. Kelly, P. L. "Characteristics of United
States Ambassadors to Latin America."
Inter-American Economic Affairs 30 (Autumn
1976): 49-79.

1977. Langley, Lester D. "Senator Kennedy on U.S.
Policy toward Latin America." **Revista
Interamericana Review** 3 (Fall 1972): 323-
329.

1978. Lowenthal, A. F. "Latin America: A Not-So-
Special Relationship." **Foreign Policy** 32
(Fall 1978): 107-126.

1979. _____. "United States and Latin America:
Ending the Hegemonic Presumption." **Foreign
Affairs** 55 (October 1976): 199-213.

1980. Morrison, DeLesseps S. **Latin American
Mission: An Adventure in Hemisphere
Diplomacy.** New York: Simon and Schuster,
1965.

1981. Needler, Martin C. "New Directions for Our
Latin American Policy." **Yale Review** 60
(March 1971): 333-341.

1982. Nichols, Roy F. "Trade Relations and the
Establishment of United States Consulates
in Spanish America, 1779-1809." **Hispanic
American Historical Review** 13 (August
1933): 289-313.

1983. Northrum, Jack. "The Trist Mission." **Journal
of Mexican American History** 3 (1973): 13-
31.

1984. Oliver, Covey T. "Foreign and Human Relations with Latin America." **Foreign Affairs**
47 (April 1969): 521-531.

1985. Parker, James R., and Terry G. Summons. "The
Rise and Fall of the Good Neighbor Policy:
The North American View." **Maryland
Historian** 1 (Spring 1970): 31-41.

1986. Perez, L. A. "International Dimensions of

Inter-American Relations, 1944-1960."
Inter-American Economic Affairs 27 (Summer 1973): 47-68.

1987. Perkins, Dexter. **The United States and Latin America.** Baton Rouge: Louisiana State University, 1961.

1988. Petras, J. "U.S.-Latin American Studies: A Critical Assessment." **Science and Society** 32 (Spring 1968): 148-168.

1989. Pike, Frederick B. "Corporatism and Latin American-United States Relations." **Review of Politics** 36 (January 1974): 132-170.

1990. _____. "Can We Slow Our Loss of Latin America?" **Inter-American Economic Affairs** 15 (Summer 1961): 3-29.

1991. Pletcher, David M. "Inter-America Trade in the Early 1870's--A State Department Survey." **Americas** 33 (April 1977): 593-612.

1992. _____. "Reciprocity and Latin America in the Early 1890's: A Foretaste of Dollar Diplomacy." **Pacific Historical Review** 47 (February 1978): 53-89.

1993. _____. "United States Relations with Latin America: Neighborliness and Exploitation." **American Historical Review** 82 (February 1977): 39-59.

1994. Rabe, Stephen G. "The Elusive Conference: United States Economic Relations with Latin America, 1945-1952." **Diplomatic History** 2 (Summer 1978): 279-294.

1995. Reagan, Ronald. "Canal as Opportunity: A New Relationship with Latin America." **Orbis** 21 (Fall 1977): 547-563.

1996. Reno, William L. "The Monroe Doctrine in Inter-American Diplomatic Relations." Ph.D. dissertation, University of California, Berkeley,1935.

1997. Rezneck, Samuel. "An American Diplomat Writes About Latin America in 1832." **Americas** 28 (October 1971): 206-211.

1998. Robinson, D. R. "Treaty Tatelolco and the United States: A Latin American Nuclear Free Zone." **American Journal of International Law** 64 (April 1970): 282-309.

1999. Roper, C. "Inter-American Relationships." **World Today** 27 (November 1971): 486-494.

2000. Rubottom, Roy R. "The Goals of United States

Policy in Latin America." **Annals of the American Academy of Political and Social Science** 342 (July 1962): 30-40.

2001. Schneider, Ronald M. "U.S. Policy in Latin America." **Current History** 51 (November 1966): 257-263.

2002. _____. "The U.S. in Latin America." **Current History** 48 (January 1965): 1-8, 50.

2003. Sealander, Judith. "In the Shadow of Good Neighbor Diplomacy: The Women's Bureau and Latin America." **Prologue** 11 (Winter 1979): 237-250.

2004. Slater, Jerome. "Democracy Versus Stability: The Recent Latin American Policy of the United States." **Yale Review** 55 (December 1965): 169-181.

2005. _____. "The United States and Latin America: Premises for the New Administration." **Yale Review** 64 (October 1974): 1-10.

2006. Sloan, J. W. "Three Views of Latin America: President Nixon, Governor Rockefeller, and the Latin American Consensus of Vina del Mar." **Orbis** 14 ((Winter 1971): 934-950.

2007. Smith, Robert F. "Social Revolution in Latin America--The Role of United States Policy." **International Affairs** 41 (October 1965): 637-649.

2008. _____. "The United States and Latin-American Revolutions." **Journal of Interamerican Studies and World Affairs** 4 (January 1962): 89-103.

2009. Stepan, Alfred. "The United States and Latin America: Vital Interests and the Instruments of Power." **Foreign Affairs** 58 (1979): 659-692.

2010. Stottlemire, Marvin G. "Measuring Foreign Policy: Determinants of U.S. Military Assistance to Latin America." Ph.D. dissertation, Rice University, 1975.

2011. Thomas, A. B. "Latin American Nationalism and the United States." **Journal of Inter-American Studies** 7 (January 1965): 5-13.

2012. Tillapaugh, James E. "From War to Cold War: United States Policies toward Latin America, 1943-1948." Ph.D. dissertation, Northwestern University, 1973.

2013. Trask, Roger R. "The Impact of the Cold War

on United States-Latin American Relations, 1945-1949." **Diplomatic History** 1 (Summer 1977): 271-284.

2014. Tulchin, Joseph S. "Dollar Diplomacy and Non-Intervention: The Latin American Policy of the United States, 1919-1924." Ph.D. dissertation, Harvard University, 1965.

2015. Varg, Paul A. "The Economic Side of the Good Neighbor Policy: The Reciprocal Trade Program and South America." **Pacific Historical Review** 45 (February 1976): 47-71.

2016. Weischandle, David E. "Paternalism: A View of the Latin American Foreign Policy of the United States, 1823-1934." **Social Studies** 61 (November 1970): 263-269.

2017. Whitaker, Arthur P. "The American Idea and the Western Hemisphere: Yesterday, Today, and Tomorrow." **Orbis** 20 (Spring 1976): 161-177.

2018. Wood, Bryce. **The Making of the Good Neighbor Policy.** New York: Columbia University Press, 1961.

2019. Woods, R. B. "Conflict or Community? The United States and Argentina's Admission to the United Nations." **Pacific Historical Review** 46 (August 1977): 361-386.

Mexico

2020. Beelen, George D. "Harding and Mexico: Diplomacy by Economic Persuasion." Ph.D. dissertation, Kent State University, 1971.

2021. Berbusse, Edward J. "Unofficial Intervention of the United States in Mexico's Religious Crisis, 1926-1930." **Americas** 23 (July 1966): 28-62.

2022. Bodayla, Stephen D. "Financial Diplomacy: The United States and Mexico, 1919-1933." Ph.D. dissertation, New York University, 1975.

2023. Clements, Kendrick A. "Woodrow Wilson's Mexican Policy, 1913-15." **Diplomatic History** 4 (Spring 1980): 113-136.

2024. Fagen, Richard R. "Realities of U.S.-Mexican Relations." **Foreign Affairs** 55 (July 1977): 685-700.

2025. Gibbs, William E. "Spadework Diplomacy:
       United States-Mexican Relations During the
       Hayes Administration, 1877-1881." Ph.D.
       dissertation, Kent State University, 1973.
2026. Gonzales, Heliodoro. "The Ultimate Cosmetic
       Touch for U.S.-Mexican Relations." **Inter-
       American Economic Affairs** 33 (Winter
       1979): 85-96.
2027. Grieb, Kenneth J. "A Badger General's Foray
       into Diplomacy: General Edward S. Bragg in
       Mexico." **Wisconsin Magazine of History** 53
       (Fall 1969): 21-32.
2028. _____. "Role of the Mexican Revolution in
       Contemporary American Policy." **Midwest
       Quarterly** 10 (January 1969): 113-129.
2029. Hill, Larry D. "Woodrow Wilson's Executive
       Agents in Mexico: From the Beginning of
       His Administration to the Recognition of
       Venustiano Carranza." Ph.D. dissertation,
       Louisiana State University, 1971.
2030. Horn, James J. "Did the United States Plan an
       Invasion of Mexico in 1927." **Journal of
       Interamerican Studies and World Affairs** 15
       (November 1973): 454-471.
2031. _____. "Diplomacy by Ultimatum: Ambassador
       Sheffiel and Mexican-American Relations,
       1924-1927." Ph.D. dissertation, State
       University of New York, Buffalo, 1969.
2032. _____. "Diplomacy and the Specter of
       Boshevism in Mexico (1924-1927)." **Americas**
       32 (July 1975): 31-45.
2033. Kane, N. Stephen. "American Businessmen and
       Foreign Policy: The Recognition of Mexico,
       1920-1923." **Political Science Quarterly** 90
       (Summer 1975): 293-313.
2034. _____. "Bankers and Diplomats: The Diplo-
       macy of the Dollar in Mexico, 1921-1924."
       Business History Review 47 (Autumn 1973):
       335-352.
2035. _____. "Corporate Power and Foreign Policy:
       Efforts of American Oil Companies to
       Influence United States Relations with
       Mexico, 1921-1928." **Diplomatic History** 1
       (Spring 1973): 335-352.
2036. Lane, Janet A. "United States-Mexican
       Diplomatic Relations, 1917-1942." Ph.D.
       dissertation, Georgetown University, 1972.
2037. Lyon, Jessie C. "Diplomatic Relations

Between the United States, Mexico and Japan: 1913-1917." Ph.D. dissertation, Claremont Graduate School, 1975.

2038. Nelson, Anna L. "The Secret Diplomacy of James K. Polk During the Mexican War, 1946-1847." Ph.D. dissertation, George Washington University, 1972.

2039. Pitchford, Louis C. "The Diplomatic Representatives from the United States to Mexico from 1836-1848." Ph.D. dissertation, University of Colorado, 1965.

2040. Pletcher, David M. "Consul Warner P. Sutton and American-Mexican Border Trade during the Early Diaz Period." **Southwestern Historical Quarterly** 79 (April 1976): 373-399.

2041. Raat, William D. "The Diplomacy of Suppression: **Los Revoltosos**, Mexico, and the United States, 1906-1911." **Hispanic American Historical Review** 56 (November 1976): 529-550.

2042. Rausch, George J. "Poison-Pen Diplomacy: Mexico, 1913." **Americas** 24 (January 1968): 272-280.

2043. Reynolds, Curtis R. "The Deterioration of Mexican-American Diplomatic Relations, 1833-1845." **Journal of the West** 11 (April 1972): 214-224.

2044. Rice, M. Elizabeth. "The Diplomatic Relations between the United States and Mexico, as Affected by the Struggle for Religious Liberty in Mexico, 1925-1929." Ph.D. dissertation, Catholic University, 1959.

2045. Ring, Jeremiah J. "American Diplomacy and the Mexico Oil Controversy, 1938-1943." Ph.D. dissertation, University of New Mexico, 1974.

2046. Sandos, James A. "The Plan of San Diego: War and Diplomacy on the Texas Border, 1915-1916." **Arizona and the West** 14 (Spring 1972): 5-24.

2047. Shoemaker, Raymond L. "Henry Lane Wilson and Republican Policy toward Mexico, 1913-1920." **Indiana Magazine of History** 76 (June 1980): 103-122.

2048. Smith, Robert F. "The Morrow Mission and the International Committee of Bankers on

Mexico: The Interaction of Finance Diplomacy and the New Mexican Elite." **Journal of Latin America Studies** 1 (November 1969): 149-166.

2049. Trow, C. W. "Woodrow Wilson and the Mexican Interventionist Movement of 1919." **Journal of American History** 58 (June 1971): 46-72.

2050. Tyler, R. C. "Fugitive Slaves in Mexico." **Journal of Negro History** 57 (January 1972): 1-12.

2051. Young, Paul P. "Mexican Oil and American Diplomacy." Ph.D. dissertation, University of Texas, Austin, 1934.

Central America

2052. Baker, George W. "Ideals and Realities in the Wilson Administration's Relations with Honduras." **Americas** 21 (July 1964): 3-19.

2053. _____. "The Wilson Administration and Nicaragua, 1913-1921." **Americas** 22 (April 1966): 339-376.

2054. _____. "The Wilson Administration and Panama, 1913-1921." **Journal of Interamerican Studies and World Affairs** 8 (April 1966): 279-292.

2055. _____. "The Woodrow Wilson Administration and El Salvadoran Relations 1913-1921." **Social Studies** 56 (March 1965): 97-102.

2056. _____. "The Woodrow Wilson Administration and Guatemalan Relations." **Historian** 27 (February 1965): 155-169.

2057. Block, Robert H. "Southern Congressmen and Wilson's Call for Repeal of the Panama Canal Tolls Exemption." **Southern Studies** 17 (Spring 1978): 91-100.

2058. Burbach, R. "Central America: The End of U.S. Hegemony?" **Monthly Review** 33 (January 1982): 1-18.

2059. Cameron, Duncan H. "The Panama Canal Policy of the United States." **Midwest Quarterly** 11 (January 1970): 141-152.

2060. Cochrane, James D. "U.S. Attitudes toward Central American Integration." **Inter-American Economic Affairs** 18 (Autumn 1964): 73-92.

2061. Coker, W. S. "Panama Canal Tolls Controversy: A Different Perspective." **Journal** of American History 55 (December 1968): 555-564.

2062. Crowell, J. "United States and a Central American Canal, 1869-1877." **Hispanic American Historical Review** 49 (February 1969): 27-52.

2063. Dinwoodie, David H. "Expedient Diplomacy: The United States and Guatemala, 1898-1920." Ph.D. dissertation, University of Colorado, 1966.

2064. _____. "Dollar Diplomocy in the Light of the Guatemalan Loan Project, 1909-1913." **Americas** 26 (January 1970): 237-253.

2065. Fletcher, William G. "Canal Site Diplomacy: A Study in American Political Geography." Ph.D. dissertation, Yale University, 1940.

2066. Gordon, M. "Case History of US Subversion: Guatemala, 1954." **Science & Society** 35 (Summer 1971): 129-155.

2067. Grieb, Kenneth J. "United States and the Central American Federation." **Americas** 24 (October 1967): 107-121.

2068. Kamman, William. "A Search for Stability: United States Dipolmacy toward Nicaragua, 1925-1933." Ph.D. dissertation, Indiana University, 1962.

2069. Koch, E. I., and R. J. McCloskey. "On U.S. Relations with El Salvador: The Doch-State Department Correspondence." **American Economic Affairs** 30 (Summer 1976): 79-83.

2070. Kuhn, Gary G. "Central American Diplomatic Rivalry within the United States, 1862-1865." **North Dakota Quarterly** 47 (Winter 1979): 34-40.

2071. Lael, Richard L. "Dilemma Over Panama: Negotiation of the Thomson-Urrutia Treaty." **Mid-America** 61 (January 1979): 35-45.

2072. Langley, Lester D. "The United States and Panama, 1933-1941: A Study in Strategy and Diplomacy." Ph.D. dissertation, University of Kansas, 1965.

2073. Langley, Lester D. "U.S.-Panamanian Relations since 1941." **Journal of Interamerican Studies and World Affairs** 12 (July 1970): 339-365.

2074. _____. "The World Crisis and the Good Neighbor Policy in Panama, 1936-1941." **Americas** 24 (October 1967): 137-152.

2075. Leonard, Thomas M. "Commissary Issue in
       American-Panamanian Relations, 1900-1936."
       Americas 30 (July 1973): 83-109.
2076. _____. "United States and Panama
       Negotiating the Aborted 1926 Treaty." **Mid-
       America** 61 (October 1979): 188-203.
2077. Naughton, William A. "Panama Versus the
       United States: A Case Study in Small State
       Diplomacy." Ph.D. dissertation, American
       University, 1972.
2078. Randall, S. J. "Colombia, the United States,
       and Interamerican Aviation Rivalry, 1927-
       1940." **Journal of Interamerican Studies
       and World Affairs** 14 (August 1972): 297-
       324.
2079. Ropp, Steve C. "Ratification of the Panama
       Canal Treaties: The Muted Debate." **World
       Affairs** 141 (Spring 1979): 283-292.
2080. Rosenfeld, Stephen S. "The Panama
       Negotiations--A Close-Run Thing." **Foreign
       Affairs** 54 (October 1975): 1-13.
2081. Russell, William. "Diplomatic Relations
       between the United States and Nicaragua,
       1920-1933." Ph.D. dissertation, University
       of Chicago, 1953.
2082. Ryan, Paul B. "Canal Diplomacy and U.S.
       Interests." **United States Naval Institute
       Proceedings** 103 (January 1977): 43-53.
2083. Sparks, Dade. "Central America and Its
       Diplomatic Relations with the United
       States, 1860-1893." Ph.D. dissertation,
       Duke University, 1934.
2084. Stansifer, C. L. "Application of the Tobar
       Doctrine to Central America." **Americas** 23
       (January 1967): 251-272.
2085. _____. "E. George Squier and the Honduras
       Inter-oceanic Railroad Project." **Hispanic
       American Historical Review** 46 (February
       1966): 1-27.
2086. Sudol, Ronald A. "The Thetoric of Strategic
       Retreat: Carter and the Panama Canal
       Debate." **Quarterly Journal of Speech** 65
       (December 1979): 379-391.
2087. Tierney, J. J. "US Intervention in
       Nicaragua, 1927-1933: Lessons for Today."
       Orbis 14 (Winter 1971): 1012-1028.
2088. Van Alstyne, Richard W. "Panama Canal: A
       Classical Case of An Imperial Hangover."

Journal of Contemporary History 15 (April
1980): 299-316.

South America

2089. Barnard, A. "Chilean Communists, Radical
Presidents and Chilean Relations with the
United States, 1940-1947." **Journal of
Latin American Studies** 13 (November 1981):
347-374.
2090. Beck, William F. "Anglo-United States Rela-
tions with Chile During the War of the
Pacific, 1879-1883: A Study in Diplomatic
History." Ph.D. dissertation, University
of Pittsburgh, 1942.
2091. Blasier, C. "United States, Germany, and the
Bolivian Revolutionaries (1941-1946)."
Hispanic American Historical Review 52
(February 1972): 26-54.
2092. Cantero, M. "Lessons of Chile." **World
Marxist Review** 20 (August 1977): 42-52.
2093. Cortada, James W. "Diplomatic Rivalry
between Spain and the United States over
Chile and Peru, 1864-1871." **Inter-American
Economic Affairs** 27 (Spring 1974): 47-57.
2094. Deaton, Ronny H. "The Impact of United Private Investment, Aid, and Trade Policies
toward Brazil during the Alliance for
Progress." Ph.D. dissertation, University
of Kansas, 1973.
2095. Dye, R. W. "Peru, the United States, and
Hemisphere Relations." **Inter-American
Economic Affairs** 26 (Autumn 1972): 69-87.
2096. Fagen, Richard R. "The United States and
Chile: Roots and Branches." **Foreign
Affairs** 53 (January 1975): 297-313.
2097. Fishlow, Albert. "Flying Down to Rio: Perspectives on U.S.-Brazil Relations."
Foreign Affairs 57 (Winter 1978-79): 387-
405.
2098. _____. "United States and Brazil: The Case
of the Missing Relationship." **Foreign
Affairs** 60 (Spring 1982): 904-914.
2099. Frederick, Richard G. "United States Foreign
Aid to Bolivia, 1953-1972." Ph.D. dissertation, University of Maryland, 1976.
2100. Froehlich, Richard C. "The United States
Navy and Diplomatic Relations with Brazil,

1822-1871." Ph.D. dissertation, Kent State University, 1971.

2101. Gray, William H. "The Diplomatic Relations between the United States and Venezuela, 1830-1864." Ph.D. dissertation, Univeristy of Chicago, 1938.

2102. Hendrickson, Embert J. "Roosevelt's Second Venezuelan Controversy." **Hispanic American Historical Review** 50 (August 1970): 482-498.

2103. Hilton, Stanley E. "United States, Brazil, and the Cold War, 1945-1960: End of the Special Relationship." **Journal of American History** 68 (December 1981): 599-624.

2104. Holbo, Paul S. "Perilous Obscurity: Public Diplomacy and the Press in teh Venezuelan Crisis, 1902-1903." **Historian** 32 (May 1970): 428-448.

2105. House, Lewis. "Edwin V. Morgan and Brazilian-American Diplomatic Relations 1912-1933." Ph.D. dissertation, New York University, 1969.

2106. Jaquette, Jane. "The Impact of the U.S. on Peruvian Developoment Policy." Ph.D. dissertation, Cornell University, 1971.

2107. Jordan D. C. "Marxism in Chile: An Interim View of Its Implicaiton for US Latin American Policy." **Orbis** 15 (Spring 1971): 315-337.

2108. Leacock, R. "JFK, Business, and Brazil." **Hispanic American Historical Review** 59 (November 1979): 636-673.

2109. Mcarver, Charles H. "Mining and Diplomacy: United States Interests at Cerro De Pasco, Peru, 1876-1930." Ph.D. dissertation, University of North Dakota, 1977.

2110. McGill, Margaret. "Diplomatic Relations between the United States and Argentina, 1830-1860." Ph.D. dissertation, University of Texas, Austin, 1936.

2111. McCann, Frank D. "Aviation Diplomacy: The United States and Brazil 1939-1941." **Inter-American Economic Affairs** 21 (Spring 1968): 35-50.

2112. _____. "Brazil, the United States, and World War II: A Commentary." **Diplomatic History** 3 (Winter 1979): 59-76.

2113. Mackaman, Frank H. "United States Loan

Policy, 1920-1930: Diplomatic Assumptions, Governmental Politics, and Conditions in Peru and Mexico." Ph.D. dissertation, University of Missouri, Columbia, 1977.

2114. Mathews, Joseph J. "Informal Diplomacy in the Venezuelan Crisis of 1896." **Journal of American History** 50 (September 1963): 195-212.

2115. Morris, M. "Trends in US-Brazilian Maritime Relations." **Inter-American Economic Affairs** 27 (Winter 1973): 3-24.

2116. Nolan, Louis C. "The Diplomatic and Commercial Relations of the United States and Peru, 1826-1875." Ph.D. dissertation, Duke University, 1935.

2117. Peterson, Dale W. "The Diplomatic and Commercial Relations between the United States and Peru from 1883-1918." Ph.D. dissertation, University of Minnesota, 1969.

2118. Peterson, Harold F. "Diplomatic Relations between the United States and Argentina, 1810-1870." Ph.D. dissertation, Duke University, 1933.

2119. Rosenberg, Emily S. "Anglo-American Economic Rivalry in Brazil during World War I." **Diplomatic History** 2 (Spring 1978): 131-152.

2120. _____. "Dollar Diplomacy under Wilson: An Ecuadorean Case." **Inter-American Economic Affairs** 25 (Autumn 1971): 47-54.

2121. Sherman, William R. "The Diplomatic and Commercial Relations of the United States and Chile, 1820-1914." Ph.D. dissertation, Clark University, 1923.

2122. Snyder, J. R. "William S. Culbertson in Chile: Opening the Door to a Good Neighbor, 1928-1933." **Inter-American Economic Affairs** 26 (Summer 1972): 81-96.

2123. Stewart, Watt. "Early United States-Argentine Diplomatic Relations." Ph.D. dissertation, University of Chicago, 1928.

2124. Strauss, Norman T. "Brazil in the 1870's as Seen by American Diplomats." Ph.D. dissertation, New York University, 1971.

2125. Van Cleve, John V. "The Latin American Policy of President Kennedy, A Reexamination: Case: Peru." **Inter-American**

Economic Affairs 30 (Spring 1977): 29-44.

Europe

General

2126. Aron, Raymond. "America and Euorpe: The
       Logic of Interdependence." **Survey** 19
       (Summer 1973): 1-4.
2127. _____. "Europe & the United States."
       Commentary 38 (August 1964): 54-60.
2128. Ball, George W. "America and Europe: The
       Logic of Unilateralism." **Survey** 19 (Summer
       1973): 5-11.
2129. Benoit, Emile. "The United States and a
       United Europe." **Current History** 42 (March
       1962): 172-178.
2130. Birrenbach, Kurt. "The United States and
       Western Europe: Partners or Rivals?" **Orbis**
       17 (Summer 1973): 405-414.
2131. Brosio, Manlio. "Europe and the Atlantic
       Alliance Today." **Atlantic Community
       Quarterly** 10 (Fall 1972): 285-294.
2132. Brzezinski, Zibniew K. "America and a Larger
       Europe." **World Today** 21 (October 1965):
       419-427.
2133. _____. "America and Europe." **Foreign
       Affairs** 49 (October 1970): 11-30.
2134. Bundy, McGeorge. "America;s Enduring Links
       with Europe." **Atlantic Community Quarterly**
       8 (Spring 1970): 17-30.
2135. Church, Frank. "U.S. Policy and the 'New
       Europe'." **Foreign Affairs** 45 (October
       1966): 49-57.
2136. Cottrell, Alvin J. "Nato: Cornerstone of
       U.S. Foreign Policy." **Current History** 39
       (September 1960): 136-146.
2137. Craig, G. M. "The Campaign, Nixon, and
       American Atlantic Policy." **International
       Journal** (Canada) 24 (Spring 1969): 302-
       309.
2138. Cromwell, W. C. "Europe and the Structure of
       Peace." **Orbis** 22 (Spring 1978): 11-36.
2139. Davis, Gerald H. "The Diplomatic Relations
       between the United States and Austria-
       Hungary, 1913-1917." Ph.D. dissertation,
       Vanderbilt University, 1958.
2140. Duroselle, Jean-Baptiste. "The Future of the

Atlantic Community." International Journal (Canada) 21 (Autumn 1966): 421-446.

2141.   Edwards, Owen D. "American Diplomats and Irish Coercion, 1880-1883." Journal of American Studies 1 (October 1967): 213-232.

2142.   Enthoven, Alain C. "U.S. Forces in Europe: How Many? Doing What." Foreign Affairs 53 (April 1975): 513-532.

2143.   France, Boyd. "Washington's New Look at the European Community." Atlantic Community Quarterly 8 (Summer 1970): 242-250.

2144.   Franko, L. G. "Carter Administration's Clash with Euorpean Economic Interests." Atlantic Community Quarterly 16 (Winter 1978-79): 440-451.

2145.   Friedlander, R. A. "Europe and America: The Dialogue of Disagreement." South Atlantic Quarterly 65 (Summer 1966): 303-313.

2146.   Gaddis, John L. "Was the Truman Doctrine a Real Turning Point?" Foreign Affairs 52 (January 1974): 386-402.

2147.   Garnett, John. "The United States and Europe: Defence, Technology and the Western Alliance." International Affairs 44 (April 1968): 282-287.

2148.   Gasteyger, C. "Europe and America at the Crossroads." Atlantic Community Quarterly 10 (Summer 1972): 154-166.

2149.   Gelber, Lionel. "The United States and Europe: A Marriage of Inconvenience." Foreign Affairs 41 (January 1963): 310-322.

2150.   George, James H. "United States Postwar Relief Planning: The First Phase, 1941-1943." Ph.D. dissertation, University of Wisconsin, 1970.

2151.   Gieger, Theodore. "Trends in Atlantic Relations during the 1970's." Atlantic Community Quarterly 8 (Summer 1970): 210-223.

2152.   Goodman, Elliott R. "America's Continuing Stake in Europe." Polity 4 (Summer 1972): 541-547.

2153.   Griffith, Robert. "Truman and the Historians: The Reconstruction of Postwar American History." Wisconsin Magazine of History 59 (Autumn 1975): 20-50.

2154.   Hallstein, Walter. "The European Community

and Atlantic Partnership." **International Organization** 17 (Summer 1963): 771-786.

2155. Helmreich, Jonathan A. "The Diplomacy of Apology: U.S. Bombings of Switzerland during World War II." **Air University Review** 28 (May/June 1977): 19-37.

2156. Hogan, Michael J. "The United States and the Problem of International Economic Control: American Attitudes Toward European Reconstruction, 1918-1920." **Pacific Historical Review** 44 (February 1975): 84-103.

2157. Howe, R. "Democrat Hopefuls Look at Europe." **Atlantic Community Quarterly** 10 (Summer 1972): 145-153.

2158. Huizinga, J. H. "Quiet American and the New Europe." **Atlantic Community Quarterly** 4 (Winter 1966/67): 479-486.

2159. Huntley, J. R. "United States and the European Community." **Atlantic Community Quarterly** 10 (Winter 1972-73): 527-540.

2160. Jamison, Edward A. "Irish-Americans, the Irish Question and American Diplomacy, 1895-1921." Ph.D. dissertation, Harvard University, 1944.

2161. Jenkins, R. "United States and a Uniting Europe." **Atlantic Community Quarterly** 15 (Summer 1977): 209-220.

2162. Johnson, L. B. "Making Europe Whole: An Unfinished Task." **Atlantic Community Quarterly** 4 (Winter 1966-67): 487-493.

2163. Joshua, Wynfred. "A Strategic Concept for the Defense of Europe." **Orbis** 17 (Summer 1973): 448-462.

2164. Kaiser, Karl. "U.S. and European Security in the 1970's." **Survey** 19 (Spring 1973): 11-40.

2165. Kitchens, Joseph. "Theodore Roosevelt and the Politics of War 1914-1918." **International Review of History and Political Science** 13 (May 1976): 1-16.

2166. Kohl, Wilfred L., and W. Taubman. "American Policy Toward Europe: The Next Phase." **Orbis** 17 (Spring 1973): 51-74.

2167. Korbel, Josef. "Changes in Eastern Europe and New Opportunities for American Policy." **World Politics** 18 (July 1966): 749-757.

2168. Leffler, Melvyn P. "American Policy Making

and European Stability, 1921-1933." **Pacific Historical Review** 46 (May 1977): 207-228.

2169. Lindberg, Leon N. "Decisionmaking and Integration in the European Community." **International Organization** 19 (Winter 1965): 56-80.

2170. McCloy, John J. "American Interests and Europe's Future." **Texas Quarterly** 9 (Autumn 1966): 160-175.

2171. Mahncke, D. "Europe and the United States." **Atlantic Community Quarterly** 15 (Spring 1977): 57-66.

2172. Merchant, Livingston T. "Contribution to the North American Dialogue." **Atlantic Community Quarterly** 5 (Winter 1967-68): 578-585.

2173. Morgan, Roger. "Can Europe Have a Foreign Policy?" **World Today** 30 (February 1974): 43-50.

2174. Nerlich, Uwe. "Western Europe's Relations with the United States." **Daedalus** 108 (Winter 1979): 87-111.

2175. O'Grady, Joseph P. "Religion and American Diplomacy: An Incident in Austro-American Relations." **American Jewish Historical Quarterly** 59 (June 1970): 407-423.

2176. Pfaltzgraff, Robert L. "The United States and Europe: Partners in a Multipolar World?" **Orbis** 17 (Spring 1973): 31-74.

2177. Pick, O. "Atlantic Defense and the Integration of Europe." **Atlantic Community Quarterly** 10 (Summer 1972): 174-184.

2178. Pierre, Andrew J. "What Happened to the Year of Europe?" **World Today** 30 (March 1974): 110-119.

2179. Reges, Stephen G. "Diplomatic Relations between the United States and Norway, 1933-1944." Ph.D. dissertation, Georgetown University, 1959.

2180. Richardson, R. C. "Can NATO Fashion a New Strategy." **Orbis** 17 (Summer 1973): 415-438.

2181. Roper, Elmo. "The Future of the Atlantic Community." **Atlantic Community Quarterly** 1 (Fall 1963): 316-323.

2182. Rostow, Eugene V. "Europe and the United States--the Partnership of Necessity."

Atlantic Community Quarterly 6 (Summer 1968): 216-227.

2183. _____. "Prospects for the Alliance." Atlantic Community Quarterly 3 (Spring 1965): 34-42.

2184. Serfaty, S. "America and Europe in the 1970's: Integration or Disintegration?" Orbis 17 (Spring 1973): 95-109.

2185. Smith, M. "From the Year of Europe to a Year of Carter: Continuing Patterns and Problems in Euro-American Relations." Journal of Common Market Studies 17 (September 1978): 26-44.

2186. Stanley, Timothy W., and Darnell M. Whitt. Detente Diplomacy: United States and European Security in the 1970's. Cambridge, Mass.: University Press of Cambridge, 1970.

2187. Stinchcombe, William. "Talleyrand and the American Negotiations of 1797-1798." Journal of American History 62 (December 1975): 575-590.

2188. Stock, Leo F.,ed. Consular Relations between the United States and the Papal States: Instructions and Despatches. Washington, D.C.: American Catholic Historical Association, 1945.

2189. Toskova, Vitka. "The Policy of the United States towards the Axis Satellites (1943-1944)." Bulgarian Historical Review 7 (1979): 3-26.

2190. Trask, David F. The United States in the Supreme War Council: American War Aims and Inter-Allied Strategy, 1917-1918. Middleton, Conn.: Wesleyan University Press, 1961.

2191. Truitt, Wesley B. "The Troops to Europe Decision: The Process, Politics, and Diplomacy of a Strategic Commitment." Ph.D. dissertation, Columbia University, 1968.

2192. Van Campen, S. I. P. "NATO: A Balance Sheet after Thirty Years." Orbis 23 (Summer 1979): 261-279.

2193. Van Der Beugel, Ernest H. "Relations between Europe and the United States." Atlantic Community Quarterly 5 (Summer 1967): 173-176.

2194. Vest, G. S. "Review of U.S. Policy in

Europe." **Atlantic Community Quarterly** 17
(Fall 1979): 19-36.

2195. Wohlsletter, Albert. "Threats and Promises
of Peace: Europe and American in the New
Era." **Orbis** 17 (Winter 1974): 1107-1144.

France

2196. Ambrosious, Lloyd E. "Wilson, Clemenceau and
the German Problem at the Paris Peace
Conference of 1919." **Rocky Mountain Social
Science Journal** 12 (April 1975): 69-79.
2197. _____. "Wilson, the Republicans, and French
Security After World War I." **Journal of
American History** 59 (September 1972): 341-
352.
2198. Blumenthal, Henry. "Diplomatic Relations
between the United States and France,
1836-1861." Ph.D. dissertation, University
of California, 1949.
2199. Bowman, Albert H. "The Struggle for Neutrality: A History of the Diplomatic
Relations Between the United States and
France, 1790-1801." Ph.D. dissertation,
Columbia University, 1954.
2200. Destler, I. M. "Treaty Troubles: Versailles
in Reverse." **Foreign Policy** 33 (Fall 1978-
79): 45-65.
2201. Duroselle, Jean-Baptiste. "Relations between
Two Peoples: The Singular Example of the
United States and France." **Review of
Politics** 41 (October 1979): 483-500.
2202. Gould, Lewis L. "Diplomats in the Lobby:
Franco-American Relations and the Dingley
Tariff of 1897." **Historian** 39 (August
1977): 659-680.
2203. Hamon, L. "Relations between Europe and
America--A French Viewpoint." **Atlantic
Community Quarterly** 6 (Spring 1968):29-34.
2204. Hoffmann, Stanley. "Perceptions, Reality,
and the Franco-American Conflict." **Journal
of International Affairs** 21 (1967): 57-71.
2205. Kleber, L. C. "XYZ Affair." **History Today** 23
(October 1973): 715-723.
2206. Lancaster, John E. "France and the United
States, 1870-1871: Diplomatic Relations
During the Franco-Prussian War and the
Insurrection of the Commune." Ph.D.

dissertation, University of Georgia, 1972.

2207. Loveland, Willaim A. "Deliverance from Dictatorship: American Diplomacy towards France During the 1940s." Ph.D. dissertation, Rutgers University, 1979.

2208. Miller, David H. "Some Legal Aspects of the Visit of President Wilson to Paris." **Harvard Law Review** 36 (November 1922): 51-78.

2209. Murphy, James T. "A History of American Diplomacy at the Paris Peace Conference of 1898." Ph.D. dissertation, American University, 1965.

2210. Noble, George B. "Policies and Opinions at Paris, 1919: Wilsonian Diplomacy, the Versailles Peace, and French Public Opinion." Ph.D. dissertation, Columbia University, 1935.

2211. Piore, M. " American Economist in Paris." **Massachusetts Review** 17 (Summer 1976): 219-230.

2212. Pitz, Arthur H. "United States Diplomatic Relations with Vichy France from 1940 to 1942." Ph.D. dissertation, Northern Illinois University, 1975.

2213. Rakove, Jack N. "French Diplomacy and American Politics: The First Crisis, 1779." **Mid-America** 60 (April 1979): 27-36.

2214. Redman, Margaret E. "Franco-American Diplomatic Relations, 1919-1926." Ph.D. dissertation, Stanford University 1946.

2215. Rhodes, Benjamin D. "Reassessing Uncle Shylock: The United States and the French War Debt, 1917-1929." **Journal of American History** 55 (March 1969): 787-803.

2216. Sabrier, Jules G. "United States Atlantic Alliance Policy and the Problem of France, 1963-1969." Ph.D. dissertation, Tulane University 1979.

2217. Serfaty, S. "International Anomaly: The United States and the Communist Parties in France and Italy, 1945-1947." **Studies in Comparative Communism** 8 (Spring/Summer 1975): 123-146.

2218. Solovieff, Georges. "Franco-American Relations from 1775-1800." **American Society Legion of Honor Magazine** 48 (1977): 112-117.

2219. Thomas, Robert C. "Andrew Jackson versus

France: American Policy toward France, 1834-36." **Tennessee Historical Quarterly** 35 (Spring 1975) 51-64.
2220.   Ullmann, M. "Security Aspects in French Foreign Policy." **Atlantic Community Quarterly** 12 (Spring 1974): 12-21.

Germany

2221.   Backer, John H. **The Decision to Divide Germany: American Foreign Policy in Transition.** Durham, N.C.: Duke University Press, 1978.
2222.   Baecker, T. "Arms of the Ypiranga: The German Side." **Americas** 30 (July 1973): 1-17.
2223.   Barker, Elizabeth. "The Berlin Crisis 1958-1962." **International Affairs** 39 (January 1963): 59-73.
2224.   Berbusse, Edward J. "Diplomatic Relations Between the United States and Weimar Germany: 1919-1929." Ph.D. dissertation, Georgetown University, 1952.
2225.   Buckingham, Peter H. "Diplomatic and Economic Normalcy: America's Open Door Peace with the Former Central Powers, 1921-1929." Ph.D. dissertation, Washington State University, 1980.
2226.   Burke, Bernarad V. "American Diplomats and Hitler's Rise to Power, 1930-1033: The Mission of Ambassador Sackett." Ph.D. dissertation, University of Washington, 1966.
2227.   _____. "American Economic Diplomacy and the Weimar Republic." **Mid-America** 54 (October 1972): 211-233.
2228.   Craddock, Walter R. "United States Diplomacy and the Saar Dispute, 1949-1955." **Orbis** 12 (Spring 1968): 247-267.
2229.   Doerries, Reinhard D. "Imperial Berlin and Washington: New Light on Germany's Foreign Policy and America's Entry into World War I." **Central European History** 11 (March 1978): 23-49.
2230.   Erler, Fritz. "The Alliance and the Future of Germany." **Foreign Affairs** 43 (April 1965): 436-446.
2231.   Gimbel, John. "On the Implementation of the Potsdam Agreement: An Essay on U.S. Postwar German Policy." **Political Science**

Quarterly 87 (June 1972): 242-267.
2232. Girard, Jolyon P. "American Diplomacy and the Ruhr Crisis of 1920." **Military Affairs** 39 (April 1975): 59-61.
2233. _____. "Bridge on the Rhine: American Diplomacy and the Rhineland, 1919-1923." Ph.D. dissertation, University of Maryland, 1973.
2234. _____. "Congress and Presidential Military Policy: The Occupation of Germany, 1919-1923." **Mid-America** 56 (October 1974): 211-220.
2235. Glass, George A. "The United States and West Germany: Cracks in the Security Foundation?" **Orbis** 23 (Fall 1979): 535-547.
2236. Jessup, Philip C. "Park Avenue Diplomacy—Ending the Berlin Blockage." **Political Science Quarterly** 87 (September 1972): 377-400.
2237. Johnson, Paul M. "Washington and Bonn: Dimensions of Change in Bilateral Relations." **International Organization** 33 (Autumn 1979): 451-480.
2238. Kaiser, Karl. "Great Nuclear Debate: German-American Disagreements." **Foreign Policy** 30 (Spring 1978): 83-110.
2239. Kaiser, Karl and Hans-Peter Schwarz, eds. **America and Western Europe: Problems and Prospects.** Lexington, Mass.: Lexington Books, 1978.
2240. Kalterfeliter, W. "Europe and the Nixon Doctrine: A German Point of View." **Atlantic Community Quarterly** 11 (Winter 1973/74): 456-469.
2241. Kreider, John K. "Diplomatic Relations Between Germany and the United States 1906-1913." Ph.D. dissertation, Pennsylvania State University, 1969.
2242. Kuklick, B. "Division of Germany and American Policy on Reparations." **Western Political Quarterly** 23 (June 1970): 276-293.
2243. Leader, Stefan H. "Intellectual Processes in Foreign Policy Decision-Making: The Case of German-American Relations, 1933-1941." Ph.D. dissertation, State University of New York, 1971.
2244. McGeehan, Robert J. "American Diplomacy and

the German Rearmament Question, 1950-1953." Ph.D. dissertation, Columbia University, 1969.

2245. Marks, Sally, and Denis Dulude. "German-American Relations, 1918-1921." **Mid-American** 53 (October 1971): 211-226.

2246. Martin, Curtis H. "United States Diplomacy and the Issue of Representative Government in the Former German Satellite States 1943-1946: A Study of Foreign Policy and the Foreign Policy Process." Ph.D. dissertation, Fletcher School of Law and Diplomacy, 1974.

2247. Meyer, M. C. "Mexican-German Conspiracy of 1915." **Americas** 23 (July 1966): 76-89.

2248. Morgan, Roger. "Washington and Bonn: A Case Study in Alliance Politics." **International Affairs** 46 (July 1971): 489-502.

2249. Moss, Kenneth B. "Bureaucrat as Diplomat: George S. Messersmith and the State Department's Approach to War, 1933-1941." Ph.D. dissertation, University of Minnesota, 1978.

2250. _____. "George S. Messersmith's: An American Diplomat and Nazi Germany." **Delaware History** 17 (Fall-Winter 1977): 236-249.

2251. _____. "United States, the Open Door, and Nazi Germany: 1933-1938." **South Atlantic Quarterly** 78 (Autumn 1979): 489-506.

2252. Offner, Arnold A. "American Diplomacy and Germany, 1933-1938." Ph.D. dissertation, Indiana University, 1964.

2253. Paeffgen, Hans. "The Berlin Blockade and Airlift: A Study of American Diplomacy." Ph.D. dissertation, University of Michigan, 1979.

2254. Parr, W. Grant. "The State Department and Germany." **American-German Review** 30 (February-March 1964): 4-7.

2255. Parsons, Edward B. "German-American Crisis of 1902-1903." **Historian** 33 (May 1971): 436-452.

2256. Pastusiak, Longin. "Evolution of Relations Between the United States and Federal Republic of Germany After World War II." **Polish Western AFfairs** 14 (1973): 199-223.

2257. Plischke, Elmer. "Resolving the `Berlin Question'--An Options Analysis." **World**

Affairs 131 (July-September 1968): 91-100.
2258.   _____. "Reunifying Germany--An Options
Analysis." **World Affairs** 132 (June 1969):
28-38.
2259.   _____. "West German Foreign and Defense
Policy." **Orbis** 12 (Winter 1969): 1098-
1136.
2260. Rearden, Steven L. "American Policy toward
Germany, 1944-1946." Ph.D. dissertation,
Harvard University, 1975.
2261. Schick, Jack M. "American Diplomacy and the
Berlin Negotiations." **Western Political
Quarterly** 18 (December 1965): 803-820.
2262. Small, Melvin." United States and the German
Threat to the Hemisphere, 1905-1914."
Americas 28 (January 1972) 152-170.
2263. Snyder, L. L. "Bismarck and the Lasker
Resolution, 1884." **Review of Politics** 29
(January 1967): 41-64.
2264. Spencer, F. "United States and Germany in
the Aftermath of War." **International
Affairs** 43 (October 1967): 693-703.
2265. Vardamis, A. A. "German-American Military
Fissures." **Foreign Policy** 34 (Spring
1979): 87-106.
2266. Windsor, Philip. "The Berlin Crises."
History Today 12 (June 1962): 375-384.

Great Britain

2267. Anderson, Stuart. "British Threats and the
Settlement of the Oregon Boundary
Dispute." **Pacific Northwest Quarterly** 66
(October 1975): 153-160.
2268. Birn, Donald S. "Open Diplomacy at the
Washington Conference of 1921-2: The
British and French Experience."
Comparative Studies in Society and History
12 (July 1970): 297-319.
2269. Christy, Florence J. "Anglo-American Diplo-
macy and the Decline of the British Em-
pire, 1919-1930: The British View." Ph.D.
dissertation, University of Georgia, 1970.
2270. Cooper, John M. "British Response to the
House-Grey Memorandum: New Evidence and
New Questions." **Journal of American
History** 59 (March 1973): 958-971.
2271. Duncan, Francis. "Atomic Energy and Anglo-

American Relations, 1946-1954." **Orbis** 12 (Winter 1969): 1188-1203.

2272. Gelber, Lionel. "America, the Global Balance and Britain." **Atlantic Community Quarterly** (Fall 1968): 383-402.

2273. Gray, Gertrude M. "Oil in Anglo-American Diplomatic Relations, 1920-1928." Ph.D. dissertation, University of California, 1950.

2274. Harley, Lewis R. "Our Diplomatic Relations with Great Britain--the Fisheries." Ph.D. dissertation, University of Pennsylvania, 1895.

2275. Henderson, Conway W. "The Anglo-American Treaty of 1862 in Civil War Diplomacy." **Civil War History** 15 (December 1969): 308-319.

2276. Ishii, Osamu. "Cotton-Textile Diplomacy: Japan, Great Britain and the United States, 1930-1936." Ph.D. dissertation, Rutgers University, 1977.

2277. Keck, Daniel N. "Designs for the Postwar World: Anglo-American Diplomacy, 1941-1945." Ph.D. dissertation, University of Connecticut, 1967.

2278. Kimball, Warren F. "Lend-Lease and the Open Door: The Temptation of British Opulence, 1937-1942." **Political Science Quarterly** 86 (June 1971): 232-259.

2279. Lester, Malcolm. "Anglo-American Diplomatic Problems Arising from British Naval Operations in American Waters, 1793-1802." Ph.D. dissertation, University of Virginia, 1954.

2280. Lowe, James T. "American Diplomacy within the British Empire." Ph.D. dissertation, Georgetown University, 1935.

2281. Meaney, Neville K. "The American Attitude Towards the British Empire from 1919 to 1922--A Study in the Diplomatic Relations of the English-Speaking Nations." Ph.D. dissertation, Duke University, 1959.

2282. Morrow, Rising L. "Citizenship in Anglo-American Diplomacy form 1790 to 1870." Ph.D. dissertation, Harvard University, 1932.

2283. Offner, Arnold A. "Appeasement Revisited: The United States, Great Britain, and

Germany, 1933-1940." Journal of American
History 64 (September 1977): 373-393.

2284. Pierre, Andrew J. "Nuclear Diplomacy:
Britain, France and America." Foreign
Affairs 49 (January 1971): 283-301.

2285. Rowland, Benjamin M. "Commercial Conflict
and Foreign Policy: A Study in Anglo-
American Relations, 1932-1938." Ph.D.
dissertation, Johns Hopkins University,
1975.

2286. Sargent, Thomas A. "America, Britain and the
Nine Power Treaty: A Study of Inter-War
Diplomacy and Great Power Relationships."
Ph.D. dissertation, Fletcher School of Law
and Diplomacy, 1969.

2287. Williams, Joyce E. "Colonel House and Sir
Edward Grey: A Study in Anglo-American
Diplomacy." Ph.D. dissertation, Indiana
University, 1972.

2288. Williams, Mary W. "Anglo-American Isthmian
Diplomacy, 1815-1915." Ph.D. dissertation,
Stanford University, 1914.

Mediterranean

2289. Adams, T. W., and Alvin J. Cottrell.
"American Foreign Policy and the UN
Peacekeeping force in Cyprus." Orbis 12
(Summer 1968): 490-503.

2290. Anthem, T. "Greek Colonels and the U.S.A."
Contemporary Review 216 (April 1970): 178-
183.

2291. _____. "Greek Horizon Grows Brighter." Contemporary Review 218 (Fall 1971): 57-61.

2292. Berutti, John M. "Italo-American Diplomatic
Relations, 1922-1928." Ph.D. dissertation,
Stanford University, 1960.

2293. Cortada, James W. "Conflict Diplomacy:
United States-Spanish Relation, 1855-
1868." Ph.D. dissertation, Florida State
University, 1973.

2294. Coufoudakis, Van. "U.S. Foreign Policy and
the Cyprus Question: An Interpretation."
Millenium 5 (Winter 1976): 245-268.

2295. Fischer, Leroy H., and B. J. Chandler.
"United States-Spanish Relations During
the American Civil War." Lincoln Herald 75
(Winter 1973): 134-147.

2296. Fusco, Jeremiah N. "Diplomatic Relations Between Italy and the United states, 1913-1917." Ph.D. dissertation, George Washington University, 1969.

2297. Herrick, Robert. "United States Foreign Policy and Portugal: A Reevaluation." **New Scholar** 3 (1972): 125-164.

2298. Hourihan, William J. "Marlinspike Diplomacy: The Navy in the Mediterranean, 1904." **United States Naval Institute Proceedings** 105 (January 1979): 42-51.

2299. Little, Douglas J. "Twenty Years of Turmoil: ITT, The State Department, and Spain, 1924-1944." **Business History Review** 53 (Winter 1979): 449-472.

2300. Macridis, R. C. "Greek Political Freedom and United States Foreign Policy." **Massachusetts Review** 9 (Winter 1968): 147-154.

2301. Nigro, Louis J. "Propaganda, Politics and the New Diplomacy: The Impact of Wilsonian Propaganda on Politics and Public Opinion in Italy, 1917-1919." Ph.D. dissertation, Vanderbilt University, 1979.

2302. Page, Thomas N. **Italy and the World War.** New York: Scribner, 1920.

2303. Palmer, M. "Arms Control and the Mediterranean." **World Today** 27 (November 1971): 495-502.

2304. Papandreou, A. "Greece: An American Problem." **Massachusetts Review** 12 (Autumn 1971): 655-671.

2305. Parson, Edward B. "Admiral Sims' Mission in Europe in 1917-1919 and Some Aspects of United States Naval and Foreign Wartime Policy." Ph.D. dissertation, State University of New York, 1971.

2306. Platt, Alan A., and Robert Leonardi. "American Foreign Policy and the Postwar Italian Left." **Political Science Quarterly** 93 (Summer 1978): 197-215.

2307. Pollis, Adamantia. "United States Foreign Policy towards Authoritarian Regimes in the Mediterranean." **Millennium** 4 (Spring 1975): 28-51.

2308. Powers, Richard J. "Containment: From Greece to Vietnam--and Back?" **Western Political Quarterly** 22 (December 1969): 846-861.

2309. Stern, L. "Bitter Lessons: How We Failed in

Cyprus." **Foreign Policy** 19 (Summer 1975): 34-78.
2310. Szulc, Tad. "Lisbon and Washington: Behind the Portuguese Revolution." **Foreign Policy** 21 (Winter 1975-76): 3-62.
2311. Traina, Richard P. "American Diplomacy and the Spanish Civil War, 1936-1939." Ph.D. dissertation, University of California, Berkeley, 1964.
2312. Trauth, M. Philip. ""Italo-American Diplomatic Relations, 1861-1882." Ph.D. dissertation, Catholic University 1958.
2313. Wayne, George G. "The U.S. and the Roman States." **Foreign Service Journal** 44 (February 1967): 28-31, 47-49.
2314. Winn, Thomas H. "To Embrace a Corpse: American Diplomacy and the Greek War of Independence,1821-1833." E. D. D., Ball State University, 1974.
2315. Wittner, Lawrence S. "American Policy Toward Greece During World War II." **Diplomatic History** 3 (Spring 1979): 129-150.

Soviet Union

2316. Armstrong, J. A. "Soviet-American Confrontation: A New Phase?" **Survey** 21 (Autumn 1975): 40-51.
2317. Barnet, Richard J. "U.S.-Soviet Relations: The Need for A Comprehensive Approach." **Foreign Affairs** 57 (Spring 1979): 779-795.
2318. Barnett, Roger W. "Trans-SALT: Soviet Strategic Doctrine." **Orbis** 19 (Summer 1975): 533-561.
2319. Bernath, S. L. "Squall Across the Atlantic: The Peterhoff Episode." **Journal of Southern History** 34 (August 1968): 382-401.
2320. Bowers, Robert E. "American Diplomacy, the 1933 Wheat Conference, and Recognition of the Soviet Union." **Agricultural History** 49 (January 1966): 39-52.
2321. Brown, S. "Cooling-off Period for U.S.-Soviet Relations." **Foreign Policy** 28 (Fall 1977): 3-21.
2322. Brumberg, A. "Dissent in Russia." **Foreign Affairs** 52 (July 1974): 781-798.
2323. Buhite, Russell D. "Soviet-American Rela-

tions and the Repatriation of Prisoners of War, 1945." **Historian** 35 (May 1973): 384-397.

2324. Burt, Richard. "The Scope and Limits of SALT." **Foreign Affairs** 56 (July 1978): 751-770.

2325. Campbell, John C. "Soviet-American Relations." **Current History** 61 (October 1971): 193-197, 246.

2326. _____. "Soviet-American Relations: Conflict and Cooperation." **Current History** 53 (October 1967): 193-202, 241.

2327. Clemens, Walter C. "Nicholas II to SALT II: Change and Continuity in East-West Diplomacy." **International Affairs** 48 (July 1973): 385-401.

2328. Cottrell, Alvin J., and R. M. Burell. "Soviet-U.S. Naval Competition in the Indian Ocean." **Orbis** 18 (Winter 1975): 1109-1128.

2329. Danaher, K. "Namibia: Profits, Racism and the Soviet Threat." **Monthly Review** 33 (January 1982): 36-47.

2330. Dawson, Raymond H. **The Decision to Aid Russia, 1941: Foreign Policy and Domestic Politics.** Chapel Hill: University of North Carolina Press, 1959.

2331. De Luca, Anthony R. "Soviet-American Politics and the Turkish Straits." **Political Science Quarterly** 92 (Fall 1977): 503-524.

2332. De Santis, Hugh S. "The Diplomacy of Silence: The American Foreign Service, The Soviet Union and the Cold War, 1933-1946." Ph.D. dissertation, University of Chicago, 1978.

2333. Dobriansky, Lev E. "Review Of U.S. Policy Toward the USSR: A Major Theme for the 1967 Captive Nations Week." **Ukrainian Quarterly** 23 (Spring 1967): 27-42.

2334. _____. "Revived Interest in U.S. Diplomatic Relations with Ukraine and Byelorussia." **Ukrainian Quarterly** 18 (Autumn 1962): 225-232.

2335. Dukes, Paul. "Two Great Nations, 1815-50: Russia and the United States." **History Today** 20 (February 1970): 94-106.

2336. Egan, Clifford L. "Pressure Groups, the Department of State, and the Abrogation of the Russian-American Treaty of 1832." **Proceedings of the American Philosophical Society** 115 (August 1971): 328-334.

2337. Elegant, Robert S. "China, the U.S. and Soviet Expansionism." **Commentary** 61 (February 1976): 39-46.

2338. Elliott, M. "United States and Forced Repatriation of Soviet Citizens, 1944-47." **Political Science Quarterly** 88 (June 1973): 253-275.

2339. Fainsod, Merle. "Some Reflections on Soviet-American Relations." **American Political Science Review** 62 (December 1968): 1093-1103.

2340. Finley, D. D. "Detente and Soviet-American Trade: An Approach to a Political Balance Sheet." **Studies in Comparative Communism** 8 (Spring 1975): 66-97.

2341. Fusfeld, Herbert I. "US-USSR Technological Interactions." **Survey** 23 (Spring 1977-78): 105-111.

2342. Garver, J. W. "Sino-Vietnamese Conflict and the Sino-American Rapprochement." **Political Science Quarterly** 96 (Fall 1981): 445-464.

2343. Gelber, Harry G. "Sino-Soviet Relationship and the United States." **Orbis** 15 (Spring 1971): 118-133.

2344. Gilbert, Stephen P. "Soviet-American Military Aid Competition in the Third World." **Orbis** 13 (Winter 1970): 1117-1137.

2345. Goldwater, Barry M. "Perilous Conjuncture: Soviet Ascendancy and American Isolationism." **Orbis** 15 (Spring 1971): 53-64.

2346. Griffiths, David M. "American Commercial Diplomacy in Russia, 1780 to 1783." **William and Mary Quarterly** 27 (July 1970): 379-410.

2347. Hagan, Kenneth J., and Jacob W. Kipp. "U.S. and U.S.S.R. Naval Strategy." **United States Naval Institute Proceedings** 99 (November 1973): 38-44.

2348. Hanson, Betty C. "American Diplomatic Reporting from the Soviet Union, 1934-1941." Ph.D. dissertation, Columbia University, 1966.

2349. Harriman, W. Averell. **America and Russia in a Changing World: A Half Century of Per-**

sonal Observation. New York: Doubleday,
         1971.
2350.   _____. **Peace with Russia?** New York: Simon
         and Schuster, 1959.
2351.   Hildt, John C. "Early Diplomatic Negotia-
         tions of the United States with Russia."
         Ph.D. dissertation, Johns Hopkins Univer-
         sity, 1906.
2352.   Hopmann, P. Terrence, and T. C. Smith. "Ap-
         plication of a Richardson Process Mode:
         Soviet-American Interactions in the Test
         Ban Negotiations 1962-1963." **Journal of
         Conflict Resolution** 21 (December 1977):
         701-726.
2353.   Humphrey, Hubert H. "The Course of Soviet
         Foreign Policy and Soviet-American
         Relations in the 1970's." **Orbis** 15 (Spring
         1971): 65-71.
2354.   Husband, William B. "Soviet Perceptions of
         US 'Positions-of-Strength' Diplomacy in
         the 1970's." **World Politics** 31 (July
         1979): 495-517.
2355.   Ikle, F. D. "What to Hope for and Worry
         About in SALT." **Atlantic Community
         Quarterly** 15 (Winter 1977-78): 450-459.
2356.   Irani, Robert G. "The Azerbaijan Crisis,
         1945-1946: An Options Analysis of United
         States Policy." Ph.D. dissertation,
         University of Maryland, 1973.
2357.   Kaufman, Burton I. "The United States
         Response to the Soviet Economic Offensive
         of the 1950's." **Diplomatic History** 2
         (Spring 1978): 153-165.
2358.   Kennan, George F. "The United States and the
         Soviet Union, 1917-1976." **Foreign Affairs**
         54 (July 1976): 670-690.
2359.   Killen, Linda. "The Search for a Democratic
         Russia: Bakhmetev and the United States."
         Diplomatic History 2 (Summer 1978): 237-
         256.
2360.   Kintner, William R. "US and the USSR: Con-
         flict and Cooperation." **Atlantic Community
         Quarterly** 12 (Spring 1974): 81-102.
2361.   Kushner, Howard I. "The Russian-American
         Diplomatic Contest for the Pacific Basin
         and the Monroe Doctrine." **Journal of the
         West** 15 (April 1976): 65-80.
2362.   _____. "Russian Fleet and the American

Civil War: Another View." **Historian** 34
(August 1972): 633-649.

2363. Laird, Roy D. "Grain as a Foreign Policy
Tool in Dealing with the Soviets: A
Contingency Plan." **Policy Studies Journal**
6 (Summer 1978): 533-537.

2364. Langer, John D. "The Formulation of American
Aid Policy Toward the Soviet Union, 1940-
1943: The Hopkins Shop and the Department
of State." Ph.D. dissertation, Yale
niversity, 1975.

2365. Latting, James T. "The U.S. Approach to
SALT." **Millennium** 3 (Spring 1974): 76-82.

2366. Lensen, G. A. "Russia and the United States
in Asia." **Russian Review** 24 (April 1965):
99-110.

2367. Lieberman, B. "Coalitions and Conflict
Resolution." **American Behavioral Scientist**
18 (March 1975): 557-581.

2368. Lodal, Jan M. "Salt II and American
Security." **Foreign Affairs** 57 (Winter
1978-79): 245-268.

2369. McCauley, B. "Hungary and Suez, 1956: The
Limits of Soviet and American Power."
Journal of Contemporary History 16
(October 1981): 777-800.

2370. McDuffee, Ray W. "The State Department and
the Russian Revolutions, March-November,
1917." Ph.D. dissertation, Georgetown
University, 1954.

2371. McGeehan, Robert J. "American Policies and
the US-Soviet Relationship." **World Today**
34 (September 1978): 346-354.

2372. Maddox, Robert J. "Woodrow Wilson, the
Russian Embassy and Siberian Inter-
vention." **Pacific Historical Review** 36
(November 1967): 435-448.

2373. Maddux, Thomas R. "American Diplomats and
the Soviet Experiment: The View from the
Moscow Embassy, 1934-1939." **South Atlantic
Quarterly** 74 (Autumn 1975): 468-487.

2374. ———. "Watching Stalin Maneuver Between
Hitler and the West: American Diplomats
and Soviet Diplomacy, 1934-39." **Diplomatic
History** 1 (Spring 1977): 140-154.

2375. Manning, Donald. "Soviet-American
Relations." Ph.D. dissertation, Michigan
State University, 1979.

2376. Matlock, Jack F. "US-Soviet Relations in the
       1970's." **Survey** 19 (Spring 1973): 132-139.
2377. Metzl, L. "Reflections in the Soviet Secret
       Police and Intelligence Services." **Orbis**
       18 (Fall 1974): 917-930.
2378. Mitchell, D. W. "Soviet Naval Challenge."
       Orbis 14 (Spring 1970): 129-153.
2379. Nitze, Paul H. "The Vladivostok Accord and
       Salt II." **Review of Politics** 37 (April
       1975): 147-160.
2380. Payne, R. J. "Soviet/Cuban Factor in the New
       United States Policy toward Southern
       Africa." **Africa Today** 25 (April 1978): 7-
       26.
2381. Pfaltzgraff, Robert L. "Multi-polarity,
       Alliances, and US-Soviet-Chinese
       Relations." **Orbis** 17 (Fall 1973): 720-736.
2382. Pipes, Richard. "America, Russia and Europe
       in the Light of the Nixon Doctrine."
       Survey 19 (Summer 1973): 30-40.
2383. ———. "Russia's Mission, America's Des-
       tiny." **Encounter** 35 (October 1970): 3-11.
2384. Plischke, Elmer. "Eisenhower's 'Correspon-
       dence Diplomacy' with the Kremlin: Case
       Study in Summit Diplomatics." **Journal of
       Politics** 30 (February 1968): 137-159.
2385. Radosh, R. "John Spargo and Wilson's Russian
       Policy, 1920." **Journal of American History**
       52 (December 1965): 548-565.
2386. Rockefeller, Nelson A. "Purpose and Policy."
       Foreign Affairs 38 (April 1960): 370-390.
2387. Schwartz, Harry. "The Moscow-Peking-
       Washington Triangle." **Annals of the
       American Academy of Political and Social
       Science** 414 (July 1974): 41-50.
2388. Scott, Robert. "China, Russia and the United
       States." **Foreign Affairs** 48 (January
       1970): 334-343.
2389. Sonnenfeldt, H. "Russia, America and
       Detente." **Foreign Affairs** 56 (January
       1978): 275-294.
2390. Stults, T. "Roosevelt, Russian Persecution
       of Jews, and American Public Opinion."
       Jewish Social Studies 33 (January 1971):
       13-22.
2391. Trani, Eugene P. "Russia in 1905: The View
       from the American Embassy." **Review of
       Politics** 31 (January 1969): 48-65.

2392. _____. "Woodrow Wilson and the Decision to Intervene in Russia: A Reconsideration." **Journal of Modern History** 48 (September 1976): 440-461.

2393. Triska, Jan F., and David D. Finley. "Soviet-American Relations: A Multiple Symmetry Mode." **Journal of Conflict Resolution** 9 (March 1965): 37-53.

2394. Tynbee, A. J. "Russian-American Relations: The Case for Second Thoughts." **Journal of International Affairs** 22 (1968): 1-4.

2395. Ulam, Adam B. "Detente under Soviet Eyes." **Foreign Policy** 24 (Fall 1976): 145-159.

2396. _____. "U.S.-Soviet Relations: Unhappy Coexistence." **Foreign Affairs** 57 (1978): 555-571.

2397. Veron, G. D. "Controlled Conflict: Soviet Perceptions of Peaceful Coexistence." **Orbis** 23 (Summer 1979): 271-297.

2398. Walters, R. S. **American and Soviet Aid: A Comparative Analysis.** Pittsburgh: University of Pittsburgh Press, 1970.

2399. Weise, E. "Mr. X, Russia, and Vietnam." **Modern Age** 19 (Fall 1975): 397-406.

2400. Weissman, B. M. "Aftereffects of the American Relief Mission to Soviet Russia." **Russian Review** 29 (October 1970): 411-421.

2401. Wessel, Thomas R. "Wheat for the Soviet Masses: M. L. Wilson and the Montana Connection." **Montana** 31 (April 1981): 42-53.

2402. Wessell, Hils H. "Changing Soviet-American Relations." **Current History** 77 (October 1979): 97-100, 132.

2403. _____. "Political and International Implications of Soviet Dissent." **Orbis** 17 (Fall 1973): 793-802.

2404. Whiting, Alan S. "Sino-American Detente." **China Quarterly** 82 (June 1980): 334-341.

2405. Zagoria, D. S. "Into the Breach: New Soviet Alliances in the Third World." **Foreign Affairs** 57 (Spring 1979): 733-754.

2406. Zimmerman, William, and R. Axelrod. "Lessons of Vietnam and Soviet Foreign Policy." **World Politics** 34 (October 1981): 1-24.

Eastern Europe

2407. Bromke, Adam. "The United States and Eastern

Europe." **International Journal** 21 (Spring 1966): 211-217.

2408. Brzezinski, Zbigniew K. "The Framework of East-West Reconciliation." **Foreign Affairs** 46 (January 1968): 256-275.

2409. Chandler, Harriette L. "The Transition to Cold Warrior: The Evolution of W. Averell Harriman's Assessment of the U.S.A.'s Polish Policy, October 1943--Warsaw Uprising." **East European Quarterly** 10 (Summer 1976): 229-245.

2410. Costigliola, Frank. "American Foreign Policy in the 'Nut Cracker': The United States and Poland in the 1920's." **Pacific Historical Review** 48 (February 1979): 85-105.

2411. Davis, Lynn E. "United States Policy Toward Eastern Europe, 1941-1945: The Escalation of Conflict and Commitment." Ph.D. dissertation, Columbia University, 1971.

2412. De Santis, Hugh S. "Conflicting Images of the USSR: American Career Diplomats and the Balkans, 1944-1946." **Political Science Quarterly** 94 (Fall 1979): 475-494.

2413. _____. "In Search of Yugoslavia: Anglo-American Policy and Policy-making 1943-45." **Journal of Contemporary History** 16 (July 1981): 541-563.

2414. Devasia, A. Thomas. "The United States and the Formation of Greater Romania, 1914-1918: A Study in Diplomacy and Propaganda." Ph.D. dissertation, Boston College, 1970.

2415. Fascell, Dante B. "The Helsinki Accord: A Case Study." **Annals of the American Academy of Political and Social Science** 442 (March 1979): 69-76.

2416. Garrett, Stephen A. "Eastern European Ethnic Groups and American Foreign Policy." **Political Science Quarterly** 93 (Summer 1978): 301-323.

2417. _____. "On Dealing with National Communism: The Lessons of Yugoslavia." **Western Political Quarterly** 26 (September 1973): 529-549.

2418. Gibson, Hugh S., and Samuel M. Vauclain. **Poland: Her Problems and Her Future.** New York: American-Polish Chamber of Commerce and Industry, 1920.

2419. Hammersmith, Jack L. "American Diplomacy and the Polish Question, 1943-1945." Ph.D. dissertation, University of Virginia, 1970.

2420. Hammett, Hugh B. "America's Non-Policy in Eastern Europe and the Origins of the Cold War." **Survey** 19 (Autumn 1973): 144-162.

2421. Hayden, Eric W. **Technology Transfer to East Europe: United States Corporate Experience.** New York: Praeger, 1976.

2422. Holzman, Franklyn D., and Robert Legvold. "The Economics and Politics of East-West Relations." **International Organization** 29 (Winter 1975): 275-320.

2423. Kaczurba, Janusz. "Polish-American Economic Relations." **Polish Western Affairs** 20 (1979): 64-78.

2424. Korbonski, Andrzej. "U.S. Policy in East Europe." **Current History** 48 (March 1965): 129-134, 182.

2425. Kousoulas, D. George. "Truman Doctrine and the Stalin-Tito Rift: A Reappraisal." **South Atlantic Quarterly** 72 (Summer 1965): 560-577.

2426. Kutolowski, John. "The Effect of the Polish Insurrection of 1863 on the American Civil War Diplomacy." **Historian** 27 (August 1965): 560-577.

2427. Lerski, George J. "Sources for the Diplomatic History of Polish-American Relations." **Polish American Studies** 27 (Spring-Summer 1970): 20-32.

2428. Licklider, R. E. "Soviet Control of Eastern Europe: Morality Versus American National Interest." **Political Science Quarterly** 91 (Winter 1976/77): 619-629.

2429. London, Kurt. **The Making of Foreign Policy-- East and West.** Philadelphia: Lippincott, 1965.

2430. Lukaszewski, J. "United States, the West, and the Future of Eastern Europe." **Journal of International Affairs** 22 (1968): 16-25.

2431. McWhinney, Edward, ed. **Law, Foreign Policy, and the East-West Detente.** Toronto: University of Toronto Press, 1964.

2432. Marinescu, Beatrice, and Serband Radulescu-Zoner. "American Consular Reports About Romania's Struggle to Win Independence."

East European Quarterly 9 (Fall 1978): 349-358.
2433. Markovich, Stephen C. "American Foreign Aid and Yugoslav Internal Policies." **East European Quarterly** 9 (Summer 1975): 185-195.
2434. Mosely, Philip E. "The U.S. and East-West Detente: The Range of Choice." **Journal of International Affairs** 22 (1968): 5-15.
2435. Moss, Kenneth B. "United States and Central Europe, 1861-1871: Some American Approaches to National Development and the Balance of Power." **Historian** 39 (February 1977): 248-269.
2436. Orzell, Laurence J. "A 'Painful Problem': Poland in Allied Diplomacy, February-July, 1945." **Mid-America** 59 (October 1977): 147-169.
2437. Rhodes, Benjamin D. "The Origins of Finnish-American Friendship, 1919-1941." **Mid-America** 54 (January 1972): 3-29.
2438. Scowcroft, Brent. "Congress and Foreign Policy: An Examination of Congressional Attitudes Toward the Foreign Aid Programs to Spain and Yugoslavia." Ph.D. dissertation, Columbia University, 1967.
2439. Thomas, J. R. "U.S.-East European Relations: Strategic Issues." **Orbis** 12 (Fall 1968): 754-773.
2440. Ullmann, W. "Some Aspects of American-Czechoslovakian Relations, 1945-1947." **Eastern European Quarterly** 10 (Spring 1976): 65-76.
2441. Whitcomb, Roger S. "The United States and East Europe." **Current History** 60 (May 1971): 263-268, 307.
2442. White, Merril A. "Some Considerations of United States Foreign Policy Toward Eastern Europe: 1941-1964." **Polish Review** 10 (Winter 1965): 3-42.

Far East and Pacific

General

2443. Adams, F. C. "Road to Pearl Harbor: A Reexamination of American Far Eastern Policy, July 1937-December 1938." **Journal**

of **American History** 58 (June 1971): 73-92.
2444. Albinski, H. S. "American-Australian Security Policies: The Current Phase." **Pacific Affairs** 51 (Winter 1978-79): 606-619.
2445. Allen, Horace N. **Korea: Fact and Fancy.** Seoul, Korea: Press of Methodist Publishing House, 1904.
2446. Barnett, A. Doak. "The New Multipolar Balance in East Asia: Implications for United States Policy." **Annals of the American Academy of Political and Social Science** 390 (July 1970): 73-86.
2447. Baron, Dona G. "Policy for 'Paradise': A Study of United States Decision-Making Processes Respecting the Trust Territories of the Pacific Islands and the Impact Thereupon of United Nations Oversight." Ph.D. dissertation, Columbia University, 1973.
2448. Buhite, Russell D. "'Major Interests': American Policy toward China, Taiwan, and Korea, 1945-1950." **Pacific Historical Review** 47 (August 1978): 425-451.
2449. Clubb, O. Edmund. "Sino-American Relations and the Future of Formosa." **Political Science Quarterly** 80 (March 1965): 1-21.
2450. Clyde, Paul H. "Historical Reflections on American Relations with the Far East." **South Atlantic Quarterly** 61 (Autumn 1962): 437-449.
2451. Dennett, Tyler. **Americans in Eastern Asia.** New York: Barnes and Noble, 1941.
2452. Fithian, F. J. "Dollars without the Flag: The Case of Sinclair and Sakhalin Oil." **Pacific Historical Review** 39 (May 1970): 205-222.
2453. Fleming, D. F. "What Is Our Role in East Asia?" **Western Political Quarterly** 18 (March 1965): 73-86.
2454. Garver, J. W. "Taiwan's Russian Option: Image and Reality." **Asian Survey** 18 (July 1978): 751-766.
2455. Gordon, Bernard K. "Asian Angst and American Policy." **Foreign Policy** 47 (Summer 1982): 46-65.
2456. Gordon, Lincoln. "American Planning for Taiwan, 1942-1945." **Pacific Historical Review** 37 (May 1968): 201-228.

2457.   Greene, F. "United States and Asia in 1981."
        Asian Survey 22 (January 1982): 1-12.
2458.   Hackler, Rhoda. "Our Men in the Pacific: A
        Chronicle of U.S. Consular Officers at
        Seven Ports in the Pacific Islands and
        Australia During the 19th Century." Ph.D.
        dissertation, University of Hawaii, 1979.
2459.   Ham, Yung-Chul. "The Carter Administration's
        Policy Toward East Asia: With Focus on
        Korea." **American Studies International** 18
        (Autumn 1979): 35-48.
2460.   Harriman, W. Averell. "The United States and
        the Far East." **Annals of the American
        Academy of Political and Social Science**
        342 (July 1962): 89-104.
2461.   Hart, Robert A. **The Eccentric Tradition:
        American Diplomacy in the Far East.** New
        York: Charles Scribner's Sons, 1976.
2462.   Holsinte, Jon D. "American Diplomacy in
        Samoa 1884-1889." Ph.D. dissertation,
        Indiana University, 1971.
2463.   Hornbeck, Stanley K. **The United States and
        the Far East.** Boston: World Peace
        Foundation, 1942.
2464.   Hoxie, R. Gordon. "Presidential Leadership
        and American Foreign Policy: Some
        Reflections on the Taiwan Issue, with
        Particular Considerations on Alexander
        Hamilton, Dwight Eisenhower, and Jimmy
        Carter." **Presidential Studies Quarterly** 9
        (Spring 1979): 131-143.
2465.   Hunt, C. L., and L. Lacar. "Social Distance
        and American Policy in the Philippines."
        Sociology and Social Research 57 (July
        1973): 495-509.
2466.   Karnow, S. "East Asia in 1978: The Great
        Transformation." **Foreign Affairs** 57
        (1978): 589-612.
2467.   Kash, Don E. "United States Policy for
        Quemoy and Matsu: Pros, Cons, and Pros-
        pects." **Western Political Quarterly** 16
        (December 1963): 912-923.
2468.   Klein, David H. "Anglo-American Diplomacy
        and the Pacific War: The Politics of
        Confrontation." Ph.D. dissertation,
        University of Pennsylvania, 1977.
2469.   Lai, Nathan. "United States Policy and the
        Diplomacy of Limited War in Korea: 1950-

1951." Ph.D. dissertation, University of Massachusetts, 1974.

2470. Laitin, D. D. "Somali Territorial Claims in International Perspective." **Africa Today** 23 (April 1976): 29-38.

2471. Langley, Harold D. "Gideon Nye and the Formosa Annexation Scheme." **Pacific Historical Review** 34 (November 1965): 397-420.

2472. Mackirdy, K. A. "Fear of American Intervention as a Factor in British Expansion: Western Australia and Natal." **Pacific Historical Review** 35 (May 1966): 123-139.

2473. Martin, James R. "Institutionalization and Professionalization of the Republic of Korea Army: The Impact of United States Military Assistance Through Development of a Military Schools System." Ph.D. dissertation, Harvard University, 1973.

2474. Matray, James A. "An End to Indifference: America's Korean Policy during World War II." **Diplomatic History** 2 (Spring 1978): 181-196.

2475. Matsuda, Takeshi. "Woodrow Wilson's Dollar Diplomacy in the Far East: The New Chinese Consortium, 1917-1921." Ph.D. dissertation, University of Wisconsin, 1979.

2476. Minger, Ralph E. "From Law to Diplomacy: The Summons to the Philippines." **Mid-America** 53 (April 1971): 103-120.

2477. Neu, C. E. "Theodore Roosevelt and American Involvement in the Far East, 1901-1909." **Pacific Historical Review** 35 (November 1966): 433-449.

2478. Paige, Glenn D. **The Korea Decision.** New York: Free Press, 1968.

2479. Park, Chang J. "American Foreign Policy in Korea and Vietnam: Comparative Case Studies." **Review of Politics** 37 (January 1975): 20-47.

2480. Patterson, Wayne. "Sugar-Coated Diplomacy: Horace Allen and Korean Immigration to Hawaii, 1902-1905." **Diplomatic History** 3 (Winter 1979): 19-38.

2481. Poon-Kim, Shee. "A Decade of ASEAN, 1967-1977." **Asian Survey** 17 (August 1977): 753-770.

2482. Pratt, L. "Anglo-American Naval Conversations on the Far East of January, 1938."

International Affairs 47 (October 1971):
745-763.
2483. Ravenal, Earl C. "The Nixon Doctrine and Our
Asian Commitments." **Foreign Affairs** 49
(January 1971): 201-217.
2484. Reed, John J. "American Diplomatic Relations
with Australia During the Second World
War." Ph.D. dissertation, University of
Southern California, 1969.
2485. Reischauer, Edwin O. **Toward A New Far
Eastern Policy.** New York: Foreign Policy
Association, 1950.
2486. _____. **Wanted: An Asian Policy.** New York:
Knopf, 1955.
2487. Roebuck, James R. "The United States and
East Asia, 1909-1913: A Study of the Far
Eastern Diplomacy of William Howard Taft."
Ph.D. dissertation, University of
Virginia, 1977.
2488. Roucek, J. S. "Pacific in Geopolitics."
Contemporary Review 206 (February 1965):
63-76.
2489. Sbrega, John J. "Anglo-American Relations an
the Politics of Coalition Diplomacy in the
Far East During the Second World War."
Ph.D. dissertation, Georgetown University,
1974.
2490. Scalapino, Robert A. "The United States and
Asia." **Air University Review** 21 (March-
April 1970): 37-51.
2491. Shepardson, Donald E. "American Policy in
Asia: Tenacity in the Pursuit of Folly
(1973)." **Midwest Quarterly** 21 (Autumn
1979): 33-45.
2492. Siracusa, Joseph M. "Australian-American
Relations, 1980: A Historical Perspec-
tive." **Orbis** 24 (Summer 1980): 271-287.
2493. Snyder, Richard C., and Glenn D. Paige. "The
United States Decision to Resist Aggres-
sion in Korea: The Application of an
Analytic Scheme." **Administrative Science
Quarterly** 3 (December 1958): 341-378.
2494. Tate, Merze. "Twisting the Lion's Tail over
Hawaii." **Pacific Historical Review** 36
(February 1967): 27-46.
2495. _____. "U.S. Diplomacy: Influence of
Sandwich Islands Missionaries and the
ABCFM." **Oregon Historical Quarterly** 68

(March 1967): 53-74.
2496. Treadgold, Donald W. "The United States and East Asia: A Theme with Variations." **Pacific Historical Review** 49 (February 1980): 1-27.
2497. Utley, Jonathan G. "The Department of State and the Far East, 1937-1941: A Study of the Ideas Behind Its Diplomacy." Ph.D. dissertation, University of Illinois, Urbana-Champaign, 1970.
2498. Walker, Richard L. "The Future of U.S. Trans-Pacific Alliances." **Orbis** 19 (Fall 1975): 904-924.
2499. Weiss, Thomas J. "Taiwan and U.S. Policy." **Orbis** 12 (Winter 1969): 1165-1187.
2500. Wilson, Dick. "The American Quarter-Century in Asia." **Foreign Affairs** 51 (July 1973): 811-830.
2501. Woodard, Kim. "The Second Transition: America in Asia under Carter." **SAIS Review** 6 (Winter 1981): 129-148.
2502. Yoder, A. "Options for a New Policy in East Asia." **Asian Survey** 16 (May 1976): 478-491.
2503. Young, Kenneth T. "Asia and America at the Crossroads." **Annals of the American Academy of Political and Social Science** 384 (July 1969): 53-65.

China

2504. Alvarez, David J. "The Department of State and the Abortive Papal Mission to China, August, 1918." **Catholic Historical Review** 62 (July 1976): 455-463.
2505. Anderson, David L. "China Policy and Presidential Policies, 1952." **Presidential Studies Quarterly** 10 (Winter 1980): 79-90.
2506. Armstrong, Hamilton F. "Thoughts Along the China Border: Will Neutrality Be Enough?" **Foreign Affairs** 38 (January 1960): 238-260.
2507. Arnold, Julean H. **China Through the American Window.** Shanghai: American Chamber of Commerce, 1932.
2508. Aspaturian, Vernon D. "The USSR, the USA and China in the Seventies." **Survey** 19 (Spring 1973): 103-131.

2509. Barnett, A. Doak. "Military-Security Relations between China and the United States." **Foreign Affairs** 55 (April 1977): 584-597.

2510. Berger, Roland. "China's Policy and the Nixon Visit." **Journal of Contemporary Asia** 2 (1972): 3-16.

2511. Bethell, T. N. "China at Eye-level: Stripping Away the Stereotypes While There's Still Time." **Washington Monthly** 11 (October 1979): 18-28.

2512. Bobrow, D. B. "Chinese Communist Conflict System." **Orbis** 9 (Winter 1966): 930-952.

2513. Brecht, Arnold. "Fairness in Foreign Policy: The Chinese Issue." **Social Research** 28 (Spring 1961): 95-104.

2514. Briggs, Herbert W. "American Consular Rights in Communist China." **American Journal of International Law** 44 (April 1950): 243-258.

2515. Brown, R. G. "Chinese Politics and American Policy: A New Look at the Triangle." **Foreign Policy** 23 (Summer 1976): 3-23.

2516. Buhite, Russell D. "Missed Opportunities: American Policy and the Chinese Communists, 1949." **Mid-America** 61 (October 1979): 179-199.

2517. _____. "Nelson Johnson and American Policy toward China, 1925-1928." **Pacific Historical Review** 35 (November 1966): 451-466.

2518. Callis, Helmut G. "The Chinese-United States Stalemate." **Current History** 37 (December 1959): 339-344.

2519. Chadbourn, Charles C. "Sailors and Diplomats: U.S. Naval Operations in China, 1865-1877." Ph.D. dissertation, University of Washington, 1976.

2520. Chan, Steve. "Rationality, Bureaucratic Politics and Belief System: Explaining the Chinese Policy Debate, 1964-1966." **Journal of Peace Research** 16 (1979): 333-347.

2521. Chiao, Joseph M. "The Beginning of American-Chinese Diplomatic Relations: The Cushing Mission and the Treaty of Wanghia of 1844." Ph.D. dissertation, University of Notre Dame, 1954.

2522. Chong, K. R. "Abortive American-Chinese Project for Chinese Revolution, 1908-

1911." **Pacific Historical Review** 41 (February 1972): 54-70.

2523. Choundhury, G. W. "China Revisited." **Orbis** 20 (Fall 1976): 601-612.

2524. Clubb, O. Edmund. "China and the United States: Beyond Ping-Pong." **Current History** 61 (September 1971): 129-134, 180.

2525. Cohen, Jerome A. "China Policy for the Next Administration." **Foreign Affairs** 55 (October 1976): 20-37.

2526. _____. "Recognizing China." **Foreign Affairs** 50 (October 1971): 30-43.

2527. Cohen, Warren I. "America and the May Fourth Movement: The Response to Chinese Nationalism, 1917-1921." **Pacific Historical Review** 35 (Fall 1966): 83-100.

2528. _____. "Development of Chinese Communist Policy toward the United States, 1922-1933." **Orbis** 11 (Spring 1967): 219-237.

2529. _____. "Development of Chinese Communist Policy toward the United States, 1934-1945." **Orbis** 11 (Summer 1967): 551-569.

2530. De Dubnic, Vladimir R. "Europe and the New U.S. Policy Toward China." **Orbis** 16 (Spring 1972): 85-104.

2531. Fairbank, John K. "China Missions in History: Some Introductory Remarks." **Journal of Presbyterian History** 49 (Winter 1971): 283-286.

2532. _____. "'American China Policy' to 1898: A Misconception." **Pacific Historical Review** 39 (November 1970): 409-420.

2533. _____. "The New China and the American Connection." **Foreign Affairs** 51 (October 1972): 31-43.

2534. Fall, Bernard B., Richard N. Goodwin, George McGovern, and John P. Roche. "Containing China: A Round-Table Discussion." **Commentary** 41 (May 1966): 23-41.

2535. Fleming, D. F. "Can We Escape from Containing China?" **Western Political Quarterly** 24 (March 1971): 163-177.

2536. Ford, Andrew T. "The Diplomacy of the Boxer Uprising, with Special Reference to American Foreign Policy." Ph.D. dissertation, University of Wisconsin, 1971.

2537. Gandhi, Shanti S. "United States Diplomatic Relations with China, 1869-1882." Ph.D.

dissertation, Georgetown University, 1954.
2538. Gass, Oscar. "China and the United States."
Commentary 34 (November 1962): 369-397.
2539. Gelber, Harry G. "Limiting Factors in a
Reconsideration of U.S. China Policies."
Orbis 14 (Fall 1970): 599-626.
2540. _____. "United States and China: The
Evolution of Policy." **International
Affairs** 46 (October 1970): 682-697.
2541. George, Brian T. "The State Department and
Sun Yat-sen: American Policy and the
Revolutionary Disintegration of China,
1920-1924." **Pacific Historical Review** 46
(August 1977): 387-408.
2542. Ghosh, Partha S. "Passage of the Silver Pur-
chase Act of 1934: The China Lobby and the
Issue of China Trade." **Indian Journal of
American Studies** 6 (January/July 1976):
18-29.
2543. Guhin, Michael A. "The United States and the
Chinese People's Republic: The Non-Recog-
nition Policy Reviewed." **International
Affairs** 45 (January 1969): 44-63.
2544. Halperin, Morton H. "America and Asia: The
Impact of Nixon's China Policy." **Foreign
Service Journal** 49 (August 1972): 12-19,
28.
2545. Holdcamper, Forrest R. "A History of
American Diplomatic Relations Regarding
Manchuria." Ph.D. dissertation, Clark
University, 1934.
2546. Hubert, Mary G. "The Role of Nelson Trusler
Johnson in Sino-American Diplomatic
Relations, 1930-1935." Ph.D. dissertation,
Catholic University, 1964.
2547. Hunt, M. H. "American Remission of the Boxer
Indemnity: A Reappraisal." **Journal of
Asian Studies** 31 (May 1972): 539-559.
2548. Kalicki, J. H. "China, America, and Arms
Control." **World Today** 26 (April 1970):
147-155.
2549. _____. "Sino-American Relations after
Cambodia." **World Today** 26 (September
1970): 383-392.
2550. Kennedy, Edward M. "Normal Relations with
China: Good Law, Good Policy." **Policy
Review** 8 (Spring 1979): 125-134.
2551. Lampton, D. M. "US Image of Peking in Three

International Crises." **Western Political Quarterly** 26 (March 1973): 28-50.

2552. Levine, Steven I. "China Policy During Carter's Year One." **Asian Survey** 18 (May 1978): 437-447.

2553. Li, Victor H., and John W. Lewis. "Resolving the China Dilemma: Advancing Normalization, Preserving Security." **International Security** 2 (Summer 1977): 11-23.

2554. Long, Ronald B. "The Role of American Diplomats in the Fall of China, 1941-1949." Ph.D. dissertation, St. John's University, 1961.

2555. McCutcheon, James M. "The Missionary and Diplomat in China." **Journal of Presbyterian History** 41 (December 1963): 224-236.

2556. McGee, Gale W. "A China Policy for the United States." **South Atlantic Quarterly** 76 (Autumn 1977): 424-437.

2557. Moorsteen, Richard, and Morton Abramowitz. **Remaking China Policy: United States-China Relations and Governmental Decision-making.** Cambridge, Mass.: Harvard University Press, 1971.

2558. Newman, Robert P. **Recognition of Communist China? A Study in Argument.** New York: Macmillan, 1961.

2559. Niemeyer, Gerhart. "Ideological Dimensions of the New China Policy." **Orbis** 15 (Fall 1971): 808-817.

2560. Ninkovich, Frank. "Cultural Relations and American China Policy, 1942-1945." **Pacific Historical Review** 49 (August 1980): 471-498.

2561. Oksenberg, Michael, and Robert B. Oxnam. "China and America: Past and Future." **Headline Series** 235 (April 1977): 3-77.

2562. Overholt, W. H. "President Nixon's Trip to China and Its Consequences." **Asian Survey** 13 (July 1973): 707-721.

2563. Pan, Stephen C. "American Diplomacy Concerning Manchuria." Ph.D. dissertation, Catholic University, 1938.

2564. Papageorge, Linda M. "The United States Diplomats' Response to Rising Chinese Nationalism, 1900-1912." Ph.D. dissertation, Michigan State University, 1973.

2565. Paulsen, George E. "The Szechwan Riots of
       1895 and American 'Missionary Diplomacy'."
       Journal of Asian Studies 28 (February
       1969): 285-298.
2566. Price, Allen T. "American Missions and
       American Diplomacy in China, 1830-1900."
       Ph.D. dissertation, Harvard University,
       1934.
2567. Pruden, George B. "Issachar Jacox Roberts
       and American Diplomacy in China During the
       Taiping Rebellion." Ph.D. dissertation,
       American University, 1977.
2568. Pugach, Noel H. "American Friendship for
       China and the Shantung Question at the
       Washington Conference." **Journal of
       American History** 64 (June 1977): 67-86.
2569. Rhee, T. C. "Peking and Washington in a New
       Balance of Power." **Orbis** 18 (Spring 1974):
       151-178.
2570. Robinson, T. W. "View from Peking: China's
       Policies towards the United States, the
       Soviet Union and Japan." **Pacific Affairs**
       45 (Fall 1972): 333-355.
2571. Schiebel, Joseph. "The Soviet Union and the
       Sino-American Relationship." **Orbis** 21
       (Spring 1977): 77-94.
2572. Sigal, Leon V. "The 'Rational Policy' Model
       and the Formosa Straits Crisis." **Inter-
       national Studies Quarterly** 14 (June 1970):
       121-156.
2573. Sim, Y. "Sino-American Detente: A Note on
       Afro-Americans' Views." **Journal of Black
       Studies** 5 (September 1974): 77-85.
2574. Solomon, R. H. "Parochialism and Paradox in
       Sino-American Relations." **Asian Survey** 7
       (December 1967): 831-850.
2575. _____. "Thinking Through the China
       Problem." **Foreign Affairs** 56 (January
       1978): 324-356.
2576. Starr, Daniel P. "Nelson Trusler Johnson:
       The United States and the Rise of
       Nationalist China, 1925-1937." Ph.D.
       dissertation, Rutgers University, 1967.
2577. Steiner, H. Arthur. "Re-thinking U.S. China
       Policy: A Review Article." **Pacific Affairs**
       45 (Summer 1972): 255-267.
2578. Stoessinger, John G. "China and America: The
       Burden of Past Misperceptions." **Journal of**

International Affairs 21 (1967): 72-91.
2579. Tan, Shao H. "The Diplomacy of American Investments in China." Ph.D. dissertation, University of Chicago, 1927.
2580. Taylor, A. H. "Opium and the Open Door." South Atlantic Quarterly 69 (Winter 1970): 79-95.
2581. Tong, Te-King. "Diplomatic Relations Between China and the United States, 1844-1860." Ph.D. dissertation, Columbia University, 1959.
2582. Torregrosa, Manuel F. "United States Dollar Diplomacy in China, 1909-1913." Ph.D. dissertation, Georgetown University, 1951.
2583. Tozer, Warren W. "Last Bridge to China: The Shanghai Power Company, the Truman Administration and the Chinese Communists." Diplomatic History 1 (Winter 1977): 64-78.
2584. Tsou, Tang. "The Quemoy Imbroglio: Chiang Kai-Shek and the United States ." Western Political Quarterly 12 (December 1959): 1075-1091.
2585. Tuchman, Barbara W. Stilwell and the American Experience in China, 1911-1945. New York: Macmillan, 1970.
2586. Van Alstyne, Richard W. "The United States and the Chinese Revolution: 1949-1972." Current History 65 (September 1973): 97-101.
2587. Vevier, Olson. "The United States and China: Diplomacy and Finance 1906-1913." Ph.D. dissertation, University of Wisconsin, 1953.
2588. Vinacke, Harold M. "United States Policy Towards China: An Appraisal." Far Eastern Survey 29 (May 1960): 65-69.
2589. Vinson, J. Chal. "The United States and China." Current History 43 (November 1962): 290-294.
2590. Wu, Ting-fang. America and the Americans from a Chinese Point of View. London: Duckworth, 1914.
2591. Yahuda, Michael. "American Policy Towards China in Historical Perspective." International Affairs 47 (July 1972): 450-456.
2592. Yee, Herbert S. "Decisions to Establish Diplomatic Relations with China: Environmental Variables in Foreign Policy

Decisions-Making." Ph.D. dissertation,
University of Hawaii, 1976.

Japan

2593. Bernstein, Barton J. "Perils and Politics of
Surrender: Ending the War with Japan and
Avoiding the Third Atomic Bomb." **Pacific
Historical Review** 46 (February 1977): 1-
27.
2594. Borton, H. "Preparation for the Occupation
of Japan." **Journal of Asian Studies** 25
(February 1966): 203-212.
2595. Boyle, J. H. "Drought-Walsh Mission to
Japan." **Pacific Historical Review** 34 (May
1965): 141-161.
2596. Burns, Richard D., and Edward M. Bennett.
**Diplomats in Crisis: United States-
Chinese-Japanese Relations, 1919-1941.**
Santa Barbara, Calif.: ABC-Clio, 1974.
2597. Caruthers, Sandra C. "Charles Legendre,
American Diplomacy, and Expansionism in
Meiji Japan, 1868-1893." Ph.D. disser-
tation, University of Colorado, 1966.
2598. Church, Deborah C. "The Role of the American
Diplomatic Advisers to the Japanese
Foreign Ministry, 1872-1887." Ph.D.
dissertation, University of Hawaii, 1978.
2599. Clemens, W. C. "SALT, the NPT, and US-
Japanese Security Relations." **Asian
Studies** 10 (December 1970): 1037-1045.
2600. Cohen, Bernard C. **The Political Process and
Foreign Policy: The Making of the Japanese
Peace Settlement.** Princeton, N.J.:
Princeton University Press, 1957.
2601. Daniels, Roger. **The Decision to Relocate the
Japanese Americans.** Philadelphia:
Lippincott, 1975.
2602. Epp, Robert. "The U.S.-Japanese Treaty
Crisis." **Current History** 58 (April 1970):
202-208, 243.
2603. Esthus, Raymond A. "Diplomatic Relations
Between the United States and Japan."
Ph.D. dissertation, Duke University, 1956.
2604. Foster, William C. "The Japanese Mass
Movement." **Political Affairs** 39 (July
1960): 13-23.
2605. Fry, M. G. "North Atlantic Triangle and the

Abrogation of the Anglo-Japanese Alliance." **Journal of Modern History** 39 (March 1967): 46-64.

2606. Gall, Morris. "The United States and Japan." **Social Education** 32 (December 1968): 785-788.

2607. Gordon, Bernard K. "Japan, the United States, and Southeast Asia." **Foreign Affairs** 56 (April 1978): 579-600.

2608. _____. "Loose Cannon on a Rolling Deck? Japan's Changing Security Policies." **Orbis** 22 (Winter 1979): 967-1005.

2609. Haight, J. M. "Franklin D. Roosevelt and a Naval Quarantine of Japan." **Pacific Historical Review** 40 (May 1971): 203-226.

2610. Holland, Harrison M. "The U.S.-Japan Alliance--A Post Viet Nam Assessment." **Pacific Community** 7 (January 1976): 199-215.

2611. Iriye, Akira. "American Diplomacy and Sino-Japanese Relations, 1926-1931." Ph.D. dissertation, Harvard University, 1961.

2612. Ishii, John D. "Japanese-American Diplomatic Relations, 1919-1929." Ph.D. dissertation, Georgetown University, 1950.

2613. Kawahara, Hattie M. "Diplomatic Relations Between the United States and Japan from 1931 to 1941." Ph.D. dissertation, University of Minnesota, 1949.

2614. Kelley, Donald R., Kenneth R. Stunkel, and Richard R. Wescott. "The Politics of the Environment: The United States, the USSR, and Japan." **American Behavioral Scientist** 17 (May-June 1974): 751-770.

2615. Kobayashi, T. "Great Debate in Japan: The Fate of the U.S.-Japan Security Treaty in 1970." **Journal of Politics** 30 (August 1968): 749-779.

2616. More, Lois A. "American Diplomacy in Japan, 1853-1869: From Advantage Gained to Advantage Lost." ED.D., Columbia University, 1963.

2617. Okita, Saburo. "Japan, China and the United States: Economic Relations and Prospects." **Foreign Affairs** 57 (Summer 1979): 1090-1110.

2618. Park, Y. H. "Japan's Perspectives and Expectations Regarding America's Role in

Korea." **Orbis** 20 (Fall 1976): 761-784.
2619. Parsons, Edward B. "Roosevelt's Containment of the Russo-Japanese War." **Pacific Historical Review** 38 (February 1969): 21-43.
2620. Pfaltzgaff, Robert L. "American-European-Japanese Relationship: Prospects for the Late 1970s." **Orbis** 19 (Fall 1975): 809-826.
2621. Pillsbury, M. "Japanese Card?" **Foreign Policy** 33 (Winter 1978/79): 3-30.
2622. Reischauer, Edwin O. **The United States and Japan.** Cambridge, Mass.: Harvard University Press, 1965.
2623. Safford, Jeffrey J. "Experiment in Containment: The United States Steel Embargo and Japan, 1917-1918." **Pacific Historical Review** 39 (November 1970): 439-451.
2624. Schonberger, Howard. "The Japan Lobby in American Diplomacy 1947-1952." **Pacific Historical Review** 46 (August 1977): 327-359.
2625. Stockwin, J. A. A. "Continuity and Change in Japanese Foreign Policy." **Pacific Affairs** 46 (Spring 1973): 77-93.
2626. Suttmeier, R. P. "Japanese Reactions to U.S. Nuclear Policy: The Domestic Origins of an International Negotiating Position." **Orbis** 22 (Fall 1978): 651-680.
2627. Ushiba, Nobuhiko. "Relationship Between Japan and the United States." **Air University Review** 22 (September-October 1971): 2-16.

Indochina

2628. Baral, Jaya K. **The Pentagon and the Making of U.S. Foreign Policy: A Case Study of Vietnam, 1960-1968.** Atlantic Highlands, N.J.: Humanities Press, 1978.
2629. Brown, M., and J. J. Zasloff. "Laos 1976: Faltering First Steps toward Socialism." **Asian Survey** 17 (February 1977): 107-115.
2630. Chomsky, Noam, H. J. Morgenthau, and M. Walzer. "Vietnam and Cambodia." **Dissent** 25 (Fall 1978): 386-391.
2631. Cooper, Chester L. **The Lost Crusade: America in Vietnam.** New York: Dodd, Mead, 1970.
2632. Darling, Frank C. "America and Thailand."

Asian Studies 7 (April 1967): 213-225.

2633. _____. "American Policy in Vietnam: Its Role in the Quabeland Theory and International Peace." **Asian Survey** 11 (August 1971): 818-839.

2634. _____. "Political Functions of the United States Embassy in Thailand." **Asian Survey** 18 (November 1978): 1191-1207.

2635. Duncanson, Dennis J. "South Vietnam: Detente and Reconciliation." **International Affairs** 49 (October 1973): 554-566.

2636. Fall, Bernard B. "Vietnam: The Agonizing Reappraisal." **Current History** 48 (February 1965): 95-102, 116.

2637. Fleming, D. F. "Vietnam and After." **Western Political Quarterly** 21 (March 1968): 141-151.

2638. Garfield, Gene J. "The Truman Policy in Indochina: A Study in Decision-Making." Ph.D. dissertation, Southern Illinois University, 1972.

2639. Gerberding, William P. "Vietnam and the Future of United States Foreign Policy." **Virginia Quarterly Review** 44 (Winter 1968): 19-42.

2640. Goldstein, W. "American Political System and the Next Vietnam." **Journal of International Affairs** 25 (1971): 91-119.

2641. Gordon, Bernard K. "Viet Nam and Indochina in U.S. Policy." **Pacific Community** 8 (July 1977): 575-587.

2642. Grinter, Lawrence E. "Bargaining Between Saigon and Washington: Dilemmas of Linkage Politics During War." **Orbis** 18 (Fall 1974): 837-867.

2643. Halperin, Morton H. "After Vietnam: Security and Intervention in Asia." **Journal of International Affairs** 22 (1968): 236-246.

2644. Heckscher, August. "Democracy and Foreign Policy: The Case of Vietnam." **American Scholar** 35 (Autumn 1966): 613-620.

2645. Herring, George C. "Vietnam Syndrome and American Foreign Policy." **Virginia Quarterly Review** 57 (Autumn 1981): 594-612.

2646. Hess, G. R. "Franklin Roosevelt and Indochina." **Journal of American History** 59 (September 1972): 353-368.

2647. Hill, K. L. "President Kennedy and the

Neutralization of Laos." **Review of Politics** 31 (July 1969): 353-369.

2648. Hunter, Robert E., and P. Windsor. "Vietnam and United States Policy in Asia." **International Affairs** 44 (April 1968): 202-213.

2649. Javits, Jacob K. "United States and Europe--After Vietnam." **Atlantic Community Quarterly** 6 (Fall 1968): 361-367.

2650. Kattenburg, Paul M. "Viet Nam and U.S. Diplomacy, 1940-1970." **Orbis** 15 (Fall 1971): 818-841.

2651. Lunch, W. L., and P. W. Sperlich. "American Public Opinion and the War in Vietnam." **Western Political Quarterly** 32 (March 1979): 21-44.

2652. Mahajani, U. "President Kennedy and United States Policy in Laos, 1961-63." **Journal of Southeast Asian Studies** 2 (September 1971): 87-99.

2653. Martin, James V. "A History of the Diplomatic Relations Between Siam and the United States of America, 1833-1929." Ph.D. dissertation, Fletcher School of Law and Diplomacy, 1948.

2654. Mecklin, John F. **Mission in Torment: An Intimate Account of the U.S. Role in Vietnam.** Garden City, N.Y.: Doubleday, 1965.

2655. Nicholas, H. G. "Vietnam and the Traditions of American Foreign Policy." **International Affairs** 44 (April 1968): 189-201.

2656. Patrick, Richard. "Presidential Leadership in Foreign Affairs Reexamined: Kennedy and Laos without Radical Revisionism." **World Affairs** 140 (Winter 1978): 245-258.

2657. Race, J. "Unlearned Lessons of Vietnam." **Yale Review** 66 (Winter 1977): 161-177.

2658. Reischauer, Edwin O. **Beyond Vietnam: The United States and Asia.** New York: Knopf, 1967.

2659. Sethachuay, Vivat. "United States-Thailand Diplomatic Relations During World War II." Ph.D. dissertation, Brigham Young University, 1977.

2660. Solomon, R. H. "Rise and Fall of Laotian and Vietnamese Opiate Trades." **Journal of Psychedelic Drugs** 11 (July 1979): 159-171.

2661. Summers, Laura. "Cambodia: Model of the Nixon Doctrine." **Current History** 65

(December 1973): 252-256, 276.
2662. Thies, Wallace J. "Coercion and Diplomacy: Force and Foreign Policy in the Vietnam Conflict, 1964-1968." Ph.D. dissertation, Yale University, 1977.
2663. Thompson, James C. " How Could Vietnam Happen? An Autopsy." **Atlantic Monthly** 221 (April 1968): 47-53.
2664. Thompson, W. S. "Indochinese Debacle and the United States." **Orbis** 19 (Fall 1975): 990-1011.
2665. Trivers, Howard. "Myths, Slogans, and Vietnam." **Virginia Quarterly Review** 48 (Winter 1972): 1-23.
2666. Warner, Geoffrey. "United States and Vietnam 1945-65." **International Affairs** 48 (July 1972): 379-394.
2667. _____. "The United States and Vietnam 1945-1965." **International Affairs** 47 (October 1972): 593-615.
2668. Watt, David C. "American Foreign Policy and Vietnam." **Political Quarterly** 43 (January 1972): 89-102.
2669. Young, Kenneth T. "United States Policy and Vietnamese Political Viability, 1954-1967." **Asian Studies** 7 (August 1967): 507-514.

Africa

2670. Allen, G. "Report on the Growing Crisis in Southern Africa." **American Opinion** 22 (April 1979): 11-17.
2671. Aluko, O. "Nigeria, the United States and Southern Africa." **African Affairs** 78 (January 1979): 91-102.
2672. Asante, S. K. B. "The Politics of Confrontation and Indifference: United States and Africa." **Utafiti** 4 (1979): 65-84.
2673. Baker, R. K. "The 'Back Burner' Revisited: America's African Policy." **Orbis** 15 (Spring 1971): 428-447.
2674. Berman, Edward H. "Foundations, United States Foreign Policy, and African Education, 1945-1975." **Harvard Educational Review** 49 (May 1970): 145-179.
2675. Bissell, Richard E. "United States Policy in Africa." **Current History** 73 (December

1977): 193-195, 224-225.

2676. Bowles, Chester. "Africa, Asia, and Berlin." **Department of State Bulletin** 45 (September 1961): 479-490.

2677. Bowman, L. W. "South Africa's Southern Strategy and Its Implications for the United States." **International Affairs** 47 (January 1971): 19-30.

2678. Brenen, Henry. "U.S. Foreign Policy in a Changing Africa." **Political Science Quarterly** 93 (Fall 1978): 443-464.

2679. Browne, Robert S. "US-Africa Economic Relations: A Brief Overview." **Review of Black Political Economy** 8 (Winter 1978): 167-183.

2680. Coker, C. "United States and National Liberation in Southern Africa." **African Affairs** 78 (July 1979): 319-330.

2681. Darlington, Charles F., and Alice B. Darlington. **African Betrayal.** New York: McKay, 1968.

2682. Doku, Maurice K. "Economics, Foreign Aid, and Foreign Policy: Case Studies in Three Contiguous West African Countries." Ph.D. dissertation, Claremont Graduate School, 1972.

2683. Emerson, Rupert. "American Policy in Africa." **Foreign Affairs** 40 (January 1962): 303-315.

2684. Ferguson, C., and W. R. Cotter. "South Africa: What Is to Be Done." **Foreign Affairs** 56 (January 1978): 253-274.

2685. Ferguson, John H. "American Diplomacy and the Boer War." Ph.D. dissertation, University of Pennsylvania, 1937.

2686. Foltz, William J. "United States Policy toward Southern AFrica: Economic and Strategic Constraints." **Political Science Quarterly** 92 (Spring 1977): 47-64.

2687. Girling, J. L. S. "Nixon's Algeria--Doctrine and Disengagement in Indochina." **Pacific Affairs** 44 (Winter 1971-72): 527-544.

2688. Goldstein, Myra S. "The Genesis of Modern American Relations with South Africa, 1895-1914." Ph.D. dissertation, State University of New York, 1972.

2689. Houser, G. "US Policy in Southern Africa." **Christianity & Crisis** 37 (September 1977):

197-201.

2690. Irwin, Ray W. "The Diplomatic Relations of the United States with the Barbary Powers, 1776-1816." Ph.D. dissertation, New York University, 1929.

2691. Kaplan, Lawrence S. "United States, Belgium, and the Congo Crisis of 1960." **Review of Politics** 29 (April 1967): 239-256.

2692. Kraus, Jon. "American Foreign Policy in Africa." **Current History** 80 (March 1981): 97-100, 129, 138.

2693. Lefever, Ernest W. "U.S. Policy, the UN and the Congo." **Orbis** 11 (Summer 1967): 394-413.

2694. Lemarchand, R. "C.I.A. in Africa: How Central? How Intelligent?" **Journal of Modern African Studies** 14 (September 1976): 401-426.

2695. Libby, Ronald T. "Anglo-American Diplomacy and the Rhodesia Settlement: A Loss of Impetus." **Orbis** 23 (Spring 1979): 185-211.

2696. Lockwood, E. "Reagan and South Africa: Drifting Toward Alliance?" **Christianity & Crisis** 41 (November 1981): 323-327.

2697. Logan, Rayford W. "Discrimination: Weakness of Our African Policy." **Current History** 42 (January 1962): 28-35, 48.

2698. McKay, Vernon. "American Policy in Africa: From Old Dilemmas to New." **SAIS Review** 5 (Spring 1961): 23-30.

2699. McMurty, Virginia A. "Foreign Aid and Political Development: The American Experience in West Africa." Ph.D. dissertation, University of Wisconsin, 1974.

2700. Morris, Milton D. "Black Americans and the Foreign Policy Process: The Case of Africa." **Western Political Quarterly** 25 (September 1972): 451-463.

2701. Murapa, R. "Political Economy of the United States Policy in Southern Africa." **Review of Black Political Economy** 7 (Spring 1977): 238-265.

2702. Nicol, D. "Africa and the U.S.A. in the United Nations." **Journal of Modern African Studies** 16 (September 1978): 365-395.

2703. Nurse, R. J. "Critic of Colonialism: JFK and Algerian Independence." **Historian** 39 (February 1977): 307-326.

2704. Nyerere, J. K. "America and Southern Africa." **Foreign Affairs** 55 (July 1977): 671-684.

2705. Obiozor, George A. "The Development of Nigeria--United States Diplomacy, 1960-1975." Ph.D. dissertation, Columbia University, 1976.

2706. Ottaway, David. "Africa: U.S. Policy Eclipse." **Foreign Affairs** 58 (1979): 637-658.

2707. Pahad, E. "Commentary: Washington's Stake in Southern Africa." **World Marxist Review** 21 (March 1978): 24-32.

2708. Rustin, B., and C. Gershman. "Africa, Soviet Imperialism and the Retreat of American Power." **Commentary** 64 (October 1977): 33-43.

2709. Savage, Marie A. "American Diplomacy in North Africa, 1776-1817." Ph.D. dissertation, Georgetown University, 1949.

2710. Schaufele, William E. "U.S. Relations in Southern Africa." **Annals of the American Academy of Political and Social Science** 432 (July 1977): 110-119.

2711. Shepherd, George W. "The Conflict of Interests in American Policy on Africa." **Western Political Quarterly** 12 (December 1959): 996-1004.

2712. _____. "Origins of America's Africa Policy." **American Review** 1 (Spring 1961): 130-145.

2713. Skurnik, W. A. E. "Ivoirien Student Perceptions of U.S. Africa Policy." **Journal of Modern African Studies** 17 (September 1979): 409-432.

2714. Smith, T. "South Africa: The Churches vs. the Corporations." **Business and Society Review** 15 (Fall 1975): 54-64.

2715. Walters, R. E. "Apartheid and the Atom: The United States and South Africa's Military Potential." **Africa Today** 23 (July 1976): 25-35.

2716. Walters, R. W. "Nuclear Arming of South Africa." **Black Scholar** 8 (September 1976): 25-32.

2717. Warren, H. "U.S. Role in the Eritrean Conflict." **Africa Today** 23 (April 1976): 39-53.

2718. Williams, G. Mennen. "Basic United States
       Policy in Africa." **Department of State
       Bulletin** 45 (October 1961): 600-603.
2719. _____. "Diplomatic Rapport between Africa
       and the United States." **Annals of the
       American Academy of Political and Social
       Science** (July 1964): 54-64.
2720. Zingg, Paul J. "American and North Africa: A
       Case Study in United States-Third World
       Relations." **History Teacher** 12 (February
       1979): 153-270.
2721. _____. "The Cold War in North Africa:
       American Foreign Policy and Postwar Muslim
       Nationalism, 1945-1962." **Historian** 39
       (November 1976): 40-61.

Middle East

2722. Adler, Selig. "United States Policy on
       Palestine in the FDR Era." **American Jewish
       Historical Quarterly** 62 (September 1972):
       11-29.
2723. Ajami, F. "Struggle for Egypt's Soul."
       Foreign Policy 35 (Summer 1979): 3-30.
2724. Alvarez, David J. "The United States and
       Turkey 1945-1946: The Bureaucratic Deter-
       minants of Cold War Diplomacy." Ph.D.
       dissertation, University of Connecticut,
       1975.
2725. Ashhab, N. "Anti-popular Policy in the
       Middle East: Dead-end." **World Marxist
       Review** 25 (February 1982): 14-21.
2726. Ball, George W. "Coming Crisis in Israeli-
       American Relations." **Foreign Affairs** 58
       (Winter 1979/80): 231-256.
2727. Baram, Phillip. "Undermining the British:
       Department of State Policies in Egypt and
       the Suez Canal Before and During World War
       II." **Historian** 40 (August 1978): 631-649.
2728. Ben-zvi, Abraham. "The Carter Presidency and
       the Palestinian Question." **Wiener Library
       Bulletin** 33 (1980): 55-65.
2729. Bill, J. A. "Iran and the Crisis of '78."
       Foreign Affairs 57 (Winter 1978-79): 323-
       342.
2730. Blechman, Barry M. "The Quantitative
       Evaluation of Foreign Policy Alternatives:
       Sinai, 1956." **Journal of Conflict**

Resolution (10 December 1966): 408-426.
2731.   Boll, M. M. "Turkey's New National Security
        Concept: What It Means for NATO." **Orbis** 23
        (Fall 1979): 609-631.
2732.   Bonham, G. M., et al. "October War: Changes
        in Cognitive Orientation toward the Middle
        East Conflict." **International Studies
        Quarterly** 23 (March 1979): 3-44.
2733.   Brundage, W. H., and W. A. Mitchell. "Toward
        an Understanding of Opium Poppy Production
        in Turkey." **Journal of Asian and African
        Studies** 12 (January/October 1977): 259-
        267.
2734.   Campbell, John C. "The Arab-Israeli
        Conflict: An American Policy." **Foreign
        Affairs** 49 (October 1970): 51-69.
2735.   _____. **Defense of the Middle East: Problems
        of American Policy.** New York: Harper,
        1960.
2736.   Chaibane, Antoine. "Crisis Diplomacy:
        America's Decision or Failure in the
        Middle East." Ph.D. dissertation, Florida
        State University, 1980.
2737.   Chomsky, Noam. "Reflections on the Arab-
        Israeli Conflict." **Journal of Contemporary
        Asia** 5 (1975): 337-344.
2738.   Cohen, M. J. "American Influence on British
        Policy in the Middle East during World War
        Two: First Attempts at Coordinating Allied
        Policy on Palestine." **American Jewish His-
        torical Quarterly** 67 (September 1977): 50-
        70.
2739.   Cohen, R. "Israel and the Soviet-American
        Statement of October 1, 1977: The Limits
        of Patron-Client Influence." **Orbis** 22
        (Fall 1978): 613-633.
2740.   Curtis, Michael. "Soviet-American Relations
        and the Middle East Crisis." **Orbis** 15
        (Spring 1971): 403-427.
2741.   Daniel, Robert L. "American Influences in
        the Near East Before 1861." **American
        Quarterly** 16 (Spring 1964): 72-84.
2742.   Denovo, John A. "Petroleum and American
        Diplomacy in the Near East, 1908-1928."
        Ph.D. dissertation, Yale University, 1948.
2743.   Dinstein, Yoram. **Consular Immunity from
        Judicial Process: With Particular Re-
        ference to Israel.** Jerusalem: Institute

for Legislative Research and Comparative Law, 1966.

2744.   Draper, Theodore. "How Not to Make Peace in the Middle East." **Commentary** 67 (March 1979): 23-39.

2745.   _____. "The United States & Israel: Tilt in the Middle East?" **Commentary** 59 (April 1975): 29-45.

2746.   Ferrell, Robert H. "American Policy in the Middle East." **Review of Politics** 37 (January 1975): 3-19.

2747.   Fulbright, J. William. "Getting Tough With Israel." **Washington Monthly** 6 (February 1975): 23-27.

2748.   Griffith, W. E. "Fourth Middle East War, the Energy Crisis and US Policy." **Orbis** 17 (Winter 1974): 1161-1188.

2749.   Gruen, G. E. "Ambivalence in the Alliance: U.S. Interests in the Middle East and the Evolution of Turkish Policy." **Orbis** 24 (Summer 1980): 363-378.

2750.   Hart, Parker T. "An American Policy Toward the Middle East." **Annals of the American Academy of Political and Social Science** 390 (July 1970): 98-113.

2751.   Hayes, Stephen D. "Joint Economic Commissions as Instruments of US Foreign Policy in the Middle East." **Middle East Journal** 31 (Winter 1977): 16-30.

2752.   Hess, G. R. "Iranian Crisis of 1945-46 and the Cold War." **Political Science Quarterly** 89 (March 1974): 117-146.

2753.   Irani, Robert H. "U.S. Strategic Interests in Iran and Saudi Arabia." **Parameters** 7 (1977): 21-34.

2754.   Issawi, C. "Oil and the Middle East Politics." **Proceedings of the Academy of Political Science** 31 (December 1973): 111-122.

2755.   Kerner, Howard J. "Turco-American Diplomatic Relations, 1860-1880." Ph.D. dissertation, Georgetown University, 1948.

2756.   Kerr, M. "Coming to Terms with Nasser: Attempts and Failures." **International Affairs** 43 (January 1967): 65-84.

2757.   Krasner, Stephen D. "Statist Interpretation of American Oil Policy toward the Middle East." **Political Science Quarterly** 94

(Spring 1979): 77-96.
2758.   Malone, J. J. "America and the Arabian
        Peninsula: The First Two Hundred Years."
        Middle East Journal 30 (Summer 1976): 406-
        424.
2759.   Mangold, P. "America, Israel and Middle East
        Peace: The Limits of Bilateral Influence."
        World Today 34 (December 1978): 458-466.
2760.   Matthews, Robert O. "The Suez Canal Dispute:
        A Case Study in Peaceful Settlement."
        International Organization 21 (Winter
        1967): 79-101.
2761.   Mazuzan, George T. "United States Policy
        Toward Palestine at the United Nations,
        1947-1948: An Essay." **Prologue** 7 (Fall
        1975): 163-176.
2762.   Morano, L. "Multinationals and Nation-
        States: The Case of Aramco." **Orbis** 23
        (Summer 1979): 447-469.
2763.   Noer, T. J. "American Government and the
        Irish Question during World War I." **South
        Atlantic Quarterly** 72 (Winter 1973): 95-
        114.
2764.   Parzen, Herbert. "The Roosevelt Palestine
        Policy, 1943-1945: An Exercise in Dual
        Diplomacy." **American Jewish Archives** 26
        (April 1974): 31-65.
2765.   Pfau, Richard. "Containment in Iran, 1946:
        The Shift to an Active Policy." **Diplomatic
        History** 1 (Fall 1977): 359-372.
2766.   Podet, Allen H. "Anti-Zionism in a Key
        United States Diplomat: Loy Henderson at
        the End of World War II." **American Jewish
        Archives** 30 (November 1978): 155-187.
2767.   Ramazani, R. K. "Who Lost America: The Case
        of Iran." **Middle East Journal** 36 (Winter
        1982): 5-21.
2768.   Rosen, S. J., and M. Moustafine. "Does
        Washington Have the Means to Impose a
        Settlement in Israel?" **Commentary** 64
        (October 1977): 25-32.
2769.   Rostow, Eugene V. "American Stake in
        Israel." **Commentary** 63 (April 1977): 32-
        46.
2770.   _____. "America, Europe, and the Middle
        East." **Commentary** 57 (February 1974): 40-
        55.
2771.   Rubin, Barry. "Anglo-American Relations in

Saudi Arabia, 1941-45." **Journal** of **Contemporary History** 14 (April 1979): 253-267.

2772. Rustow, D. A. "Turkey's Travails." **Foreign Affairs** 58 (Fall 1979): 82-102.

2773. Sabki, Hisham. "Woodrow Wilson and Self-Determination in the Arab Middle East." **Journal of Social and Political Studies** 4 (Winter 1979): 381-399.

2774. Sagan, S. D. "Lessons of the Yom Kippur Alert." **Foreign Policy** 36 (Fall 1979): 160-177.

2775. Schoenbaum, David. "The United States and the Birth of Israel." **Wiener Library Bulletin** 31 (1978): 87-100.

2776. Schulz, Ann. "United States Policy in the Middle East." **Current History** 68 (February 1975): 54-57, 81-82.

2777. Smolansky, O. M. "The United States and the Soviet Union in the Middle East." **Proceedings of the Academy of Political Science** 33 (1978): 99-109.

2778. Statterthwaite, Joseph C. "The Truman Doctrine: Turkey." **Annals of the American Academy of Political and Social Science** 401 (May 1972): 74-84.

2779. Stevens, Richard P. "The Political and Diplomatic Role of American Zionists as a Factor in the Creation of the State of Israel." Ph.D. dissertation, Georgetown University, 1960.

2780. Tarr, David W. "American Power and Diplomacy in the Middle East." Ph.D. dissertation, University of Chicago, 1961.

2781. Thorpe, James A. "United States and the 1940-1940 Anglo-Iraqi Crisis: American Policy in Transition." **Middle East Journal** 25 (Winter 1971): 79-89.

2782. Trice, Robert H. "Congress and the Arab-Israeli Conflict: Support for Israel in the U.S. Senate, 1970-1973." **Political Science Quarterly** 92 (Fall 1977): 443-463.

2783. _____. "Foreign Policy Interest Groups, Mass Public Opinion, and the Arab-Israeli Dispute." **Western Political Quarterly** 31 (June 1978): 238-252.

2784. Tucker, R. W. "Behind Camp David." **Commentary** 66 (November 1978): 25-33.

2785.   _____. "Is Peace Still Possible in the
          Middle East? The Role of the United
          States." **Commentary** 66 (July 1978): 17-78.
2786.   _____. "Middle East: Carterism Without
          Carter?" **Commentary** 72 (September 1981):
          27-36.
2787.   Ullman, Richard H. "After Rabat: Middle East
          Risks and American Roles." **Foreign Affairs**
          53 (January 1975): 284-296.
2788.   Warne, William E. **Mission for Peace: Point
          Four in Iran.** Indianapolis: Bobbs-Merrill,
          1956.
2789.   Whetten, Lawrence L. "Lessons of Iran."
          World Today 35 (October 1979): 391-399.
2790.   Yaffe, Richard. "U.S. Policy and the Syrian-
          Israel Conflict." **Israel Horizons** 10 (May
          1962): 8-13.

South Asia

2791.   Ahmad, Zubair. "The United States Decision
          on Military Aid to Pakistan." Ph.D. dis-
          sertation, University of Pennsylvania,
          1975.
2792.   Artner, Stephen J. "Detente Policy Before
          and After Afghanistan." **Aussenpolitik** 31
          (1980): 134-146.
2793.   Ashton, Charles H. "Congressional Decision-
          Making in the Foreign Policy-Making Pro-
          cess: The Case of the Bokaro Steel Mill
          Project in Indo-American Relations." Ph.D.
          dissertation, University of Pennsylvania,
          1972.
2794.   Badgley, John H. "The American Territorial
          Presence in Asia." **Annals of the American
          Academy of Political and Social Science**
          390 (July 1970): 38-47.
2795.   Bandyopadhaya, Jayantanuja. "Making of
          Foreign Policy: A Tentative Subsystematic
          Model of South Asia." **South Asian Studies**
          3 (July 1968): 27-39.
2796.   Barnds, William J. "India and America at
          Odds." **International Affairs** 49 (July
          1973): 371-384.
2797.   _____. "United States Policy toward South
          Asia: Shifting Perceptions and Policy
          Choices." **Pacific Community** 8 (July 1977):
          645-659.

2798. Bell, Peter, and Stephen Resnick. "The
       Contradicitons of Post-War Development in
       Southeast Asia." **Journal of Contemporary
       Asia** 1 (Autumn 1970): 37-49.
2799. Belohlavek, John M. "Andrew Jackson and the
       Malaysian Pirates: A Question of Diplomacy
       and Politics." **Tennessee Historical
       Quarterly** 36 (Spring 1977): 19-29.
2800. Bozeman, Adda B. "Iran: U.S. Foreign Policy
       and the Tradition of Persian Statecraft."
       Orbis 23 (Summer 1979): 387-402.
2801. Caldwell, M. "ASEANisation." **Journal of
       Contemporary Asia** 4 (1974): 36-70.
2802. _____. "Luddites and Lemmings in South-east
       Asia." **International Affairs** 41 (July
       1965): 421-440.
2803. Chapin, W. "United States and South East
       Asia." **World Today** 23 (August 1967): 348-
       354.
2804. Downum, Garland. "The Madagascan Mission to
       the United States in 1883: Diplomacy and
       Public Relations." **Historian** 39 (May
       1977): 472-489.
2805. Frankel, F. R. "India's Promise." **Foreign
       Policy** 38 (Spring 1980): 51-66.
2806. Haendel, Dan. **The Process of Policy
       Formation: U.S. Foreign Policy in the
       Indo-Pakistani War of 1971.** Boulder,
       Colo.: Westview, 1978.
2807. Holdridge, J. H. "Department of State, US
       Policy Towards Southeast Asia." **Journal of
       Contemporary Asia** 11 (1981): 515-519.
2808. Hoyt, Edwin C. "Foreign Policies of India
       and the United States: A Comparison."
       India Quarterly 17 (July/September 1961):
       277-293.
2809. Johnstone, William C. "A New Look at
       American Policy in Southeast Asia." **SAIS
       Review** 5 (Spring 1961): 31-36.
2810. _____. "United States Policy in Southern
       Asia." **Current History** 46 (February 1964):
       65-70, 116.
2811. Jordan, Amos A. **Foreign Aid and the Defense
       of Southeast Asia.** New York: Praeger,
       1962.
2812. Kennedy, Edward M. "The Persian Gulf: Arms
       Race or Arms Control?" **Foreign Affairs** 54
       (October 1975): 14-35.

2813. Long, David E. "United States Policy toward
      the Persian Gulf." **Current History** 69
      (February 1975): 69-73, 85.
2814. Montgomery, John D. **The Politics of Foreign
      Aid: American Experience in Southeast
      Asia.** New York: Praeger, 1962.
2815. Mullins, Frances H. "United States Diplomacy
      Concerning the Indian Independence Move-
      ment, 1940-1945." Ph.D. dissertation,
      Fletcher School of Law and Diplomacy,
      1971.
2816. Nuetcherlein, D. E. "US National Interests
      in Southeast Asia: A Reappraisal." **Asian
      Studies** 11 (November 1971): 1054-1070.
2817. Palmer, Norman D. "Alternative Futures for
      South Asia and United States Policy."
      Orbis 15 (Spring 1971): 351-380.
2818. _____. "Indo-American Relations: The
      Politics of Encounter." **Orbis** 23 (Summer
      1979): 403-420.
2819. _____. "South Asia and the Great Powers."
      Orbis 17 (Fall 1973): 989-1009.
2820. Park, R. L. "Coming to Grips with India."
      Asian Survey 17 (December 1977): 1158-
      1166.
2821. Peritz, R. "American-Malaysian Relations:
      Substance and Shadows." **Orbis** 11 (Summer
      1967): 532-550.
2822. Plischke, Elmer. "United States Southeast
      Asian Policy--An Options Analysis." **Social
      Studies** 18 (Fall 1971): 18-31.
2823. Porter, Gareth. "The Decline of U.S.
      Diplomacy in Southeast Asia." **SAIS Review**
      24 (Winter 1981): 149-159.
2824. Power, P. F. "Indo-American Nuclear
      Controversy." **Asian Survey** 19 (June 1979):
      574-596.
2825. Rao, R. V. R. C. "Searching for a Mature
      Relationship: The United States and
      India." **Round Table** 263 (July 1976): 249-
      260.
2826. Park, R. L. "Can India Be Reported?
      Journalists, Diplomats, and Scholars in
      Cross-Cultural Communication." **Journal of
      Asian Studies** 39 (November 1979): 11-19.
2827. Smith, Douglas L. "The Misspaugh Mission and
      American Corporate Diplomacy in Persia,
      1922-1927." **Southern Quarterly** 14 (January

1976): 151-172.

2828. Stillman, James P. "Foreign Aid, Ideology and Bureaucratic Politics: The Bokaro Steel Mill and Indian-American Relations." Ph.D. dissertation, Columbia University, 1975.

2829. Srinivasachary, M. S. "Commerce, Peace, and Security: United States Foreign Policy toward India, 1947-1954." Ph.D. dissertation, Kansas State University, 1975.

2830. Talbot, Phillips. "The American Posture Toward India and Pakistan." **Annals of the American Academy of Political and Social Science** 390 (July 1970): 87-97.

2831. Trager, Frank N. "Alternative Futures for Southeast Asia and United States Policy." **Orbis** 15 (Spring 1971): 381-402.

2832. _____. "The United States and Pakistan: A Failure of Diplomacy." **Orbis** 9 (Fall 1965): 613-629.

2833. Van Cleave, William R., and S. T. Cohen. "Nuclear Aspects of Future U.S. Security Policy in Asia." **Orbis** 19 (Fall 1975): 1152-1180.

2834. Weatherbee, Donald E. "U.S. Policy and the Two Southeast Asias." **Asian Survey** 18 (April 1978): 408-421.

2835. Weinstein, Franklin B. "U.S.-Vietnam Relations and the Security of Southeast Asia." **Foreign Affairs** 56 (July 1978): 842-856.

2836. Wilcox, Wayne. "American Policy towards South Asia." **Asian Affairs** 60 (June 1973): 127-139.

2837. Wolf, Charles. **Foreign Aid: Theory and Practice in Southern Asia.** Princeton, N.J.: Princeton University Press, 1960.

2838. Yeselson, Abraham. "United States-Persian Diplomatic Relations, 1883-1921." Ph.D. dissertation, Brown University, 1954.

BIOGRAPHICAL MATERIALS

2839. Adams, Charles F. **Diary**. Edited by Marc Friedlaender and L. H. Butterfield. Cambridge, Mass.: Belknap, 1964-74.

2840. Adams, D. K. "Messersmith's Appointment to Vienna in 1943: Presidential Patronage or Career Promotion?" **Delaware History** 18 (Spring-Summer 1978): 17-27.

2841. Adams, John. **Diary and Autobiography**. Edited by L. H. Butterfield. Cambridge, Mass.: Belknap, 1961.

2842. _____. **The John Adams Papers**. Edited by Frank Donovan. New York: Dodd, Mead, 1965.

2843. Allen, Horace N. **Things Korean: A Collection of Sketches and Anecdotes, Missionary and Diplomatic**. New York: Revell, 1908.

2844. Allen, Katharine M. **Foreign Service Diary**. Washington, D.C.: Potomac, 1967.

2845. Allen, Max P. "The Early Career of William Pinkney, Diplomat and Constitutional Lawyer." Ph.D. dissertation, Indiana University, 1944.

2846. Allison, John M. **Ambassador From the Prairie--Or, Allison Wonderland**. Boston: Houghton Mifflin, 1973.

2847. Anderson, David L. "Anson Burlingame: American Architect of the Cooperative Policy in China, 1961-1871." **Diplomatic History** 1 (Summer 1977): 239-256.

2848. _____. "Anson Burlingame: Reformer and Diplomat." **Civil War History** 25 (December 1979): 293-308.

2849. Anderson, Larz. **Larz Anderson: Letters and Journals of a Diplomat**. Edited by Isabel Anderson. New York: Revell, 1940.

2850. Anderson, Richard C. **The Diary and Journal of Richard Clough Anderson, Jr., 1814-1826**. Edited by Alfred Rischendorf and E. Taylor Parks. Durham, N.C.: Duke University Press, 1964.

2851. Andrews, Christopher C. **Recollections, 1829-1922**. Edited by Alice E. Andrews. Cleveland: Clark, 1928.

2852. Angell, James B. **Reminiscences**. New York: Longmans, Green, 1912.

2853. _____. **Selected Addresses by James Burrill Angell**. New York: Longmans, Green, 1912.

2854.   Armstrong, Hamilton F. **Those Days.** New York:
        Harper and Row, 1963.
2855.   Attwood, William. **The Reds and the Blacks: A
        Personal Adventure.** New York: Harper and
        Row, 1967.
2856.   Baker, Ray S. **American Chronicle: The Auto-
        biography of Ray Stannard Baker.** New York:
        Scribner, 1945.
2857.   Baldridge, Letitia. **Of Diamonds and Diplo-
        mats.** Boston: Houghton Mifflin 1968.
2858.   _____. **Roman Candle.** Boston: Houghton Mif-
        flin, 1956.
2859.   Baldwin, C. F. "Dog's Life in the Foreign
        Service." **Virginia Quarterly Review** 55
        (Autumn 1979): 716-723.
2860.   Ball, George W. **Diplomacy for a Crowded
        World: An American Foreign Policy.** Boston:
        Little, Brown, 1976.
2861.   Barlow, Joel. **Life and Letters of Joel
        Barlow, LL.D.** Edited by Charles Burr Todd.
        New York: Burt Franklin, 1972.
2862.   Bartlett, Merrill L. "Commodore James Biddle
        and the First Naval Mission to Japan,
        1845-1846." **American Neptune** 41 (January
        1981): 25-35.
2863.   Bax, Emily. **Miss Bax of the Embassy.** Boston:
        Houghton Mifflin, 1939.
2864.   Beaulac, Willard L. **Career Ambassador.** New
        York: Macmillan, 1951.
2865.   _____. **Career Diplomat: A Career in the
        Foreign Service of the United States.** New
        York: Macmillan, 1964.
2866.   _____. **A Diplomat Looks at Aid to Latin
        America.** Carbondale: Southern Illinois
        University Press, 1970.
2867.   Belmont, August. **Letters, Speeches and Ad-
        dresses of August Belmont.** New York:
        Privately printed, 1890.
2868.   Belohlavek, John M. "George Mifflin Dallas
        (1792-1864): A Political and Diplomatic
        Biography." Ph.D. dissertation, University
        of Nebraska, Lincoln, 1970.
2869.   _____. "A Philadelphian and the Canal: The
        Charles Biddle Mission to Panama, 1835-
        1836." **Pennsylvania Magazine of History
        and Biography** 104 (October 1980): 450-461.
2870.   Benet, Stephen V. **Selected Letters.** Edited
        by Charles A. Fenton. New Haven, Conn.:
        Yale University Press, 1960.

2871. Berle, Adolf A. **Latin America: Diplomacy and Reality.** New York: Harper and Row, 1962.

2872. _____. **Navigating the Rapids, 1918-1971: From the Papers of Adolf A. Berle.** Edited by Beatrice Bishop Berle and Travis B. Jacobs. New York: Harcourt Brace Jovanovich, 1973.

2873. _____. **New Directions in the New World.** New York: Harper, 1940.

2874. Berquist, Harold E. "Russo-American Economic Relations in the 1820's: Henry Middleton as a Protector of American Economic Interests in Russia and Turkey." **East European Quarterly** 11 (Spring 1977): 27-41.

2875. Biddle, Cordelia D. **My Philadelphia Father: As Told to Kyle Crichon.** Garden City, N.Y.: Doubleday, 1955.

2876. Bigelow, John. **Retrospections of an Active Life.** New York: Baker and Taylor, 1909-1913.

2877. Bilainkin, G. "Joseph P. Kennedy: The Truth." **Contemporary Review** 216 (February 1970): 64-70.

2878. Bjerk, Roger C. W. "Kennedy at the Court of St. James: The Diplomatic Career of Joseph P. Kennedy, 1938-1940." Ph.D. dissertation, Washington State University, 1971.

2879. Bland, Larry I. "W. Averell Harriman: Businessman and Diplomat, 1891-1945." Ph.D. dissertation, University of Wisconsin, 1972.

2880. Blayney, Michael S. "Diplomat and Humanist: The Diplomatic Career of Herbert Claiborne Pell." Ph.D. dissertation, Washington State University, 1973.

2881. Bohlen, Charles E. **Witness to History, 1929-1969.** New York: Norton, 1973.

2882. Bonsal, Stephen. **Unfinished Business: Paris-Versailles, 1919.** Garden City, N.Y.: Doubleday, 1944.

2883. Boswell, George T. "The Roller-Coaster Career of William C. Bullitt." Ph.D. dissertation, Texas Christian University, 1972.

2884. Bowen, Herbert W. **Recollections, Diplomatic and Undiplomatic.** New York: Hitchcock, 1926.

2885. Bowers, Claude G. **Chile Through Embassy Windows, 1929-1953.** New York: Simon and

Schuster, 1958.

2886. _____. **My Life: The Memoirs of Claude Bowers.** New York: Simon and Schuster, 1962.

2887. _____. **My Mission to Spain: Watching the Rehearsal for World War II.** New York: Simon and Schuster, 1954.

2888. Bowles, Chester. **Africa's Challenge to America.** Berkeley: University of California Press, 1956.

2889. _____. **Ambassador's Report.** New York: Harper, 1954.

2890. _____. **American Politics in a Revolutionary World.** Cambridge, Mass.: Harvard University Press, 1956.

2891. _____. **Ideas, People, and Peace.** New York: Harper, 1958.

2892. _____. **The Makings of a Just Society: What the Postwar Years Have Taught Us About National Development.** Delhi, India: University of Delhi, 1963.

2893. _____. **The New Dimensions of Peace.** New York: Harper, 1955.

2894. _____. **Promises to Keep: My Years in Public Life, 1941-1969.** New York: Harper and Row, 1971.

2895. _____. **Tomorrow Without Fear.** New York: Simon and Schuster, 1946.

2896. _____. **A View From the New Delhi: Selected Speeches and Writings, 1963-1969.** New Haven, Conn.: Yale University Press, 1969.

2897. Boyce, Richard F. **The Diplomat's Wife.** New York: Harper, 1956.

2898. Braden, Spruille. **Diplomats and Demagogues: The Memoirs of Spruille Braden.** New Rochelle, N.Y.: Arlington House, 1971.

2899. Brauer, Kinley J. "The Appointment of Carl Schurz as Minister for Spain." **Mid-America** 56 (April 1974): 75-84.

2900. Briceland, Alan V. "Ephraim Kirby: Mr. Jefferson's Emissary on the Tombigbee-Mobile Frontier in 1804." **Alabama Review** 24 (April 1971): 83-113.

2901. Brooks, Neal A. "The Diplomatic Career of Whitelaw Reid." Ph.D. dissertation, Case Western Reserve University, 1974.

2902. Brown, James S. "Eugene Schuyler, Observer of Russia: His Years as a Diplomat in Russia, 1867-1875." Ph.D. dissertation, Vanderbilt University, 1971.

2903. Buchanan, Wiley T. **Red Carpet at the White House.** New York: Dutton, 1964.

2904. Buchanan, William. **The Central American Peace Conference Held at Washington, D.C., 1907: Report of Mr. William Buchanan Representing the United States of America.** Washington, D.C.: Government Printing Office, 1908.

2905. Buhite, Russell D. **Patrick J. Hurley and American Foreign Policy.** Ithaca, N.Y.: Cornell University Press, 1973.

2906. _____. "Patrick J. Hurley and American Policy toward China." **Chronicles of Oklahoma** 45 (Winter 1967-68): 376-392.

2907. Bullitt, Orville, H., ed. **For the President: Personal and Secret--Correspondence Between Franklin D. Roosevelt and William C. Bullitt.** Boston: Houghton Mifflin, 1972.

2908. Bullitt, William C. **The Great Globe Itself: A Preface to World Affairs.** New York: Scribner, 1946.

2909. Burke, Lee H. **Ambassador at Large: Diplomat Extraordinary.** The Hague: Nijhoff, 1972.

2910. Burnside, William H. "Powell Clayton: Ambassador to Mexico, 1897-1905." **Arkansas Historical Quarterly** 38 (Winter 1979): 328-344.

2911. Caldwell, John C., and Mark Gayn. **American Agent.** New York: Holt, 1947.

2912. Carmona, Israel. "Anatomy of a Diplomatic Failure: A Study of the Tenure of Ambassador James Rockwell Sheffield in Mexico, 1924-1927." Ph.D. dissertation, University of Southern California, 1969.

2913. Carpenter, W. B. "The Equipment of American Students for Foreign Service." **Annals of the American Academy of Political and Social Science** 122 (November 1925): 124-130.

2914. Carroll, John M. "A Pennsylvanian in Paris: James A. Longa, Jr., Unofficial Diplomat 1919-1925." **Pennsylvania History** 45 (January 1978): 3-18.

2915. Cathcart, James L. **The Diplomatic Journal and Letter Book of James Leander Cathcart, 1788-1796.** Worcester, Mass.: American

Antiquarian Society, 1864.
2916. Cerwin, Herbert. **In Search of Something: The Memoirs of a Public Relations Man.** Los Angeles: Sherbourne, 1966.
2917. Child, Maude P. **The Social Side of Diplomatic Life.** Indianapolis: Bobbs-Merrill, 1926.
2918. Child, Richard W. **A Diplomat Looks at Europe.** New York: Duffield, 1925.
2919. Childs, James R. **Foreign Service Farewell: My Years in the Near East.** Charlottesville: University of Virginia Press, 1969.
2920. Choate, Joseph H. **Arguments and Addresses of Joseph Hodges Choate.** Edited by Frederick C. Hicks. St. Paul, Minn.: West, 1926.
2921. _____. **Life of Joseph Hodges Choate as Gathered Chiefly from His Letters.** Edited by Edward Sandford Martin. New York: Scribner, 1927.
2922. Coffin, Frank M. **Witness for Aid.** Boston: Houghton Mifflin, 1964.
2923. Collier, William M. **At the Court of His Catholic Majesty.** Chicago: McClurg, 1912.
2924. Conant, James B. **Germany and Freedom: A Personal Appraisal.** Cambridge, Mass.: Harvard University Press, 1958.
2925. _____. **My Several Lives: Memoirs of a Social Inventor.** New York: Harper and Row, 1970.
2926. Conway, John S. "Myron C. Taylor's Mission to the Vatican 1940-1950." **Church History** 44 (March 1975): 85-99.
2927. Coolidge, Harold J. **Archibald Cary Coolidge: Life and Letters.** New York: Houghton Mifflin, 1932.
2928. Coolidge, John G. **Random Letters from Many Countries.** Boston: Marshall Jones, 1924.
2929. _____. **A War Diary in Paris, 1914-1917.** Cambridge, Mass.: Riverside, 1931.
2930. Coolidge, Thomas J. **The Autobiography of T. Jefferson Coolidge, 1831-1920.** Boston: Houghton Mifflin, 1923.
2931. Cortissoz, Royal. **The Life of Whitelaw Reid.** New York: Scribner, 1921.
2932. Corwin, Thomas. **Life and Speeches of Thomas Corwin: Orator, Lawyer, and Statesman.** Edited by Josiah Morrow. Cincinnati: Anderson, 1896.

2933.   _____. Speeches of Thomas Corwin, with a
         Sketch of His Life. Edited by Isaac
         Strohm. Dayton, Ohio: Comley, 1859.
2934.   Cox, Samuel S. Diversions of a Diplomat in
         Turkey. New York: Webster, 1887.
2935.   Crane, Katharine. Mr. Carr of State: Forty
         Seven Years in the Department of State.
         New York: St. Martin's Press, 1960.
2936.   Cresson, William P. Francis Dana: A Puritan
         Diplomat at the Court of Catherine the
         Great. New York: Dial, 1930.
2937.   Croly, Herbert D. Willard Straight. New
         York: Macmillan, 1924.
2938.   Cronon, David E. Josephus Daniels in Mexico.
         Madison: University of Wisconsin Press,
         1960.
2939.   Crowe, Philip K. Diversions of a Diplomat in
         Ceylon. London: Macmillan, 1957.
2940.   Cudahy, John. The Armies March: A Personal
         Report by John Cudahy. New York: Scribner,
         1941.
2941.   Cushing, Caleb. The Cushing Reports. Edited
         by Margaret Diamont Benetz. Salisbury,
         N.C.: Documentary Publications, 1976.
2942.   _____. Outlines of the Life and Public Ser-
         vices, Civil and Military, of William
         Henry Harrison of Ohio. Boston: Weeks,
         Jordan, 1840.
2943.   Dahl, Victor C. "Granville Stuart in Latin
         America: A Montana Pioneer's Diplomatic
         Career." Montana Magazine of Western
         History 21 (July 1971): 18-33.
2944.   _____. "Montana Pioneer Abroad: Granville
         Stuart in South America." Journal of the
         West 4 (July 1965): 345-366.
2945.   Dallas, George M. Diary of George Mifflin
         Dallas, United States Minister to Russia,
         1837-39. Edited by Susan Dallas. Phila-
         delphia: Lippincott, 1892.
2946.   _____. A Series of Letters From London
         Written During the Years 1856, '57, '58,
         '59, '60. Edited by Julia Dallas. Phila-
         delphia: Lippincott, 1869.
2947.   Dallek, Robert. "Beyond Tradition: The
         Diplomatic Careers of William E. Dodd and
         George S. Messersmith, 1933-1938." South
         Atlantic Quarterly 66 (Spring 1967): 233-
         244.

2948. _____. "Roosevelt's Ambassador: The Public
       Career of William E. Dodd." Ph.D. disser-
       tation, Columbia University, 1964.
2949. Daniels, Jonathan. The End of Innocence.
       Philadelphia: Lippincott, 1954.
2950. Daniels, Josephus. Shirt-Sleeve Diplomat.
       Chapel Hill: University of North Carolina
       Press, 1947.
2951. Davidson, John W. "Brand Whitlock and the
       Diplomacy of Belgian Relief." Prologue 2
       (Winter 1970): 143-160.
2952. Davies, John P. Foreign and Other Affairs.
       New York: Norton, 1964.
2953. Davies, Joseph E. Mission to Moscow. New
       York: Simon and Schuster, 1941.
2954. _____. Our Soviet Ally in War and Peace.
       New York: National Council of American-
       Soviet Friendship, 1944.
2955. Davis, Kenneth P. "The Diplomatic Career of
       Jacob Gould Schurman." Ph.D. dissertation,
       University of Virginia, 1975.
2956. Dawes, Charles G. Essays and Speeches.
       Boston: Houghton Mifflin, 1915.
2957. _____. Journal as Ambassador to Great
       Britain. New York: Macmillan, 1939.
2958. _____. A Journal of Reparations. London:
       Macmillan, 1939.
2959. _____. A Journal of the Great War. Boston:
       Houghton Mifflin, 1921.
2960. Day, Donald E. "A Life of Wilson Shannon,
       Governor of Ohio, Diplomat, Territorial
       Governor of Kansas." Ph.D. dissertation,
       Ohio State University, 1978.
2961. Deane, John R. The Strange Alliance: The
       Story of Our Efforts at Wartime Coopera-
       tion with Russia. New York: Viking, 1947.
2962. Deane, Silas. Paris Papers: Or, Mr. Silas
       Deane's Late Intercepted Letters to his
       Brothers, and Other Intimate Friends in
       America. New York: Rivington, 1782.
2963. DeLeon, Edwin. Thirty Years of My Life on
       Three Continents. London: Ward and Downey,
       1890.
2964. Denby, Charles. China and Her People: Being
       the Observations, Reminiscences and Con-
       clusions of an American Diplomat. Boston:
       Page, 1906.
2965. Dennett, Raymond, and Joseph E. Johnson,

eds. **Negotiating with the Russians.**
Boston: World Peace Foundations, 1951.
2966. De Novo, John A. "The Enigmatic Alvery A.
Adee and American Foreign Relations, 1870–
1924." **Prologue** 7 (Summer 1975): 69–80.
2967. Dix, John A. **Memoirs of John Adams Dix.** Compiled by Morgan Dix. New York: Harper,
1883.
2968. Dobney, Frederick J., ed. **Selected Papers of
Will Clayton.** Baltimore: Johns Hopkins
University Press, 1971.
2969. Dodd, Martha. **My Years in Germany.** London:
Golancz, 1940.
2970. _____. **Through Embassy Eyes.** New York:
Harcourt, Brace, 1939.
2971. Dodd, William E. **Ambassador Dodd's Diary,
1933–1938.** Edited by Martha Dodd. New
York: Harcourt, Brace, 1941.
2972. Donovan, James B. **Strangers on a Bridge: The
Case of Colonel Abel.** New York: Atheneum,
1964.
2973. Donovan, Theresa A. "Difficulties of a Diplomat: George Mifflin Dallas in London."
**Pennsylvania Magazine of History and
Biography** 92 (October 1968): 421–440.
2974. _____. "President Pierce's Ministers at the
Court of St. James." **Pennsylvania Magazine
of History and Biography** 91 (October
1967): 457–470.
2975. Dorwart, Jeffery M. "The Independent Minister: John M. B. Sill and the Struggle
against Japanese Expansion in Korea, 1894–
1897." **Pacific Historical Review** 44
(November 1975): 485–502.
2976. Douglass, Frederick. **A Black Diplomat in
Haiti: The Diplomatic Correspondence of
U.S. Minister Frederick Douglass from
Haiti, 1889–1891.** Edited by Norma Brown.
Salisbury, N.C.: Documentary Publications,
1977.
2977. _____. **Frederick Douglass: Selections From
His Writings.** Edited by Philip S. Foner.
New York: International Publishers, 1964.
2978. _____. **The Life and Writings of Frederick
Douglass.** Edited by Philip S. Foner. New
York: International Publishers, 1950–55.
2979. _____. **The Mind and Heart of Frederick
Douglass: Excerpts from Speeches of the**

Great Negro Orator. Edited by Barbara Ritchie. New York: Crowell, 1968.

2980. Draper, William F. Recollections of a Varied
Career. Boston: Little, Brown, 1908.

2981. Dufault, David V. "Francis B. Sayre and the
Commonwealth of the Philippines, 1936-
1942." Ph.D. dissertation, University of
Oregon, 1972.

2982. Duley, Eleanor I. "George Bancroft, Diplomat." Ph.D. dissertation, Radcliffe College, 1939.

2983. Dunham, Donald. Envoy Unextraordinary. New
York: Day 1944.

2984. _____. Zone of Violence: The Brutal, Shock-
ing Story Lived by an American Diplomat
Behind the Red Curtain. New York: Belmont,
1962.

2985. Eagles, Keith D. "Ambassador Joseph E.
Davies and American-Soviet Relations,
1937-1941." Ph.D. dissertation, University
of Washington, 1966.

2986. Egan, Clifford L. "An American Diplomat in
Spain: Selected Civil War Letters of
Horatio J. Perry." Lincoln Herald 73
(Summer 1971): 62-74.

2987. Egan, Maurice F. Recollections of a Happy
Life. New York: Doran, 1924.

2988. Eggert, G. G. "Our Man in Havana: Fitzhugh
Lee." Hispanic American Historical Review
47 (November 1967): 463-485.

2989. Einstein, Lewis. A Diplomat Looks Back.
Edited by Lawrence E. Gelfand. New Haven,
Conn.: Yale University Press, 1968.

2990. _____. Inside Constantinople: A Diplomatist's Diary During the Dardanelles Expedition, April-September 1915. New York:
Dutton, 1918.

2991. Eitler, Warren J. "Diplomacy of the Graves
Mission to Siberia." Ph.D. dissertation,
Georgetown University, 1953.

2992. Eppinga, Richard J. "Aristocrat, Nation-
alist, Diplomat: The Life and Career of
Huntington Wilson." Ph.D. dissertation,
Michigan State University, 1972.

2993. Esherick, Joseph W., ed. Lost Change in
China: The World War II Despatches of John
S. Service. New York: Random House, 1974.

2994. Farley, Foster M. "William B. Reed: President Buchanan's Minister to China 1857-1858." **Pennsylvania History** 37 (July 1970): 269-280.

2995. Farnsworth, Beatrice. **William C. Bullitt and the Soviet Union.** Bloomington: Indiana University Press, 1967.

2996. Ferrell, Robert H. "A Dawes Diplomatic Dinner." **Journal of the Illinois State Historical Society** 55 (Autumn 1962): 250-254.

2997. Fischer, Robert. "Henry Cabot Lodge and the Taft Arbitration Treaties." **South Atlantic Quarterly** 78 (Spring 1979): 244-258.

2998. Fitz-Simons, Daniel W. "Henry A. Wallace: Diplomat, Ideologue, and Administrator, 1940-1945." Ph.D. dissertation, St. John's University, 1977.

2999. Fonzi, Gaeton. **Annenberg: A Biography of Power.** New York: Weybright and Talley, 1970.

3000. Foster, John W. **Diplomatic Memoirs.** Boston: Houghton Mifflin, 1909.

3001. Francis, David R. **Russia From the American Embassy, April, 1916-November, 1918.** New York: Scribner, 1921.

3002. Fry, Joseph A. "An American Abroad: The Diplomatic Career of Henry Shelton Sanford." Ph.D. dissertation, University of Virginia, 1974.

3003. Gade, John A. **All My Born Days: Experiences of Naval Intelligence Officer in Europe.** New York: Scribner, 1942.

3004. Galbraith, John K. **Ambassador's Journal.** Boston: Houghton Mifflin, 1969.

3005. _____. "Plain Tales from the Embassy." **American Heritage** 20 (October 1969): 6-13, 97-111.

3006. Gallatin, Abraham A. A. **The Writings of Albert Gallatin.** Edited by Henry Adams. New York: Antiquarian, 1960.

3007. Gallatin, James. **A Great Peacemaker.** Edited by Count Gallatin. New York: Scribner, 1914.

3008. Gallman, Waldemar J. **Iraq Under General Nuri: My Recollections of Nuri Al-Said, 1954-58.** Baltimore: Johns Hopkins University Press, 1964.

3009. Garwood, Ellen C. **Will Clayton: A Short Biography.** Austin: University of Texas

Press, 1958.

3010. Gerard, James W. **Face to Face with Kaiserism**. New York: Doran, 1918.

3011. _____. **My First Eighty-Three Years in America: The Memoirs of James W. Gerard**. Garden City, N.Y.: Doubleday, 1951.

3012. _____. **My four Years in Germany**. New York: Doran, 1917.

3013. Geren, Paul F. **Burma Diary**. New York: Harper, 1943.

3014. Gibbs, William E. "Diaz Executive Agents and United States Foreign Policy." **North Dakota Quarterly** 45 (Spring 1977): 36-53.

3015. Gibson, Hugh S. **A Diplomatic Diary**. New York: Hodder and Stoughton, 1917.

3016. _____. **Hugh Gibson, 1883-1954: Extracts from His Letters and Anecdotes from His Friends**. Edited by Perrin C. Galpin. New York: Belgian-American Educational Foundation, 1956.

3017. _____. **A Journal From Our Legation in Belgium**. Garden City, N.Y.: Doubleday, 1917.

3018. Gilderhus, Mark T. "Henry P. Fletcher in Mexico, 1917-1920: An Ambassador's Response to Revolution." **Rocky Mountain Social Science Journal** 10 (October 1973): 61-70.

3019. Gill, G. J. "Edward Everett and the Northeastern Boundary Controversy." **New England Quarterly** 42 (June 1969): 201-213.

3020. Goldberg, Joyce S. "Patrick Egan: Irish-American Minister to Chile, 1889-93." **Eire-Ireland** 14 (Fall 1979): 83-95.

3021. Goopman, Allan E., ed. **Negotiating While Fighting: The Diary of Admiral C. Turner Joy at the Korean Armistice Conference**. Stanford, Calif.: Hoover Institution, 1978.

3022. Graff, Frank W. "The Strategy of Involvement: A Diplomatic Biography of Sumner Welles 1933-1943." Ph.D. dissertation, University of Michigan, 1971.

3023. Gregory, Ross. "The Superfluous Ambassador: Walter Hine's Page Return to Washington 1916." **Historian** 28 (May 1966): 389-404.

3024. Grew, Joseph C. **Report From Tokyo: A Message to the American People**. New York: Simon and Schuster, 1942.

3025. _____. Report From Tokyo: A Warning to the United Nations. London: Hammond, 1943.

3026. _____. Ten Years in Japan. New York: Simon and Schuster, 1944.

3027. Griffis, Stanton. Lying in State. Garden City, N.Y.: Doubleday, 1952.

3028. Griffiths, John L. The Greater Patriotism: Public Addresses by John Lewis Griffiths, American Consul General at London: Delivered in England and America. New York: Lane, 1918.

3029. Griscom, Lloyd C. Dipolmatically Speaking. Boston: Little, Brown, 1940.

3030. Hagerman, Herbert J. Letters of a Young Diplomat. Santa Fe, N.M.: Rydal, 1937.

3031. Hale, Edward E. Franklin in France: From Original Documents, Most of Which Are Now Published for the First Time. Boston: Roberts, 1887-88.

3032. Hale, Richard W., ed. Letters of Warwick Greene, 1915-1928. Boston: Houghton Mifflin, 1931.

3033. Halstead, Charles R. "Diligent Diplomat: Alexander W. Weddell as American Ambassador to Spain, 1939-1942." Virginia Magazine of History and Biography 82 (January 1974): 3-38.

3034. Hamby, A. L. "Henry A. Wallace, the Liberals, and Soviet-American Relations." Review of Politics 30 (April 1968): 153-169.

3035. Hardy, Arthur S. Things Remembered. Boston: Houghton Mifflin, 1923.

3036. Harper, James W. "Hugh Lenox Scott: Soldier, Diplomat, 1876-1917." Ph.D. dissertation, University of Virginia, 1968.

3037. Harriman, Florence J. Mission to the North. Philadelphia: Lippincott, 1941.

3038. Harriman, W. Averell, and Elie Abel. Special Envoy to Churchill and Stalin, 1941-1946. New York: Random House, 1975.

3039. Harris, Townsend. The Complete Journal of Townsend Harris, First American Consul General and Minister to Japan. Garden City, N.Y.: Doubleday, 1930.

3040. _____. Some Unpublished Letters of Townsend Harris. Edited by Shio Sakanshi. New York: Japan Reference Library, 1941.

3041. Harrison, Thomas S. **The Homely Diary of a Diplomat in the East, 1897-1899.** Boston: Houghton Mifflin, 1917.

3042. Hatch, Alden. **Ambassador Extraordinary: Clare Boothe Luce.** New York: Macmillan, 1945.

3043. Hayes, Carlton J. **Wartime Mission in Spain, 1942-1945.** New York: Macmillan, 1945.

3044. Heinrichs, Waldo H. **American Ambassador: Joseph C. Grew and the Development of the United Diplomatic Tradition.** Boston: Little, Brown, 1966.

3045. Henderson, H. J. "Congressional Factionalism and the Attempt to Recall Benjamin Franklin." **William and Mary Quarterly** 27 (April 1970): 246-267.

3046. Hendrick, Burton J. **The Life and Letters of Walter Hines Page.** Garden City, N.Y.: Doubleday, 1922-25.

3047. Hill, Larry D. "The Progressive Politician as a Diplomat: The Case of John Lind in Mexico." **Americas** 27 (April 1971): 355-372.

3048. Hilliard, Henry W. **Speeches and Addresses, 1839-1954.** New York: Harper, 1855.

3049. Hilton, Stanley E. "The Welles Mission to Europe, February-March 1940: Illusion or Realism?" **Journal of American History** 58 (June 1971): 93-120.

3050. Himelhoch, Myra. "Herman Allen's Mission to Chile, 1823-1827." **Vermont History** 42 (Spring 1974): 155-169.

3051. Hooker, Nancy H., ed. **The Moffat Papers: Selections From the Diplomatic Journals of Jay Pierrepont Moffat, 1919-1943.** Cambridge, Mass.: Harvard University Press, 1956.

3052. Horton, George. **Recollections Grave and Gay: The Story of a Mediterranean Consul.** Indianapolis: Bobbs-Merrill, 1927.

3053. House, Edward M., and Charles Seymour, eds. **What Really Happened at Paris: The Story of the Peace Conference, 1918-1919, By American Delegates.** New York: Scribner, 1921.

3054. Howe, M. A. DeWolfe. **George Von Lengerke Meyer.** New York: Dodd, Mead, 1919.

3055. Howells, William D. **Life and Letters of Wil-**

liam Dean Howells. Edited by Mildred
Howells. Garden City, N.Y.: Doubleday,
1928.

3056. _____. Selected Edition of William Dean
Howells. Bloomington: Indiana University
Press, 1968.

3057. _____. Selected Writings of William Dean
Howells. Edited by Henry Steele Commager.
New York: Random House, 1950.

3058. Hubbell, John T. "Jeremiah Sullivan Black
and the Great Secession Winter." Western
Pennsylvania Historical Magazine 57 (July
1974): 255-274.

3059. Hudson, Randall O. "The Filibuster Minister:
The Career of John Hill Wheeler as United
States Minister to Nicaragua, 1854-1856."
North Carolina Historical Review 49 (July
1971): 280-297.

3060. Humphreys, David. The Miscellaneous Works of
David Humphreys. Gainesville, Fla.: Scholar's Facsimiles--Reprints, 1968.

3061. Huntington-Wilson, Francis M. Memoirs of an
Ex-Diplomat. Boston: Humphries, 1945.

3062. Huntley, Theodore A. The Life of John W.
Davis. New York: Duffield, 1924.

3063. Irving, Washington. Letters From Sunnyside
and Spain. Edited by Stanley T. Williams.
New Haven, Conn.: Yale University Press,
1938.

3064. _____. Spanish Papers. New York: Putnam,
1895.

3065. _____. Washington Irving Diary, Spain,
1828-29. New York: Hispanic Society of
America, 1926.

3066. Izard, Ralph. Correspondence of Mr. Ralph
Izard of South Carolina. Edited by Anne
Izard Dess. New York: Francis and Co.,
1844.

3067. Joerger, Pauline N. King. "A Political Biography of David Lawrence Gregg: American
Diplomat and Hawaiian Official." Ph.D.
dissertation, University of Hawaii, 1976.

3068. Johnson, Arthur M. Winthrop W. Aldrich:
Lawyer, Banker, Diplomat. Cambridge,
Mass.: Harvard University Press, 1968.

3069. Johnson, Hallett. Diplomatic Memoirs:
Serious and Frivolous. New York: Vantage,
1963.

3070. Johnson, Paul W. "The Journalist as Diplomat: E. J. Dillon and the Portsmouth Peace Conference." **Journalism Quarterly** 53 (Winter 1976): 689-693.

3071. Johnson, Robert U. **Remembered Yesterdays.** Boston: Little, Brown, 1923.

3072. Johnson, Willis F. **George Harvey--A Passionate Patriot.** Boston: Houghton Mifflin, 1929.

3073. Kaplan, Lawrence S. "The Brahmin as Diplomat in Nineteenth Century America: Everett, Bancroft, Motley, Lowell." **Civil War History** 19 (March 1973): 5-28.

3074. _____. "The Paris Mission of William Harris Crawford 1813-1815." **Georgia Historical Quarterly** 60 (Spring 1976): 9-22.

3075. Kateb, George. "George F. Kennan: The Heart of a Diplomat." **Commentary** 45 (January 1968): 21-26.

3076. Kehoe, Barbara B. "William Patterson Jones: American Consul in China, 1862-1868." **Journal of the Illinois State Historical Society** 73 (Spring 1980): 45-52.

3077. Kennan, George F. "Diplomacy as a Profession." **Foreign Service Journal** 38 (May 1961): 23-26.

3078. _____. **From Prague and Munich: Diplomatic Papers, 1938-1940.** Princeton, N.J.: Princeton University Press, 1968.

3079. _____. **Memoirs, 1925-1950.** Boston: Little, Brown, 1967.

3080. _____. **Memoirs, 1950-1963.** Boston: Little, Brown, 1972.

3081. _____. **Realities of American Foreign Policy.** Princeton, N.J.: Princeton University Press, 1954.

3082. Kim, Samuel S. "America's First Minister to China, Anson Burlingame and the Tsungli Ymen." **Maryland Historian** 3 (Fall 1972): 87-104.

3083. _____. "Anson Burlingame: A Study in Personal Diplomacy." Ph.D. dissertation, Columbia University, 1966.

3084. King, Rufus. **The Life and Correspondence of Rufus King.** Edited by Charles R. King. New York: Putnam, 1894-1900.

3085. Kirk, Lydia. **Postmarked Moscow.** New York: Scribner, 1952.

3086. Kist, Glenn J. "The Role of Thomas C. Dawson in United States-Latin American Diplomatic Relations: 1897-1912." Ph.D. dissertation, Loyola University of Chicago, 1971.

3087. Kitchens, Allen H. "Ambassador Extraordinary: The Diplomatic Career of Joseph Hodges Choate." Ph.D. dissertation, George Washington University, 1971.

3088. Knight, Jonathan. "George Frost Kennan and the Study of American Foreign Policy: Some Critical Comments." **Western Political Quarterly** 20 (March 1967): 149-160.

3089. Koerner, Gustav P. **Memoirs of Gustav Koerner, 1809-1896.** Edited by Thomas J. McCormac. Cedar Rapids, Iowa: Torch, 1909.

3090. Koskoff, David E. **Joseph P. Kennedy: A Life and Times.** Englewood Cliffs, N.J.: Prentice-Hall, 1974.

3091. Langley, Harold D. "The Tragic Career of H. G. Rogers, Pennsylvania Politician and Jacksonian Diplomat." **Pennsylvania History** 31 (January 1964): 30-61.

3092. Land, Arthur B. I **Saw Freedom Betrayed.** London: Regency, 1949.

3093. Larkin, Thomas O. **The Larkin Papers: Personal, Business, and Official Correspondence of Thomas Loiver Larkin, Merchant and U.S. Consul in California.** Edited by George P. Hammons. Berkeley: University of California Press, 1951.

3094. Laurens, Henry. **Correspondence of Henry Laurens of South Carolina.** New York: Zenger Club, 1861.

3095. _____. "A Narrative of the Capture of Henry Laurens, of His Confinement in the Tower of London." **South Carolina Historical Society Collection** 1 (1857): 18-68.

3096. _____. **The Papers of Henry Laurens.** Edited by Philip M. Hamer and George C. Rogers. Columbia: University of South Carolina Press, 1972.

3097. Laurens, John. **A Succinct Memoir of the Life and Public Service of Colonel John Laurens, Aide-De-Camp to General Washington and Special Envoy to the French Court During the War of the American Revolution** . . . Albany, N.Y.: Williamstadt, 1867.

3098.   Lauter, Beatrice B. "William C. Bullitt and
        the Soviet Union: The Education of a
        Diplomat." Ph.D. dissertation, Yale
        University, 1959.
3099.   Lawrence, May V. A Diplomat's Helpmate. San
        Francisco: Crocker, 1918.
3100.   Leach, Paul R. That Man Dawes. Chicago:
        Reilly and Lee, 1930.
3101.   Leahy, William D. I Was There: The Personal
        Story of the Chief of Staff to Presidents
        Roosevelt and Truman--Based on His Notes
        and Diaries Made at the Time. New York:
        Whittlesey, 1950.
3102.   Lee, William. Letters of William Lee,
        Sheriff and Alderman of London: Commercial
        Agent of the Continental Congress in
        France, and Minister to the Courts of
        Vienna and Berlin, 1766-1783. Edited by
        Worthington Chauncey Ford. Brooklyn:
        Historical Printing Club, 1891.
3103.   _____. A Yankee Jeffersonian: Selections
        From the Diary and Letters of William Lee
        of Massachusetts Written From 1796-1840.
        Cambridge, Mass.: Belknap, 1958.
3104.   Lester, Charles E. My Consulship. New York:
        Cornish Lamport, 1953.
3105.   Levine, Erwin L. Theodore Francis Green.
        Providence, R.I.: Brown University Press,
        1971.
3106.   Lewin, Howard. "A Frontier Diplomat: Andrew
        Montour." Pennsyylvania History 33 (April
        1966): 153-186.
3107.   Libhart, Lemar L. "Simon Cameron's Political
        Exile as United States Minister to Rus-
        sia." Journal of the Lancaster County
        Historical Society 72 (1968): 189-228.
3108.   Lisagor, Peter, and Marguerite Higgins.
        Overtime in Heaven: Adventures in the
        Foreign Service. Garden City, N.Y.:
        Doubleday, 1964.
3109.   Liston, Ann E. "W. C. Rives: Diplomat and
        Politician, 1829-1853." Ph.D. disserta-
        tion, Ohio State University, 1972.
3110.   Lockmiller, David A. Enoch H. Crowder:
        Soldier, Lawyer, Statesman. Columbia:
        University of Missouri Press, 1955.
3111.   Lodge, Henry C. The Storm Has Many Eyes: A
        Personal Narrative. New York: Norton,

1973.
3112. Lohbeck, Don. **Patrick J. Hurley.** Chicago:
Regnery, 1956.
3113. Long, Breckinridge. **The War Diary of Breckinridge Long.** Edited by Fred L. Israel.
Lincoln: University of Nebraska Press,
1966.
3114. Loring, George B. **A Year in Portugal, 1889-
1890.** New York: Putnam, 1891.
3115. Lowell, James R. **Letters of James Russell
Lowell.** Edited by Charles Eliot Norton.
New York: Harper, 1894.
3116. _____. **New Letters of James Russell Lowell.**
Edited by M. A. DeWolfe Howe. New York:
Harper, 1932.
3117. McBride, David. "Solomon Porter Hood, 1853-
1943: Black Missionary, Educator and Minister to Liberia." **Journal of the Lancaster County Historical Society** 84
(1980): 2-9.
3118. McCormick, T. "Wilson-McCook Scheme of 1896-
1897." **Pacific Historical Review** 36
(February 1967): 47-58.
3119. McDonald, James G. **My Mission in Israel,
1948-1951.** New York: Simon and Schuster,
1951.
3120. Maclean, Elizabeth K. "Joseph E. Davies and
Soviet-American Relations, 1941-43."
Diplomatic History 4 (Winter 1980): 73-93.
3121. Marsh, Caroline C. **Life and Letters of
George Perkins Marsh.** New York: Scribner,
1888.
3122. Martin, E. S. **Life of Joseph H. Choate.** New
York: Constable, 1920.
3123. Masingill, Eugene F. "The Diplomatic Career
of Henry Lane Wilson in Latin America."
Ph.D. dissertation, Louisiana State
University, 1957.
3124. Megaree, Richard. "The Diplomacy of John
Bassett Moore: Realism in American Foreign
Policy." Ph.D. dissertation, Northwestern
University, 1963.
3125. Mende, Elsie. **An American Soldier and
Diplomat, Horace Porter.** New York: Stokes,
1927.
3126. Meriwether, Lee. **After Thoughts: A Sequel to
My Yesteryears.** Webster Groves, Mo.:
International Mark Twain Society, 1945.

3127. _____. **My Yesteryears: An Autobiography of Lee Meriwether.** Webster Groves, Mo.: International Mark Twain Society, 1942.

3128. _____. **The War Diary of a Diplomat.** New York: Dodd, Mead, 1919.

3129. Mesta, Perle S., and Robert Cahn. **Perle--My Story.** New York: McGraw-Hill, 1960.

3130. Meyer, Armin H. **Assignment--Tokyo: An Ambassador's Journal.** Indianapolis: Bobbs-Merrill, 1974.

3131. Miller, David H. **My Diary at the Conference of Paris.** New York: Appeal, 1924.

3132. Miller, William J. **Henry Cabot Lodge: A Biography.** New York: Heinemen, 1967.

3133. Millspaugh, Arthur C. **Americans in Persia.** Washington, D.C.: Brookings Institution, 1946.

3134. Minger, Ralph E. "Taft's Mission to Japan: A Study in Personal Diplomacy." **Pacific Historical Review** 30 (August 1961): 279-294.

3135. Miscamble, Wilson D. "George F. Kennan, the Policy Planning Staff and the Origins of the Marshall Plan." **Mid-America** 62 (April-July 1980): 75-89.

3136. Mitchell, Eleanor S. **Postscript to Seven Homes.** Francestown, N.H.: Jones, 1960.

3137. _____. **Seven Homes Had I: Experiences of a Foreign Service Wife.** New York: Exposition, 1955.

3138. Mitchell, Kell F. "Frank L. Polk and Continued American Participation in the Paris Peace Conference, 1919." **North Dakota Quarterly** 41 (Spring 1973): 50-61.

3139. Mitchell, Lee C. "'But This History': Henry Adams' 'Education' in London Diplomacy." **New England Quarterly** 53 (September 1979): 358-376.

3140. Moffatt, Jay P. **The Moffat Papers: Selections From the Diplomatic Journals of Jay Pierrepont Moffat, 1919-1943.** Edited by Nancy Harrison Hooker. Cambridge, Mass.: Harvard University Press, 1956.

3141. Monti, Luigi. **Adventures of a Consul Abroad.** Boston: Lee and Shepard, 1878.

3142. Moran, Benjamin. **The Journal of Benjamin Moran.** Edited by Sarah Agnes Wallace and Frances Elma Gillespie. Chicago: University of Chicago Press, 1949.

3143. Morgenthau, Henry. **Ambassador Morgenthau's Story**. Garden City, N.Y.: Doubleday, Page, 1918.

3144. _____. **All in a Lifetime**. Garden City, N.Y.: Doubleday, Page, 1922.

3145. _____. **I Was Sent to Athens**. Garden City, N.Y.: Doubleday, Page, 1929.

3146. Morris, Gouverneur. **The Diary and Letters of Gouverneur Morris**. Edited by Anne Cary Morris. New York: Scribner, 1888.

3147. Morris, Ira N. **From an American Legation**. New York: Knopf, 1923.

3148. _____. **Heritage From My Father**. New York: I. N. Morris, 1947.

3149. Morrow, Elizabeth C. **The Mexican Years: Leaves From the Diary of Elizabeth Cutter Morrow**. New York: Spiral, 1953.

3150. Morrow, John H. **First American Ambassador to Guinea**. New Brunswick, N.J.: Rutgers University Press, 1967.

3151. Motley, John L. **John Lathrop Motley and His Family: Further Letters and Records**. Edited by Herbert St. John Mildmay. New York: Lane, 1910.

3152. _____. **The Writings of John Lathrop Motley**. New York: Harper, 1900.

3153. Mott, Thomas B. **Myron T. Herrick, Friend of France**. Garden City, N.Y.: Doubleday, Doran, 1929.

3154. _____. **Twenty Years as Military Attache**. New York: Oxford, 1937.

3155. Murphy, Robert D. **Diplomat Among Warriors**. Garden City, N.Y.: Doubleday, 1964.

3156. Murray, William V. **Political Sketches: Inscribed to His Excellency John Adams, Minister Plenipotentiary From the United States to the Court of Great Britain by a Citizen of the United States**. London: Dilly, 1787.

3157. Nevins, Allan. **Henry White: Thirty Years of American Diplomacy**. New York: Harper, 1930.

3158. Nicolson, Harold. **Dwight Morrow**. New York: Harcourt, Brace, 1935.

3159. O'Grady, Joseph P. "Politics and Diplomacy: The Appointment of Anthony M. Keiley to Rome in 1885." **Virginia Magazine of History and Biography** 76 (April 1968):

191-220.
3160. O'Shaughnessy, Edith L. Diplomatic Days. New
       York: Harper, 1917.
3161. _____. A Diplomat's Wife in Mexico. New
       York: Harper, 1916.
3162. _____. Viennese Medley. New York: Huebsch,
       1924.
3163. Pace, Antonio. Benjamin Franklin and Italy.
       Philadelphia: American Philosophical
       Society, 1958.
3164. Paddock, Paul. China Diary: Crisis Diplomacy
       in Dairen. Ames: Iowa State University
       Press, 1977.
3165. Page, Walter H. The Life and Letters of
       Walter Hines Page. Edited by Burton J.
       Hendrick. Garden City, N.Y.: Doubleday,
       Page, 1923-26.
3166. Palmer, Frederick. America in France. New
       York: Dodd, Mead, 1918.
3167. _____. Bliss, Peacemaker: The Life and Let-
       ters of Tasker Howard Bliss. New York:
       Dodd, Mead, 1934.
3168. Parker, Maude. Impersonation of a Lady.
       Boston: Houghton Mifflin, 1934.
3169. _____. Secret Envoy. Indianapolis: Bobbs-
       Merrill, 1930.
3170. Parker, Peter. The Journal of Peter Parker.
       London: Smith, Elder, 1838.
3171. Patterson, Jefferson. Diplomatic Terminus:
       An Experience in Uruguay. Cambridge, Mass:
       Riverside, 1962.
3172. Petrov, Vladimir. A Study in Diplomacy: The
       Story of Arthur Bliss Lane. Chicago: Reg-
       nery, 1971.
3173. Pfaller, Louis L. "Indian Diplomat at Large:
       Two Incidents in the Career of Major
       McLaughlin." North Dakota History 42
       (Spring 1975): 4-17.
3174. Phelps, Edward J. Orations and Essays of Ed-
       ward John Phelps--Diplomat and Statesman.
       Edited by J. G. McCullough. New York:
       Harper, 1901.
3175. Pitre, M. "Frederick Douglas and the Annex-
       ation of Santo Domingo." Journal of Negro
       History 62 (October 1977): 390-400.
3176. Poinsett, Joel R. The Present Political
       State of Mexico: A Previously Unpublished
       Confidential Report on the Political Con-

dition of Mexico in 1822, Prepared for the U.S. Secretary of State. Edited by L. Smith Lee. Salisbury, N.C.: Documentary Publications, 1976.

3177. Powers, Richard J. "Kennan Against Himself: From Containment to Disengagement: a Decade of U.S. Foreign Policy Making as Focused on the Ideas and Concepts of George F. Kennan, 1947-1957." Ph.D. dissertation, Claremont College, 1967.

3178. Prisco, Salvatore. "John Barrett, Exponent of Commercial Expansion: A Study of a Progressive Era Diplomat, 1887-1920." Ph.D. dissertation, Rutgers University, 1969.

3179. _____. "John Barrett's Plan to Mediate the Mexican Revolution." **Americas** 27 (April 1971): 413-425.

3180. _____. "Lloyd C. Griscom, New Jersey Patrician in Diplomatic Service, 1893-1909." **New Jersey History** 98 (Spring/Summer 1980): 65-80.

3181. _____. "A Vermonter in Siam: How John Barrett Began his Diplomatic Career." **Vermont History** 37 (Spring 1969): 83-93.

3182. Pugach, N. "Making the Open Door Work: Paul S. Reinsch in China, 1913-1919." **Pacific Historical Review** 38 (May 1969): 157-175.

3183. Rankin, Karl L. **China Assignment.** Seattle: University of Washington Press, 1964.

3184. Reed, James E. "American Foreign Policy, the Politics of Missions and Josiah Strong, 1890-1900." **Church History** 41 (June 1972): 230-245.

3185. Reed, Joseph V. **To the Embassy.** New York: Duell, Sloan, and Pearce, 1963.

3186. Reinsch, Paul S. **An American Diplomat in China.** Garden City, N.Y.: Doubleday, 1922.

3187. Richardson, Norval. **My Diplomatic Education.** New York: Dodd, Mead, 1923.

3188. _____. **Living Abroad: The Adventures of an American Family.** New York: Lippincott, 1938.

3189. Roider, Karl A. "William Lee, Our First Envoy in Vienna." **Virginia Magazine of History and Biography** 86 (April 1978): 163-168.

3190. Rosenau, James N. **The Nomination of Charles "Chip" Bohlen.** New York: Holt, 1958.

3191.   Rosenwaike, Ira. "Bernard Henry: His Naval
         and Diplomatic Career." **American Jewish
         History** 69 (June 1980): 488-496.
3192.   Rostow, Walt W. **View from the Seventh Floor.**
         New York: Harper and Row, 1964.
3193.   Rounds, Frank W. **A Window on Red Square.**
         Boston: Houghton Mifflin, 1953.
3194.   Rowe, Joseph M. "William Howard Taft: Diplo-
         matic Trouble-Shooter." Ph.D. disser-
         tation, Texas A & M University, 1977.
3195.   Rubin, Barry. "Ambassador Laurence A.
         Steinhardt: The Perils of a Jewish
         Diplomat, 1940-1945." **American Jewish
         History** 70 (March 1981): 331-346.
3196.   Rush, Richard. **Narrative of a Residence at
         the Court of London.** London: Bailey, 1833.
3197.   _____. Occasional Productions: Political,
         Diplomatic, and Miscellaneous.
         Philadelphia: Lippincott, 1860.
3198.   Russell, Beatrice. **Living in State.** New
         York: McKay, 1959.
3199.   Safford, Jeffrey J. "Edward Hurley and
         American Shipping Policy: An Elaboration
         on Wilsonian Diplomacy, 1918-1919."
         Historian 35 (August 1973): 568-586.
3200.   Sanders, Neill F. "Freeman Harlow Morse and
         the Forber-Aspinwall Mission: An Aberra-
         tion in Union Foreign Policy." **Lincoln
         Herald** 80 (Spring 1978): 15-25.
3201.   Sands, William F. **Undiplomatic Memories.** New
         York: Whittlesey, 1930.
3202.   Sawyer, Charles. **Concerns of a Conservative
         Democrat.** Carbondale: Southern Illinois
         University Press, 1968.
3203.   Sayre, Francis B. **Glad Adventure.** New York:
         Macmillan, 1957.
3204.   Schneider, Laurence A. "Humphrey Marshall,
         Commissioner to China, 1853-1854." **Regis-
         ter of the Kentucky Historical Society** 63
         (April 1965): 97-120.
3205.   Schrier, William. **Gerrit J. Diekema, Orator:
         A Rhetorical Study of the Political and
         Occasional Addresses of Gerrit J Diekema.**
         Grand Rapids, Mich.: Aerdmans, 1950.
3206.   Schurz, Carl. **Autobiography: By Wayne
         Andrews.** New York: Scribner, 1961.
3207.   _____. **The Intimate Letters of Carl Schurz,
         1941-1969.** Edited by Joseph Schafer.

Madison: State Historical Society of Wisconsin, 1928.
3208. _____. The Reminiscences of Carl Schurz. New York: McClure, 1907-8.
3209. _____. Speeches, Correspondence, and Political Papers of Carl Schurz. Edited by Frederick Bancroft. New York: Putnam, 1913.
3210. Schuyler, Eugene. Selected Essays: with a Memoir by Evelyn Shuyler Schaeffer. New York: Scribner, 1901.
3211. Sebald, William J. With MacArthur in Japan. New York: Norton, 1965.
3212. Seward, Frederick W. Reminiscences of a War-Time Statesman and Diplomat, 1830-1915. New York: Putnam, 1916.
3213. Seymour, Charles, ed. The Intimate Papers of Colonel House. Boston: Houghton Mifflin, 1927-28.
3214. Sharp, William G. War Memories. Edited by Warrington Dawson. London:Constable, 1931.
3215. Shaw, Smauel. The Journals of Major Samuel Shaw, The First American Consul at Canton. Taipei, Taiwan: Ch'eng-Wen, 1968.
3216. Sherrill, Charles H. A Year's Embassy to Mustafa Kemal. New York: Scribner, 1934.
3217. Shotwell, James T. At the Paris Peace Conference. New York: Macmillan, 1937.
3218. Shuster, W. Morgan. Strangling of Persia. New York: Century, 1912.
3219. Simpson, Bertram L. Indiscreet Letters from Peking. New York: Dodd, Mead, 1907.
3220. Skinner, Robert P. Abyssinia of Today: An Account of the First Mission Sent by the American Government to the Court of the King of Kings, 1903-1904. New York: Longmans, Green, 1906.
3221. _____. Our Mission to Abyssinia: Consul General Skinner's Report. Washington, D.C.: Government Printing Office, 1904.
3222. Smith, Arthur D. Mr. House of Texas. New York: Funk and Wagnalls, 1940.
3223. _____. The Real Colonel House. New York: Doran, 1918.
3224. Smith, Dwight L. "Josiah Harmar, Diplomatic Courier." Pennsylvania Magazine of History and Biography 87 (October 1963): 420-430.
3225. Smith, Earl E. The Fourth Floor: An Account

of the Castro Communist Revolution. New York: Random House, 1962.

3226. Smith, Jean E. "Selection of a Proconsul for Germany: The Appointment of Gen. Lucius D. Clay, 1945." **Military Affairs** 40 (October 1976): 123-129.

3227. Smith, Walter B. **My Three Years in Moscow.** Philadelphia: Lippincott, 1950.

3228. Smith, William L. **Observations on China and the Chinese.** New York: Carleton, 1763.

3229. Smylie, Robert F. "John Leighton Stuart: A Missionary Diplomat in the Sino-Japanese Conflict, 1937-1941." **Journal of Presbyterian History** 53 (Fall 1975): 256-276.

3230. Smythe, David M. **American Vice-Consul.** Boston: Christopher, 1942.

3231. Southern, David W. "The Ordeal of Brand Whitlock, Minister to Belgium, 1914-1922." **Northwest Ohio Quarterly** 41 (Summer 1969): 113-127.

3232. Stackman, Ralph R. "Lawrence A. Steinhart: New Deal Diplomat, 1933-1945." Ph.D. dissertation, Michigan State University, 1967.

3233. Standley, William H., and Arthur A. Ageton. **Admiral Ambassador to Russia.** Chicago: Regnery, 1955.

3234. Stanley, Ruth M. "Nathan kirk Griggs, Consul to Chemnitz, Germany, 1876-1882." **Nebraska History** 57 (Winter 1976): 439-459.

3235. Stanton, Edwin F. **Brief Authority: Excursions of a Common Man in an Uncommon World.** New York: Harper, 1956.

3236. Stourzh, Gerald. **Benjamin Franklin and American Foreign Policy.** 2nd ed. Chicago: University of Chicago Press, 1969.

3237. Straus, Oscar S. **Under Four Administrations: From Cleveland to Taft.** Boston: Houghton Mifflin, 1922.

3238. Stern, Sheldon M. "Henry Cabot Lodge and Louis A. Collidge in Defense of American Sovereignty, 1898-1920." **Proceedings of the Massachusetts Historical Society** 87 (1975): 118-134.

3239. Strong, Theron G. **Joseph H. Choate--New Englander, New Yorker, Lawyer, Ambassador.** New York: Dodd, Mead, 1917.

3240. Stuart, John L. **Fifty Years in China: The**

Memoirs of John Leighton Stuart, Missionary and Ambassador. New York: Random
House, 1954.

3241. Swerczek, Ronald E. "The Diplomatic Career
of Hugh Gibson, 1908-1938." Ph.D. dissertation, University of Iowa, 1972.

3242. Sylvester, John A. "Arthur Bliss Lane:
American Career Diplomat." Ph.D. dissertation, University of Wisconsin, 1967.

3243. Taylor, Maxwell D. Responsibility and
Response. New York: Harper and Row, 1967.

3244. _____. The Uncertain Trumper. New York:
Harper, 1960.

3245. Thayer, Charles W. Bears in the Caviar.
Philadelphia: Lippincott, 1951.

3246. _____. Diplomat. New York: Harper, 1959.

3247. _____. Guerilla. New York: New American,
1963.

3248. Thompson, Waddy. Recollections of Mexico.
New York: Wiley, 1846.

3249. Thorpe, James A. "The Mission of Arthur C.
Millspaugh to Iran, 1943-1945." Ph.D. dis-
sertation, University of Wisconsin,
Madison, 1973.

3250. Timmons, Bascom N. Portrait of an American:
Charles Gates Dawes. New York: Holt, 1953.

3251. Towell, William P. "Cognitive Complexity of
a Foreign Policy Decision-Maker Under Conditions of Rising Threat: Joseph Grew and
U.S.-Japan Relations, 1938-1941." Ph.D.
dissertation, University of Illinois, Urbana, 1975.

3252. Ullman, Richard H. "Realities of George F.
Kennan." Foreign Policy 28 (Fall 1977):
139-155.

3253. Vare, Daniele. The Laughing Diplomat. Garden
City, N.Y.: Doubleday, 1938.

3254. Varg, Paul A. Open Door Diplomat: The Life
of W. W. Rockhill. Urbana: University of
Illinois Press, 1952.

3255. Viereck, George S. The Strangest Friendship
in History: Woodrow Wilson and Colonel
House. New York: Liverright, 1932.

3256. Villard, Henry S. Affairs at State. New
York: Crowell, 1965.

3257. Walker, J. Samuel. "The Confessions of a
Cold Warrior: Clinton P. Anderson and
American Foreign Policy, 1945-1972." New

Mexico Historical Review 52 (April 1977): 117-134.
3258. Wallace, Hugh C. The Speeches of the Honorable American Ambassador to France, 1919-1921. Paris: Plon Nourrit, 1921.
3259. Wallace, Lewis. Lew Wallace: An Autobiography. New York: Harper, 1906.
3260. Weber, Ralph E. "Joel R. Poinsett's Secret Mexican Dispatch Twenty." South Carolina Historical Magazine 75 (April 1974): 67-76.
3261. Welles, Sumner. The Time for Decision. New York: Harper, 1944.
3262. _____. We Need Not Fail. Boston: Houghton Mifflin, 1948.
3263. _____. Where Are We Heading? New York: Harper, 1946.
3264. _____. World of the Four Freedoms. New York: Columbia University Press, 1943.
3265. White, Andrew D. The Autobiography of Andrew Dickson White. New York: Century, 1905.
3266. _____. The First Hague Conference. Boston: World Peace Foundation, 1912.
3267. Whitlock, Brand. Belgium: A Personal Narrative. New York: Appleton, 1919.
3268. _____. The Letters and Journal of Brand Whitlock. Edited by Allan Nevins. New York: Appleton-Century, 1936.
3269. Whitney, Thomas P. Russia in My Life. New York: Reynal, 1962.
3270. Whittemore, Bert R. "A Quiet Triumph: The Mission of John Gilbert Winant to London, 1941." Historical New Hampshire 30 (Spring 1975): 1-11.
3271. Wikoff, Henry. The Adventures of a Roving Diplomat. New York: Petridge, 1857.
3272. _____. A New Yorker in the Foreign Office and His Adventures in Paris. London: Truebner, 1858.
3273. _____. The Reminiscences of an Idler. New York: Fords, Howard, and Hulbert, 1880.
3274. Williams, John B. The New Zealand Journal, 1842-1844, of John Brown Williams of Salem, Massachusetts, Edited by Robert W. Kenny. Salem, Mass.: Peabody Museum of Salem, 1956.
3275. Williams, Samuel W. A Journal of the Perry Expedition to Japan (1853-1854). Edited by

Frederick Wells Williams. Yokohama: Kelly and Walsh, 1910.
3276. Williams, Walter L. "Nineteenth Century Pan-Africanist: John Henry Smyth, United States Minister to Liberia, 18780-1885." **Journal of Negro History** 63 (January 1978): 18-25.
3277. Williamson, John G. Adolphus. **Caracas Diary, 1835-1840.** Edited by Jane Lucas de Grumond. Baton Rouge: Camelia, 1954.
3278. Willson, Beckles. **America's Ambassadors to France (1777-1927).** New York: Stokes, 1928.
3279. Wilson, Francis M. H. **Memoirs of an Ex-Diplomat.** Boston: Bruce Humphries, 1945.
3280. Wilson, Henry L. **Diplomatic Episodes in Mexico, Belgium, and Chile.** Garden City, N.Y.: Doubleday, 1927.
3281. Wilson, Hugh R. **A Career Diplomat: The Third Chapter--The Third Reich.** Edited by Hugh R. Wilson. New York: Vantage, 1960.
3282. _____. **Diplomacy as a Career.** Cambridge, Mass.: Riverside, 1941.
3283. _____. **Diplomat Between Wars.** New York: Longmans, Green, 1941.
3284. _____. **The Education of a Diplomat.** New York: Longmans, Green, 1938.
3285. Winant, John G. **Letter From Grosvernor Square: An Account of a Stewardship.** Boston: Houghton Mifflin, 1947.
3286. _____. **Our Greatest Harvest: Selected Speeches.** London: Hodder, 1950.
3287. Winfield, Louise. **Living Overseas.** Washington, D.C.: Public Affairs, 1962.
3288. Wolf, Charles. **Indonesian Assignment.** University: University of Alabama Press, 1952.
3289. Wood, Eric F. **The Note-Book of an Attache: Seven Months in the War Zone.** New York: Century, 1915.
3290. Woolsey, Lester H. "The Personal Diplomacy of Colonel House." **American Journal of International Law** 21 (October 1927): 706-715.
3291. Wright, C. Ben. "George F. Kennan, Scholar-Diplomat: 1926-1946." Ph.D. dissertation, University of Wisconsin, Madison, 1972.
3292. Wright, Esmond, ed. **Benjamin Franklin: A**

Profile. New York: Hill and Wang, 1970.
3293. Yost, Bartley. **Memoirs of a Consul.** New York: Vantage, 1955.
3294. Young, John R. **Men and Memories: Personal Reminiscences.** Edited by Mary D. Young. New York:P. Neeley, 1901.
3295. Younger, Edward E. "The Early Diplomatic Career of John A. Kasson." Ph.D. dissertation, George Washington University, 1943.
3296. Zeiger, Henry A. **The Remarkable Henry Cabot Lodge.** New York: Popular Library, 1964.

Dean Acheson

3297. Acheson, Dean G. "Danger in the World--And What to Do About It." **U.S. News and World Report** 48 (June 1960): 116-119.

3298. _____. "The Eclipse of the State Department." **Foreign Affairs** 49 (July 1971): 593-606.

3299. _____. **Fragments of My Fleece**. New York: Norton, 1971.

3300. _____. **Morning and Noon**. Boston: Houghton Mifflin, 1965.

3301. _____. **The Pattern of Responsibility: From the Record of Dean Acheson**. Edited by McGeorge Bundy. Boston: Houghton Mifflin, 1952.

3302. _____. **Power and Diplomacy**. Cambridge, Mass.: Harvard University Press, 1958.

3303. _____. "The Premises of American Policy." **Orbis** 3 (October 1959): 269-281.

3304. _____. **Present at the Creation: My Years in the State Department**. New York: Norton, 1969.

3305. _____. "Responsibility for Decision in Foreign Policy." **Yale Review** 44 (Autumn 1954): 1-12.

3306. _____. **Sketches From Life of Men I Have Known**. New York: Harper, 1961.

3307. _____. **Strengthening the Forces of Freedom: Selected Speeches and Statements . . . February 1949-April 1950**. Washington, D.C.: Government Printing Office, 1950.

3308. _____. "The United States and Europe: The Practice of Partnership." **Foreign Affairs** 41 (January 1963): 247-260.

3309. _____. **This Vast External Realm**. New York: Norton, 1973.

3310. Loss, Richard A. "Secretary of State Dean Acheson as Political Executive: Administrator of Personnel Security." **Public Administration Review** 34 (July 1974): 352-358.

3311. _____. "Secretary of State Dean Acheson: The Political Dimension." Ph.D. dissertation, Cornell University, 1971.

3312.　McLellan, David. S. "Dean Acheson and the Korean War." **Political Science Quarterly** 83 (March 1968): 16-39.

3313.　_____. "The 'Operational Code' Approach to the Study of Political Leaders: Dean Acheson's Philosophical and Instrumental Beliefs." **Canadian Journal of Political Science** 4 (March 1971): 52-75.

3314.　Perlmutter, Oscar W. "Acheson and the Diplomacy of World War II." **Western Political Quarterly** 14 (December 1961): 896-911.

3315.　_____. "Acheson vs. Congress." **Review of Politics** 22 (January 1960): 5-44.

3316.　Smith, Gaddis. **Dean Acheson.** New York: Cooper Square, 1972.

3317.　Stupak, Ronald J. "Dean Acheson: The Secretary of State as a Policy-Maker." Ph.D. dissertation, Ohio State University, 1967.

3318.　_____. **The Shaping of Foreign Policy: The Role of the Secretary of State as Seen By Dean Acheson.** New York: Odyssey, 1969.

John Quincy Adams

3319.　Adams, John Quincy. **The Diary of John Quincy Adams, 1794-1845: American Diplomacy, and Political, Social, and Intellectual Life From Washington to Polk.** Edited by Allen Nevins. New York: Ungar, 1928.

3320.　_____. **Writings of John Quincy Adams.** Edited by Worthington Chauncey Ford. New York: Macmillan, 1913-17.

3321.　Appleby, Joyce. "The Jefferson-Adams Rupture and the First French Translation of John Adams' Defence." **American Historical Review** 73 (April 1968): 1084-1091.

3322.　Aring, Charles D. "Adams and Jefferson, a Correspondence." **History Today** 21 (September 1971): 609-618.

3323.　Banninga, Jerald L. "John Quincy Adams' Address of July 4, 1821." **Quarterly Journal of Speech** 53 (February 1967): 44-49.

3324.　Bergquist, Harold E. "John Quincy Adams and the Promulgation of the Monroe Doctrine, October-december 1823." **Essex Institute Historical Collections** 111 (January 1975): 37-52.

3325.　Crapol, Edward P. "John Quincy Adams and the

Monroe Doctrine: Some New Evidence." **Pacific Historical Review** 48 (August 1979): 413-418.

3326. Glick, Wendell. "The Best Possible World of John Quincy Adams." **New England Quarterly** 37 (March 1964): 3-17.

3327. Macoll, John D. "John Quincy Adams's Compromise Tariff of 1832." **Capitol Studies** 1 (Fall 1972): 41-58.

3328. Mirak, Robert. "John Quincy Adams, Jr., and the Reconstruction Crisis." **New England Quarterly** 35 (June 1962): 187-202.

3329. Morgan, William G. "John Quincy Adams versus Andrew Jackson: Their Biographers and the 'Corrupt Bargain' Charge." **Tennessee Historical Quarterly** 26 (Spring 1967): 43-58.

3330. Tatum, Edward H. **The United States and Europe, 1815-1823: A Study in the Background of the Monroe Doctrine.** Berkeley: University of California Press, 1936.

Robert Bacon

3331. Bacon, Robert. **Robert Bacon: Life and Letters.** Edited by James Brown Scott. Garden City, N.Y.: Doubleday, 1923.

3332. Scott, James B. **Robert Bacon: Life and Letters.** Garden City, N.Y.: Doubleday, 1923.

Thomas Francis Bayard

3333. Bayard, Richard H. **Bayard Papers.** Washington, D.C.: American Historical Association, 1913.

James Gillespie Blaine

3334. Ford, Trowbridge H. "The Political Crusade Against Blaine in 1884." **Mid-America** 57 (January 1975): 38-55.

3335. Spetter, Allan. "Harrison and Blaine: Foreign Policy, 1889-1893." **Indiana Magazine of History** 65 (September 1969): 215-228.

3336. Strobel, Edward H. **Mr. Blaine and His Foreign Policy: An Examination of His Most Important Dispatches While Secretary of**

State. Boston: Hall, 1884.

James Buchanan

3337. Bobr-Tylingo, Stanislaw. "James Buchanan and
        Poland in 1854." **Antemurale** 23 (1979): 75-
        93.
3338. Davis, Robert R. "James Buchanan and the
        Suppression of the Slave Trade, 1859-
        1861." **Pennsylvania History** 33 (October
        1966): 446-459.
3339. Fufita, Fumiko. "Foreign Policy in a Demo-
        cracy: Polk, Buchanan and Oregon." **Amer-
        ican Review** 7 (1973): 107-144.
3340. Hillman, Franklin P. "The Diplomatic Career
        of James Buchanan." Ph.D. dissertation,
        George Washington University, 1953.
3341. Horton, Rushmore G. **The Life and Public Ser-
        vices of James Buchanan: Late Minister to
        England and Formerly Minister to Russia .
        . . and Secretary of State, Including the
        Most Important of His State Papers.** New
        York: Derky and Jackson, 1856.
3342. Klein, Frederic S. "James Buchanan--Man on a
        Tightrope." **American History Illustrated** 1
        (May 1966): 13-20, 24.
3343. Klein, Philip S. "James Buchanan--Selfish
        Politician or Christian Statesman?"
        Journal of Presbyterian History 42 (March
        1964): 1-18.
3344. Mackinnon, William P. "The Buchanan Spoils
        System and the Utah Expedition: Careers of
        W. M. F. Magraw and John M. Hockaday."
        Utah Historical Quarterly 31 (Spring
        1963): 127-150.
3345. Rosenberger, Homer T. "To What Extent Did
        Harriet Lane Influence the Public Policies
        of James Buchanan." **Journal of the Lan-
        caster County Historical Society** 74
        (1970): 1-22.

William Jennings Bryan

3346. Bryan, William Jennings. **Heart to Heart
        Appeals.** New York: Revell, 1917.
3347. Bryan, William Jennings, and Mary B. Bryan.
        The Memoirs of William Jennings Bryan.
        Philadelphia: Winston, 1925.

3348.   _____. The Old World and Its Ways. St.
         Louis: Thompson, 1907.
3349.   _____. Speeches of William Jennings Bryan,
         Revised and Arranged by Himself. New York:
         Funk and Wagnals, 1909.
3350.   Clements, Kendrick A. "'A Kindness to Car-
         ranza': William Jennings Bryan, Inter-
         national Harvester and Intervention in
         Yucatan." Nebraska History 57 (Winter
         1976): 479-490.
3351.   _____. "William Jennings Bryan and Demo-
         cratic Foreign Policy, 1896-1915." Ph.D.
         dissertation, University of California,
         1970.
3352.   Coletta Paolo E. "Bryan, Anti-Imperialism
         and Missionary Diplomacy." Nebraska
         History 44 (September 1963):167-188.
3353.   _____. "Bryan at Baltimore, 1912: Wilson's
         Warwick?" Nebraska History 57 (Summer
         1976): 201-225.
3354.   _____. "'The Most Thankless Task': Bryan
         and the California Alien Land Legis-
         lation." Pacific Historical review 36 (May
         1967): 163-188.
3355.   _____. "The Patronage Battle Between Bryan
         and Hitchcock." Nebraska History 49
         (Summer 1968): 121-137.
3356.   _____. "Secretary of State William Jennings
         Bryan and 'Deserving Democrats'." Mid-
         America 48 (April 1966): 75-98.
3357.   _____. "William Jennings Bryan and Currency
         and Banking Reform." Nebraska History 45
         (March 1964): 31-58.
3358.   _____. "William Jennings Bryan and the
         United States-Colombia Impasse, 1903-
         1921." Hispanic American Historical Review
         47 (November 1967): 486-501.
3359.   _____. "William Jennings Bryan's Plans for
         World Peace." Nebraska History 58 (Summer
         1977): 193-217.
3360.   Curti, Merle E. Bryan and World Peace.
         Northampton, Mass.: Department of History,
         Smith College, 1931.
3361.   Daly, James J. "William Jennings Bryan and
         the Red River Valley Press, 1890-1896."
         North Dakota History 42 (Winter 1975): 26-
         37.
3362.   Daniels, Roger. "William Jennings Bryan and

the Japanese." **Southern California
Quarterly** 48 (Fall 1966): 227-240.
3363. Fite, Gilbert C. "William Jennings Bryan and
the Campaign of 1896: Some Views and
Problems." **Nebraska History** 47 (September
1966): 247-264.
3364. Glad, Paul W., ed. **William Jennings Bryan: A
Profile.** New York: Hill and Wang, 1968.
3365. Himmelberg, Robert F., and Raymond J. Cunningham, eds. "William Jennings Bryan, Or-
lando Jay Smith, and the Founding of the
Commoner: Some New Bryan Letters."
Nebraska History 48 (Spring 1967): 69-79.
3366. Kaplan, Edward S. "William Jennings Bryan
and the Panama Canal Tolls Controversy."
Mid-America 56 (April 1974): 100-108.
3367. Lindeen, Shirley A., and James Walter
Lindeen. "Bryan, Norris and the Doctrine
of Party Responsibility." **American Studies**
11 (Spring 1970): 45-53.
3368. Long, John C. **Bryan: The Great commoner.** New
York: Appleton, 1928.
3369. Ogle, Arthur B. "Above the World: William
Jennings Bryan's View of the American
Nation in International Affairs." **Nebraska
History** 61 (Summer 1980): 152-171.
3370. Russell, C. Allyn. "William Jennings Bryan:
Statesman--Fundamentalist." **Journal of
Presbyterian History** 53 (Summer 1975): 93-
119.
3371. Schruben, F. W. "William Jennings Bryan,
Reformer." **Social Studies** 55 (January
1964): 12-16.
3372. Smith, Willard H. "William Jennings Bryan
and Racism." **Journal of Negro History** 53
(April 1969): 127-149.
3373. _____. "William Jennings Bryan and the
Social Gospel." **Journal of American
History** 53 (June 1966): 41-60.
3374. _____. "The Pacifist Thought of William
Jennings Bryan." **Mennonite Quarterly
Review** 45 (April 1971): 152-181.
3375. Sutton, Walter A. "Bryan, LaFollette,
Norris: Three Mid-Western Politicians."
Journal of the West 8 (October 1969): 613-
658.
3376. Vivian, James F. "Wilson, Bryan, and the
American Delegation to the Abortive Fifth

Pan American Conference, 1914." **Nebraska History** 59 (Spring 1978): 56-69.
3377. Williams, Wayne C. **William Jennings Bryan**. New York: Revell, 1923.
3378. Worthen, Edward H. "The Mexican Journeys of William Jennings Bryan, a Good Neighbor." **Nebraska History** 59 (Winter 1978): 485-500.

James Francis Byrnes

3379. Byrnes, James F. **All in One Lifetime**. New York: Harper, 1958.
3380. _____. **Speaking Frankly**. New York: Harper, 1947.
3381. Byrnes, Robert F. "United States Policy Towards Eastern Europe: Before and After Helsinki." **Review of Politics** 37 (October 1975): 435-463.
3382. Gormly, James L. "Secretary of State James F. Byrnes, An Initial British Evaluation." **South Carolina Historical Magazine** 79 (July 1978): 198-205.
3383. Partin, John W. "Roosevelt, Byrnes and the 1944 Vice-Presidential Nomination." **Historian** 42 (November 1979): 85-100.
3384. Paterson, Thomas G. "Potsdam, the Atomic Bomb, and the Cold War: A Discussion with James F. Byrnes." **Pacific Historical Review** 41 (May 1972): 225-230.
3385. Theoharis, Athan. "James F. Byrnes: Unwitting Yalta Myth-Maker." **Political Science Quarterly** 81 (December 1966): 581-592.

John Caldwell Calhoun

3386. Barsness, Richard W. "John C. Calhoun and the Military Establishment, 1817-1825." **Wisconsin Magazine of History** 50 (Autumn 1966): 43-53.
3387. Baskin, Darryl. "The Pluralist Vision of John C. Calhoun." **Polity** 2 (Fall 1969): 49-64.
3388. Bergeron, Paul H., ed. "A Tennessean Blasts Calhoun and Nullification." **Tennessee Historical Quarterly** 26 (Winter 1967): 383-386.
3389. Boller, P. F. "Calhoun on Liberty." **South**

Atlantic Quarterly 66 (Summer 1967): 395-408.

3390.   Harrison, Lowell H. "'A Cast-Iron Man': John C. Calhoun." American History Illustrated 9 (February 1975): 4-9, 43-49.

3391.   Kaleb, George. "Majority Principle: Calhoun and His Antecedents." Political Science Quarterly 84 (December 1969): 583-605.

3392.   Marmor, T. R. "Anti-industrialism and the Old South: The Agrarian Perspective of John C. Calhoun." Comparative Studies in Society and History 9 (July 1967): 377-406.

3393.   Silbey, Joel H. "John C. Calhoun and the Limits of Southern Congressional Unity, 1841-1850." Historian 30 (November 1967): 58-71.

3394.   Skeen, C. Edward. "Calhoun, Crawford, and the Politics of Retrenchment." South Carolina Historical Magazine 73 (July 1972): 141-155.

Lewis Cass

3395.   Carmony, Donald F., and Francis P. Prucha, eds. "A Memorandum of Lewis Cass Concerning a System for the Regulation of Indian Affairs." Wisconsin Magazine of History 52 (Autumn 1968): 35-50.

3396.   Miriani, Ronald G. "Lewis Cass and Indiana Administration in the Old Northwest, 1815-1836." Ph.D. dissertation, University of Michigan, 1974.

3397.   Shewmaker, Kenneth E. "The 'War of Words': The Cass-Webster Debate of 1842-43." Diplomatic History 5 (Spring 1981): 151-163.

3398.   Spencer, Donald S. "Lewis Cass and Symbolic Intervention: 1848-1852." Michigan History 53 (Spring 1969): 1-17.

3399.   Stevens, Walter W. "Lewis Cass and the Presidency." Michigan History 49 (June 1965): 123-134.

3400.   _____. "Michigan's Lewis Cass." Filson Club Historical Quarterly 39 (October 1965): 320-325.

Henry Clay

3401. Campbell, Randolph B. "Henry Clay and the
Poinsett Pledge Controversy of 1826."
Americas 28 (April 1972): 429-440.
3402. _____. "The Spanish American Aspect of
Henry Clay's American System." **Americas** 24
(June 1967): 3-17.
3403. Clay, Henry. **The Life and Speeches of the
Honorable Henry Clay.** Edited by Daniel
Mallory. Hartford, Conn.: Andrus, 1855.
3404. _____. **The Papers of Henry Clay.** Edited by
James F. Hopkins. Lexington: University of
Kentucky Press, 1959-73.
3405. _____. **The Works of Hery Clay: Comprising
His Life, Correspondence and Speeches.**
Edited by Calvin Colton. New York: Putnam,
1904.
3406. Corts, Paul R. "Randolph vs. Clay: A Duel of
Words and Bullets." **Filson Club Historical
Quarterly** 43 (April 1969): 151-157.
3407. Jones, Thomas B. "Henry Clay and Continental
Expansion, 1820-1844." **Register of the
Kentucky Historical Society** 73 (July
1975): 241-262.
3408. Lightfoot, Alfred. "Henry Clay and the Missouri Question 1819-1821." **Missouri
Historical Review** 61 (January 1967): 143-
165.
3409. Neely, Mark E. "American Nationalism in the
Image of Henry Clay: Abraham Lincoln's Eu-
logy on Henry Clay in Context." **Register
of the Kentucky Historical Society** 73
(January 1975): 31-60.
3410. Morgan, William G. "The 'Corrupt Bargain'
Charge Against Clay and Adams: An Historiographical Analysis." **Filson Club Historical Quarterly** 42 (April 1968): 132-149.
3411. _____. "Henry Clay's Biographers and the
'Corrupt Bargain' Charge." **Register of the
Kentucky Historical Society** 66 (July
1968): 242-258.
3412. Picklesimer, Dorman. "To Campaign or Not to
Campaign: Henry Clay's Speaking Tour
Through the South." **Filson Club Historical
Quarterly** 42 (July 1968): 235-242.
3413. Spaulding, Thomas M. "Clay Versus Randolph."
Michigan Quarterly Review 1 (Winter 1962):

8-13.

3414.   Winkler, James R. "Henry Clay: A Current As-
         sessment." **Register of the Kentucky His-
         torical Society** 70 (July 1972): 179-186.

John Middleton Clayton

3415.   Wire, Richard A. "John M. Clayton and the
         Search for Order: A Study in Whig Politics
         and Diplomacy." Ph.D. dissertation,
         University of Maryland, 1971.

Bainbridge Colby

3416.   Smith, Daniel M. "Bainbridge Colby and the
         Good Neighbor Policy, 1920-1921." **Journal
         of American History** 50 (June 1963): 56-78.

William Rufus Day

3417.   Duncan, George W. "The Diplomatic Career of
         William Rufus Day, 1897-1898." Ph.D. dis-
         sertation, Case Western Reserve Univer-
         sity, 1976.

John Foster Dulles

3418.   Beal, John Robinson. **John Foster Dulles,
         1888-1959.** New York: Harper, 1959.
3419.   Bell, Coral. "The Diplomacy of Mr. Dulles."
         International Journal 20 (Winter 1964-65):
         90-96.
3420.   Berding, Andrew H. **Dulles of Diplomacy.**
         Princeton, N.J.: Van Nostrand, 1965.
3421.   Challener, Richard D. "John Foster Dulles:
         The Moralist Armed." **Proceedings of the
         Fourth Military History Symposium** (1973):
         1431-1461.
3422.   _____, and John Fenton. "Which Way,
         America? Dulles Always Knew." **American
         Heritage** 22 (June 1971): 12-13, 84-93.
3423.   Cheng, Peter Ping-Chii. "A Study of John
         Foster Dulles: Diplomatic Strategy in The
         Far East." Ph.D. dissertation, Southern
         Illinois University, 1964.
3424.   Drummond, Roscoe, and Gaston Coblentz. **Duel
         at the Brink: John Foster Dulles' Command
         of American Power.** New York: Doubleday,

1960.

3425. Dulles, Allen W. **The Secret Surrender.** New York: Harper and Row, 1966.

3426. Dulles, Eleanor L. **American Foreign Policy in the Making.** New York: Harper and Row, 1968.

3427. _____. **John Foster Dulles: The Last Year.** New York: Harcourt, Brace, and World, 1963.

3428. Dulles, John Foster. **A Peace Treaty in the Making: Japanese Peace Conference, San Francisco, September 4-8, 1951.** Washington, D. C.: Government Printing Office, 1951.

3429. _____. "The Role of Negotiation." **Department of State Bulletin** 38 (February 1958): 159-168.

3430. _____. **The Spiritual Legacy of John Foster Dulles: Selections from His Articles and Addresses.** Philadelphia: Westminster, 1960.

3431. Dulles, Michael G. **John Foster Dulles: A Statesman and His Time.** The Hague: Nijhoff, 1972.

3432. Finer, Herman. **Dulles Over Suez: The Theory and Practice of His Diplomacy.** Chicago: Quadrangle, 1964.

3433. Fujiyama, Aiichiro. "The Late Mr. John Foster Dulles and Japan." **Contemporary Japan** 26 (August 1959): 1-4.

3434. Gerson, Louis L. **John Foster Dulles.** New York: Cooper Square, 1967.

3435. Gilbert, Jerry D. "John Foster Dulles' Perceptions of the People's Republic of China: A Study of Belief Systems and Perception in the Analysis of Foreign Policy Decision-Making." Ph.D. dissertation, Texas Tech University, 1973.

3436. Goold-Adams, Richard. **John Foster Dulles: A Reappraisal.** New York: Appleton-Century Crofts, 1962.

3437. _____. **The Time of Power: A Reappraisal of John Foster Dulles.** London: Weidenfield, 1962.

3438. Guhin, Michael A. "Dulles' Thoughts on International Politics: Myth and Reality." **Orbis** 13 (Fall 1969): 865-889.

3439. _____. **John Foster Dulles: A Statesman and**

His Times. New York: Columbia University Press, 1972.

3440.   Heller, Deane, and David Heller. **John Foster Dulles: Soldier for Peace.** New York: Holt, Rinehart and Winston, 1960.

3441.   Holsti, Ole R. "The Belief System and National Images: John Foster Dulles and the Soviet Union." Ph.D. dissertation, Stanford University, 1962.

3442.   _____. "The 'Operational Code' Approach to the Study of Political Leaders: John Foster Dulles' Philosophical and Instrumental Beliefs." **Canadian Journal of Political Science** 3 (March 1970): 123-137.

3443.   Hoopes, Townsend. **The Devil and John Foster Dulles.** Boston: Little, Brown, 1973.

3444.   _____. "God and John Foster Dulles." **Foreign Policy** 13 (Winter 1973-74): 154-177.

3445.   Hostetter, John H. "John Foster Dulles and the French Defeat in Indochina." Ph.D. dissertation, Rutgers University, 1972.

3446.   Jones, Henry P. "John Foster Dulles and United States Involvement in Vietnam." Ph.D. dissertation, University of Oklahoma, 1972.

3447.   Keim, Albert N. "John Foster Dulles and the Protestant World Order Movement on the Eve of World War II." **Journal of Church and State** 21 (Winter 1979): 73-89.

3448.   Ladenburger, John F. "The Philosophy of International Politics of John Foster Dulles, 1919-1952." Ph.D. dissertation, University of Connecticut, 1969.

3449.   Leab, Daniel. "Dulles at the Brink: Some Diverse Reactions form 10 Years Ago." **Journalism Quarterly** 43 (Autumn 1966): 547-550.

3450.   Marushkin, B. "Dulles' Suez Script." **International Affairs** 5 (May 1955): 57-64.

3451.   May, Joseph T. "John Foster Dulles and the European Defense Community." Ph.D. dissertation, Kent State University, 1969.

3452.   Monroe, Elizabeth. "John Foster Dulles and the Middle East: Appraisal of the Late Secretary of State's Accomplishments." **Western World** 2 (August 1959): 41-44.

3453.   Mosley, Leonard. **Dulles: A Biography of Eleanor, Allen, and John Foster Dulles and**

Their Family Network. New York: Dial, 1978.

3454. Mulder, John M. "The Moral World of John Foster Dulles: A Presbyterian Layman and International Affairs." **Journal of Presbyterian History** 49 (Summer 1971): 157-182.

3455. Newcomer, James R. "Acheson, Dulles, and Rusk: Information, Coherence and Organization in the Department of State." Ph.D. dissertation, Stanford University, 1976.

3456. Nimer, Benjamin. "Dulles, Suez, and Democratic Policy." **Western Political Quarterly** 12 (September 1959): 784-798.

3457. Peeters, Paul. "John Foster Dulles: The Man and His Work." **Modern Age** 4 (Summer 1960): 235-242.

3458. Pruessen, Ronald W. "Woodrow Wilson to John Foster Dulles: A Legacy." **Princeton University Library Chronicle** 34 (Winter 1973): 109-130.

3459. Rushkoff, B. C. "Eisenhower, Dulles and the Quemoy-Matsu Crisis, 1954-1955." **Political Science Quarterly** 96 (Fall 1981): 465-480.

3460. Smith, Gaddis. "The Shadow of John Foster Dulles." **Foreign Affairs** 52 (January 1974): 403-408.

3461. Stassen, G. H. "Individual Preference versus Role-Constraint in Policy-Making: Senatorial Response to Secretaries Acheson and Dulles." **World Politics** 25 (October 1972): 96-119.

3462. Thomas, I. B. " Unfair to Foster Dulles?" **Twentieth Century** 177 (1969): 39-40.

3463. Thompson, Dean K. "World Community 'Epitomized': Henry Pitney Van Dusen on John Foster Dulles and Dag Hammarskjold." **Journal of Presbyterian History** 48 (Winter 1970): 293-315.

3464. Van Dusen, Henry P., ed. **The Spiritual Legacy of John Foster Dulles.** Philadelphia: Westminster, 1960.

3465. Wright, Esmond. "Foreign Policy Since Dulles." **Political Quarterly** 33 (April/June 1962): 114-128.

William Maxwell Evarts

3466. Barrows, Chester L. "William M. Evarts,

Lawyer, Diplomat, Statesman." Ph.D. dissertation, Columbia University, 1942.

Hamilton Fish

3467. Hanks, Richard K. "Hamilton Fish and
American Isolationism, 1920-1944." Ph.D.
dissertation, University of California,
Riverside, 1971.

Frederick Theodore Frelinghuysen

3468. Rollins, John W. "Frederick Theodore
Frelinghuysen and the Politics and Diplo-
macy of Stewartship." Ph.D. dissertation,
University of Wisconsin, Madison, 1974.

Walter Quintin Gresham

3469. Goll, Eugene W. "The Diplomacy of Walter Q.
Gresham, Secretary of State, 1893-1895."
Ph.D. dissertation, Pennsylavnia State
University, 1974.
3470. Paulsen, George E. "The Abrogation of the
Gresham-Yank Treaty." **Pacific Historical
Review** 40 (November 1971): 457-477.
3471. _____. "Secretary Gresham, Senator Lodge,
and American Good Offices in China, 1894."
Pacific Historical Review 36 (May 1967):
123-142.

Alexander Haig

3472. Chanda, N. "Haig Turns the Screw." **Far Eastern Economic Review** 112 (June 26-July 2,
1981): 10-12.
3473. Haig, A. M. "New Directions in U.S. Foreign
Policy." **Atlantic Community Quarterly** 19
(Summer 1981): 131-137.

John Hay

3474. Bishop, Joseph B. **Johy Hay, Scholar, Statesman: An Address Delivered Before the
Alumni Association of Brown University,
June 19, 1906.** Providence, R.I.: Standard,
1906.
3475. Dennett, Tyler. **John Hay: From Poetry to**

Politics. New York: Dodd, Mead, 1933.

3476. Godson, Susan H. "John Hay and the Hay-Pauncefote Treaties of 1900 and 1901." **Southern Humanities Review** 1 (Fall 1975): 49-76.

3477. Hay, John M. **Letters of John Hay and Extracts From Diary.** Edited by Clara Louis Stone Hay. Washington, D.C.: Gordian Press, 1908.

3478. _____. **The Life and Letters of John Hay.** Edited by William Roscoe Thayer. Boston: Houghton Mifflin, 1915.

Christian Archibald Herter

3479. Herter, Christian A. "Basic Concepts of United States Foreign Policy.' **American Bar Association Journal** 46 (October 1960): 1099-1102.

3480. _____. "Department Recommends Senate Approval of Mutual Security Treaty with Japan." **Department of State Bulletin** 42 (June 1960): 1029-1032.

3481. _____. "Fifteenth Anniversary of the United Nations." **Department of State Bulletin** 43 (November 1960): 739-741.

3482. _____. "National Security with Arms Limitation." **Department of State Bulletin** 42 (March 1960): 354-361.

3483. _____. "New Dimensions in Diplomacy." **Department of State Bulletin** 37 (November 1957): 831-834.

3484. _____. "Official Account of the U-2 and the 'Summit' Breakup." **U.S. News & World Report** 48 (June 6, 1960): 68-70.

3485. _____. "Role of the Department of State in the National Policy Machinery." **Department of State Bulletin** 43 (July 1960): 3-7.

3486. _____. "Secretary Herter Reports to Foreign Relations Committee on Events at Paris." **Department of State Bulletin** 42 (June 1960): 947-955.

3487. _____. "The United States and Europe: Atlantica." **Foreign Affairs** 41 (January 1963): 299-309.

3488. Noble, George B. **Christian A. Herter.** New York: Cooper Square, 1970.

Charles Evans Hughes

3489.   Ellis, Lewis E. "Charles Evans Hughes, a
         Profile." **American History Illustrated** 3
         (October 1968): 28-37.
3490.   Glad, Betty. **Charles Evans Hughes and the
         Illustions of Innocence: A Study in
         American Diplomacy.** Urbana: University of
         Illinois Press, 1966.
3491.   Greer, Virginia L. "Charles Evans Hughes and
         Nicaragua, 1921-1925." Ph.D. dissertation,
         University of New Mexico, 1954.
3492.   Hill, Leslie B. "Charles Evans Hughes and
         United States Adherence to an Interna-
         tional Court: A Rhetorical Analysis."
         Ph.D. dissertation, University of Il-
         linois, 1968.
3493.   Hughes, Charles Evans. "Some Observations of
         the Conduct of Our Foreign Relations."
         American Journal of International Law 16
         (July 1922): 365-374.
3494.   Huthamcher, J. Joseph. "Charles Evans Hughes
         and Charles Francis Murphy: The Metamor-
         phosis of Progressivism." **New York History**
         46 (January 1965): 25-40.
3495.   Kane, N. Stephen. "Charles Evans Hughes and
         Mexican-American Relations, 1921-1924."
         Ph.D. dissertation, University of
         Colorado, 1970.
3496.   Navarrete, George. "The Latin American
         Policy of Charles Evans Hughes, 1921-
         1925." Ph.D. dissertation, University of
         California, Berkeley, 1964.
3497.   Pusey, Merlo J. **Charles Evans Hughes.** New
         York: Macmillan, 1951.
3498.   Woodard, Nelson E. "Postwar Reconstruction
         and International Order: A Study of the
         Diplomacy of Charles Evans Hughes, 1921-
         1925." Ph.D. dissertation, University of
         Wisconsin, 1970.

Cordell Hull

3499.   Bowers, Robert E. "Hull, Russian Subsersion
         in Cuba, and Recognition of the U.S.S.R."
         Journal of American History 53 (December
         1966): 542-554.
3500.   Buell, Raymond L. **The Hull Trade Agreement**

Program and the American Slave System. New
York: Foreign Policy Association, 1938.

3501. Burns, Richard D. "Cordell Hull: A Study in
Diplomacy, 1933-1941." Ph.D. dissertation,
University of Illinois, 1960.

3502. Chu, Power Yung-Chao. "A History of the Hull
Trade Program, 1934-1939." Ph.D. dissertation, Columbia University, 1957.

3503. Furdell, William J. "Cordell Hull and the
London Economic Conference of 1933." Ph.D.
dissertation, Kent State University, 1970.

3504. Grollman, Catherina A. "Cordell Hull and His
Concept of a World Organization." Ph.D.
dissertation, University of North Carolina, 1965.

3505. Hinton, Harold B. Cordell Hull: A Biography.
Garden City, N.Y.: Doubleday, 1942.

3506. Hull, Cordell. The Memoirs of Cordell Hull.
New York: Macmillan, 1948.

3507. Jablon, Howard. "Cordell Hull, His 'Associ-
ates,' and Relations with Japan, 1933-
1936." Mid-America 56 (July 1974): 160-
174.

3508. _____. "Cordell Hull, the State Department,
and the Foreign Policy of the First
Roosevelt Administration, 1933-1936."
Ph.D. dissertation, Rutgers University,
1967.

3509. Milner, Cooper. "The Public Life of Cordell
Hull, 1907-1924." Ph.D. dissertation,
Vanderbilt University, 1960.

3510. Pratt, Julius W. Cordell Hull, 1933-1944.
New York: Cooper Square, 1964.

3511. _____. "The Ordeal of Cordell Hull." Review
of Politics 28 (January 1966): 76-98.

3512. Schatz, Arthur W. "The Anglo-American Trade
Agreement and Cordell Hull's Search for
Peace, 1936-1938." Journal of American
History 57 (June 1970): 85-103.

3513. _____. "Cordell Hull and the Struggle for
the Reciprocal Trade Agreements Program,
1932-1940. Ph.D. dissertation, University
of Oregon, 1965.

3514. Stanley, Judith M. "Cordell Hull and
Democratic Party Unity." Tennessee
Historical Quarterly 32 (Summer 1973):
169-187.

3515. Woods, R. B. "Hull and Argentina: Wilsonian

Diplomacy in the Age of Roosevelt."
**Journal of Interamerican Studies and World
Affairs** 16 (August 1974): 350-371.

John Jay

3516. Bhagat, G. "The Jay Treaty and Indian
Trade." **Essex Institute Historical
Collections** 208 (April 1972): 153-172.
3517. Clarfield, Gerard. "Postscript to the Jay
Treaty: Timothy Pickering and Anglo-
American Relations, 1795-1797." **William
and Mary Quarterly** 23 (January 1966): 106-
120.
3518. Farnham, Thomas J. "The Virginia Amendments
of 1795: An Episode in the Opposition to
Jay's Treaty." **Virginia Magazine of His-
tory and Biography** 75 (January 1967): 75-
88.
3519. Gruver, Rebecca B. "The Diplomacy of John
Jay." Ph.D. dissertation, University of
California, Berkeley, 1964.
3520. Hammett, Hugh B. "The Jay Treaty: Crisis
Diplomacy in the New Nation." **Social
Studies** 65 (January 1974): 10-17.
3521. Jay, John. **The Correspondence and Public
Papers of John Jay.** Edited by Henry P.
Johnston. New York: Putnam, 1890-93.
3522. _____. **The Diary of John Jay During the
Peace Negotiations of 1782.** New Haven,
Conn.: Yale University Library, 1934.
3523. _____. **The Life of John Jay, with Selec-
tions From His Correspondence and Miscel-
laneous Papers.** Edited by William Jay. New
York: Harper, 1833.
3524. Morris, Richard B., ed. "The Jay Papers:
Mission to Spain." **American Heritage** 19
(February 1968): 8-21, 85-96.

Thomas Jefferson

3525. Alexander, Edward P. "Jefferson and
Kosciuszko: Friends of Liberty and of
Man." **Pennsylvania Magazine of History and
Biography** 92 (January 1968): 87-103.
3526. Allison, John M. **Adams and Jefferson: The
Story of a Friendship.** Norman: University
of Oklahoma Press, 1966.

3527. Andrews, Stuart. "Jefferson and the French
       Revolution." **History Today** 18 (May 1968):
       299-306, 368.
3528. Arrowood, Charles F. **Thomas Jefferson and
       Education in a Republic.** New York: McGraw-
       Hill, 1930.
3529. Banning, Lance. "Jeffersonian Ideology and
       the French Revolution: A Question of Li-
       berticide at Home." **Studies in Burke and
       His Time** 17 (Winter 1976): 5-26.
3530. Berkhofer, Robert F. "Jefferson, the Ordi-
       nance of 1784, and the Origins of the
       American Territorial System." **William and
       Mary Quarterly** 29 (April 1972): 231-262.
3531. Bowling, Kenneth R. "Dinner at Jefferson's:
       A Note on Jacob E. Cooke's 'The Compromise
       of 1790'." **William and Mary Quarterly** 28
       (October 1971): 629-648.
3532. Brodie, Fawn M. "Jefferson Biographers and
       the Psychology of Canonization." **Journal
       of Interdisciplinary History** 2 (Summer
       1971): 155-172.
3533. _____. **Thomas Jefferson: An Intimate
       History.** New York: Norton, 1974.
3534. Chaudhuri, J. "Jefferson's Unheavenly City:
       A Bientennial Look." **American Journal of
       Economics and Sociology** 34 (October 1975):
       397-410.
3535. Chiang, C. Y. Jesse. "Understanding Thomas
       Jefferson." **International Review of
       History and Political Science** 14 (August
       1977): 51-61.
3536. Clark, K. "Thomas Jefferson and the Italian
       Renaissance." **Virginia Quarterly Review** 48
       (Autumn 1972): 519-531.
3537. Cooke, Jacob E. "The Collaboration of Tench
       Coxe and Thomas Jefferson." **Pennsylvania
       Magazine of History and Biography** 100
       (October 1976): 468-490.
3538. Dearmont, Nelson S. "Federalist Attitudes
       Toward Governmental Secrecy in the Age of
       Jefferson." **Historian** 37 (February 1975):
       222-240.
3539. Hay, Robert P. "The Glorious Departure of
       the American Patriarchs: Contemporary
       Reactions to the Deaths of Jefferson and
       Adams." **Journal of Southern History** 35
       (November 1969): 543-555.

3540. Hoskins, Janina W. "'A Lesson which All Our
       Countrymen Should Study': Jefferson Views
       Poland." **Quarterly Journal of the Library
       of Congress** 33 (January 1976): 29-46.

3541. Jefferson, Thomas. **The Writings of Thomas
       Jefferson.** Edited by Paul L. Ford. New
       York: Putnam, 1892-1900.

3542. _____. **The Writings of Thomas Jefferson.**
       Edited by Andrew J. Lipscomb, and Albert
       Ellery Bergh. Washington, D.C.: Thomas
       Jefferson Memorial Association of the
       United States, 1905.

3543. Kaplan, Lawrence S. "Consensus of 1789: Jef-
       ferson and Hamilton on American Foreign
       Policy." **South Atlantic Quarterly** 71
       (Winter 1972): 91-105.

3544. _____. "Jefferson's Foreign Policy and
       Napoleon's Ideologues." **William and Mary
       Quarterly** 19 (July 1962): 344-359.

3545. Luttrell, C. B. "Thomas Jefferson on Money
       and Banking: Disciple of David Hume and
       Forerunner of Some Modern Monetary Views."
       History of Political Economy 7 (Summer
       1975): 156-173.

3546. Lynd, Staughton. "Beard, Jefferson and the
       Tree of Liberty." **American Studies** 9
       (Spring 1968): 8-22.

3547. McLoughlin, William G. "Thomas Jefferson and
       the Beginning of Cherokee Nationalism,
       1806 to 1809." **William and Mary Quarterly**
       32 (October 1975): 547-580.

3548. Malone, Dumas. "Mr. Jefferson and the Tradi-
       tions of Virginia." **Virginia Magazine of
       History and Biography** 75 (April 1967):
       131-142.

3549. Mannix, Richard. "Gallatin, Jefferson, and
       the Embargo of 1808." **Diplomatic History** 3
       (Spring 1979): 151-172.

3550. Midgley, Louis. "The Brodie Connection:
       Thomas Jefferson and Joseph Smith."
       Brigham Young University Studies 19 (Fall
       1979): 59-67.

3551. Morgan, R. J. "Time Hath Found Us: The Jef-
       fersonian Revolutionary Vision." **Journal
       of Politics** 38 (August 1976): 20-36.

3552. Muller, H. N. "Smuggling into Canada: How
       the Champlain Valley Defied Jefferson's
       Embargo." **Vermont History** 38 (Winter

1970): 5-21.

3553. Peterson, Merrill D. "Adams and Jefferson: A Revolutionary Dialogue." **Wilson Quarterly** 1 (Autumn 1976): 108-125.

3554. _____. ed. **Thomas Jefferson: A Profile.** New York: Hill and Wang, 1967.

3555. _____. "Thomas Jefferson and Commercial Policy, 1783-1793." **William and Mary Quarterly** 22 (October 1965): 584-610.

3556. Prince, Carl E. "The Passing of the Aristocracy: Jefferson's Removal of the Federalists, 1801-1805." **Journal of American History** 57 (December 1970): 563-575.

3557. Scanlon, James E. "A Sudden Conceit: Jefferson and the Louisiana Government Bill of 1804." **Louisiana History** 9 (Spring 1968): 139-162.

3558. Sestanovich, Stephen. "Thomas Jefferson, Pao." **Foreign Service Journal** 43 (July 1966): 23-25.

3559. Shalhope, Robert E. "Thomas Jefferson's Republicanism and Antebellum Southern Thought." **Journal of Southern History** 42 (November 1976): 529-556.

3560. Shurr, George H. "Thomas Jefferson and the French Revolution." **American Society of Legion of Honor Magazine** 50 (Winter 1979-1980): 161-182.

3561. Spivak, Burton. "Jefferson, England, and the Embargo: Trading Wealth and Republican Value in the Shaping of American Diplomacy, 1804-1809." Ph.D. dissertation, University of Virginia, 1975.

3562. Stuart, R. C. "Thomas Jefferson and the Function of War: Policy or Principle?" **Canadian Journal of History** 11 (August 1976): 155-171.

3563. Szasz, Paul C. "Thomas Jefferson Conceives an International Organization." **American Journal of International Law** 75 (January 1981): 138-140.

3564. Weymouth, Lally, ed. **Thomas Jefferson: The Man...His World...His Influence.** London: Weidenfeld and Nicolson, 1973.

3565. Winston, Alexander. "Mr. Jefferson in Paris." **American Society Legion of Honor Magazine** 35 (1964): 139-150.

3566. Wood, G. S. "Problem of Jefferson." **Virginia**

Quarterly Review 47 (Winter 1971): 137-
141.

3567.   Woolery, William K. The Relations of Thomas
Jefferson to American Foreign Policy,
1783-1793. Baltimore: Johns Hopkins
University Press, 1927.

Frank Billings Kellogg

3568.   Bryn-Jones, David. Frank B. Kellogg: A
Biography. New York: Putnam, 1937.

3569.   Cleaver, Charles G. "Frank B. Kellogg: Attitudes and Assumptions Influencing His
Foreign Policy Decisions." Ph.D. dissertation, University of Minnesota, 1956.

3570.   Debenedetti, Charles. "Borah and the
Kellogg-Briand Pact." Pacific Northwest
Quarterly 63 (January 1972): 22-29.

3571.   Ellis, Lewis E. Frank B. Kellogg and American Foreign Relations, 1925-1929. New
Brunswick, N.J.: Rutgers University Press,
1961.

3572.   Ferrell, Robert H. Frank B. Kellogg and
Henry L. Stimson. New York: Cooper Square,
1963.

3573.   Traphagen, Jeanne C. "The Inter-American
Diplomacy of Frank B. Kellogg." Ph.D. dissertation, University of Minnesota, 1956.

Henry Alfred Kissinger

3574.   Allison, Graham T. "Cold Dawn and the Mind
of Kissinger." Washington Monthly 6 (March
1974): 39-47.

3575.   Alroy, Gil C. "Kissinger Delivers Another
Israeli Withdrawal." Midstream 21
(November 1975): 8-18.

3576.   Bell, Coral. The Diplomacy of Detente: The
Kissinger Era. New York: St. Martin's
Press, 1977.

3577.   _____. "Kissinger in Retrospect: The
Diplomacy of Power-Concert?" International
Affairs 53 (April 1977): 202-216.

3578.   Blumenfeld, Ralph. Henry Kissinger: The
Private and Public Story. Bergenfield,
N.J.: New American Library, 1974.

3579.   Brown, Seyom. The Crisis of Power: An Interpretation of United States Foreign Policy

During the Kissinger Years. New York: Columbia University Press, 1979.

3580. Buchan, Alastair. "Irony of Henry Kissinger." International Affairs 50 (July 1974): 367-379.

3581. Bull, Hedley. "Kissinger." International Affairs (London) 56 (Summer 1980): 484-487.

3582. Dickson, Peter. Kissinger and the Meaning of History. New York: Cambridge University Press, 1978.

3583. "Dr. Kissinger on World Affairs: Interview." Encounter 51 (November 1978): 9-25.

3584. Draper, Theodore. "Ghosts of Vietnam." Dissent 26 (Winter 1979): 30-42.

3585. _____. "Kissinger's Apologia." Dissent 27 (Spring 1980): 233-254.

3586. Dunn, Keith A. "Detente and Deterrence: From Kissinger to Carter." Parameters 7 (1977): 46-55.

3587. Gelb, L. H. "Story of a Flap." Foreign Policy 16 (Fall 1974): 165-181.

3588. Girling, J. L. S. "Kissingerism: The Enduring Problems." International Affairs 51 (July 1975): 323-343.

3589. Golan, Matti. The Secret Conversations of Henry Kissinger: Step-By-Step Diplomacy in the Middle East. New York: Quadrangle, 1976.

3590. Gordon, Murray. "Kissinger's Travails." Midstream 21 (May 1975): 7-17.

3591. Gottlieb, S. "Scoop & Henry--The Arms Debate." Dissent 21 (Fall 1974): 473-477.

3592. Graebner, Norman A. "Henry Kissinger and American Foreign Policy: A Contemporary Appraisal." Australian Journal of Politics and History 22 (April 1976): 7-22.

3593. Graubard, Stephen R. Kissinger: Portrait of a Mind. New York: Norton, 1973.

3594. Hallett, Douglas. "Kissinger Dolosus: The Domestic Politics of SALT." Yale Review 65 (December 1975): 161-174.

3595. Hanson, S. G. "Kissinger on the Chilean Coup." Inter-American Economic Affairs 27 (Winter 1973): 61-85.

3596. Holbrooke, R. "New Battle Lines." Foreign Policy 13 (Winter 1973-74): 178-185.

3597. Hsiung, James C. "U.S. Relations with China

in the Post-Kissingerian Era: A Sensible Policy for the 1980s." **Asian Survey** 17 (August 1977): 691-710.

3598. Joiner, Harry M. **American Foreign Policy: The Kissinger Era.** Hunsville, Ala.: Strode, 1977.

3599. Kalb, Marvin, and Bernard Kalb. **Kissinger.** Boston: Little, Brown, 1974.

3600. Kessler, Francis P. "Kissinger's Legacy: A Latin American Policy." **Current History** 72 (February 1977): 76-78, 86-88.

3601. _____. "Kissinger's 'New Dialogue' with Latin America: New Beginnings vs. Old Realities." **Midwest Quarterly** 16 (Winter 1975): 119-134.

3602. Kimche, Jon. "Kissinger Diplomacy and the Art of Limited War." **Midstream** 20 (November 1974): 3-12.

3603. Kissinger, Henry A. **American Foreign Policy.** 3rd ed. New York: Norton, 1974.

3604. _____. "Arms Control, Inspection and Surprise Attack." **Foreign Affairs** 38 (July 1960): 557-575.

3605. _____. "Coalition Diplomacy in a Nuclear Age." **Foreign Affairs** 42 (July 1964): 525-545.

3606. _____. "Communist Parties in Western Europe: Challenge to the West." **Atlantic Community Quarterly** 15 (Fall 1977): 261-274.

3607. _____. "Domestic Structure and Foreign Policy." **Daedalus** 95 (Spring 1966): 503-529.

3608. _____. "Moral Foundations of Foreign Policy." **Atlantic Community Quarterly** 13 (Fall 1975): 270-281.

3609. _____. "NATO: Evolution or Decline." **Texas Quarterly** 9 (Autumn 1966): 110-118.

3610. _____. **The Necessity for Choice: Prospects of American Foreign Policy.** New York: Harper, 1961.

3611. _____. **Nuclear Weapons and Foreign Policy.** New York: Harper, 1957.

3612. _____. "Permanent Challenge of Peace: United States Policy Toward the Soviet Union." **Atlantic Community Quarterly** 14 (Spring 1976): 20-36.

3613. _____. "The Policymaker and the Intellectual." **Reporter** 20 (March 1959): 30-35.

3614.   _____. "Secretary Kissinger Announces New
         Steps for Improvement of Department's
         Resource Allocation and Personnel
         Systems." **Department of State Bulletin** 73
         (July 1975): 85-90.
3615.   _____. **The Troubled Partnership.** New York:
         McGraw-Hill, 1965.
3616.   _____. "The Viet Nam Negotiations." **Foreign
         Affairs** 47 (January 1969): 211-234.
3617.   _____. "What About the Future?" **Atlantic
         Community Quarterly** 4 (Fall 1966): 317-
         329.
3618.   _____. **The White House Years.** Boston:
         Little, Brown, 1979.
3619.   _____. **Years of Upheaval.** Boston: Little,
         Brown, 1982.
3620.   Kohl, Wilfred L. "The Nixon-Kissinger
         Foreign Policy System and U.S.-European
         Relations: Patterns of Policy Making."
         World Politics 28 (October 1975): 1-43.
3621.   Kornegay, F. A. "Kissinger and Africa."
         Africa Report 20 (November 1975): 37-40.
3622.   Klein, David H. "Chou En-Lai--Henry
         Kissinger Talks: Continuity, Revolution
         and 'Pacific' Diplomacy." **Peace and Change**
         1 (Fall 1972): 63-66.
3623.   Kushner, Rose. "In Search of the Real Henry
         Kissinger." **Times of Israel** 1 (October
         1974): 16-24.
3624.   Labedz, L. "USA and the World Today:
         Kissinger and After." **Survey** 22 (Winter
         1976): 1-37.
3625.   LaFeber, Walter. "Kissinger and Acheson: The
         Secretary of State and the Cold War."
         Political Science Quarterly 92 (Summer
         1977): 189-197.
3626.   Lanau, David. **Kissinger: The Uses of Power.**
         Boston: Houghton Mifflin, 1972.
3627.   Laqueur, Walter. "Kissinger & the Politics
         of Detente." **Commentary** 56 (December
         1973): 46-52.
3628.   Lin, C. Y. **Kissinger's Diplomacy.** Brunswick,
         Ohio: King's Court, 1975.
3629.   Liska, George. **Beyond Kissinger: Ways of
         Conservative Statecraft.** Baltimore: Johns
         Hopkins University Press, 1975.
3630.   Lockwood, T. "Lone Ranger Rides Again:
         Kissinger in Africa." **Christianity &**

Crisis 36 (November 1976): 247-252.

3631. Luttwak, Edward N., and Walter Laqueur. "Kissinger & the Yom Kippur War." **Commentary** 58 (September 1974): 33-40.

3632. Madar, Daniel R. "Patronage, Position, and Policy Planning: S/P and Secretary Kissinger." **Journal of Politics** 42 (November 1980): 1066-1084.

3633. Magunbane, B. "What Is Kissinger Up to in Southern Africa?" **Freedomways** 16 (1976): 162-171.

3634. Mazrui, Ali A. "Nationalists and Statesmen: From Nkrumah and DeGaulle to Nyerere and Kissinger." **Journal of African Studies** 6 (Winter 1979/80): 199-205.

3635. Montgomery, John D. "Education of Henry Kissinger." **Journal of International Affairs** 29 (Spring 1975): 49-62.

3636. Morris, Roger. "Kissinger and Brothers Kalb." **Washington Monthly** 6 (July/August 1974): 51-60.

3637. _____. Uncertain Greatness: Henry Kissinger and American Foreign Policy. New York: Harper and Row, 1977.

3638. Noer, T. J. "Henry Kissinger's Philosophy of History." **Modern Age** 19 (Spring 1975): 180-189.

3639. Perlmutter, Amos. "Crisis Management: Kissinger's Middle East Negotiations (October 1973-June 1974)." **International Studies Quarterly** 19 (September 1975): 316-343.

3640. Quandt, W. B. "Kissinger and the Arab-Israeli Disengagement Negotiations." **Journal of International Affairs** 29 (Spring 1975): 33-48.

3641. Rosecrance, Richard. "Kissinger, Bismarck and the Balance of Power." **Millennium** 3 (Spring 1974): 45-52.

3642. Rubin, Barry. "Kissinger." **Contemporary Review** 232 (May 1978): 239-245.

3643. Schulzinger, Robert D. "The Naive and Sentimental Diplomat: Henry Kissinger's Memoirs." **Diplomatic History** 4 (Summer 1980): 303-315.

3644. Serfaty, S. "Kissinger Legacy: Old Obsessions and New Look." **World Today** 33 (March 1977): 81-89.

3645. Sheehan, E. R. F. "How Kissinger Did It:
       Step by Step in the Middle East." **Foreign
       Policy** 22 (Spring 1976): 3-70.
3646. Starr, Harvey. "The Kissinger Years: Study-
       ing Individuals and Foreign Policy."
       International Studies Quarterly 24
       (December 1980): 465-496.
3647. Stern, L. "Two Henrys Descending." **Foreign
       Politics** 18 (Spring 1975): 168-176.
3648. Stoessinger, John G. **Henry Kissinger: The
       Anguish of Power.** New York: Norton, 1976.
3649. Szulc, Tad. "How Kissinger Did It: Behind
       the Vietnam Cease-Fire Agreement." **Foreign
       Policy** 15 (Summer 1974): 21-69.
3650. Todd, O. "Who's in Charge Here?" **Atlas** 21
       (April 1972): 28-31.
3651. Valeriani, Richard. **Travels with Henry.**
       Boston: Houghton Mifflin, 1979.
3652. Van Hollen, C. "The Tilt Policy Revisited:
       Nixon-Kissinger Geopolitics in South
       Asia." **Asian Survey** 20 (April 1980): 339-
       361.
3653. Walker, S. G. "Interface Between Beliefs and
       Behavior: Henry Kissinger's Operational
       Code and the Vietnam War." **Journal of Con-
       flict Resolution** 21 (March 1977): 129-168.
3654. Watt, David C. "Henry Kissinger: An Interim
       Judgement." **Political Quarterly** 48
       (January 1977): 3-13.
3655. _____. "Kissinger's Track Back." **Foreign
       Policy** 37 (Winter 1979/80): 59-66.
3656. Weber, William T. "Kissinger as Historian: A
       Historiographical Approach to Statesman-
       ship." **World Affairs** 141 (Summer 1978):
       40-56.

Philander Chase Knox

3657. Mulhollan, Paige E. "Philander C. Knox and
       Dollar Diplomacy, 1909-1913." Ph.D. dis-
       sertation, University of Texas, Austin,
       1966.

Robert Lansing

3658. Barany, G. "Wilsonian Central Europe:
       Lansing's Contribution." **Historian** 28
       (February 1966): 224-251.

3659.   Beers, Burton F. Vain Endeavor: Robert
        Lansing's Attempts to End the American-
        Japanese Rivalry. Durham, N.C.: Duke
        University Press, 1962.
3660.   Glaser, David. "1910: William Jenkins,
        Robert Lansing, and the Mexican Inter-
        lude." Southwestern Historical Quarterly
        74 (January 1971): 337-356.
3661.   Lansing, Robert. Big Four and Others of the
        Peace Conference. Boston: Houghton
        Mifflin, 1921.
3662.   _____. The Peace Negotiations: A Personal
        Narrative. Boston: Houghton Mifflin, 1921.
3663.   _____. War Memoirs of Robert Lansing.
        Indianapolis: Bobbs-Merrill, 1935.
3664.   Zivojinovic, Dragan. "Robert Lansing's Com-
        ments on the Pontifical Peace Noted of
        August 1, 1917." Journal of American
        History 56 (December 1969): 556-571.

Edward Livington

3665.   Carosso, Vincent P., and Lawrence H. Leder.
        "Edward Livingston and Jacksonian Diplo-
        macy." Louisiana History 7 (Summer 1966):
        241-248.
3666.   Mackey, Philip E. "Edward Livingston and the
        Origins of the Movement to Abolish Capital
        Punishment in America." Louisiana History
        16 (Spring 1975): 145-166.

James Madison

3667.   Bell, Rudolph M. "Mr. Madison's War and
        Long-Term Congressional Voting Behavior."
        William and Mary Quarterly 36 (July 1979):
        373-395.
3668.   Bradley, Jared W. "W. C. C. Claiborne and
        Spain: Foreign Affairs under Jefferson and
        Madison, 1801-1811." Louisiana History 12
        (Fall 1971): 297-314.
3669.   _____. "W. C. C. Claiborne and Spain:
        Foreign Affairs under Jefferson and
        Madison, 1801-1811." Louisiana History 13
        (Winter 1972): 5-28.
3670.   Brant, Irving. "Madison and the War of
        1812." Virginia Magazine of History and
        Biography 74 (January 1966): 51-67.

3671. Dewey, Donald O. "Madison's Views on Electoral Reform." **Western Political Quarterly** 15 (March 1962): 140-145.
3672. Ingersoll, D. E. "Machiavelli and Madison: Perspectives on Political Stability." **Political Science Quarterly** 85 (June 1970): 259-280.
3673. Kaplan, Lawrence S. "France and Madison's Decision for War, 1812." **Journal of American History** 50 (March 1964): 652-671.
3674. Madison, James. **The Papers of James Madison.** Edited by William Hutchinson, Robert Rutland, and William M. E. Rachal. Chicago: University of Chicago Press, 1962-77.
3675. Mead, Sidney E. "Neither Church Nor State: Reflections on James Madison's 'Line of Separation'." **Journal of Church and State** 10 (Autumn 1968): 349-364.
3676. Skeen, C. Edward. "Mr. Madison's Secretary of War." **Pennsylvania Magazine of History and Biography** 100 (July 1976): 336-355.
3677. Stagg, J. C. A. "James Madison and the Coercion of Great Britain: Canada, the West Indies, and the War of 1812." **William and Mary Quarterly** 38 (January 1981): 3-34.
3678. _____. "James Madison and the 'Malcontents': The Political Origins of the War of 1812." **William and Mary Quarterly** 33 (October 1976): 557-585.

William Learned Marcy

3679. Scribner, Robert L. "The Diplomacy of William L. Marcy, Secretary of State, 1853-1857." Ph.D. dissertation, University of Virginia, 1949.

George Catlett Marshall

3680. Ambrose, Stephen E. "General George C. Marshall." **American History Illustrated** 4 (February 1970): 4-11, 48.
3681. Edelstein, Alex S. "The Marshall Plan Information Program in Western Europe as an Instrument of United States Foreign Policy, 1948-1952." Ph.D. dissertation, University of Minnesota, 1958.

3682.   Ferrell, Robert H. **George C. Marshall.** New
        York: Cooper Square, 1965.
3683.   Geiger, Theodore. "The Lessons of the
        Marshall Plan." **Atlantic Community
        Quarterly** 5 (Fall 1967): 419-426.
3684.   Haglung, David G. "George C. Marshall and
        the Question of Military Aid to England,
        May-June 1940." **Journal of Contemporary
        History** 15 (October 1980): 745-760.
3685.   Jackson, Scott. "Prologue to the Marshall
        Plan: The Origins of the American Commit-
        ment for a European Recovery Program."
        Journal of American History 65 (March
        1979): 1043-1068.
3686.   Johnson, James H. "The Marshall Plan: A Case
        Study in American Foreign Policy Formula-
        tion and Implementation." Ph.D. disserta-
        tion, University of Oklahoma, 1966.
3687.   Marshall, George C. **Marshall's Mission to
        China, Dec. 1945-Jan. 1947: The Report and
        Appended Documents.** Arlington, Va.:
        University Publications of America, 1976.
3688.   Price, Harry B. **The Marshall Plan and Its
        Meaning.** Ithaca, N.Y.: Cornell University
        Press, 1955.
3689.   Tsou, Tang. "Civil Strife and Armed Inter-
        vention: Marshall's China Policy." **Orbis** 6
        (Spring 1962): 76-101.
3690.   Van Der Beugel, Ernest H. "From Marshall Aid
        to Atlantic Partnership." **Atlantic Com-
        munity Quarterly** 4 (Spring 1966): 5-16.
3691.   Wilson, Theodore A. **The Marshall Plan: An
        Atlantic Venture of 1947-51.** New York:
        Foreign Policy Association, 1977.
3692.   Winham, Gilbert R. "An Analysis of Foreign
        Aid Decision-making: the Case of the
        Marshall Plan." Ph.D. dissertation,
        University of North Carolina, 1968.

James Monroe

3693.   Ammon, Harry. "James Monroe and the Election
        of 1808 in Virginia." **William and Mary
        Quarterly** 20 (January 1963): 33-56.
3694.   _____. "The Monroe Doctrine: Domestic
        Politics or National Decision?" **Diplomatic
        History** 5 (Winter 1981): 53-73.
3695.   Berkeley, Dorothy S., and Edmund Berkeley.

"'The Piece Left Behind': Monroe's Authorship of a Political Pamphlet Revealed." **Virginia Magazine of History and Biography** 75 (April 1967): 174-180.

3696. Bond, Beverly W. **The Monroe Mission to France, 1794-1796.** Baltimore: Johns Hopkins University Press, 1907.

3697. Manning, Clarence A. "The Meaning of the Monroe Doctrine." **Ukrainian Quarterly** 18 (Autumn 1962): 246-254.

3698. May, Ernest R. **The Making of the Monroe Doctrine.** Cambridge, Mass.: Harvard University Press, 1979.

3699. Monroe, James. **Autobiography.** Edited by Stuart Berry Brown. Syracuse, N.Y.: Syracuse University Press, 1959.

3700. _____. **The Memoirs of James Monroe, Esq. Relating to His Unsettled Claims Upon the People and Government of the United States.** Charlottesville, Va.: Gilmer, Davis, 1828.

3701. _____. **The Writings of James Monroe.** Edited by Stanislaus Murray Hamilton. New York: Putnam, 1898-1903.

3702. Nadler, Solomon. "The Green Bag: James Monroe and the Fall of De Witt Clinton." **New York Historical Society Quarterly** 59 (July 975): 202-225.

Timothy Pickering

3703. Clarfield, Gerald H. **Timothy Pickering and American Diplomacy, 1795-1800.** Columbia: University of Missouri Press, 1969.

3704. _____. "Timothy Pickering and French Diplomacy, 1795-1796." **Essex Institute Historical Collections** 104 (January 1968): 58-74.

3705. _____. "Victory in the West: A Study of the Role of Timothy Pickering in the Successful Consummation of Pickney's Treaty." **Essex Institute Historical Collections** 101 (October 1965): 333-353.

3706. Phillips, Edward H. "Salem, Timothy Pickering, and the American Revolution." **Essex Institute Historical Collections** 111 (January 1975): 65-78.

3707. _____. "Timothy Pickering at His Best: Indian Commissioner, 1790-1794." **Essex In-**

stitute Historical Collections 102 (July 1966): 163-202.

3708. Wheaton, Henry. **Some Account of the Life, Writings, and Speeches of William Pinkney.** Philadelphia: Small, 1826.

3709. Wilbur, W. Allan. "Timothy Pickering, Federalist Politician: An Historiographical Perspective." **Historian** 34 (February 1972): 278-292.

Edmund Randolph

3710. Clifford, John G. "A Muddy Middle of the Road: The Politics of Edmund Randolph, 1790-1795." **Virginia Magazine of History and Biography** 80 (July 1972): 282-311.

3711. Reardon, John J. "'The Heart is Gnawed': Edmund Randolph and American Independence." **Virginia Cavalcade** 26 (Summer 1976): 20-29.

3712. Thomas, Emory M. "Edmund Randolph." **Virginia Cavalcade** 18 (Spring 1969): 5-12.

William Pierce Rogers

3713. Brecher, Michael. "Israel and the Rogers Peace Initiatives." **Orbis** 18 (Summer 1974): 402-426.

3714. Rogers, William P. "Desegregation in the Schools: The Citizen's Responsibility." **Cornell Law Quarterly** 45 (Spring 1960): 488-513.

3715. _____. "Growing Ties Between Science and Foreign Policy." **Department of State Bulletin** 64 (June 1971): 766-768.

3716. _____. "The New Foreign Service and the Job of Modern Diplomacy." **Department of State Bulletin** 65 (December 1971): 675-676.

3717. _____. "Our Permanent Interests in Europe." **Atlantic Community Quarterly** 10 (Spring 1972): 21-26.

3718. _____. **The Twilight Struggle: The Alliance for Progress and the Politics of Development in Latin America.** New York: Random House, 1967.

3719. _____. "U.S. Foreign Policy in a Technological Age." **Department of State Bulletin** 64 (February 1971): 198-202.

3720.   _____. "U.S. Foreign Policy, 1969-70: A
         Report of the Secretary of State." **Depart-
         ment of State Bulletin** 64 (April 1971):
         465-477.
3721.   _____. "U.S. Foreign Policy, 1971: A Report
         of the Secretary of State." **Department of
         State Bulletin** 66 (March 1972): 459-470.
3722.   _____. "U.S. Policy Toward Latin America:
         An Official Statement." **Revista Inter-
         americana Review** 2 (Fall 1972): 263-271.

Elihu Root

3723.   Cantor, Louis. "Elihu Root and the National
         Guard: Friend or Foe?" **Military Affairs** 33
         (December 1969): 371-373.
3724.   Cummins, Lejeune. "The Origin and Develop-
         ment of Elihu Root's Latin American
         Diplomacy." Ph.D. dissertation, University
         of California, Berkeley, 1964.
3725.   Davis, Jack. "The Latin American Policy of
         Elihu Root." Ph.D. dissertation, Univer-
         sity of Illinois, 1956.
3726.   Defroscia, Patrick D. "The Diplomacy of
         Elihu Root, 1905-1909." Ph.D. disserta-
         tion, Temple University, 1976.
3727.   Dubin, Martin D. "Elihu Root and the Ad-
         vocacy of a Legue of Nations, 1914-1917."
         Western Political Quarterly 19 (September
         1966): 439-455.
3728.   Hendrickson, Embert J. "Root's Watchful
         Watiing and the Venezuelan Controversy."
         Americas 23 (October 1966): 115-129.
3729.   Hewes, James E. **From Root to McNamara: Army
         Organization and Administration, 1900-
         1963.** Washington, D.C.: U.S. Army Center
         of Military History, 1975.
3730.   Hopkins, C. Howard, and John W. Long. "Amer-
         ican Jews and the Root Mission to Russia
         in 1917: Some New Evidence." **American
         Jewish History** 69 (March 1980): 342-354.
3731.   Ingram, Alton E. "The Root Mission to Rus-
         sia, 1917." Ph.D. dissertation, Louisiana
         State University, 1970.
3732.   Jessup, Philip C. **Elihu Root.** New York:
         Dodd, Mead, 1938.
3733.   Leopold, Richard W. **Elihu Root and the Con-
         servative Tradition.** Boston: Little,

Brown, 1954.

3734. Muth, Edwin A. "Elihu Root: His Role and Concepts Pertaining to United States Policies of Intervention." Ph.D. dissertation, Georgetown University, 1966.

3735. Root, Elihu. **Addresses on Government and Citizenship.** Edited by Robert Bacon and James Brown Scott. Cambridge, Mass.: Harvard University Press, 1916.

3736. _____. **Addresses on International Subjects.** Edited by Robert Bacon and James Brown Scott. Cambridge, Mass.: Harvard University Press, 1916.

3737. _____. **Men and Policies: Addresses by Elihu Root.** Edited by Robert Bacon and James Brown Scott. Cambridge, Mass.: Harvard University Press, 1925.

3738. _____. **The Military and Colonial Policy of the United States: Addresses and Reports by Elihu Root.** Edited by Robert Bacon and James Brown Scott. Cambridge, Mass.: Harvard University Press, 1916.

3739. _____. "A Requisite for the Success of Popular Diplomacy." **Foreign Affairs** 1 (September 1922): 3-10.

3740. _____. **The United States and War: The Mission to Russia, Political Addresses by Elihu Root.** Edited by Robert Bacon and James Brown Scott. Cambridge, Mass.: Harvard University Press, 1918.

3741. Semsch, Philip L. "Elihu Root and the General Staff." **Military Affairs** 27 (Spring 1963): 16-27.

3742. Scott, James B. **Elihu Root's Services to International Law.** New York: Carnegie Endowmen for International Peace, 1925.

Dean Rusk

3743. Cohen, Warren I. **Dean Rusk.** Totowa, N.J.: Cooper Square Publishers, 1980.

3744. Gutierrez, Gilbert G. "Dean Rusk and Southeast Asia: An Operational Code Analysis." Ph.D. dissertation, University of California, Riverside, 1974.

3745. Hah, Chong-Do. "Dean Rusk and Communist China." **Centennial Review** 15 (Spring 1971): 182-203.

3746. Rusk, Dean. "The Alliance for Progress i𝖓 the Context of World Affairs." **Department of State Bulletin** 46 (May 1962): 787-794.

3747. _____. "The Anatomy of Foreign Policy Decisions." **Department of State Bulletin** 52 (September 1965): 502-509.

3748. _____. "The Bases of United States Foreign Policy." **Proceedings of the Academy of Political Science** 27 (January 1962): 98-110.

3749. _____. "Basic Issues Underlying the Present Crisis." **Department of State Bulletin** 47 (December 1962): 867-973.

3750. _____. "Building the Frontiers of Freedom." **Department of State Bulletin** 44 (June 1961): 947-955.

3751. _____. "Disarmament and Arms Control." **Department of State Bulletin** 47 (July 1962): 3-7.

3752. _____. "Foreign Policy Aspects of Space Communications." **Department of State Bulletin** 47 (August 1962)L: 315-319.

3753. _____. "Four Central Threads of U.S. Foreign Policy." **Department of State Bulletin** 45 (October 1961): 625-630.

3754. _____. "A Fresh Look at the Formulation of Foreign Policy." **Department of State Bulletin** 44 (March 1961): 395-399.

3755. _____. "Methods of Diplomacy." **Department of State Bulletin** 45 (August 1961): 287-288.

3756. _____. "Old-Fashioned Diplomacy." **Department of State Bulletin** 44 (April 1961): 522.

3757. _____. "Parliamentary Diplomacy: Debate vs. Negotiation." **World Affairs Interpreter** 26 (July 1955): 121-138.

3758. _____. "A Plan for International Development." **Department of State Bulletin** 44 (June 1961): 1000-1008.

3759. _____. "The Realities of Foreign Policy." **Department of State Bulletin** 46 (March 1962): 487-494.

3760. _____. "Secretary of State Cites Value of Privacy in Use of Diplomatic Channel." **Department of State Bulletin** 44 (February 1961): 214.

3761. _____. "Trade and Aid--Essentials of Free-

World Leadership." **Department of State Bulletin** 46 (March 1962): 403-409.

3762.   _____. "Views of Dean Rusk--Next Secretary of State." **U.S. News and World Report** 49 (December 26, 1960): 64-70.

3763.   _____. "U.S. Foreign Policy: Four Major Issues." **Department of State Bulletin** 45 (October 1961): 702-709.

3764.   _____. "U.S. Outlines Initial Proposals of Program for General and Complete Disarmament." **Department of State Bulletin** 46 (April 1962): 531-536.

3765.   _____. **The Winds of Freedom: Selections From the Speeches and Statements of Secretary of State Dean Rusk, January 1961-August 1962.** Edited by Ernest K. Lindley. New York: Beacon, 1963.

3766.   Stillman, Edmund. "Dean Rusk: In the American Grain." **Commentary** 45 (May 1968): 31-37.

William Henry Seward

3767.   Brauer, Kinley J. "Seward's 'Foreign War Panacea': An Interpretation." **New York History** 55 (April 1974): 133-157.

3768.   Cooney, Charles F. "Seward's Savior: George F. Robinson." **Lincoln Herald** 75 (Fall 1973): 93-96.

3769.   Coulter, E. Merton. "Seward and the South: His Career as a Georgia Schoolmaster." **Georgia Historical Quarterly** 53 (June 1969): 147-164.

3770.   Curran, Thomas J. "Seward and the Know-Nothings." **New York Historical Society Quarterly** 51 (April 1967): 141-159.

3771.   Dibble, Ernest F. "War Averters: Seward, Mallory, and Fort Pickens." **Florida Historical Quarterly** 49 (January 1971): 232-244.

3772.   Goldwert, M. "Matias Romero and Congressional Opposition to Seward's Policy toward the French Intervention in Mexico." **Americas** 22 (July 1965): 22-40.

3773.   Hinckley, Ted C. "William H. Seward Visits His Purchase." **Oregon Historical Quarterly** 72 (June 1971): 127-147.

3774.   Kushner, Howard I. "'Seward's Folly'?:

American Commerce in Russian America and
the Alaska Purchase." **California Historical Quarterly** 54 (Spring 1975): 4-26.
3775. Nalty, Bernard C., and Truman R. Strobridge.
"Mission to Peking, 1870: Captain McLane
Tilton's Letter Describing His Trip with
the Seward Party to Peking." **American
Neptune** 25 (April 1965): 116-127.
3776. O'Rourke, Mary M. "The Diplomacy of William
H. Seward During the Civil War: His Policies as Related to International Law."
Ph.D. dissertation, University of California, Berkeley, 1963.
3777. Sharrow, Walter G. "William Henry Seward and
the Basis for American Empire, 1850-1860."
Pacific Historical Review 36 (August
1967): 325-342.

Edward Reilly Stettinius, Jr.

3778. Campbell, Thomas M. "The Role of Edward R.
Stettinius, Jr., in the Founding of the
United Nations." Ph.D. dissertation,
University of Virginia, 1964.
3779. Campbell, Thomas M., and George C. Herring,
eds. **The Diaries of Edward R. Stettinius,
Jr., 1943-1946.** New York: New Viewpoints,
1975.
3780. Stettinius, Edward R. **Lend-Lease: Weapon for
Victory.** New York: Macmillan, 1944.
3781. _____. "Reorganization of the Office of the
Foreign Service." **Department of State
Bulletin** 12 (April 1945): 777-784.
3782. _____. **Roosevelt and the Russians: The
Yalta Conference.** Edited by Walter
Johnson. Garden City, N.Y.: Doubleday,
1949.
3783. Vloyantes, John P. "Edward R. Stettinius,
Jr. as Secretary of State." Ph.D. disser-
tation, University of Utah, 1954.
3784. Walker, Richard L., and George Curry. **Edward
R. Stettinius and James F. Brynes.** New
York: Cooper Square, 1965.

Henry Lewis Stimson

3785. Current, Richard N. **Secretary Stimson: A**

Study in Statecraft. New Brunswick, N.J.:
Rutgers University Press, 1954.

3786.   Hecht, R. A. "Great Britain and the Stimson
Note of January 7, 1932." Pacific
Historical Review 38 (May 1969): 177-191.

3787.   Langer, Robert. "Seizure of Territory, the
Stimson Doctrine and Related Principles in
Legal Theory and Diplomatic Practice,"
Ph.D. dissertation, Columbia University,
1948.

3788.   Morison, Elting E. Turmoil and Tradition: A
Study of the Life and Times of Henry L.
Stimson. Boston: Houghton Mifflin, 1960.

3789.   Ostrower, Gary B. "Secretary of State Stimson and the League." Historian 41 (May
1979): 467-482.

3790.   Redmond, Kent G. "Henry L. Stimson and the
Question of League Membership." Historian
25 (February 1963): 200-212.

3791.   Robertson, Charles L. "The American Secretary of State: A Study of the Office Under
Henry L. Stimson and Cordell Hull." Ph.D.
dissertation, Princeton University, 1959.

3792.   Schultejann, Mary A. "Henry L. Stimson's
Latin American Policy, 1929-1933." Ph.D.
dissertation, Georgeton University, 1967.

3793.   Smith, Michael J. "Henry L. Stimson and the
Philippines." Ph.D. dissertation, Indiana
University, 1970.

3794.   _____. "Henry L. Stimson and the
Philippines: American Withdrawal from
Empire, 1931-1935." Michigan Academician 5
(Winter 1973): 335-348.

3795.   Sternsher, Bernard. "The Stimson Doctrine:
F.D.R. Versus Moley and Tugwell." Pacific
Historical Review 31 (August 1962): 281-
290.

3796.   Stimson, Henry L. American Policy in
Nicaragua. New York: Scribner, 1927.

3797.   _____. "Decision to Use the Atomic Bomb."
Harper's Magazine 196 (February 1947): 97-
107.

3798.   _____. The Far Eastern Crisis: Recollections and Observations. New York: Harper,
1936.

3799.   Stimson, Henry L., and McGeorge Bundy. On
Active Service in Peace and War. New York:
Harper, 1948.

Cyrus Roberts Vance

3800. Schweid, B. "Interview with Secretary of
       State Cyrus R. Vance, February 3, 1977."
       Atlantic Community Quarterly 15 (Spring
       1977): 112-121.

Elihu Benjamin Washburne

3801. Clifford, Dale. "Elihu Benjamin Washburne:
       An American Diplomat in Paris, 1870-71."
       Prologue 2 (Winter 1970): 161-174.
3802. Washburne, Elihu B. **Recollections of a Min-
       ister to France, 1869-1877**. New York:
       Scribner, 1887.
3803. _____. **United States Embassy, France**.
       Washington, D.C.: Government Printing Of-
       fice, 1878.

Daniel Webster

3804. Barlett, Irving H. "Daniel Webster as a Sym-
       bolic Hero." **New England Quarterly** 45
       (December 1972): 484-507.
3805. Brauer, Kinley J. "The Webster-Lawrence
       Feud: A Study in Politics and Ambitions."
       Historian 29 (November 1966): 34-59.
3806. Brown, Norman D. "Webster-Jackson Movement
       for Constitution and Union Party in 1833."
       Mid-America 46 (July 1964): 147-171.
3807. Dubofsky, Melvyn. "Daniel Webster and the
       Whig Theory of Economic Growth, 1828-
       1848." **New England Quarterly** 42 (December
       1969): 551-572.
3808. Eichert, Magdalen. "Daniel Webster's Western
       Land Investments." **Historical New Hamp-
       shire** 26 (Fall 1971): 29-39.
3809. Elitzer, Michael R. "A Study of Greatness:
       Daniel Webster and the African Slave Trade
       Cases." **Journal of Historical Studies** 4
       (1980): 43-63.
3810. Etulain, Richard W. "Peter Harvey: Confidant
       and Interpreter of Daniel Webster."
       Vermont History 39 (Winter 1971): 21-30.
3811. Leduc, Thomas. "The Webster-Ashburton Treaty

and the Minnesota Iron Ranges." **Journal of American History** 51 (December 1964): 476-481.

3812.   Mondale, Clarence. "Daniel Webster and Technology." **American Quarterly** 14 (Spring 1962): 37-47.

3813.   Nathans, Sydney. "Daniel Webster, Massachusetts Man." **New England Quarterly** 39 (June 1966): 161-181.

3814.   Parish, Peter J. "Daniel Webster, New England, and the West." **Journal of American History** 63 (September 1976): 303-315.

3815.   Shewmaker, Kenneth E. "Daniel Webster and the Politics of Foreign Policy, 1850-1852." **Journal of American History** 63 (September 1976): 303-315.

3816.   _____ "'Untaught Diplomacy': Daniel Webster and the Lobos Islands Controversy." **Diplomatic History** 1 (Fall 1977): 321-340.

3817.   Wilson, Major L. "Of Time and the Union: Webster and His Critics in the Crisis of 1850." **Civil War History** 14 (December 1968): 293-306.

3818.   Wiltse, Charles M. "Daniel Webster and the British Experience." **Massachusetts Historical Society Proceedings** 85 (1973): 58-77.

INDEXES

Index of Authors

Batchelder, Robert C., 903
Bauer, Raymond A., 904,
    1774
Bax, Emily, 2863
Bax, Frans R., 1264
Bay, C., 1507
Bayard, Richard H., 3333
Beal, John Robinson, 3418
Beam, Jacob D., 639
Bean, Elizabeth A., 554
Beard, Charles A., 905
Beard, Edmund, 1453
Beaulac, Willard L., 210,
    326, 2864-2866
Bechhoefer, Bernhard G.,
    1508
Beck, William F., 2090
Becker, Joseph D., 684
Becker, William H., 1775,
    1803
Beckman, Peter R., 1426
Beelen, George D., 2020
Beers, Burton F., 3659
Beichman, Arnold, 174
Bell, Coral, 1081, 3419,
    3576, 3577
Bell, Harry H., 327
Bell, Peter, 2798
Bell, Rudolph M., 3667
Bell, Sidney, 211
Belmont, August, 2867
Belmont, Perry, 455
Beloff, Max, 702
Belohlavek, John M., 1082,
    2799, 2868, 2869
Bemis, Samuel F., 126,
    212, 703
Ben-Eliezer, M., 426
Bender, Lynn D., 1879
Bendiner, Robert, 3
Benet, Stephen V., 2870
Benham, Frederic, 1549
Bennet, Doublas J., 1265
Bennett, Edward M., 2596
Bennett, John A., 1427
Bennett, Meridian, 625
Bennett, S. E., 1743
Bennett, W. S., 1804

Benoit, Emile, 2129
Benson, Robert S., 1266
Benton, William, 1938
Ben-zvi, Abraham, 2728
Berbusse, Edward J., 2021,
    2224
Berding, Andrew H., 427,
    704 842, 3420
Berger, E., 1389
Berger, Henry W., 1345
Berger, Raoul, 1140
Berger, Roland, 2510
Berger, William E., 1428
Bergeron, Paul H., 3388
Bergman, Helen A., 428
Bergsten, C. Fred. 1550-
    1552
Berkeley, Dorothy S., 3695
Berkeley, Edmund, 3695
Berkhofer, Robert F., 3530
Berkowitz, Morton, 843
Berle, Adolf A., 705, 1880
    2871-2873
Berman, Edward H., 2674
Bernardo, C. Joseph, 1429
Bernath, S. L., 2319
Bernstein, Barton J.,
    1083, 1509, 1510, 1713,
    1881, 2593
Bernstein, Robert A., 1017
Berquist, Harold E., 2874,
    3324
Berry, John M., 1267
Berry, Nicholas O., 213
Berutti, John M., 2292
Bess, Demaree C., 4
Bestor, Arthur, 1141
Bethell, T. N., 2511
Bhagat, G., 3516
Bhagwati, Jagdish, 1182
Bhatachurya, Anindya K.,
    1553
Biddle, Cordelia D., 2875
Bigelow, John, 2876
Biglow, Frank W., 1939
Bilainkin, G., 2877
Bilder, Richard B., 43
Bill, J. A., 2729

Torregrosa, Manuel F.,
  2582
Toskova, Vitka, 2189
Toth, Charles W., 1925
Toulmin, Harry A., 1383
Towell, William P., 3251
Tower, J. G. 1322
Toynbee, A. J., 2393
Tozer, Warren W., 2583
Trachtenberg, Marc, 1073
Tracy, Thomas M., 541
Trager, Frank N., 1446,
  2831, 2832
Traina, Richard P., 2311
Trani, Eugene P., 2391,
  2392
Traphagen, Jeanne C., 3573
Trask, David F., 2190
Trask, Roger R., 2013
Trauth, M. Philip, 2313
Treadgold, Donald W., 2496
Trice, Robert H., 2782,
  2783
Triska, Jan F., 2393
Trivers, Howard, 898, 2665
Trotter, Richard G., 1926
Trout, B. T., 1770
Trow, C. W., 2049
Truitt, Wesley B., 2191
Truman, David B., 1771
Tsou, Tang, 2584, 3689
Tuchman, Barbara W., 2585
Tucker, R. W., 1500, 1737,
  2784-2786
Tuerck, David G., 1600
Tulchin, Joseph S., 2014
Turpin, William N., 825
Tuthill, John W., 826
Tyler, R. C., 2050
Tyler, Robert L., 827
Tynan, Thomas M., 1873

Ulam, Adam B., 2395, 2396
Ullman, Richard H., 366,
  2787, 3252
Ullmann, M., 2220
Ullmann, W., 2440
Unger, L., 958

Urban, George, 1260
Urbany, R., 828
U.S. Bureau of the Budget,
  65
U.S. Department of
  Justice, 692
U.S. Department of State,
  31-35, 125, 142, 170,
  198, 367, 499-501, 543,
  544, 583-585, 610-612,
  633, 670, 682
Ushiba, Nobuhiko, 2627
Uslaner, Eric M., 956
U.S. Library of Congress.
  Congressional Research
  Service, 313
U.S. Secretary of State,
  586
Utley, Jonathan G., 109,
  2497

Valeriani, Richard, 3651
Van Alstyne, Richard W.,
  2088, 2586
Van Campen, S. I. P., 2192
Vance, C. R., 1855
Van Cleave, William R.,
  2833
Van Cleve, John V., 2125
Van Deburg, William L.,
  1340
Van der Beugel, Ernst H.,
  2193, 3690
Van de Velde, W., 1405
Van Dusen, Henry P., 3464
Van Dyne, Frederick, 545
Van Hollen, C., 3652
Vannicelli, M., 1905
Vansittart, Lord, 368
Vardamis, A. A., 2265
Vare, Daniele, 3253
Varg, Paul A., 829, 2015,
  3254
Vauclain, Samuel M., 2418
Vayrynen, Raimo, 959
Veron, G. D., 2397
Vest, G. S., 2194
Vevier, Olson, 2587

Index of Subjects